P9-CDA-740

PROGRAMMING IN THE KEY OF

C#

A PRIMER FOR ASPIRING PROGRAMMERS

Microsoft®
.net™

Charles Petzold

PUBLISHED BY
Microsoft Press
A Division of Microsoft Corporation
One Microsoft Way
Redmond, Washington 98052-6399

Copyright © 2004 by Charles Petzold

All rights reserved. No part of the contents of this book may be reproduced or transmitted in any form or by any means without the written permission of the publisher.

Library of Congress Cataloging-in-Publication Data
Petzold, Charles
    Programming in the Key of C# / Charles Petzold.
        p. cm.
    Includes index.
    ISBN 0-7356-1800-3
    1. C# (Computer progam language).   I. Title.

    QA76.73.C154P45   2003
    005.13'3--dc21   2003052699

Printed and bound in the United States of America.

1 2 3 4 5 6 7 8 9   QWE   8 7 6 5 4 3

Distributed in Canada by H.B. Fenn and Company Ltd.

A CIP catalogue record for this book is available from the British Library.

Microsoft Press books are available through booksellers and distributors worldwide. For further information about international editions, contact your local Microsoft Corporation office or contact Microsoft Press International directly at fax (425) 936-7329. Visit our Web site at www.microsoft.com/mspress. Send comments to *mspinput@microsoft.com*.

DirectX, Microsoft, Microsoft Press, MS-DOS, MSDN, Visual Basic, Visual C#, Visual C++, Visual Studio, Windows, and Windows Media are either registered trademarks or trademarks of Microsoft Corporation in the United States and/or other countries. Other product and company names mentioned herein may be the trademarks of their respective owners.

The example companies, organizations, products, domain names, e-mail addresses, logos, people, places, and events depicted herein are fictitious. No association with any real company, organization, product, domain name, e-mail address, logo, person, place, or event is intended or should be inferred.

Acquisitions Editor: Danielle Bird
Project Editor: Denise Bankaitis
Technical Editor: Jim Fuchs

Body Part No. X08-81850

Table of Contents

Prelude

This is a book for people who want to learn the C# programming language. I've tried my best to avoid making assumptions about any prior programming experience you might or might not have had. The book begins with variables and ends with a program that plays music.

C# is a modern, object-oriented programming language designed at Microsoft. The language is part of a major collection of software technologies collectively called .NET (pronounced "dot net"), unveiled in the summer of 2000 and released about a year and a half later. You can use C# and .NET for Web programming or for writing programs that run under Microsoft Windows.

C# is not the only programming language you can use for .NET programming. Microsoft published a Common Language Specification (CLS) that defines a minimum standard of features that a programming language must have to use .NET. It is expected that many programming languages will be adapted in accordance with the CLS. But C# is the programming language designed specifically for .NET and the language that has the closest fit with the features of .NET.

As the name of the language suggests, C# is a descendent of sorts of the C and C++ programming languages, and it also bears some similarity with Java, a language that was also influenced by C and C++. These C-family languages (as they're now called) all have similar syntax, but the differences deepen on closer inspection. In particular, C# is part of a trend toward the use of programming languages that sacrifice a little efficiency in favor of safety. As I'll discuss in the first chapter, C and C++ became popular partially because programs written in these languages are often fast and use a minimum amount of memory. These languages achieve this efficiency by assuming that the programmer is very smart and doesn't make mistakes; the languages themselves don't provide any checks to determine if the program is doing anything wrong, such as accessing memory it shouldn't be accessing. C and C++ programs may be fast, but they can often have bugs that are difficult to diagnose.

Nowadays, machines are fast enough and memory is cheap enough that program efficiency is not a primary concern. What we care about more than efficiency is that programs be as free from bugs as possible. While no programming language lets programmers write entirely bug-free programs, C# goes a long way in comparison with C and C++. For that reason, C# programs are safer to run.

C# programs are also safer in another respect. As programs are transferred over the Internet, users need to be assured that the programs won't damage their computers or data in some way. C# (like Java) helps out here as well. Traditionally, the primary tool a programmer uses is a compiler that converts the program source code (what the programmer writes) into an executable (which the computer runs). In contrast, the C# compiler converts program source code into a file that contains intermediate language (IL), which cannot be directly executed on a computer. Before the program is actually run, the IL can be examined to determine whether it's capable of doing anything bad. The IL is then converted into an executable file. This latter process is the province of the .NET common language runtime (CLR).

As I began working with C# in 2000, it quickly became my preferred programming language. C# duplicates much of the concise syntax of C that I've enjoyed since first learning C in 1985. But C# also adds modern, object-oriented features while retaining very little unnecessary baggage from C. The language has combined the old and the new in an almost perfect balance.

Soon after I began working with C#, I also realized that it qualifies as a good *first* programming language for new programmers. C# is elegant and powerful, and it often protects the new programmer against common errors. Hence, I decided to write this book.

I mentioned earlier that you use C# to write .NET Web or Windows-based applications. But these are really user interface options, and that's not what this book is about. This book is about the C# programming language itself. Consequently, I've tried to write this book so that you can focus entirely on C# without distractions. What you later decide to use C# for is up to you. Still, programs need *some* way to communicate with the outside world. For this book, I've chosen to use a type of user interface known as the *console*. The advantage of the console is that it's simple, and what you learn is applicable to any type of programming you'll eventually do. If you'd like to write Windows-based applications after you've finished this book, for example, you can jump right into Chapter 2 of my book *Programming Microsoft Windows with C#* (Microsoft Press, 2001).

System Requirements

You can write and compile your C# programs using a variety of tools, and more will become available in the future. I've tried to write a book that is independent of the tool you eventually use. However, in those few instances where I found it necessary to describe how to create your C# programs, I've focused on two approaches.

The standard way to program in C# is to buy any version of Microsoft Visual C# .NET Standard Edition (which retails for about $100) or any version of Microsoft Visual Studio .NET Professional Edition (which retails for about $1000). Visual Studio .NET also includes support for C++ and Microsoft Visual Basic .NET, among other advanced features. In this book, I use the term Visual C# .NET to refer to either package, except when I need to differentiate them. To run Visual C# .NET, you need to be running Windows 2000 or Windows XP. A 600-Mhz Pentium III is recommended with at least 160 megabytes of memory, 2 gigabytes of free disk space (4.2 gigabytes for Visual Studio .NET), and a video display capable of a resolution at least 1024 by 768 with 256 colors.

If you're specifically running Visual C# .NET Version 2002 (but not Visual C# .NET Version 2003 or later editions, or any version of Visual Studio .NET) you'll need to add a little file to your installation that lets you create empty projects. Go to my Web site at *http://www.charlespetzold.com* and then to the *Programming in the Key of C#* page for details.

I'm not sure Visual C# .NET is the best tool for the beginning programmer. It's big, complex, and overwhelming, and it does much more than what the beginning programmer needs. For that reason, I have put together a little program that you can use instead. It's called Key of C#, and you can download it for free from my Web site. To use Key of C#, you first need to download and install the .NET Framework Software Development Kit (SDK), which you can find at *http://msdn.microsoft.com/downloads/list/netdevframework.asp*. Any version of the .NET Framework SDK is fine for this book. You need to be running Windows 2000 or Windows XP, or a later version of Windows. The download size is about 100 megabytes. You can then go to *http://www.charlespetzold.com* and navigate to the *Programming in the Key of C#* page, and install Key of C#.

If you've previously installed Visual C# .NET, you can also install and use Key of C# without downloading the .NET Framework SDK. Everything in the SDK is included in Visual C# .NET.

If you're comfortable working on the MS-DOS command line under Windows and you want to get a better feel for how programmers worked back in the old days, you can simply download and install the .NET Framework SDK (or install Visual C# .NET) and open up an MS-DOS Command Prompt window. The *Programming in the Key of C#* page on my Web site has more information about using this book with the command-line C# compiler

Support

The sample programs for this book are downloadable from the Microsoft Press Web site at *http://www.microsoft.com/mspress/books/6261.asp.* To download the sample files, click the Companion Content link in the More Information menu on the right side of the Web page. This will load the Companion Content page, which includes links for downloading the sample files. (There's also a link to the Microsoft Press Web site from the *Programming in the Key of C#* page on my Web site at *http://www.charlespetzold.com.*) The program files include solution files (.sln) and C# project files (.csproj) for Visual C# .NET, and also Key of C# project files (.kcsproj) for my Key of C# program.

Every effort has been made to ensure the accuracy of this book and the contents of the source code. Microsoft Press provides corrections for books through the World Wide Web at the following address:

http://www.microsoft.com/mspress/support

To connect directly to the Microsoft Press Knowledge Base and enter a query regarding a question or issue that you might have, go to

http://www.microsoft.com/mspress/support/search.asp

If you have comments, questions, or ideas regarding this book, please send them to Microsoft Press using either of the following methods:

Postal Mail:
Microsoft Press
Attn: Programming in the Key of C#
One Microsoft Way
Redmond, WA 98052-6399

E-Mail:
mspinput@microsoft.com

Please note that product support is not offered through the above mail addresses. For support regarding Visual C# .NET, Visual Studio .NET, or the .NET Framework, please visit the Microsoft Product Support Web site at

http://support.microsoft.com

For support with the Key of C# program, visit my Web site at

http://www.charlespetzold.com

Although I obviously don't have the resources of a corporation, I'll try my best to support this program.

Special Thanks

This book would have been impossible without the love and support of Deirdre, and the comfort and calm of the home that we have built together.

Also indispensable are those Sunday, Tuesday, and Thursday gatherings of friends that continue to help and support me in a myriad of ways.

My agent Claudette Moore of the Moore Literary Agency and Microsoft Press Acquisitions Editor Danielle Voeller got this project off the ground, and indulged me with a lopsided schedule that let me find a voice for this book. My friend Bruce Eckel helped assure me early on that I wasn't crazy for focusing on console I/O, and that it was, in fact, the only proper choice.

What's better than working with a Microsoft Press Project Editor and Technical Editor? Working with *two* Project Editors and *two* Technical Editors! Denise Bankaitis and Jim Fuchs did most of the work, but summer vacations and other scheduling shifts also caused Sally Stickney and Julie Xiao to get involved. Without the editors' stern readings of my manuscript, this book would be infested with mangled prose and buggy code. Editors do much more than eliminate non-parallel constructions, unclean monstrosities, and passages of questionable relevance. They help the writer see the work from multiple perspectives. Also indispensable in that process was author and teacher Robin A. Reynolds-Haertle, who identified many instances of implicit assumptions, awkward transitions, and stuff that just didn't make any sense. Any flaws still remaining in the book are due solely to my obstinacy.

I feel I owe a huge part of the arc of my professional life to Wendy Carlos, whose 1968 album *Switched-On Bach* introduced an inquisitive 16 year old not only to the music of Bach, but also to the technology of electronic music. A decade later, I was teaching myself digital electronics, building my own computer-controlled electronic music instruments, and slowly convincing myself I had more talent with chips and code than with composing music. I hope the program in the last chapter of this book will be accepted as an homage to Wendy Carlos and the *Switched-On Bach* tradition.

And finally, this book is dedicated to Johann Sebastian Bach himself, one of the few composers brave enough to write music in the key of C#.

Charles Petzold
New York City
June 2003

Part I

Beginnings

Preludio III.

Vivace. (♩.=92.)

```
int i = 2;
if (strNote(1) == '#')
iNote++;
```

1

You the Programmer

Late at night, when the day's work is done but the brain is still buzzing, programmers have sometimes been known to ask themselves this question: Is programming an art or a science?

Surely it seems like a bit of both. As an artist, the programmer starts with a palette of basic tools, spreads open a canvas as wide as available memory, and with a dash of inspiration begins fashioning a unique creation where once existed only random bits. But the canvas can't be decorated with complete anarchic abandon. The syntactical rules that govern the tools of programming may allow an infinite variety of constructions, but at the same time they are as strict and unrelenting as the laws of nature.

Programmers are the designers and builders, architects and bricklayers, visionaries and engineers of the modern age. The edifices we build become the global cities of the future, an ever-expanding series of links and connections between people, communities, and information, often with a beauty truly admired only by those who share our passion. To nonprogrammers, our creations are rarely respected—unacknowledged when they work correctly, cursed when they fail, and abandoned when they become superseded—even as they become ever more essential to users' lives.

A computer program is a magnificent machine. Were it to be implemented with whirling gears, levers, and pistons, it would fill our rooms with a music of breathtaking complexity. We'd see logic in motion, algebra in action, a dance of data. A strange vision, yes, but that's really the perspective the programmer sees, as pieces of a program are fitted together with a precision unmatched by machinery in the corporeal world. Few joys in life come close to the thrill of getting a new program working, seeing it suddenly blink awake and take life before your eyes.

Such joys are never experienced by the vast majority of computer users. Most people who use computers these days aren't programmers and never will be. They instead simply run applications—word processors, e-mail programs, Web browsers—that other people have programmed, or they use appliances—cell phones, DVD players, bread machines—that have computer programs embedded deep inside.

It wasn't always like this. Prior to 1970 (or so), getting something useful out of a computer without programming for it was just about impossible. The computer revolution really took place in two stages—the first stage was when computers were originally designed and built, and the second stage was several decades later when computers were made available to nonprogrammers. The computer *user* was born, and programmers and users haven't been able to communicate ever since!

The first working digital, programmable computers were built in the 1930s. By *digital*, I mean that they worked with discrete numbers, such as 0, 1, 3.14159, and $1.86{\times}10^6$. By *programmable*, I mean that the computers could carry out an entire sequence of mathematical operations based on coded instructions called a *program*. For many years, computer programs were encoded by little holes punched in paper or cardboard or some other medium. Eventually the computer became known as *hardware*, the coded instructions as *software*.

Software was given this name because it's easily changed. You don't have to rebuild the entire computer to do a different type of calculation. The hardware is designed to perform a comprehensive variety of basic arithmetical and logical operations. Which operations the hardware performs, and in what order, are governed by the program code. The computer is said to *execute* the program, to read the code and carry out the instructions.

For the first couple decades of digital computing, hardware and software were closely linked. Each machine had its own unique set of instructions. To transfer a program from one machine to a newer and faster machine, the program had to be rewritten with all new codes. These sets of machine-specific codes came to be known as *machine code* or (when English mnemonics were used to represent the codes) *assembly language*.

In the early 1950s, it began to be feasible to design computer languages that were generalized and that were *not* based on the architecture and codes of particular machines. These languages are known as *high-level* programming languages, in contrast to the *low-level* machine code. Some of these early high-level languages are still used today. FORTRAN (which stands for FORmula TRANslation) continues to attract a loyal following among scientists and engineers, while COBOL (Common Business Oriented Language) is still used extensively on large mainframe computers in financial institutions. BASIC (Beginner's All-purpose Symbolic Instruction Code), which dates from the mid-1960s, is also still popular, although in quite different form from its original version.

Computer programs created today in FORTRAN, COBOL, BASIC, or other high-level languages are basically text files consisting of a series of statements written in accordance with the strict rules of syntax defined by the language. Because the computer itself can run only machine code, the high-level program must be translated into machine code by either a *compiler* or an *interpreter* program. A compiler translates an entire program into machine code that is then executed by the computer, whereas an interpreter performs a simultaneous translation and execution of the program.

Another programming language that was developed during the late 1950s is *not* currently used today (as far as I know) but turned out to be extremely influential in the history of programming languages. This language is ALGOL, which stands for ALGOrithmic Language, but is also the name of the second brightest star in the constellation Perseus. Originally designed in the late 1950s by an international committee, ALGOL was later enhanced in 1960 and 1968. Although ALGOL is pretty much a dead language today, its spirit lives on in its descendents, including Pascal, PL/I, and C.

C was born at the Bell Telephone Laboratories. It's difficult to imagine the modern world without the influence of Bell Labs. In 1947, the transistor was invented at Bell Labs, and in the 1970s, the UNIX operating system was developed there. For many years, closely associated with UNIX was the programming language called simply C, designed largely by Dennis Ritchie. People are always curious about the name: C was called C because it derived from an earlier language named B, and B was a simplified version of BCPL (Basic CPL), which was derived from CPL (Combined Programming Language).

C is terser than most other programming languages. Whereas ALGOL (and many of its descendents) used the words BEGIN and END to block out a section of program statements, C used the left and right curly brackets. Common operations were streamlined. Programs written in C are often very efficient, which means that C programs often compile to a smaller number of machine code instructions compared with other languages. A significant part of C's appeal lay in the formalization of *pointers*, which are basically memory addresses that let programmers do certain jobs in very efficient ways. Some people even call C a "high-level assembly language" because it works well at the level of bits, bytes, and memory.

The efficiency of C comes at a price, and any programmer who has worked with C knows how dangerous it can be. Compilers for most other programming languages insert extra machine-code instructions into a program that help prevent the program from doing something wrong and crashing. For the sake of generating the fastest code possible, C compilers do not insert extra machine-code instructions. C assumes the programmer is smarter than the compiler. Consequently, C makes it very easy for even advanced programmers to write faulty code. *Bugs* are a common part of all programming, but C lets programmers write buggy code that is simply not possible in other languages. Many of these bugs are related to pointers, which have the power of letting a program write over areas of memory that it really shouldn't be messing with.

Although C is still a popular programming language, it's somewhat dated. Today we classify C as a traditional *procedural* language, a term that refers to the structure of C programs. A C program generally consists of multiple *procedures* (also known as *functions* or *subroutines*), each of which is a chunk of code that does a particular job or implements a particular algorithm. These procedures work with *data* in various ways. Data is numbers or text or combinations of numbers and text. In a traditional procedure programming language, *code crunches data*.

These days, many programmers prefer *object-oriented* languages. The beginnings of object-oriented programming (OOP) are generally associated with the language SmallTalk, developed at the Palo Alto Research Center (PARC). PARC is a research laboratory founded by Xerox that is also responsible for developing many concepts of the graphical user interface that eventually found their way into the Apple Macintosh and Microsoft Windows operating systems.

In an object-oriented language, programmers create *classes* rather than procedures, and from these classes spring objects, which are combinations of code and data. Rather than having procedures work with data, the data has the tools to work on itself. *Data crunches itself*. This change in perspective turns out to be very useful in writing code that is *reusable* for a variety of programming jobs.

Over the years, several adventurous programmers attempted to create object-oriented versions of C. The one that eventually became quite popular was developed at Bell Labs beginning in the early 1980s by Bjarne Stroustrup. This is C++ (pronounced "C plus plus"), the name of which is a bit of a joke. As you'll learn in Chapter 6, a double plus sign in C increases a number by 1.

C++ has some problems of its own. In theory, C++ is a superset of C. It didn't replace features of C but added to them. This forced C++ to introduce some odd notation that many people found ugly and awkward.

Moreover, what were once considered attractive features of C and C++— its low-level nature, the use of pointers—were looking more and more like fundamental flaws. As the programming community has matured in recent years, we have been moving beyond the era in which performance and economy are the primary criteria. Hardware has become fast enough, and memory cheap enough, that we can afford to focus on a far more pressing concern, which is creating code that is as free of bugs as possible, even if that means forfeiting some of the efficiency of C.

In the 1990s, Sun Microsystems created Java, an object-oriented language based on C with some significant differences from C++. Java cleaned up some of the ugly syntax of C++ and removed some of the dangerous stuff of C, but it retained much of C's terseness.

In 2000, Microsoft Corporation unveiled C# (pronounced "C sharp"), largely designed by Anders Hejlsberg, which continues the tradition of giving punning names to programming languages. The sharp sign almost looks like two plus signs of C++ moved together. And, of course, in music, C# is a little higher in pitch than C.

Like Java, C# has removed many dangerous features of C. Pointers haven't been entirely banished from C#, but they are unnecessary for the vast majority of programming chores.

Another similarity between Java and C# involves the role of the compiler. Traditionally, the compiler translates *source code* (the high-level language text file) into machine code. The machine code forms an *executable*, which is a file ready to be run on a computer. But because machine code is associated with a particular machine, the executable can be run on only one type of computer. This is why you can't run the same programs both on the Apple Macintosh and under Microsoft Windows.

The C# compiler, however, translates source code into an intermediate language (or IL), which is a type of generalized machine code. Only when you want to run the program on a particular machine is the IL translated into machine code. From the user's perspective, this translation is invisible. In theory, the two-step process allows the same IL programs to run on different types of computers. Also, a program in the form of IL can be examined more easily by an operating system for the presence of any malicious or destructive code. This capability is becoming more important as programs are exchanged over the Internet.

C, C++, Java, and C# are all now known as *C family* or *C-based* languages. C++ is a superset of C, which means that C++ has everything that C has plus more. Java and C# are not strict supersets of C, and they resemble each other more than they resemble C++. But they all share a lot of similar syntax that is unlike any other programming language. In this book, I'll occasionally mention whether a feature of C# has been inherited from C, how it differs from C, or whether it's not in C at all, just to give you a better idea of the legacy of C, C++, and C#.

Learning a programming language is sometimes compared to learning a foreign language. There are some similarities for sure. They both have a collection of vocabulary, for example, although the vocabularies of programming languages are comparatively quite small. C# defines only 77 *keywords*, which are listed on the inside back cover of this book. In keeping with a C tradition, all C# keywords are spelled in lowercase.

Programming languages have rules of syntax and grammar, although these are much simpler and also much stricter than human languages. After all, the syntax of a computer program must be simple enough for it to be completely and unambiguously interpreted by the compiler. No program yet can read human languages with the same ease and precision.

The big similarity between learning a programming language and learning a foreign language is that you can't learn either one just by reading a book. You have to practice. You have to practice as much as if you're learning to play a musical instrument. You have to write your own code. The first time you dream in code (usually not a pleasant experience, I'm afraid) you know that you're learning to think like a programmer.

Programming is a problem-solving activity. The single most important quality of a programmer is an ability to decompose problems, to break a problem down into little pieces. The tools that C# gives you really apply only to the little pieces. It's the programmer's responsibility to then put the little pieces back together to compose the total solution to the problem. This ability, too, improves with practice.

An attention to detail certainly helps. Programming doesn't tolerate sloppy thinking or solutions that work 99 percent of the time. Throughout this book, I'll try to get you thinking more like a programmer, but there's only so much I can do. As with all programming tutorials, many sample programs in this book are very short, designed to illustrate a single aspect of C# programming. In real life, programs are much larger. Writing large programs is something you must progressively learn how to do through practice by working your way up from smaller programs.

In this book, I have attempted to separate the actual C# language from the environments in which the language is used. You can use C# to write stand-alone programs that run under Windows, for example, or you can use C# on Web pages. As time goes on, C# will be used for other applications. These various applications of C# all involve different ways to get *input* from the user and display *output* to the user. C# does not impose any particular input/output (I/O) model. That's a whole other area beyond the scope of this book.

To keep these concerns to a minimum, this book shows you how to write C# programs for a very old-fashioned, plain-vanilla type of I/O device called the *console*. In years gone by, programmers who had graduated beyond punched cards worked on teletypewriters. Later on, early personal computers treated the video display as a console, and this is the face that operating systems such as MS-DOS showed to their users in the years before graphical interfaces such as Windows. Even under Windows, the console exists as the Command Prompt window.

Although eventually you probably won't be doing much console programming, learning the console is certainly not a worthless exercise. Many experienced programmers use the console when developing a particularly tricky piece of code, or later on, for debugging purposes. Wherever you go in your C# programming, I can assure you that nothing you learn in these pages will be unnecessary.

A tutorial such as this one can be neither complete nor totally precise. In the next chapter, for example, I make the statement, "The only type of operand allowed on the left side of an equal sign is a variable." That's not entirely true. Properties and indexer elements can also appear there. But that's much more than you'll need to know in Chapter 2. Eventually, you'll get the full story.

The formal description of C# is contained in the document *C# Language Specification*, which is available in a book published in 2001 by Microsoft Press (the book is called *C# Language Specifications* with an "s"), and is also available online. Eventually, you'll want to take a crack at reading this book, but you'll need to have a good level of familiarity with C# before you begin. I'll occasionally refer to the *C# Language Specification* in this book. All the sections in the document are conveniently numbered in outline form.

Although the *C# Language Specification* is the ultimate authority to resolve questions on the C# programming language, a more "user-friendly" guide is the *C# Programmer's Reference*, which is available online and also published by Microsoft Press in book form under the title *Microsoft Visual C# .NET Language Reference* (2002). It's useful for quick references, but it also includes some information not found anywhere else.

Both these documents, and much more programming information, are available on the MSDN (Microsoft Developer Network) Web site (*http://msdn.microsoft.com*). At the time of this writing, the C# language page is *http://msdn.microsoft.com/library/en-us/cscon/html/vcoriCStartPage.asp*. If you can't find it there, an updated link will probably be on the *Programming in the Key of C#* page on my Web site. That page is *http://www.charlespetzold.com/key*.

2

First Assignments

Computers and programming were first invented to perform numerical calculations, so it shouldn't be surprising that many programming languages have adopted certain elements of algebra, including the use of letters or words to represent numbers.

Here's a little bit of some simple algebra:

```
A = 3
B = 2
C = A + B
```

This isn't a very difficult problem, of course, but if we could persuade a computer to solve this problem, we'd be well on our way to persuading the computer to solve more difficult problems. A first step would be to convert the algebra into C#. And here's a little bit of some C# code:

```
A = 3;
B = 2;
C = A + B;
```

These three lines of code don't constitute a complete C# program, but they could easily be found within a typical C# program, possibly one that you might write yourself. As you'll begin doing in Chapter 4, you type such code into an *editor* (which is like a simplified word processor) and then run the compiler program to convert the code into an .EXE file you can then run.

The only apparent difference between the algebra and the C# is that each line of C# ends in a semicolon. Each of these three lines is called a *statement* in C#. A computer program is mostly composed of statements of various kinds. The letters *A*, *B*, and *C* are called *variables* and—if you want to get technical about it—variables symbolize locations in memory where the values of the variables are stored.

The apparent similarity between the algebra and the C# code is actually quite deceptive. The deceptive part is the role of the equal sign. Its meaning is a little different in programming than in algebra. For example, suppose somebody showed you these three statements of algebra:

```
A = 3
C = A + B
B = 2
```

You might hesitate a moment, but then say "*C* still equals 5." That's because an algebraic statement like "B = 2" indicates something intrinsic and unchangeable about *B*, similar to saying "Fluffy is a cat."

However, you don't want to mix up the statements in your C# code, like this:

```
A = 3;
C = A + B;
B = 2;
```

Statements in a C# program are executed by the computer *sequentially*, one after the other. The first statement has the effect of setting *A* to 3. Only when that statement has executed does *A* equal 3. But when the second statement executes, the value of *B* hasn't yet been set equal to 2. We don't know what *B* equals; we're looking only at a small part of a larger computer program.

In C#, the equal sign is most precisely called the *assignment operator*. An *operator* is a symbol or a short word that causes the computer to do something—to perform an operation. Operators have *operands*. The assignment operator has two operands: a variable on the left of the equal sign and an *expression* on the right. The assignment operator causes the variable on the left of the equal sign to be assigned a value calculated from the expression on the right. These three statements are all examples of *assignment statements*, a very common type of statement in many computer programs.

Assignment statements come in lots of different forms. All of the following assignment statements are legal in C#:

```
C = A + 3;
C = 27 + A + B;
C = B + A + A + B + A + B + 14;
C = 45 + 27;
```

In each case, a variable to the left of the equal sign is assigned the value of the evaluated expression on the right side of the equal sign. The plus sign is one of several *arithmetic operators* in C#. Of course, C# also lets you subtract, multiply, and divide, as I'll discuss in Chapter 6.

This is also a perfectly valid assignment statement in C#:

```
B = B + 5;
```

That statement wouldn't make any sense in algebra. But in C#, it simply means that 5 is added to the current value of the variable B. If B is equal to 17 before this statement, it's equal to 22 after the statement.

The following statement is valid in algebra but *not* in C#:

```
C + 5 = 4;
```

The only type of operand allowed on the left side of an equal sign is a variable.

The statements I've shown you so far contain variables, semicolons, assignment operators, addition operators, and also numeric *literals*, which are the numbers such as 2 and 3. More specifically, these numbers are *integer* literals, which means they are whole numbers with no decimal points and no fractional parts. You can also specify negative integers in the customary way with a minus sign:

```
A = -39;
```

But don't put commas in larger numbers:

```
A = 3,546,128;
```

That is *not* valid C# code. You might be surprised to learn that such a statement *is* valid in C, but it has the effect of setting *A* equal to 3—probably not what the programmer intended.

Variables are called variables because they can vary. Here's a sequence of statements to demonstrate how the values of variables can change:

```
A = 3;
B = 2;
C = A + B;
B = 4;
C = A + B;
```

After the third statement executes, *C* equals 5. After the fifth statement executes, *C* equals 7. When working with algebra, if you said "Now *B* equals 4" you'd really be talking about a whole different problem. In programming, variables often vary quite frequently. A particular variable might store a ZIP Code, for example, but as the program runs, it might be set to thousands of different ZIP Codes because the program deals with thousands of different addresses.

To avoid confusion between algebra and programming, programmers sometimes call the equal sign a *gets*, as in "C *gets* A plus B," or an *assigns*, as in "C is assigned A plus B." Others call it a *gozinta* as in "A plus B *goes into* C."

The use of a semicolon at the end of statements is common in programming languages that derive from ALGOL. The semicolons are required because C# allows code to be written in a rather freeform manner. You don't have to line everything up all nice and neat. You can jam all your statements together into one line, like this:

```
A=3;B=2;C=A+B;
```

Or, you can spread out your statements over multiple lines:

```
        A
=   3
; B         =
      2
    ;       C   = A
  +
      B
            ;
```

As you read this mess from left to right and top to bottom (as the compiler does without complaint), you'll encounter the same sequence of characters. When the compiler encounters a semicolon, it knows that one statement has ended and another might follow.

Blank spaces and new lines in a program are collectively known as *white space*. Programmers often use white space aesthetically—to make their programs more readable. For example, I like to pad my assignment operators and arithmetic operators with a blank on each side:

```
A = 3;
B = 2;
C = A + B;
```

But you don't have to.

Although *A*, *B*, and *C* are certainly simple and convenient variable names, you have plenty of flexibility in naming your variables:

```
HAYDN = 3;
London = 2;
Symphony104 = HAYDN + London;
```

C# is a *case-sensitive* programming language, which means you can use uppercase or lowercase letters in your variable names, but you must be consistent. *London* is not the same as *london*. This sequence of statements contains three distinct variables:

```
London = 3;
london = 2;
LONDON = London + london;
```

To keep your confusion level at a minimum, you'll probably want to avoid variable names that differ only by case.

The rules for valid variable names in C# are rather complex because they can involve characters found in other alphabets, such as Cyrillic and Arabic. For example, you can use Greek letters in your variable names:

$\alpha = 3;$
$\beta = 2;$
$\gamma = \alpha + \beta;$

If you'd like to use variable names like these, you need to install foreign language keyboard layouts from the Regional And Language Options area of the Windows Control Panel. Although you can use Greek letters in your variable names, you can't use Roman numerals for your numeric literals.

For characters you can easily type from your keyboard, the rules for naming variables are rather simple:

- Variable names must begin with a letter or an underscore character.

- Variable names must contain only letters, underscores, and numbers.

Got it? A variable name can contain numbers (such as the *Symphony104* variable I used earlier), but it can't *begin* with a number. Otherwise, it looks too much like a numeric literal to the C# compiler and to the C# programmer.

Variable names cannot contain spaces or punctuation other than the underscore. For a variable name that contains multiple words, it was once the convention to use underscores to separate the words:

```
population_of_new_jersey = 8414350;
```

These days, a more common convention is to mix uppercase and lowercase:

```
PopulationOfNewJersey = 8414350;
```

There are certain words you *cannot* use for variable names. These are called *keywords*, and they are words that C# has reserved for itself. There are 77 keywords in C#; they are listed on the inside back cover of this book.

It's best to use variable names that are meaningful in some way. Someone else might need to read your program, or you might come back to your program years after you wrote it. You'll find it's really a big help if your variable names tell you exactly what the variables are:

```
NumberOfChildMovieTicketsDesired = 3;
NumberOfAdultMovieTicketsDesired = 2;
TotalNumberOfMovieTicketsToBeIssued = NumberOfChildMovieTicketsDesired +
    NumberOfAdultMovieTicketsDesired;
```

Notice the third statement is a bit long, so I've used two lines for the statement. If a statement must be continued beyond one line, the subsequent lines are often indented to make the statement more readable. Because very explicit variable names can be quite lengthy, you might want to ease the typing drudgery with names that are shorter but almost as clear:

```
ChildTkts = 3;
AdultTkts = 2;
TotalTkts = ChildTkts + AdultTkts;
```

Although it's fairly clear to us humans what we want to do here, these three statements do *not* constitute a *complete* C# program. The compiler needs a little more information to begin, a subject we'll now turn to in Chapter 3.

Declarations of Purpose

Before you use a particular variable in a C# program, you must tell the compiler what type of variable it is. It may seem very obvious to us that a variable simply refers to a number. However, variables can be many things besides numbers, and there are even different types of numbers in C#.

C# supports three different types of numbers:

■   If you were writing a program dealing with population (for example), you would want to use whole numbers, also known as *integers*. There's no such thing as a fractional person except if you are calculating averages or something similar.

■   If you were working with money in your program (which is quite common in some industries), you would need *decimal* numbers, such as dollars and cents.

■   If you were writing a program with scientific applications, you'd probably be accustomed to expressing numbers using scientific notation. In programming, these are called *floating-point* numbers.

You can mix all three types of numbers in a single program. But for now, let's stick with integers, which are whole numbers, both positive and negative.

You inform the compiler that you wish to use a particular variable name when you *declare* the variable in a *declaration statement*. In the declaration statement, you need to specify the *type* of the variable, that is, what type of number (or whatever else) you want the variable to be. A particular variable can be declared only once.

C# (like C and C++ before it) uses the word *int* (rhymes with "mint") to denote an integer. Here's how you declare the variable *ChildTkts* to be an integer:

```
int ChildTkts;
```

The declaration statement indicates the variable's type, which must be to the left of the variable name. You can say: The type of *ChildTkts* is *int*. Or: *Child-Tkts* is a variable of type *int*. Or: *ChildTkts* is an object of type *int*.

As you can see by the list in the inside back cover of this book, *int* is a C# keyword. You can't name a variable *int* (but you can name a variable *Int* or *INT*).

When a C# program runs, the declaration statement causes a small amount of memory to be set aside specifically to store the value of the variable. It is said that memory is *allocated* for the variable.

Here's how a program might look with both declaration statements and assignment statements:

```
int ChildTkts;
int AdultTkts;
int TotalTkts;

ChildTkts = 3;
AdultTkts = 2;
TotalTkts = ChildTkts + AdultTkts;
```

The blank line in the middle isn't necessary; it's just something that helps visually structure the program—declaration statements first, then assignment statements.

You can have more than one variable in a single declaration statement:

```
int ChildTkts, AdultTkts, TotalTkts;
```

This single declaration statement is the equivalent of the three separate declaration statements. When more than one variable appears in a declaration statement, commas must separate the variable names. All the variables are declared to be the same type.

There are many different ways to write these variable declarations. The variables don't have to be declared in the same order in which you use them:

```
int TotalTkts, AdultTkts, ChildTkts;

ChildTkts = 3;
AdultTkts = 2;
TotalTkts = ChildTkts + AdultTkts;
```

You can declare some variables together in one declaration statement and others by themselves:

```
int ChildTkts, AdultTkts;
int TotalTkts;
```

You can even declare the variables as you need them:

```
int ChildTkts;
ChildTkts = 3;

int AdultTkts;
AdultTkts = 2;

int TotalTkts;
TotalTkts = ChildTkts + AdultTkts;
```

Here the declaration statements and assignment statements alternate. The only rule is that each variable must be declared sometime *before* the variable is used.

It's also possible to assign a variable a value at the same time you declare it. At first glance, the following statement might look like an assignment statement, but it's actually a declaration statement:

```
int ChildTkts = 3;
```

When a variable is assigned a value in its declaration, the variable is said to be *initialized*. You can still assign the variable a different value later in the program. There is no difference between initializing a variable in the declaration statement and assigning the variable a value right after the declaration statement:

```
int ChildTkts;
ChildTkts = 3;
```

Between the time that a variable is declared and the time it is first assigned a value, the variable is said to be *uninitialized*. It has no value, or rather it probably has some random value. The C# compiler won't allow you to use an uninitialized variable. For example, consider the following sequence of statements:

```
int ChildTkts, AdultTkts, TotalTkts;
TotalTkts = ChildTkts + AdultTkts;
```

The *ChildTkts* and *AdultTks* variables have not been assigned values, so you cannot use them to calculate *TotalTkts*.

In a single declaration statement, you can initialize some variables and not initialize others:

```
int ChildTkts, AdultTkts = 2, TotalTkts;
```

Notice that the three variables in the declaration statement are still separated by commas.

It's even possible to initialize all three variables in the same declaration statement:

```
int ChildTkts = 3, AdultTkts = 2, TotalTkts = ChildTkts + AdultTkts;
```

The initialization of *TotalTkts* is an expression involving the other two variables. In this case, *TotalTkts* must be declared and initialized after *ChildTkts* and *AdultTkts* have both been declared and initialized.

Putting too much into one declaration statement can make your program difficult to read. The following three declaration statements are both concise and clear:

```
int ChildTkts = 3;
int AdultTkts = 2;
int TotalTkts = ChildTkts + AdultTkts;
```

Concision and clarity are very admirable goals when programming.

Unfortunately, we still haven't created a complete C# program. In C#, as in many modern programming languages, code is organized into units called *classes* and *methods*. Each method contains code that performs a certain job. (In other programming languages, methods may be called *functions* or *procedures* or *subroutines*.) Related methods are grouped together into a class. The simplest C# program consists of a single class that contains a single method. At the very least, every C# program must have a method named *Main*. The *Main* method is always the first method in a program that the computer executes. *Main* is called the *entry point* to the program. For very short programs (such as the ones we'll be writing for awhile), *Main* is often the only method in the program. Although *Main* plays a special role in C#, it is not a keyword. You can name a variable *Main* if you want.

Like variables, *Main* must be declared in your program. Declaring a method is just a bit more involved than declaring a variable.

Methods often have *input* and *output*. For example, in a method that calculates sales commissions, the input to the method is a sales figure, and the output of the method is the calculated commission. The method is like a little factory that takes in raw materials and creates a product. In general, a method gets input in the form of some variables, which are called the method *parameters*. The method crunches these variables in some way and then outputs a result, which is called a *return value*.

Actual examples of parameters and return values will have to wait, however, because the version of *Main* that we'll be writing now has *no* input and *no* output. The declaration of the *Main* method must reflect that fact, and actually indicate the *absence* of parameters and a return value.

Let's begin the method declaration with its name:

```
Main
```

Remember that C# is case sensitive. *Main* must begin with an uppercase M.

Normally the method parameters are indicated by a list of variables enclosed in a pair of parentheses following the method name. Because this version of *Main* has no parameters, the word *Main* is followed by empty parentheses:

```
Main()
```

When a method has a return value, the type of that value (such as *int*) is indicated to the left of the method name in the method declaration. When a method has no return value, you use the keyword *void* to indicate that fact:

```
void Main()
```

Let me point out something of a similarity between variables and method declarations: variables are declared with the variable type to the left of the variable name; similarly, methods are declared with the return type to the left of the method name.

Yet another keyword is required in the declaration of *Main*. The keyword *static* goes to the left of the return type:

```
static void Main()
```

I'm afraid that the exact meaning and implications of the keyword *static* involve concepts of C# that are considerably more advanced than I'm prepared to discuss just yet. For now, you can think of the word *static* as implying that the method stands by itself, that it is constant and unchanging during the execution of the program.

A method declaration also includes a *body*, which is the actual code that constitutes the method. The body of the method is enclosed within a pair of *curly brackets* (also called curly *braces*) that follows the parameter list, left curly bracket first, then right:

```
static void Main()
{

}
```

I've placed these curly brackets on separate lines because it's customary. But C# is a freeform language; you can place the curly brackets on the same line as the other parts of the *Main* declaration.

The C# code that makes up the method appears inside the curly brackets. Let's use some variable declaration statements and assignment statements from earlier in this chapter:

```
static void Main()
{
int ChildTkts, AdultTkts, TotalTkts;

ChildTkts = 3;
AdultTkts = 2;
TotalTkts = ChildTkts + AdultTkts;
}
```

A group of C# statements enclosed in curly brackets is often referred to as a *block*. Thus, if you want to think of all this very formally (as the C# compiler certainly does), a method declaration consists of a modifier (which is the keyword *static* in this method), a return type (*void*), a method name (*Main*), a parameter list enclosed in parentheses, and a block, which contains the method code.

Most programmers like to indent all the statements that appear in a block:

```
static void Main()
{
    int ChildTkts, AdultTkts, TotalTkts;

    ChildTkts = 3;
    AdultTkts = 2;
    TotalTkts = ChildTkts + AdultTkts;
}
```

Visually, the indentation suggests that the statements are somehow *inside* the method, which is certainly the case. The number of spaces you indent the code is up to you. Most programmers use at least two spaces but not more than eight. Code in this book uses four spaces.

Some programmers (but not I) like to put the first curly bracket on the same line as the beginning of the method declaration:

```
static void Main() {
    int ChildTkts, AdultTkts, TotalTkts;

    ChildTkts = 3;
    AdultTkts = 2;
    TotalTkts = ChildTkts + AdultTkts;
}
```

Other programmers (including me until about 1997) like to indent the brackets as well as the code:

```
static void Main()
    {
    int ChildTkts, AdultTkts, TotalTkts;

    ChildTkts = 3;
    AdultTkts = 2;
    TotalTkts = ChildTkts + AdultTkts;
    }
```

And still other programmers indent the brackets two spaces and the code within the brackets another two spaces:

```
static void Main()
  {
    int ChildTkts, AdultTkts, TotalTkts;

    ChildTkts = 3;
    AdultTkts = 2;
    TotalTkts = ChildTkts + AdultTkts;
  }
```

The C# compiler doesn't care about your indentation style. The company you work for may enforce a particular style, and your friends who program may have their own ideas on the subject. Otherwise, just pick an indentation style you like and be consistent.

Alas, regardless of your preferred indentation style, a declaration of the *Main* method is still not a complete C# program. In a C# program, all methods must belong to a *class* or a *structure*. Classes and structures are very similar, so until I note otherwise, everything I say about classes also applies to structures.

In object-oriented programming languages such as C#, a class is the fundamental organizational unit of code and data. What this means will become more apparent as you make your way through this book. A C# program always contains one or more classes. Each class contains one or more *members*, a category that includes methods such as *Main*.

The simplest complete C# program consists of a single class that contains a single member, which is the method called *Main*.

A class declaration begins with the keyword *class* followed by the name of the class, which is a name that you (the programmer) make up:

```
class MyVeryFirstProgram
```

The rules for naming classes are the same as naming variables. Variable names and class names both come under the category of *identifiers*, which are names that you make up. All identifiers must begin with a letter or an underscore and must contain only letters, numbers, and underscores. You can't use a keyword as an identifier. Although *Main* is not a keyword, you can't use *Main* as a name of a class if the class also contains a method named *Main*.

The declaration of the class also includes a pair of curly brackets that encloses the contents of the class:

```
class MyVeryFirstProgram
{

}
```

Inside the curly brackets you can put methods, such as the *Main* method we created earlier. It is customary to indent all the members of the class, which means that the contents of the method are indented twice:

```
class MyVeryFirstProgram
{
    static void Main()
    {
        int ChildTkts, AdultTkts, TotalTkts;

        ChildTkts = 3;
        AdultTkts = 2;
        TotalTkts = ChildTkts + AdultTkts;
    }
}
```

And there it is—a complete, functional C# program. The program contains one class, named *MyVeryFirstProgram*. The *MyVeryFirstProgram* class contains one method, named *Main*. The *Main* method declares three variables of type *int*. The program concludes with three assignment statements.

The next step is to type this program into the computer, compile it, and run it, which I'll demonstrate in the next chapter.

4

Edit, Compile, Run

A computer program begins life as a text file that you (the programmer) write. This file is often referred to as the program *source code*. By convention, C# source-code files have a filename extension of .CS (which stands for *C Sharp*). A program consists of one or more source-code files.

After you create the source-code file or files, you compile the program by running the compiler. The C# compiler is a program that reads source code and creates intermediate language (IL), generally in the form of a file with the extension .EXE (which stands for *Executable*). Very often…very, *very* often, your source code won't be perfect. If the compiler detects a problem with your source code, it will tell you about it. These problems are generally known as *syntax errors* or *compile-time errors*, or simply *compile errors*. If the compiler reports any errors, you must go back and edit the source code to fix the problems. (Sometimes compile errors are called *compiler* errors, as if the compiler is at fault. Although compilers have been known to make mistakes, it's much more common for the compiler to *find* mistakes in your code.)

When you finally persuade the compiler to create an .EXE file, you can run that program. The program is now under the care of the operating system and, in the case of C# programs, the common language runtime (CLR) part of .NET. Very often…very, very, *very* often, this program will not do exactly what you wanted. Sometimes your code will attempt to do something that's not allowed (such as accessing some memory that doesn't belong to it), and the program itself in conjunction with the CLR will tell you about that problem, generally in the form of a dialog box that pops up. These problems are known as *runtime errors* or *exceptions*. Again, you must go back to the source code and attempt to fix the problem.

This whole process is known as the *edit-compile-run* cycle, and it's a major part of the process of *program development*. For all but the tiniest programs, it's extremely rare to have a finished program after going through this cycle only once. When writing a large program, you'll want to start the cycle as soon as possible. You'll begin with a much smaller program and progressively enhance it through multiple edit-compile-run cycles.

When you finally have a program that *seems* to run OK, you must test it. Often you'll find that the program still doesn't work quite right. These problems are known as *bugs*. Sometimes bugs are easy to find; sometimes they are not. Debugging is a whole science in itself (or is it an art?) that is pretty much beyond the scope of this book. Steve McConnell's *Code Complete* (Microsoft Press, 1993) has a good chapter on debugging as well as much other essential information for programmers.

As I mentioned in the Prelude, you have a choice of several ways to edit and compile your C# programs. The most conventional way is with Microsoft Visual C# .NET or (if you'll be using multiple programming languages, and you have the money) Microsoft Visual Studio .NET. I'll be using the term Visual C# .NET to refer to either package. Visual C# .NET is a sophisticated *integrated development environment*, or IDE.

In Visual C# .NET, programs are called *projects*. Projects can contain one or more source-code files. To create a new project in Visual C# .NET, select the menu item File | New | Project. In the New Project dialog box, select Visual C# Projects on the left and Empty Project on the right. Select a location and a name for your project. To create the program shown at the end of the previous chapter, you can use the name MyVeryFirstProgram. This project name will become the default name of the .EXE file. The name is not case sensitive.

Next, add a C# file to this project. Select the menu item File | Add New Item. In the Add New Item dialog box, select Local Project Items on the left and Code File on the right. Give the source-code file a name. For projects that have only one source-code file, you'll commonly give the file the same name as the project, in this case, MyVeryFirstProgram.cs. Again, the name is not case sensitive.

You will now be working in the Visual C# .NET editor, which is like a sophisticated version of Windows Notepad. Here's where you enter and fix your code. You can begin by typing the program from the previous chapter into the editor. Here it is again for your convenience:

MyVeryFirstProgram.cs

```
class MyVeryFirstProgram
{
    static void Main()
    {
        int ChildTkts, AdultTkts, TotalTkts;

        ChildTkts = 3;
        AdultTkts = 2;
        TotalTkts = ChildTkts + AdultTkts;
    }
}
```

Press Enter after each line. You'll notice that the Visual C# .NET editor displays all the keywords in blue. The editor uses different colors for different components of your program.

A couple warnings: The Visual C# .NET editor will attempt to help you with the indentation, so you probably won't have to insert them yourself. But if you misspell "class" or some other keyword, the editor won't recognize the keyword, it won't display the keyword in blue, and it won't insert the correct indentation. Also, if something in your code is syntactically impossible, the editor will display a squiggly underline. If the editor doesn't recognize what you've typed as a valid C# program, it might simply ignore any tabs that you insert yourself! Also, the editor will sometimes attempt to finish your typing by listing suggestions. At this stage of your learning, it might be best to just ignore those suggestions.

You can compile the program by selecting either Build Solution or Build MyVeryFirstProgram from the Build menu. The program saves MyVeryFirstProgram.cs to disk and compiles it. If there are any compile errors, they will be listed in the window below the editor. The errors will indicate the line numbers in the source-code file. You can also double-click the error to go to that line. Some errors are actually *warnings*. The warnings indicate a *possible* problem that is nevertheless legal and does not prevent an .EXE file from being created.

To run the program, choose Start Without Debugging from the Debug menu, or press Ctrl-F5. If any changes have been made to the source-code file since the last time the program was compiled, this option will ask whether you want the program to be recompiled. Thus, you can use this menu item exclusively to both compile and run the program.

When you run the program, a console window will appear. The console window looks like a miniature old-fashioned computer terminal with a black background and white text. The caption of the console window will display the filename of your project. In the window, you'll then see the text

```
Press any key to continue
```

which means that the program has finished running. MyVeryFirstProgram does not display any output of its own, but that's a problem we'll fix in the next chapter. Press any key to make the console window disappear.

I've suggested using the same name for the project (which becomes the .EXE filename), the C# source-code file, and the class declared in the program. All these names can be different. Generally, a project consists of multiple source-code files, which must all have unique names. A C# source-code file can also contain multiple class declarations.

Visual C# .NET actually groups projects into something it calls *solutions*. A solution can contain one or more projects. (The idea is that a solution can encompass multiple .EXE files and dynamic link libraries. Each .EXE file and DLL is a different project in the same solution.) When you create a project (as we did), Visual C# .NET creates a solution as well, containing that single project. To close that solution in Visual C# .NET, you'll want to pick Close Solution from the File menu. To later reopen the solution, use Open Solution from the File menu. (Don't open the .CS file.)

Visual C# .NET can be overwhelming for the beginning programmer. If you'd like to use something much simpler (and free), you can download my Key of C# program from my Web site. (See the Prelude of this book for details.)

To create a new project in Key of C#, select New Project from the File menu. Type in a name. If you leave items on the dialog box checked, the program will also create a C# file of the same name in this project. You'll be working in a Notepad-like editor. The program will help you by automatically indenting some lines, but it won't ever delete tabs that it's supplied or you've entered. Type in the program, and press F6 to compile it. Compile errors will appear in an area below the editor. Press F7 to run the program. Or, you can use F8 to both compile and run the program.

The example programs in this book are also available for downloading from the Microsoft Press Web site (*http://www.microsoft.com/mspress/books /6261.asp*). Rather than type the programs in yourself, you can simply open the solutions I've created, and then compile and run the programs. But don't do this. Get into the practice of typing C# code in yourself, rather like doing piano exercises.

Whatever approach you use to compile your programs, you'll want to spend a lot of time *experimenting* with your code and trying stuff out. Experimentation is probably the single most important activity in learning a programming language. The great thing about programming is that experimentation is both easy and safe. It's not like a chemistry set. You're not going to blow up your house. For example, remove one of the assignment statements from MyVeryFirstProgram. See what happens if *AdultTkts* or *ChildTkts* has no value. Get accustomed to seeing error messages from the compiler and knowing what they mean. You could also remove the assignment statement that calculates the value of *Total-Tkts*. That's not an error, but what does the compiler warn you about?

Try replacing the word *class* with the keyword *struct* (which stands for structure) in the program. The program should work just the same. There actually is quite a significant difference between classes and structures, and understanding that difference in all its implications will be one of the important aspects of C# programming you'll learn in this book. But in other ways, *class* and *struct* are identical.

If you want to give .EXE files of your C# programs to your friends to run, they'll need to have the Microsoft .NET Framework Redistributable installed, which comes with Visual C# .NET and is also available for downloading from *http://msdn.microsoft.com/downloads/list/netdevframework.asp*.

Of course, you won't want to give anybody a program that doesn't display some output. Correcting that problem will be our task in the next chapter.

5

Console Output

As a programmer writing computer programs, you must develop a very special relationship with a shadowy being who lurks just beyond the periphery of your vision. At the same time needy, confused, angry, and malicious, that person is known to you only as *the user*. At best, the user is merely compliant; at worst, the user is an adversary, a mad typist who will bang on your program until it fails.

In the early stages of program development, the only user is you. As you alternate between programming and testing, your perspective bounces back and forth between programmer and user. When your program displays output to the user, that output becomes input to the user's senses. When the user outputs text by typing on the keyboard, that text becomes input to the program.

Programs must have some way to display output to the user and get input from the user, called user input and output, or I/O. The methods for doing this, which are sometimes referred to as I/O models, differ depending on what the program is being used for. A program running under Windows gets user input from the keyboard, the mouse, and various controls such as buttons and scroll bars. A Windows program displays output to the user in the form of text and graphics. A program embedded in a microwave oven would have a much different user I/O model. The input would comprise the buttons on the front panel, and the output would be devices that turn the oven on and off, spin the platter, and turn on the light. Like C, the C# languages does not itself include any provision for user I/O. This might sound like a deficiency, but it's really not. It's more correct to say that C# does not *impose* any particular user I/O model on the programmer. You choose your I/O depending on what your program will be used for.

For the more common user I/O models—Windows, the Web, or the console—you make use of classes and methods defined in the .NET Framework. To explore these classes, you run a program under Windows that provides online .NET Framework documentation. (This program also includes C# documentation.)

If you have Visual C# .NET installed, run the Microsoft Visual Studio .NET Documentation program listed under Microsoft Visual Studio .NET in the Start Programs list. On the left of the program is an expandable tree structure. Expand Visual Studio .NET and then .NET Framework.

If you're using the .NET Framework SDK, run the Documentation program listed under Microsoft .NET Framework SDK in the Start Programs list. In the tree structure on the left, expand .NET Framework SDK.

You can also access the documentation over the Internet. Go to *http://msdn.microsoft.com/library*. On the left, select .NET Development, then .NET Framework SDK, then .NET Framework, and finally Reference.

In any case, continue by expanding the Reference item, and then Class Library. Now the most important rule is not to be frightened by the long list that appears. Much of the stuff listed here you'll never have occasion to use. What you're looking at here is a list of *namespaces*, which serve to separate the .NET classes into functional groups. The namespace that has the most basic classes and structures is the *System* namespace. If you expand that namespace, you'll see Console Class, and expanding that, you'll see the methods your program can use to read console input and write console output. That's what we'll be using here. Eventually you'll want to take a closer look at these methods; for now, just get a feel for where they're documented.

Let's begin with output; input will come later in Chapter 12. To display output to the console, you use two methods named *System.Console.Write* (which you can pronounce as "system dot console dot write") and *System.Console.WriteLine* ("write line").

For example, to display the value of *TotalTkts* to the user, you can insert the following statement in MyVeryFirstProgram right after the *TotalTkts* assignment statement:

```
System.Console.WriteLine(TotalTkts);
```

Recompile and run the program. Now you'll see the number

```
5
```

displayed on the console followed by the familiar "Press any key to continue." The program is working!

You can also try

```
System.Console.Write(TotalTkts);
```

In this case, you'll see

```
5Press any key to continue
```

The difference is that *System.Console.WriteLine* drops to the next line after displaying its output, but *System.Console.Write* does not. The latter method is useful for displaying multiple items on the same line.

Like romance novelists and T.S. Eliot's cats, every method in the .NET Framework has three names. *WriteLine* is the actual name of the method. You already have some idea what a method is because *Main* is a method. A method is a collection of code that performs a specific job. In this case, the job of the *WriteLine* method is to display program output to the console.

Console is a class. You already know what a class is because *MyVeryFirstProgram* is a class. Just as *Main* is a method in the *MyVeryFirstProgram* class, *WriteLine* is a method in the *Console* class.

System is a *namespace*. All classes in the .NET Framework are organized in namespaces that separate the classes into functional groups. There might be another namespace that has a class named *Console*, and that would be OK.

In the *C# Language Specification*, a statement such as:

```
System.Console.WriteLine(TotalTkts);
```

is referred to as an *invocation expression*, but most C# programmers would say that it's a *method call*. The program *calls* the *WriteLine* method, essentially handing over the value of the *TotalTkts* variable, which must be enclosed in parentheses after the method name. It is said that the program *passes* the *TotalTkts* variable to the *WriteLine* method—or that the *TotalTkts* variable is an *argument* to *WriteLine*.

In Chapter 3, when I discussed the declaration of the *Main* method, I said that *Main* had no input parameters. The declaration of *Main* in your program reflects this fact by using a pair of empty parentheses following the method name:

```
static void Main()
{

}
```

The *void* keyword indicates that *Main* returns no value.

In the source code that makes up the .NET Framework, the declaration of *WriteLine* probably looks something like this:

```
namespace System
{
    public sealed class Console
    {
        public static void WriteLine(int value)
        {

        }
    }
}
```

I say *probably* because the .NET Framework source code is considered proprietary by Microsoft, and I've never seen it. This little piece of imaginary code also includes several keywords here that are new to you (*namespace*, *public*, and *sealed*), which I'll discuss in more detail later in this book. The *System* namespace contains more classes than just *Console*, the *Console* class contains more methods than just *WriteLine*, and I haven't shown the body of *WriteLine*, which is responsible for actually displaying the number on the console.

The only thing I want to point out is that *WriteLine* is declared with a single parameter in parentheses following the method name:

```
public static void WriteLine(int value)
{

}
```

A program making use of the *WriteLine* method passes an argument to the method:

```
System.Console.WriteLine(TotalTkts);
```

When the program calls *WriteLine*, the *value* parameter to *WriteLine* takes on the value of the *TotalTkts* argument. The *WriteLine* method in the .NET Framework displays the *value* variable (which now has the same value of *TotalTkts*) to the console. When *WriteLine* has finished the work it has to do, the *WriteLine* method is said to *return control* back to the program that called it, which then continues.

I've been using the terms *parameter* and *argument*. I've said that the *WriteLine* method has a single parameter named *value*. I've also said that when a program calls *WriteLine*, it passes an argument to the method, which in this example is *TotalTkts*. Obviously, there's a close relationship between parameters and arguments—so close that some programmers even use the two words interchangeably. But you should keep the words straight. The difference is really one of perspective, depending on whether you're looking at things from inside the method or outside the method. If you could get inside the *WriteLine* method, you'd see code that displayed the *value* parameter to the console. But that code is not actually executed until a program calls *WriteLine* with an argument.

Let's return to the actual method call:

```
System.Console.WriteLine(TotalTkts);
```

Some programmers like to use blank spaces to separate the parentheses and the argument:

```
System.Console.WriteLine( TotalTkts );
```

What you can't do is spell *System*, *Console*, or *WriteLine* incorrectly or use the wrong case.

You can pass any numeric expression to *WriteLine*. For example, you could dispense with the *TotalTkts* variable entirely and use the statement

```
System.Console.WriteLine(ChildTkts + AdultTkts);
```

If all you really wanted to do was add 3 and 2, you could get rid of all the variables as well. *Main* would then contain the single statement

```
System.Console.WriteLine(3 + 2);
```

But even if we're just pretending that a program is doing something useful, it helps to have variable names that indicate exactly what the program is supposed to be doing.

It might seem as if *WriteLine* is simply transferring the value of the number to the console, but it's actually doing something considerably more sophisticated. The number is stored in memory as a particular pattern of bits. To be displayed on the console in a meaningful manner, the number must be converted to *text*, which is also a pattern of bits, but quite a different pattern. I'll discuss the conversion from numbers to text and back again in more detail beginning in Chapter 11.

If your program has multiple *System.Console.WriteLine* calls (as many programs in this book will), you can reduce your typing a bit by not typing the namespace part of the name (the *System* and the first dot). What you must do first is include the following *using* directive at the top of the program before the class declaration:

```
using System;
```

The keyword *using* is followed by a namespace name and a semicolon. This line is called a *directive* rather than a statement because it doesn't have any role when the program is eventually running. It merely instructs the compiler that any class referred to in the program is possibly a member of the *System* namespace.

If you include such a *using* directive in your program, you then can call *WriteLine* by specifying only the class name and method name:

```
Console.WriteLine(TotalTkts);
```

Here's a complete program that has a *using* directive and the shortened *WriteLine* call:

FirstOutputWithUsing.cs
```csharp
using System;

class FirstOutputWithUsing
{
    static void Main()
    {
        int ChildTkts, AdultTkts, TotalTkts;

        ChildTkts = 3;
        AdultTkts = 2;
        TotalTkts = ChildTkts + AdultTkts;

        Console.WriteLine(TotalTkts);
    }
}
```

The *using* directive doesn't save any typing here, but if you have multiple calls to methods declared in the *System* namespace, the savings can be considerable. Every program in the remainder of this book will begin with a *using* directive.

An actual program dealing with movie tickets would need to total the cost of the tickets. That calculation requires multiplication, which is among the arithmetic operators discussed in the next chapter.

Arithmetic and Its Shortcuts

Many computer programs must perform calculations of various sorts. For this reason, C# supports the four basic arithmetical operations: addition, subtraction, multiplication, and division. You already know how to add two variables in C#. If *A*, *B*, and *C* are all declared as integers, then:

```
C = A + B;
```

Subtracting one integer from another is just as easy:

```
C = A - B;
```

Both the plus and minus signs are known as *arithmetic operators*. These two operators are also categorized as *binary* operators because they have two operands—an expression on the left of the operator and an expression on the right. An expression can be a variable, a numeric literal, or the result of another operation.

You can use the plus and minus signs as *unary* operators as well as binary operators. Instead of typing

```
C = A - B;
```

you can type

```
C = A + -B;
```

or

```
C = -B + A;
```

In the first of these three statements, the minus sign is a binary operator meaning subtraction. In the second and third statements, the minus sign is a unary operator. These two statements add *A* and the negative of the value of *B*. The unary operator doesn't change the value of B itself, only the value that's used in the addition.

The plus sign, normally a binary operator for addition, can also be used as a unary operator:

```
C = +A - +B;
```

The unary plus sign has no effect on the variable it precedes. It's not very useful and that's the last time you'll see it in this book.

When it comes time to multiply something in your C# code, you'll notice that your PC keyboard doesn't have keys labeled × or ·, which are the traditional symbols for multiplication. But you will find an asterisk (the upper-shift 8 on American keyboards), and that's what you use instead:

```
Area = Length * Width;
```

Almost all programming languages use the asterisk for multiplication. Sometimes programmers use the word *star* to refer to the operator, as in "*Length* star *Width*," but it's probably clearer to say "*Length* times *Width*" or "*Length* mult *Width*."

Your keyboard probably doesn't have a division sign (÷) either. For that reason, division is indicated by the forward slash:

```
Hours = Minutes / 60;
```

You can say "*Minutes* slash 60" or "*Minutes* divided by 60" or "*Minutes* div 60."

Of the four basic arithmetical operations, everyone probably agrees that division is the most difficult. It's no different for computers. Division of integers on the computer also has a couple of peculiarities that you simply cannot ignore. To demonstrate, here's some code that focuses on an important distribution issue:

```
int Cookies, People, Share;

Cookies = 11;
People = 4;
Share = Cookies / People;
```

What will *Share* equal in this sequence of statements? The answer is definitely not 2.75! *Share* can't equal 2.75 because we know from the declaration statement that *Share* is an integer. The *int* simply cannot accommodate a fraction, which means that if you need a fractional result, you'll have to pursue a different approach (as I'll begin discussing in Chapter 14).

Moreover, the fact that *Share* is an integer isn't really the problem here. The problem occurs on the right side of the equal sign rather than on the left.

Cookies is an integer and *People* is also an integer, and in C#, any mathematical operation between two integers results in another integer.

When C# divides two integers, it *truncates* the result, which means that the fractional part is just stripped off and thrown away. The result of dividing 11 by 4 is not 2.75. The 0.75 is thrown away and the actual result is 2. That's two cookies apiece.

Let's look at what happens in this example:

```
Cookies = 11;
People = 12;
Share = Cookies / People;
```

Share equals zero in this case. There aren't enough cookies for everyone to get one, so nobody gets any. (Sad, but true.)

Truncation works similarly for negative numbers:

```
A = -3;
B = 2;
C = A / B;
```

In a non-integral calculation, the result would be –1.5, but C# discards the fraction and the integral result is –1. Truncation is sometimes also referred to as *rounding toward zero*. The result of an integer division is the next integer closest to zero.

Fortunately, C# supports another operator that lets you rescue the truncated part of the division. This operator is called the *remainder* operator or the *modulus* operator. The symbol used for the remainder operator is the percent sign (%), a symbol that actually contains a slash and hence seems to suggest its relationship with division. The remainder is the number *left over* after the division:

```
Cookies = 11;
People = 4;
Share = Cookies / People;
Leftover = Cookies % People;
```

Eleven cookies divided by 4 people equals 2 cookies per person with *Leftover* equal to 3. When using the remainder operator with negative numbers, the result always has the same sign as the value on the left of the remainder operator.

The remainder operator turns out to be quite handy for certain jobs. The operator can break a number apart in ways that might otherwise be difficult. For example, suppose you had an integer variable named *FourDigitYear* that stored numbers like 1985 and 2004. If you wanted to convert such numbers to two-digit years (85 or 04), you could use the following code:

```
TwoDigitYear = FourDigitYear % 100;
```

The two-digit year is the number left over after dividing the four-digit year by 100. The result is always a number from 0 through 99. Another example: you have a variable named *TotalMinutes* that contains, perhaps, the running time of a movie in minutes. If you want to separate that value into integral hours and minutes, you could use this code:

```
Hours = TotalMinutes / 60;
Minutes = TotalMinutes % 60;
```

If *TotalMinutes* were 135, then *Hours* would be set to 2 and *Minutes* would equal 15. The resultant *Minutes* variable will always range from 0 through 59.

The remainder operator is also useful for determining if a number is equally divisible by another. For example, leap years occur mostly in years equally divisible by four. If the expression

```
Years % 4
```

is equal to zero, then the year is a leap year (usually). I'll show you complete leap-year calculations later in this book.

I mentioned earlier that division has a couple peculiarities. Here's one:

```
A = 3;
B = 0;
C = A / B;
```

This code shows an occurrence called *division by zero*, and it's not allowed for integers. You may wonder what I mean by *not allowed*, so let's see what happens. Here's a program that deliberately divides by zero:

DivideByZero.cs
```
using System;

class DivideByZero
{
    static void Main()
    {
        int A, B, C;

        A = 3;
        B = 0;

        Console.WriteLine(A);
        Console.WriteLine(B);

        C = A / B;

        Console.WriteLine(C);
    }
}
```

This program will compile just fine. When you run it, you'll see it display variables *A* and *B*. Then it will pause for a moment, and a dialog box will appear with the title "Just-In-Time Debugging." Press the No button to indicate that you do *not* want to debug the program. The dialog box will go away, but on the console you'll see the message:

```
Unhandled Exception: System.DivideByZeroException: Attempted
 to divide by zero.
```

You may also get information about the line number of the statement in the DivideByZero.cs file that caused the problem. In any event, the program is terminated and never gets a chance to call the third *Console.WriteLine* statement.

Unless your typing has been perfect in entering the programs shown so far, you've probably already had experience with *compile* errors, which are syntactical errors in your code that the compiler calls attention to when compiling your program. The DivideByZero program exhibits a different kind of error called a *runtime* error (or runtime *exception*) because it occurs when the program is actually running.

When confronted with a divisor of zero, the division operation is said to *raise an exception*, which is a fancy way of saying that it complains about the problem. A program itself can be informed when an exception occurs. You'll learn about this in Chapter 25. Until then, messages such as the preceding one will refer to an "unhandled exception," which means an exception that the program doesn't trap itself. The message also makes reference to *System.DivideByZeroException*, which is a class in the *System* namespace that the division operator makes use of when raising the exception.

In the DivideByZero program, try replacing the assignment of the variable *C* with

```
C = A / 0;
```

or

```
C = 3 / 0;
```

Now recompile. You'll get the compile error

```
Divide by constant zero
```

When you put an actual zero right after the divide sign in your program, the compiler is smart enough to reject the code outright.

So far, I've been showing you statements with arithmetic operators in isolation. You can also combine different arithmetic operators in a single statement. It's helpful when analyzing or constructing such statements to have a good feel for *expressions. The C# Language Specification* §7.2 says "An expression is constructed from operands and operators." Here's a simple expression that has two operands and a binary operator:

```
operand1 + operand2
```

Either or both of these operands could themselves be an arithmetic expression involving other operands. The result of this expression is the sum of the two operands.

Here's another expression that has two operands and a binary operator:

```
operand1 = operand2
```

The equals operator causes the operand on the left (which must be a variable) to be set equal to the operand on the right (which could be an expression involving other operands). Besides causing *operand1* to change, the assignment expression also has a value. The value of the assignment expression is the final value of the operand on the left of the equal sign, in this case *operand1*, an implication that will become evident shortly.

Here are a few assignment statements, the last of which uses four arithmetic operations:

```
A = 2;
B = 3;
C = 4;
D = 5;
E = 6;
F = A + B * C / D - E;
```

In that final statement, which operation happens first? If you take a look at the inside back cover of this book, you'll see a scary-looking table entitled "Operator Precedence and Associativity." This table has all the information you need to anticipate how C# will evaluate an expression with multiple operators.

Toward the top of the table are those operations that have highest precedence; operations of lowest precedence are listed toward the bottom. Operands in the same category have equal precedence. For operands of equal precedence, the associativity column at the right shows the order in which they are evaluated. With one exception, the associativity is always left to right.

Here's the statement in question:

```
F = A + B * C / D - E;
```

The multiplication and division operands have higher precedence than addition and subtraction. For this reason, multiplication and division occur first from left to right. The first operation to be evaluated in this expression is therefore the multiplication. The expression reduces to:

```
F = A + 12 / D - E
```

The division is next:

```
F = A + 2 - E
```

Addition and subtraction also have equal precedence, so these operations occur from left to right, first the addition:

```
F = 4 - E
```

and then the subtraction, which results in *F* equaling –2.

If you want something else to happen, use parentheses:

```
F = (A + B) * C / (D - E);
```

If necessary, nest the parentheses:

```
F = (A + B) * (C / (D - E));
```

The unary plus and minus operators are also in the Operator Precedence and Associativity table. They have higher precedence than the multiplicative or additive operators.

The equal sign, otherwise known as one of the *assignment* operators (you'll encounter a few more shortly), is at the very bottom of the precedence table. Assignment operators are the only operators that associate from right to left, which means that multiple assignment operators in a row will be evaluated beginning with the rightmost. Consider the following perfectly legal statement:

```
A = B = C = 27;
```

Because the assignment operation associates from right to left, *C* is first assigned a value of 27, then *B* is assigned the value of *C*, and finally *A* is assigned the value of *B*.

Here's another example of a legal statement:

```
C = (A = 5) + (B = 6);
```

The first set of parentheses forces *A* to be assigned a value of 5; the value of the assignment expression is also 5. The second set of parentheses causes *B* to be assigned a value of 6, and the expression equals 6 also. *C* is the sum of those two expressions, or 11. This is a statement that *requires* parentheses. This version without parentheses is *not* legal C# code:

```
C = A = 5 + B = 6;
```

The problem is that the addition has higher precedence than assignment, but once that addition takes place, the left side of the third equal sign is not a variable.

Another illegal statement in C# is an expression that doesn't do anything or that doesn't save the result of an operation:

```
A + 12;
```

Such statements are legal in C and C++, but they were often mistakes on the part of the programmer, so they have been banned from C#.

Now that we know how to add and multiply, we're ready to incorporate actual prices into our movie ticket program. If the child movie tickets are $7 and the adult tickets are $10, this program calculates the dollar total of the tickets:

TicketCost.cs
```
using System;

class TicketCost
{
    static void Main()
    {
        int ChildTkts = 3;
        int AdultTkts = 2;
        int ChildPrice = 7;
        int AdultPrice = 10;

        int TotalCost = ChildTkts * ChildPrice + AdultTkts * AdultPrice;

        Console.WriteLine(TotalCost);
    }
}
```

No parentheses are required in the calculation because multiplication has higher precedence than addition; however, there's nothing wrong with using parentheses even when they're not required if they will help you (and anyone else who may look at your code) understand the statement better.

The programmers who invented C apparently didn't like to type a lot. Or perhaps they were very conscious of the high cost of storage and memory at the time. Whatever the reason, the designers of C invented several little short-cuts that became some of the most popular features of the language, and which have been inherited by C#. You never have to use these shortcuts. But they can often reduce your typing, as well as make your programs shorter, clearer, and easier to understand.

It's fairly common in programming to add a value to an existing variable, for example:

```
AnimalsMissingFromZoo = AnimalsMissingFromZoo + AnimalsEscapedToday;
```

You really shouldn't have to type the same variable twice if you're just adding something to it. This C# shortcut lets you skip the second appearance of the variable:

```
AnimalsMissingFromZoo += AnimalsEscapedToday;
```

Notice the plus sign in front of the equal sign. If you refer to it as a "plus equals," any C, C++, Java, or C# programmer will know what you're talking about. The plus equals is officially called a *compound assignment* operator. You can also use the subtraction, multiplication, division, and remainder operators in compound assignments. The statement

```
AnimalsMissingFromZoo -= AnimalsCapturedToday;
```

means that the value on the right is subtracted from the variable on the left.

You can also use the multiplicative operators in the same way. The statement

```
YourBudget /= 2;
```

means that *YourBudget* is slashed in half, whereas

```
YourExpectedWorkOutput *= 2;
```

doubles the value on the left.

The remainder operator is also valid in a compound assignment statement:

```
CookiesStillAvailable %= HungryPeople;
```

For example, if *CookiesStillAvailable* equals 11 and *HungryPeople* equals 3, and they each have the same number of cookies, then *CookiesStillAvailable* will equal 2.

Just as you can use assignment expressions within larger expressions, you can use compound assignment statements in larger expressions:

```
C = (A += 4) / (B *= 7);
```

Not only is it very common to add something to or subtract something from a variable, it's also common to add or subtract the number 1. For example, software for a voting booth might respond to the voter's lever by executing the instruction:

```
VotesForSmith = VotesForSmith + 1;
```

This is known as *incrementing* the *VotesForSmith* variable. As you already know, you can save some typing by using the alternative:

```
VotesForSmith += 1;
```

You can also add one to a variable with a pair of plus signs:

```
VotesForSmith++;
```

This is called the *increment* operator. It's a unary operator of very high precedence. The plus signs can go either after the variable (called *postfix*) or in front of the variable (*prefix*):

```
++VotesForSmith;
```

You can also use a postfix decrement:

```
VotesForSmith--;
```

or a prefix decrement:

```
--VotesForSmith;
```

In the statements shown so far, there's no difference between the postfix or prefix forms of the increment or decrement operators. But that's not the case if you use increment or decrement in the context of a larger expression. For example, suppose *A* equals 0 and your program has this statement:

```
B = A++;
```

That statement sets *B* equal to the current value of *A*, 0, and then increments *A*. After this statement executes, *B* is 0 and *A* is 1. This statement produces a different result:

```
B = ++A;
```

This statement increments *A* and then assigns that value to *B*. After this statement executes, both *A* and *B* are equal to 1. Notice that the placement of the ++ signs suggests when *A* is incremented: *A*++ means that *A* is incremented *after* its value is used in the expression, and ++*A* means *A* is incremented *before* its value is used.

7

Comments

So far the programs in this book have been very short and simple. In real life, however, programs can become very long, complex, and perhaps even obscure. Sometimes programmers get into a zone when they're writing code, and once they've emerged from the zone, they're not quite sure exactly what they've done. Very often in the real world, people must understand and maintain programs that they didn't write. As a compassionate programmer, you should provide some help for yourself and other human beings who are forced to read your code. In other words, you should *document* your code.

I've already mentioned the importance of using descriptive variable names. Names such as *WordCount*, *SquareFeetPerGallon*, and *YearlySales* help indicate exactly what the variable is being used for. But the only thing worse than a non-descriptive variable name is a descriptive variable name that's not quite accurate.

It's also helpful if you avoid the use of naked numbers. A statement such as:

```
SecondsOfPleasure = 86400 * VacationDays;
```

is not quite as clear as:

```
SecondsOfPleasure = SecondsPerDay * VacationDays;
```

Using descriptive variable names and avoiding unidentified numbers are part of what programmers sometimes refer to as writing *self-documenting* programs— programs that contain readable and comprehensible code.

You can easily go far beyond self-documenting code by including *comments* in your programs. Comments are text that is ignored by the compiler, but which offers explanatory information to the programmer and other people who might work with the code.

Very often programmers neglect to write comments when they're coding because the comments really don't contribute anything to the actual program. You can always add comments later, of course, after the program is working (*if* you can figure out your code at that time). But it's often more useful to write comments *before* you code or *as* you code, when the intended functionality and operation of the code is fresh in your mind.

C# supports two types of comments. The *single-line comment* was first introduced in C++ and became so popular that C programmers wanted to use that comment style as well. The style was then made part of C and has also been inherited by C#. A single-line comment begins with two right slashes. Anything to the right of the slashes until the end of the line is ignored by the compiler:

```
int Eggs = 24;    // That's two dozen for eight pies.
```

In most of C#, line breaks don't matter. A single statement could be spread out over multiple lines, and multiple statements could be crowded together on the same line. Line breaks are considered to be the same as any other white space. The single-line comment is an exception to this general rule because the comment ends at the end of the line. It's one of the very few elements of C# where an end-of-line is treated differently from other white space.

The *delimited comment* (which for many years was the only type of comment in C) begins with the characters /* and ends with the characters */. The delimited comment can begin on one line and end on another. Anything between the comment delimiters is ignored by the compiler:

```
/* The following code skates around the block two times
      and then comes to rest at the playground wall. */
```

The comment itself can include the characters /* and the compiler won't complain.

You can use both types of comments with abandon. Precedence between the two types of comments is based on what the compiler encounters first. For example, this is a problem:

```
// Single-line comment /* delimited comment
      And continuation of delimited comment */
```

The two slashes force the compiler to ignore the /* opening delimiter. Unless there's an opening delimiter somewhere *before* the double slashes, the */ closing delimiter has no opening, so it's an error. The following comment is not a problem:

```
/* Delimited comment // Single-line comment */
```

The compiler ignores the double slashes because they occur after the /* opening delimiter and are therefore part of a delimited comment. The comment ends at the */ closing delimiter.

Many programmers like to include a descriptive comment at the top of each source code file, such as the following:

```
/****************************************************************
  SuperWriter.cs

  Programmed by Charles Petzold, June-July 2010

  This word processor will blow Microsoft Word out of the water!
 ****************************************************************/
```

This comment begins and ends with the standard comment delimiters. The extra asterisks are simply for aesthetic purposes. You can also use the delimited comments to provide a descriptive paragraph for every class and method in your program. When you need to search through a long code listing looking for a particular method, a distinctive commenting style can help the methods stand out.

On a more micro level, you can use single-line comments to describe individual statements. Generally the comment goes right above the statement and is aligned with it:

```
// Calculate the total cost of child and adult tickets.
int TotalCost = ChildTkts * ChildPrice + AdultTkts * AdultPrice;
```

Personally, I like to indent my comments relative to the line they describe, but many people disagree with that practice.

> **Note**   The C# compiler has a special feature that's described in the *online C# Programmer's Reference*. Comments that begin with three slashes that precede classes, methods, and other structural elements of your program can contain XML (Extended Markup Language) tags. The C# compiler then generates an XML file containing all these tags that you can then display in a human-readable format. Much of the .NET documentation is reputedly generated from these tags. If you're involved in a large programming project that must be extensively documented, you'll definitely want to explore this feature.

Even if your code is entirely self-documenting through your exquisite choice of variable names and your crystal-clear coding style, comments are still useful programming tools.

For example, you may have some code working, but then you think of a more efficient way to do the same job. Well, maybe you're not quite sure, so you probably don't want to delete your first version yet. Just comment it out! Stick a couple of comment delimiters in to render the code invisible to the compiler. If you put the delimiters in the far left edge, you'll be sure that you won't forget about them:

```
/*

        RobotArmPosition *= 4;
        RobotLegPosition -= 12;

*/
```

Now try the new version. Can't make up your mind which is best? Uncomment the first one, comment out the other, and see what you think. Don't forget to add another comment explaining why one of the versions is commented out.

> **Note**   You'll find that selective commenting is a good way of exploring and testing, but eventually you may encounter a situation in which commenting works, but it's not quite convenient. For example, you may have a program with two chunks of similar code. You want to be able to compile the program using one or the other, but without altering anything in the actual source:code file. Or perhaps you have a program that exists in both a shareware and a commercial version. It's the same source code, just with different features.
>
> In such cases, you'll want to explore some of the *conditional compilation* features available with *pre-processing directives* that are described in the *C# Language Specification*, §2.5.

Experimentation may be important to programming but it is essential in learning how to program. You may wonder, for example, how high a C# program can count. That's a good question, and one that can be answered by experimentation. Let's do so.

Part II
Basic Types

Integers and the .NET Framework

Integers (represented in C# by the *int* data type) are found in virtually all types of programs. For that reason, it's important for the programmer to know exactly their strengths and their limitations. For example, how high can an integer count? Let's write a little program to see if we can figure it out. From here on, the program source code files in this book will include a three-line comment at the top of the code listing to identify the file name and the book the program appears in:

HowHigh.cs

```csharp
// -----------------------------------------------
// HowHigh.cs from "Programming in the Key of C#"
// -----------------------------------------------
using System;

class HowHigh
{
    static void Main()
    {
        int X = 2;

        Console.WriteLine(X);
        Console.WriteLine(X *= X);
        Console.WriteLine(X *= X);
        Console.WriteLine(X *= X);
        Console.WriteLine(X *= X);
        Console.WriteLine(X *= X);
```

```
        Console.WriteLine(X *= X);
        Console.WriteLine(X *= X);
        Console.WriteLine(X *= X);
        Console.WriteLine(X *= X);
    }
}
```

You'll learn about easier ways to perform repetitive tasks in a C# program in a later chapter, but for now you can simply copy and paste the repeating lines of code. Each *WriteLine* statement after the first one has an argument that consists of a compound assignment expression. The expression multiplies the variable *X* by itself, and then *WriteLine* displays the result. When you run this program, the results are:

```
2
4
16
256
65536
0
0
0
0
0
```

The program seems to work fine up to the sixth *WriteLine* statement. At that point, *X* is mysteriously set to 0. After that little glitch, the program continues to work correctly because 0 times 0 is always 0.

Why does 65,536 times 65,536 equal 0? And why, when you alter the HowHigh program so that *X* is initialized to 3, do you get negative results? Here they are:

```
3
9
81
6561
43046721
-501334399
2038349057
-1970898431
120648705
1995565057
```

Although these results look very wrong, they're not random numbers spit out by a computer gone mad. They're entirely predictable, if a bit surprising at first. To avoid being blindsided by such results in a real program, it's helpful for every programmer to know how variables of different types are stored and manipulated in the computer.

In today's digital computers, all information is encoded as a series of bits, a word that means *binary digit*. A bit is the simplest form of information. Deep down in the computer hardware, a bit is the presence or absence of a voltage. But for humans, it's helpful to symbolize the value of a bit as 0 or 1. Whether a particular bit is currently 0 or 1 is sometimes called the *state* of the bit. A single bit is capable of two different states and is therefore capable of distinguishing between two distinct possibilities: yes or no. On or off. Thumb up or thumb down, depending on how the bit is used. Two bits are capable of four states, which can be represented by a pair of bits: 00, 01, 10, and 11. Three bits increase the states to eight: 000, 001, 010, 011, 100, 101, 110, and 111. Each additional bit doubles the number of states. For a particular collection of bits, the number of states is equal to

$$2^{\text{Number of bits}}$$

Today's personal computers are called *32-bit* computers because they generally work with chunks of data that are 32 bits in size. Some early computers could handle only 8 bits at a shot, and a group of 8 bits became known as a *byte*. Bytes still show up a lot even in today's computers: memory, disk storage, and file sizes are all measured in terms of bytes.[*]

As the 0s and 1s of multiple bits are strung together, they start looking like numbers, and that's exactly what they are. Just as we write decimal numbers as combinations of the decimal digits 0 through 9, we can write binary numbers as combinations of the binary digits 0 and 1.

C# uses 32 bits (4 bytes) to represent a variable of type *int*. An *int* is capable of storing both positive and negative values, so the formal definition of an *int* is a *32-bit signed integer;* the word *signed* means that one of the bits indicates whether a number is negative or positive. Because an *int* has 32 bits, it is capable of 2^{32} (or 4,294,967,296) different values. These values are divided almost equally between positive and negative numbers. I say *almost* equally because there is one fewer positive number than negative, and that's because one of the bit combinations must represent 0. The decimal number 0 is represented by thirty-two 0 bits:

0000-0000-0000-0000-0000-0000-0000-0000

I've written the bits as a binary number with dashes every four digits just to make it somewhat easier to read. From 0, you can count upwards through the positive numbers:

0000-0000-0000-0000-0000-0000-0000-0001 is equivalent to decimal 1
0000-0000-0000-0000-0000-0000-0000-0010 is 2
0000-0000-0000-0000-0000-0000-0000-0011 is 3
0000-0000-0000-0000-0000-0000-0000-0100 is 4

---

[*] My book *Code: The Hidden Language of Computer Hardware and Software* (Microsoft Press, 2000) begins with an introduction to bits and information.

    0000-0000-0000-0000-0000-0000-0000-0101 is 5
    0000-0000-0000-0000-0000-0000-0000-0110 is 6
    0000-0000-0000-0000-0000-0000-0000-0111 is 7
    0000-0000-0000-0000-0000-0000-0000-1000 is 8

and so forth. Each of these binary numbers is the previous number plus 1. Adding binary numbers is just like adding decimal numbers: you start at the rightmost pair of digits and work toward the left. In binary, 0 plus 0 equals 0, 0 plus 1 equals 1, and 1 plus 1 equals 10, which in practical multi-digit addition is really 0, carry the 1. You may want to try out a few binary additions with pencil and paper to get the hang of it.

As you know, any decimal number that represents a power of 10 (such as ten, a thousand, a hundred thousand, or a billion) consists of a 1 followed by 0s. Similarly, any binary number that represents a power of two is written as a single 1 bit followed by 0s. For example,

    0000-0000-0000-0000-0000-0001-0000-0000 is 256 or 2^8

and

    0000-0000-0000-0001-0000-0000-0000-0000 is 65,536 or 2^{16}

This little fact provides a clue to how you can convert binary numbers to decimal. Every digit in a binary number represents a power of 2. A binary number with five 1 bits like this:

    0000-0000-0000-0001-0000-0010-0000-1101

is the sum of the following five binary numbers, each of which has a single 1 bit:

    0000-0000-0000-0000-0000-0000-0000-0001 is 2^0 or 1
    0000-0000-0000-0000-0000-0000-0000-0100 is 2^2 or 4
    0000-0000-0000-0000-0000-0000-0000-1000 is 2^3 or 8
    0000-0000-0000-0000-0000-0010-0000-0000 is 2^9 or 512
    0000-0000-0000-0001-0000-0000-0000-0000 is 2^{16} or 65,536

The total is decimal 66,061.

At any rate, if you keep incrementing 32-bit numbers, you'll eventually get up to

    0111-1111-1111-1111-1111-1111-1111-1111 is 2,147,483,647

Let's pause here for a moment. Throughout this entire exercise the bit way over on the left has remained 0. What we have done—in our minds if not on paper—is to enumerate all the combinations of the other 31 bits. There are 2^{31} or 2,147,483,648 such combinations, which represent the decimal numbers 0 through 2,147,483,647. With 31 bits, we can't count all the way up to 2,147,483,648 because we need a bit combination to represent 0. The number 2,147,483,647 is the maximum positive number that a 32-bit signed integer can represent. It's equivalent to 2^{31} minus 1.

That bit on the far left is known as the *high* bit or the *most significant* bit, and when speaking about signed integers, is also known as the *sign* bit. Any number with a sign bit of 1 is negative. The common way of representing negative integers in modern digital computers is called *two's complement*, which refers to the technique used to convert between positive and negative numbers, which I'll describe shortly. It's most revealing to begin listing the negative numbers starting with the least negative:

1000-0000-0000-0000-0000-0000-0000-0000 is $-2,147,483,648$
1000-0000-0000-0000-0000-0000-0000-0001 is $-2,147,483,647$
1000-0000-0000-0000-0000-0000-0000-0010 is $-2,147,483,646$
1000-0000-0000-0000-0000-0000-0000-0011 is $-2,147,483,645$

Earlier I described how you can add binary numbers. If you add one to each binary number in this list, you'll get the next one. There's no difference in the addition rules just because one of the numbers is negative. Keep incrementing until you approach 0:

1111-1111-1111-1111-1111-1111-1111-1100 is -4
1111-1111-1111-1111-1111-1111-1111-1101 is -3
1111-1111-1111-1111-1111-1111-1111-1110 is -2
1111-1111-1111-1111-1111-1111-1111-1111 is -1

Now if you add 1, you'll get a 33-bit number:

1-0000-0000-0000-0000-0000-0000-0000-0000

But we're dealing with 32-bit numbers here, so that 33rd bit can simply be discarded. Adding 1 to -1 thus comes out to

0000-0000-0000-0000-0000-0000-0000-0000

which is where we started, the number 0.

When working with two's complement signed integers, you negate a number (that is, change it from positive to negative or back again) in two steps. First, you flip all the bits, which is to change every 1 bit to a 0 and every 0 bit to a 1. That's called the one's complement. You then add 1. That's the two's complement.

It should now be obvious that a 32-bit signed integer can range in value from $-2,147,483,648$ to $2,147,483,647$. Some calculations (such as 65,536 times 65,536 in the HowHigh program) would normally result in a value outside this range, in this case, a 33-bit number representing 4,294,967,296:

1-0000-0000-0000-0000-0000-0000-0000-0000

But because only 32 bits are available to store the result, only the lowest 32 bits are retained. That crucial 1 at the top is discarded, and the result is 0. When dealing with 32-bit integers, the value 2^{32} is basically zip.

In a sense, the 32-bit binary representations form a circle. If you add 1 to the binary value for -1, and keep only the bottom 32 bits, you get 0. That's normal. But here's the binary value of 2,147,483,647:

0111-1111-1111-1111-1111-1111-1111-1111

Add 1 to this value and you get:

1000-0000-0000-0000-0000-0000-0000-0000

That's the binary value for −2,147,483,648. In other words, the following code

```
int X = 2147483647;
Console.WriteLine(X + 1);
```

displays the result:

```
-2147483648
```

In the version of the HowHigh program in which X was initialized to 3, the value 43,046,721 multiplied by itself resulted in a negative. Here's how that happens: The binary representation of 43,046,721 is:

0000-0010-1001-0000-1101-0111-0100-0001

Normally, that number multiplied by itself would be 1,853,020,188,851,841, which has a binary representation of:

0110-1001-0101-0100-1111-1110-0010-0001-1110-0011-1110-1000-0001

But because the *int* is a 32-bit integer, only the bottom 32 bits are preserved in the calculation:

1110-0010-0001-1110-0011-1110-1000-0001

The high bit is 1, which means that it's a negative number. To figure out what that number is, flip all the bits:

0001-1101-1110-0001-1100-0001-0111-1110

and add 1:

0001-1101-1110-0001-1100-0001-0111-1111

That's 501,334,399, which means that the result of multiplying 43,046,721 by itself, truncated to 32 bits, is −501,334,399, exactly what the program displayed.

The anomalies we are experiencing here are occurrences of integer *overflow* and *underflow*. Overflow occurs when an integer exceeds the maximum positive value; underflow occurs when an integer is less than the minimum negative value. Often the word *overflow* is used to refer to both phenomena. The normal behavior of C# programs (what is called the *default* behavior) is to allow overflow to take place. C# adds, subtracts, multiplies, and divides integers without worrying whether the results will fit in a 32-bit box. Ignoring overflow is the most efficient and quickest way for a computer to perform integer arithmetic. The computer can just blindly do the calculation without pausing to examine whether overflow occurred.

Although some specialized programming applications might take advantage of integer overflow, in most cases it represents a problem and may very well indicate a bug in your code. If your program wants to charge somebody negative billions of dollars for a couple movie tickets, overflow is undoubtedly the culprit. If you would prefer that C# not blithely allow overflow in integer calculations, there are several ways to prevent it.

The first technique involves the C# compiler itself. You can instruct the C# compiler to create code that checks for overflow. This is an example of a compiler *option*. To illustrate, let's return to the HowHigh program at the beginning of this chapter.

If you're using the Key of C# program, select Compiler Options from the Project menu and check the Check For Arithmetic Overflow checkbox.

In Visual C# .NET, click the project name at the right and select Properties from the Project menu. Or, right-click the project name at the right and select Properties from the menu. On the left of the dialog box, under Configuration Properties, select Build. On the right, set the Check For Arithmetic Overflow/Underflow item to True.

Recompile and run. Now when the HowHigh program runs, it displays the first five lines and then raises an exception. Just as with the DividebyZero program in Chapter 6, a dialog box appears, this time reporting an overflow exception. Click No to see the error described on the console as the program is terminated.

You can also perform overflow checking for individual expressions right in the source code by using the *checked* operator. The statement

```
B = checked(5 * A);
```

will raise an exception if the multiplication results in an overflow *regardless* of the compiler option. Similarly,

```
B = unchecked(5 * A);
```

will *not* raise an exception regardless of the compiler option.

You can also use the *checked* and *unchecked* keywords on *blocks*, which are sections of code enclosed in a pair of curly brackets. Here's an example:

```
checked
{
    A += 1000000;
    B = B * A;
}
```

Any statement within the block that results in an arithmetic overflow will raise an exception.

So, you have a choice. You can allow arithmetic calculations to proceed without regard to overflow (possibly causing errors in your results), or you can cause such calculations to raise an exception. For the moment, this seems like a Hobson's choice (which is no real choice at all) because exceptions terminate the program; however, in Chapter 25, I'll show you how a program can detect when exceptions are raised and recover from them gracefully.

You may be tempted to compile all your programs with the *checked* compiler option to prevent all arithmetic overflow and underflow. I'd advise against it. Enabling overflow checking for all integer arithmetic may seriously impair the performance of your program. You may want to enable overflow checking when developing and debugging your program, but then turn it off when distributing the "release" version to others. If your program performs arithmetic on user input, you may want to include the *checked* operator on statements that may be subject to overflow or underflow and implement exception handling to recover gracefully from any problems.

I've been speaking of *int* as if it were the only integral data type supported by C#. It is certainly the most popular integral data type, but C# supports seven others.

Suppose you were dealing with population data. There's no such thing as a negative person, so why bother using a *signed* integer? You'll never be using half the values that a signed integer can represent, so you may want to use an *unsigned* integer instead.

C# supports an unsigned 32-bit integer data type called *uint*, which is pronounced "you int." You declare a variable of type *uint* just as you would declare *int*:

```
uint A;
```

The unsigned integer has no sign bit. The most significant bit is treated the same as any other bit. Like *int*, *uint* begins with zero

0000-0000-0000-0000-0000-0000-0000-0000

and ascends to the highest maximum *int* value:

0111-1111-1111-1111-1111-1111-1111-1111 is 2,147,483,647

But unlike *int*, *uint* continues to get more positive

1000-0000-0000-0000-0000-0000-0000-0000 is 2,147,483,648

until its maximum positive value:

1111-1111-1111-1111-1111-1111-1111-1111 is 4,294,967,295

The *uint* data type can store values from 0 through 4,294,967,295 ($2^{32} - 1$). A *uint* is currently sufficient to store the population of any country in the world, but not the total population of the world.

The *uint* is also subject to overflow and underflow. In the following sequence of statements

```
uint A = 4294967295;
A += 1;
```

the variable *A* would equal 0 if integer overflow were not being checked and raise an exception otherwise.

If the 32 bits of *int* and *uint* are simply not sufficient for your application, you can make the leap to 64-bit integers, which are called *long* integers. The 64-bit signed integer is *long,* and the 64-bit unsigned integer is *ulong*.

You can also use integers that are smaller than 32 bits. Use the *short* and *ushort* data types to store 16-bit signed and unsigned integers. The *short* data type stores values that range from –32,768 through 32,767; the *ushort* data type stores values from 0 through 65,536. Use the *sbyte* and *byte* data types to store 8-bit signed and unsigned integers. The *sbyte* data type can have values from –127 through 128, and *byte* can have values from 0 through 256.

Data types *int*, *long*, and *short* are all signed integer types, and *uint*, *ulong*, and *ushort* are all unsigned integers. For the 8-bit integral types, the naming convention is reversed: *byte* is the unsigned type and *sbyte* is the signed type.

Generally, even if a particular integer will only be used to store values less than 32,767, it doesn't make much sense to use *short* rather than *int*. Today's 32-bit processors can actually handle 32-bit values with more ease and efficiency than 16-bit values. Where smaller integers may be of some use is in storing data in files on disk. If you have a lot of small values, you may want to store them on disk as 16-bit or 8-bit quantities rather than 32-bit quantities. Also, you may be dealing with a pre-existing disk data format that has 16-bit or 8-bit integral values.

The general rule is this: when you need an integer, start with *int*. The *int* data type will probably be the best choice for 97.5 percent of the integers you'll ever need. If you need something larger than *int*, go to *long*. If you'll be using disk files for storing or retrieving small integers, use *short* or *byte*, or whatever the disk format uses.

In Chapter 5, I described how you can access the documentation of the .NET Framework. If you browse the *System* namespace of the .NET Framework documentation, you'll find a structure named *Int32*. The *int* data type in C# is actually an alias (a nickname of sorts) for the *Int32* structure in the .NET Framework. The other seven integral data types are also aliases for other structures. Rather than declaring a variable using the C# type name

```
int A;
```

you can declare it using the .NET structure name:

```
System.Int32 A;
```

These two statements are exactly the same. If you have a

```
using System;
```

directive at the top of your program, you can also declare a 32-bit signed integer using

```
Int32 A;
```

And now, instead of saying that you're declaring a variable of type *int*, or you're creating an object of type *int*, you can say that you're creating an *instance* of the *Int32* structure. That will make you sound like a *very* sophisticated object-oriented programmer.

Here's a table of the C# integral data types, their equivalents in the .NET Framework, and their minimum and maximum values:

C# Type	.NET Structure	Minimum	Maximum
sbyte	*System.Sbyte*	-128	127
byte	*System.Byte*	0	255
short	*System.Int16*	-32,768	32,767
ushort	*System.UInt16*	0	65,535
int	*System.Int32*	-2,147,483,648	2,147,483,647
uint	*System.UInt32*	0	4,294,967,295
long	*System.Int64*	-9,223,372,036,854,775,808	9,223,372,036,854,775,807
ulong	*System.UInt64*	0	18,446,744,073,709,551,615

If you look at the documentation of these structures, you'll find that *SByte*, *UInt16*, *UInt32*, and *UInt64* all carry the warning that the data type is not "CLS compliant." CLS is the Common Language Specification and defines the minimum standard that programming languages must comply with in order to use the .NET Framework. The CLS requires programming languages to support the *Byte*, *Int16*, *Int32*, and *Int64* integral data types but not the others. Some languages (most notably Visual Basic .NET) do *not* support the other integral data types. If you are writing code that must be used by other programming languages—and in particular, if you are writing code that will be in dynamic link libraries—avoid using *sbyte*, *ushort*, *uint*, and *ulong* data types. Otherwise, a Visual Basic .NET program may not be able to use the dynamic link libraries you write.

An *int* is mostly just a 32-bit unsigned integer. But because *int* is also an alias for the *System.Int32* structure, you get some bonuses. You'll notice in the .NET Framework documentation that the integer structures all contain several methods, two of which (*ToString* and *Parse*) are very important and which I'll discuss in Chapter 11. You'll also see two *fields* in each of these eight structures named *MinValue* and *MaxValue*. A field is similar to a method in that they are both members of a class or structure. But a field is much simpler. A field is just a variable or (in this case) a constant, which is a number that has a fixed value. You can refer to fields in your program using the class (or structure) name and the field name separated by a period. The MinAndMaxLongs program displays the *MinValue* and *MaxValue* fields of the *Int64* structure:

MinAndMaxLongs.cs

```
// ------------------------------------------------------
// MinAndMaxLongs.cs from "Programming in the Key of C#"
// ------------------------------------------------------
using System;

class MinAndMaxLongs
{
    static void Main()
    {
        Console.WriteLine(Int64.MinValue);
        Console.WriteLine(Int64.MaxValue);
    }
}
```

The program displays the output:

```
-9223372036854775808
9223372036854775807
```

Those are the minimum and maximum values that a *long* data type can be. Similarly, the other structures provide their own minimum and maximum values.

In Chapter 2, I discussed integer *literals*, which are simply numbers that appear in your program, written without commas, spaces, or decimal points. The number 456,748 in this statement is an integer literal:

```
A *= -456748;
```

The negative sign is not part of the literal; it's a unary operator that negates the literal.

In general, any integer literal is assumed to be an *int*. However, if the number is too large for an *int*, it's assumed to be a *uint*, or a *long*, or a *ulong*, in that order, depending how large the number really is. You can override that assumption by appending a 'u' or 'U' to the number, in which case the compiler will assume that the integer is a *uint* or *ulong* (depending on its size). You can append an 'l' or 'L' to the literal to force the compiler to assume that the number is a *long* or *ulong* (again, depending on its size). Using both options causes the compiler to treat the literal as a *ulong*.

You can also write integer literals in hexadecimal (base 16) notation. A hexadecimal number begins with the prefix 0x or 0X and consists of hexadecimal digits, which are the decimal digits 0 through 9, plus lowercase or uppercase A, B, C, D, E, F:

```
A *= -0x6F82C;
```

If you'd like to experiment with hexadecimal numbers apart from your C# programs, the Windows Calculator program can work with binary and hexadecimal (as well as base 8 or octal, which C# does *not* support) if you switch the calculator into scientific mode from the View menu.

Within limits, you can mix different integer types in calculations. For example, suppose you declare the following two variables:

```
ushort US = 45867;
int I = 523;
```

When evaluating the expression

```
I + US
```

C# automatically converts the *ushort* to an *int* prior to the addition. This conversion is necessary because numeric operations such as addition can occur only between numbers of the same type. The conversion is known as an *implicit* conversion because it happens without anything that you—the programmer—specify in your code. Following this conversion, the addition involves two 32-bit signed integers, so the result is an *int* that you can assign to another *int*:

```
int A = I + US;
```

C# can implicitly convert the *ushort* to an *int* because an *int* can represent all the values that a *ushort* can and more. (See Chapter 15 for more information about numeric type conversions.) Likewise, if necessary, C# can implicitly convert a *byte* to any integral data type of 16 bits or more and an *sbyte* to any signed integral type of 16 bits or more. C# can implicitly convert a *ushort* to any 32-bit or 64-bit integral type and a *short* to any signed 32-bit or 64-bit integral type. C# can implicitly convert a *uint* to a *long* or *ulong* and an *int* to a *long*. These are the *only* implicit conversions C# performs between integral types. (See the *C# Language Specification*, §6.1.2.)

However, if an integer literal—or any other expression that is constant at compile time—is assigned to an 8-bit or 16-bit variable and is small enough to fit in the variable, C# implicitly converts the value. This declaration statement is legal

```
byte B = 125;
```

despite the fact that 125 is normally assumed to be a 32-bit signed integer. (See the *C# Language Specification*, §6.1.6.)

In a complex statement involving multiple operations, C# performs these conversions on an operation-by-operation basis based on the operator precedence and associativity rules. In an assignment operation, the expression on the right side of the equal sign may need to be implicitly converted to the type of the variable on the left side of the equal sign.

Keep in mind that the conversion *precedes* the actual operation. What happens during the operation—whether overflow or underflow will be ignored or raise an exception—is entirely governed by the *checked* or *unchecked* keywords or compiler option.

If you perform operations between an *int* and a *uint*, C# will implicitly convert each number to a *long* for the operation, because that's the only data type that can hold all the possible values of both an *int* and *uint*. You *cannot* assign the result of an operation between an *int* and a *uint* to another *int* or *uint*. This code will not work:

```
uint UI = 45867;
int I = 523;
int A = I + UI;      // Compile error here!
```

It doesn't look like it, but the problem here is you're trying to assign a *long* to an *int*, and that's exactly what the compiler will say:

```
Cannot implicitly convert type 'long' to 'int'
```

C# will not implicitly convert from a *long* to an *int* because an *int* can't store all the values that a *long* can.

C# simply does not allow an operation between a *long* and a *ulong* because there's no other integral type that can store all the possible values of both a *long* and a *ulong*. If you try to add a *long* and a *ulong*, for example, the compiler will complain:

```
Operator '+' is ambiguous on operands of type 'long' and 'ulong'
```

In some cases, you the programmer will know that a particular operation between variables of different types can be performed safely despite the fact that the C# compiler refuses to perform an implicit conversion. In such cases, you can specify an *explicit* conversion. The simplest way you can perform an explicit conversion is by using a *cast*. A cast is simply the desired data type in parentheses placed before the variable, literal, or expression you want to convert. For example:

```
(short) B
```

converts the value of the variable *B* (which could be an *int* or any other numeric type) to a *short*. The casting has no effect on the stored value of *B*; it only changes the perceived type of *B* when used in an expression.

Just a few paragraphs ago, I showed you an addition between an *int* and a *uint*. C# implicitly converts both values to *long*, so the result of the addition is another *long*. Here's how to convert the result of that addition to an *int*:

```
int A = (int) (I + UI);
```

You can also explicitly convert individual variables:

```
int A = I + (int) UI;
```

Now the *uint* is converted to an *int* prior to the operation. The operation is now between two 32-bit signed integers, so the result is an *int* and the assignment is fine.

Casting is represented in the Operator Precedence and Associativity table, located on the inside back cover of this book, by *(type)x* and is grouped with other unary operators.

The problem with casting is that it may result in bits being lost. If you cast an *int* to a *byte*, for example, all the bits except the lowest 8 are simply discarded. In such a case, the cast will raise an exception at runtime only if you've enabled overflow checking.

Casting is a very powerful tool, but very easily abused. Some programmers consider it a failure of program design if they are forced to cast. So whenever you cast, give it some extra thought. Perhaps it really *does* indicate a problem somewhere else in your code.

9

Text Strings

Over the seven or so decades of their existence, computers have been designed to communicate with users in a variety of ways, including blinking lights, graphs, pictures, and speech. However, by far the most common medium of communication between human and computer is text. The use of text by the human race precedes the invention of the computer by several thousand years. The long history of text makes it familiar and comfortable, and quite an efficient form of data compression. In learning to read, we have also learned to scan text quickly when necessary to search for a particular word or passage.

In computer programming, the word *character* refers to a single letter, number, punctuation mark, or other symbol. The generic term *string* denotes a series of text characters; in C#, *string* is also a keyword that you use to declare a *string* variable, like this:

```
string Composer;
```

You can say: *Composer* is a variable of type *string*. Or, *Composer* is a *string* variable.

The *string* data type in C# is an alias for the *System.String* class in the .NET Framework. You can alternatively declare a string variable using:

```
System.String Composer;
```

Or, if your program includes a *using* directive for the *System* namespace, you can use:

```
String Composer;
```

The uppercase *String* refers to the *String* class in the *System* namespace of the .NET Framework; the lowercase *string* is the C# data type, which is an alias for the *System.String* class. What you can't use is a lowercase *string* with the *System* namespace:

```
System.string Composer;    // Won't work!
```

Because *string* is an alias for *System.String*, that declaration indicates a data type of *System.System.String*, which does not exist.

You've seen how to declare a *string* variable. After it's declared, you can assign it a value using an assignment statement:

```
Composer = "Aaron Copland";
```

The expression on the right of the equal sign is known as a *string literal*. A string literal consists of zero or more characters (including letters, numbers, and punctuation marks) within double quotation marks. The quotation marks are *not* part of the stored string. The semicolon that terminates the assignment statement goes *outside* the quotation marks, contrary to the way that quotation marks and other punctuation are mixed in written language.

The string literal must be on a single line. This won't work:

```
Composer = "Aaron
                Copland";    // No good!
```

Just as with integers, you can initialize a *string* in the declaration statement:

```
string Conductor = "Leonard Bernstein";
```

To display a *string*, you use the familiar *Console.Write* or *Console.WriteLine* method:

```
Console.WriteLine(Conductor);
```

That statement displays the text

```
Leonard Bernstein
```

on the console. The quotation marks used to delimit the string literal in the program are not displayed because they are not part of the string. You can also pass a string literal directly to the *ConsoleWrite* or *ConsoleWriteLine* method:

```
Console.WriteLine("Take me to your leader.");
```

We've been using *Console.WriteLine* to display integers; now we have discovered that it can display strings as well. This is possible because *Console.WriteLine* exists in many different versions. These multiple versions of the same method are called *overloads* of the method.

Here's a program that might look strangely familiar:

AddingTextStrings.cs

```
// --------------------------------------------------------
// AddingTextStrings.cs from "Programming in the Key of C#"
// --------------------------------------------------------
using System;

class AddingTextStrings
{
    static void Main()
    {
        string A, B, C;

        A = "hello, ";
        B = "world";
        C = A + B;

        Console.WriteLine(C);
    }
}
```

This is very much like MyVeryFirstProgram in Chapter 3 except that the three variables are now declared as strings rather than integers. Instead of the program assigning numbers to the first two variables, they are assigned string literals. Consequently, the statement

```
C = A + B;
```

may look a bit odd here. After all, you know what it means to add two numbers together. But adding two strings? What does that mean?

The plus sign *concatenates* the two strings, which means to link together. The AddingTextStrings program displays the following output on the console:

```
hello, world
```

That's a fairly famous programmer greeting ever since 1978 when it appeared at the beginning of the classic book *The C Programming Language* by Brian W. Kernighan and Dennis M. Ritchie. But Kernighan and Ritchie just put the entire string in the C equivalent of the *WriteLine* method; they couldn't be clever and use string concatenation because it's not supported in C.

The use of the same operator (such as plus) for different types of operations (such as addition and concatenation) is known as *operator overloading*.

Notice that the string literal assigned to *A* includes a space after the comma. String concatenation doesn't insert its own spaces. You must provide them.

You can also use the addition assignment operator with strings:

```
string Boast = "This is a string.";
Boast += " And that's the truth!";
```

The operator concatenates the string on the right of the operator to the end of the existing string. No other arithmetic operators are allowed for strings.

String concatenation also comes in handy if you need to initialize a string variable with a very long string:

```
string DavidCopperfield =
    "Whether I shall turn out to be the hero of my own life, or " +
    "whether that station will be held by anybody else, these " +
    "pages must show. To begin my life with the beginning of my " +
    "life, I record that I was born (as I have been informed and " +
    "believe) on a Friday, at twelve o'clock at night. It was " +
    "remarked that the clock began to strike, and I began to " +
    "cry, simultaneously.";
```

You can use string concatenation to display a combination of string literals and string variables:

```
Console.WriteLine("Have you ever heard " + Conductor +
                " conduct " + Composer + "?");
```

That statement is the equivalent of these five statements:

```
Console.Write("Have you ever heard ");
Console.Write(Conductor);
Console.Write(" conduct ");
Console.Write(Composer);
Console.WriteLine("?");
```

Notice the use of *Write* rather than *WriteLine* for the first four parts of the sentence. As you'll recall, *Write* doesn't skip to the next line after displaying its argument. Both code examples display the text:

```
Have you ever heard Leonard Bernstein conduct Aaron Copland?
```

The documentation of the *System.String* class lists a *property* named *Length*. A property is very similar to a field, which I discussed in the previous chapter. You'll learn much more about properties and fields in Part IV of this book. For now, you should know that this particular property provides you with the number of characters in a particular string. The expression

```
DavidCopperfield.Length
```

returns the number of characters in the string declared above, namely 368. You'll see this property again in Chapter 10.

If C# requires that you use double quotation marks to delimit a string literal, what do you do if the string itself needs to contain a double quote? Suppose you need to display a string like this:

```
The name of the composition is "Appalachian Spring."
```

It's always been a little bit of a problem in programming languages to include special characters—such as the string delimiter—in a string. C# inherits a solution from C and C++. To include a double quote in a string literal, you preface the double quote sign with a reverse slash (also known as the backslash):

```
string StringWithQuotes =
    "The name of the composition is \"Appalachian Spring.\"";
```

The backslash is called an *escape* character in a string. An escape character alters the normal meaning of the character that follows.

Now the question becomes: what if you need a backslash character in a string? Although the backslash is a rarity in most written communication, it often appears in programs written for MS-DOS or Windows because the backslash is used as a separator for directory names.[*]

To include a backslash in a string, use two of them in a row. The declaration statement

```
string Directory = "C:\\Program Files\\Key of C#";
```

creates a string that refers to the directory name:

```
C:\Program Files\Key of C#
```

These days you don't need to use the backslash to separate directory names in programs written for MS-DOS and Windows. You can use a forward slash instead:

```
string Directory = "C:/Program Files/Key of C#";
```

Inside the computer, characters in a text string are represented by numbers and ultimately by bits. For many years, most computers used a character encoding known as ASCII (American Standard Code for Information Interchange). ASCII is a 7-bit code and thus able to represent 128 (2^7) unique characters.

---

[*] The heritage of this usage is a sad, sad story. In UNIX, directories in a fully-qualified filename are separated by the *forward* slash. The backslash was chosen as an escape character in C mostly because it wasn't used for anything else. In MS-DOS 1.0, which did *not* support a UNIX-like hierarchical file system, the forward slash was used for command line arguments. (In UNIX, command line arguments were prefaced with dashes.) So, when directories were introduced into MS-DOS 2.0, the backslash rather than the slash was chosen to separate directory names, seemingly without any thought being given to the problems this would cause in C.

If you're using a standard American English keyboard, you'll count 47 keys that generate 94 different characters (letters, numbers, and symbols) depending on the Shift key. The space bar generates another ASCII character. ASCII also defines 33 *control characters*, which have no visual representation and instead control the way in which text is displayed. Only a few control characters are commonly used today. These are the carriage return, line feed (which causes characters that follow to be displayed on the next line), backspace, tab, and escape. All ASCII control characters can be generated from the keyboard by using the Ctrl key in combination with letters and a few symbols. That means that you can type all 128 codes used in ASCII from your keyboard. (The function keys, arrow keys, and cursor movement keys are a little different. They do *not* generate ASCII codes.)

In practice, personal computers have commonly used 8 bits to represent text characters, thus allowing an additional 128 characters beyond what's defined by ASCII. These 8-bit encodings are often called *extended ASCII* character sets.

Unfortunately, there is no single standard extended ASCII character encoding. The original IBM PC used the additional characters for line drawing and simple mathematics symbols; Windows supports an encoding called Latin 1 that includes many accented characters used in Western European languages. Standards committees in many countries defined their own encodings for their own languages, some of which allow non-Latin alphabets such as Hebrew, Arabic, Greek, or Cyrillic (Russian).

The result: confusion and ambiguity. Whenever you see incorrect characters in a document or an e-mail from another country or another platform (such as the Apple Macintosh), you can be pretty sure that it's a conflict between two different 8-bit character encodings.

Beginning in the 1980s, work was commenced to eliminate all ambiguity in character encoding. The result is Unicode. Unicode defines a 16-bit encoding that allows 65,536 (2^{16}) codes, enough for all the world's languages likely to be used in computer communication, including the ideographs of Chinese, Japanese, and Korean. The first 128 characters of Unicode are the same as ASCII; the second 128 characters are the same as Latin 1. You can learn more about Unicode at *http://www.unicode.org*. The site includes an online edition of the book *The Unicode Standard, Version 3.0.*

Unicode has a long way to go before it supersedes 8-bit character encodings, but some programming languages, including C#, have already made the leap. C# strings are Unicode, which means that each character in a C# string is stored as a 16-bit character code. Unicode allows you to create strings like this:

The angle α equals 60°

Neither the Greek alpha nor the degree sign is part of ASCII.

You can enter Greek letters in your source code by switching to the Greek keyboard as I discussed in Chapter 2, but that doesn't help with the degree sign. In general, to include any Unicode character in a string, you locate the character in *The Unicode Standard, Version 3.0* or *http://www.unicode.org/charts* and preface the 4-digiPt hexadecimal character code with a backslash and an uppercase or lowercase U or X:

```
string Angle = "The angle \u03B1 equals 60\u00B0";
```

Interestingly enough, you can also use \u and the 4-digit hexadecimal character code in variable names and other identifiers. (See the *C# Language Specification*, §2.4.1 and §2.4.2.)

C# also inherits from C the following escape sequences that you can insert in strings. These mostly allow you to use common control characters without spelling out the entire hexadecimal code:

Escape Sequence	Unicode Encoding	Character Name
\0	\u0000	Null
\a	\u0007	Alert (bell or beep)
\b	\u0008	Backspace
\t	\u0009	Tab
\n	\u000A	New line
\v	\u000B	Vertical tab
\f	\u000C	Form feed
\r	\u000D	Carriage return
\"	\u0022	Double quote
\'	\u0027	Single quote
\\	\u005C	Backslash

For example,

```
Console.WriteLine("Beep the speaker\a and continue.");
```

will beep the computer's speaker halfway through the text output. The \a escape sequence works *only* on the console. The \v and \f sequences are for printers.

ASCII reveals its origins in the world of teletypewriters by the \r and \n escape sequences. The \r carriage return is supposed to move the print head to the left side of the page; the \n new line is supposed to drop the print head to the next line. In theory, both are required for moving the print head to the beginning of a new line. But this is an area of platform inconsistencies that show up in text files: In the MS-DOS and Windows environment, each line of a text file is generally terminated with a carriage return *and* line feed. Under UNIX, only a line feed is used. On the Macintosh, only a carriage return terminates each line.

In your C# console programs, you can use a line feed by itself to move to the beginning of the next line. The method call

```
Console.Write("\n");
```

is the same as this version of *WriteLine* that has no argument:

```
Console.WriteLine();
```

C# also allows an alternative to the use of the backslash as an escape character. When you preface a string literal with the *at* sign (@), there are no escape characters:

```
string Directory = @"C:\Program Files\Key of C#";
```

This is called a *verbatim string*. Backslashes are treated as any other character. Any embedded double quote must be written with two double quotes:

```
string StringWithQuotes =
    @"The name of the composition is ""Appalachian Spring.""";
```

That's how most other programming languages handle the quote-in-a-string problem.

I've already shown you how you can use the plus sign to concatenate strings. You can also use the plus sign to concatenate strings with numbers:

```
Console.WriteLine("The total number of tickets is " + TotalTkts);
```

Or:

```
Console.WriteLine(TotalTkts + " is the answer");
```

The rule here is simple: If the operand on either side of a plus sign is a string, the operand on the other side of the plus sign is converted to a string. The two strings are then concatenated.

To become a good programmer you must train yourself to think like a computer. I don't mean all the time. That would be nuts. But sometimes, when analyzing your own code or someone else's, you must be very cold, methodical, and (more often than not) not very bright. For example, consider the following code:

```
int A = 33;
int B = 22;
Console.WriteLine(A + B + " is the sum");
Console.WriteLine("The sum is " + A + B);
```

These two *WriteLine* statements may look quite similar, but the results are very different. Here's the program output:

```
55 is the sum
The sum is 3322
```

Why the difference? As the Operator Precedence and Associativity table on the inside back cover of this book indicates, addition is associated from left to right. In the first *WriteLine* call, the variables *A* and *B* are added and then converted to text to be concatenated with the string. In the second *WriteLine* call, the string is concatenated with the text representation of *A* (which is "33"), and then the string "The sum is 33" is concatenated with "22". To override the normal precedence and associativity, use parentheses:

```
Console.WriteLine("The sum is " + (A + B));
```

As I discussed in the previous chapter, all the integer types in C# are implemented by structures in the .NET Framework. The *string* date type in C# corresponds to the .NET type *System.String*, which is *not* a structure. *System.String* is instead a *class*.

Structures and classes in C# are very similar, but they have one essential difference: A structure is a *value* type, whereas a class is a *reference* type. What this means and what the difference implies will become apparent in the next chapter.

10

The Stack and the Heap

A primary reason for the invention of high-level languages was to free the programmer from worrying about the internal workings of the computer. But it never hurts to know a little something about what's going on behind the scenes. In particular, it helps to know how a computer program stores variables in memory while the program is running. To store a variable, the program must *allocate* a chunk of memory, which means to set aside a number of consecutive bytes sufficient for the variable's size. When the variable is no longer needed, the memory can be *freed*.

> **Note**   The material in this chapter is not part of the C# language specification but is strongly implied by the way the C# language works. I've undoubtedly simplified a few details. One of the simplifications I've made is to assume that *string* variables that are set from string literals are treated like other reference types.

When a method begins execution, memory for all the variables declared in the method is allocated from an area of memory called the *stack*. The memory for these variables is freed when the method reaches its end.

For example, suppose a method declares four variables:

```
int A, B;
long C;
string D;
```

These variables are stored on the stack—4 bytes for *A*, 4 bytes for *B*, 8 bytes for *C*, but now we have a problem: exactly how many bytes are needed to store a string?

It depends. Strings can be long and strings can be short, and as the code in the method executes, the string stored by a particular string variable can change its size:

```
StringVariable += StringVariable;
```

Even if the compiler looks ahead in the code and examines all the places where the *string* variable is assigned, it still can't figure out how much space is needed. The variable could be assigned from some text that the user types in, or that comes from a file, or from over the Internet. In other words, the length of the string is not known until the program actually runs.

For this reason, the string itself is not stored on the stack. Instead, as the program is running, the program allocates memory for the string from an area called the *heap*. The heap is a general-purpose area of storage organized so that chunks of memory of any size can be allocated and freed at random during program runtime. (The stack and the heap are also different in regard to prepositions: We say that something is stored *on* the stack but *in* the heap.)

The string itself is stored in the heap. However, the variable *D*, which is declared as a *string* in the preceding code, must be stored on the stack. What's actually stored on the stack is a *reference* to the location of the string in the heap. This reference is a number of some sort that links up the variable *D* with the string:

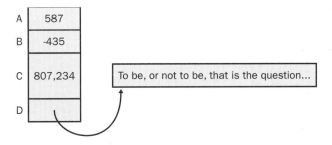

The string can grow or shrink in size in the heap, but the space on the stack required for the reference remains the same.

What is this reference exactly? It's hard to say: throughout the *C# Language Specification*, the exact nature of a reference remains vague. But consider the fact that all the bytes of memory are numbered sequentially starting with zero. These numbers are called memory *addresses*, and it's how a computer refers to a particular location in memory. The reference could very well be a memory address, also known as a *pointer*. If that is so, then we also know how much space a reference requires on the stack. These days, most people use 32-bit processors, which means that the reference is probably 32 bits wide, or 4 bytes.

So, to answer the original question: how many bytes are needed to store a string on the stack? The answer is probably four. But those four bytes are just a reference to the real string that is stored in the heap.

If programming languages have their own mantras, the mantra for C# is undoubtedly this: *Structures are value types. Classes are reference types.* It's good to memorize this mantra, but it's more important to understand it.

Structures are value types. We've already encountered several structures. All the integer types in C# are aliases for structures in the .NET Framework. The actual value of the integer is stored on the stack.

Classes are reference types. The *string* data type is an alias for the *System.String* class. It's a *class*. A class is a reference type. A reference type is stored on the stack as a reference to an area of memory allocated from the heap.

Structures are value types. Classes are reference types. Suppose a method contains the following declaration:

```
string Name;
```

When the method begins execution, memory from the stack (probably 4 bytes) is allocated for *Name*. That memory is sufficient to store a reference. But since nothing is assigned to *Name*, no memory from the heap has been allocated.

When you assign the variable a value

```
Name = "Franz Schubert";
```

memory is allocated from the heap sufficient to store the string. A reference to that heap memory is stored on the stack.

It's possible for a string literal to consist of two quote signs with no characters between them such as the following example:

```
Name = "";
```

A string with no characters is referred to as an *empty* string. Even though the string has no characters, memory is still allocated from the heap to store information about the string, including the fact that it has no characters. The *Length* property would reveal this fact: the expression *Name.Length* would return 0.

If you first assigned the string "Franz Schubert" to *Name*, and then assigned the empty string to *Name*, what happens to the memory allocated from the heap for the original string? The "Franz Schubert" string is still in the heap, but there's no reference to it, which means it's taking up unnecessary space that could be used for something else. If such is the case, the "Franz Schubert" string becomes eligible for a process called *garbage collection*. Garbage collection is a wonderful feature of C# and the common language runtime (CLR) that allows you (the programmer) to be free from worry about the heap filling up with variables your program is no longer using. The garbage collector frees this memory and allows it to be used for other variables. The memory used to store the "Franz Schubert" string may not be freed immediately, but sometime in the future as the program is running, particularly if memory gets a bit scarce, the memory in the heap will be freed and made available for other variables.

You can also assign *Name* a special value, which is the keyword *null*:

```
Name = null;
```

The keyword *null* is essentially a reference that equals 0. It means that no memory has been allocated from the heap. A string variable that does not reference any heap memory is called a *null* string. If you tried to determine the length of such a string using *Name.Length*, you'd raise an exception:

```
Unhandled Exception: System.NullReferenceException: Object reference
  not set to an instance of an object.
```

The *null* string and the empty string may initially seem pretty similar, but you can see now that they're quite different. When a string variable equals *null*, the value stored on the stack is 0, and no memory is allocated from the heap. When a string variable equals the empty string, memory has been allocated from the heap to store the string, but the string is 0 characters in length.

Now that we've seen how differently integers and strings are stored in memory, let's try to reunite the two data types by converting one to the other.

11

String Conversion

Text is the great compromise between human and computer. We force the computer to display its output in text and accept input in text solely for our own benefit. Even when a computer displays only numbers, the bit patterns of the numbers must be converted to text.

For example, if the decimal number 45 is stored in a 32-bit integer, the bits in memory are:

0000-0000-0000-0000-0000-0000-0010-1101

This is called the *binary* representation of the number. In order for a number to be displayed on the screen, it must be converted to Unicode characters. The exact number of Unicode characters depends on the magnitude of the number. The Unicode representation of the number 45 consists of the two characters '4' and '5', to which the Unicode standard assigns the two 16-bit codes:

0000-0000-0011-0100 and 0000-0000-0011-0101

As you know, the *Console.Write* and *Console.WriteLine* methods convert integers to their string representations automatically. However, it's also possible for a program to convert integers to strings directly, and also—just as importantly—to convert certain strings to integers. When you convert a string to an integer, the string must contain only characters that represent numeric digits, possibly preceded by a negative sign.

Let's begin examining the process of converting an integer to a string by declaring an integer variable and a string variable:

```
int I = 45;
string S;
```

You cannot simply assign that integer to a string:

```
S = I;    // Won't work!
```

If you try to do so, the compiler will tell you

```
Cannot implicitly convert type 'int' to 'string'
```

Nor can you cast the integer to a string:

```
S = (string) I;    // Still won't work!
```

This statement will give you the message:

```
Cannot convert type 'int' to 'string'
```

C# is characterized as a *strongly typed* language, meaning that it places many restrictions on the implicit or explicit conversion between variables of different types.

However, in some cases, the conversion of an integer to a string will be performed behind the scenes, such as when you call *Console.WriteLine*. Another way you can convert an integer to a string is to concatenate the integer with an empty string:

```
S = "" + I;
```

or

```
S = I + "";
```

In either case, C# converts the integer to text for concatenation with the string. But the string being concatenated with the integer is empty, so it doesn't affect the final result. If *I* is equal to 45, the resultant string will have two characters, '4' and '5'.

But we're still working with techniques that convert the integer to a string *behind the scenes*. To perform this conversion explicitly and aboveboard, you can call a method named *ToString* that is provided specifically for converting variables to strings:

```
S = I.ToString();    // The preferred method
```

Following this call, *S* will equal the two-character string "45".

ToString is a method. You can always tell a method by the parentheses that follow the name. Either you're declaring a method (like *Main*) or you're calling a method. The version of the *ToString* method in the previous statement has no arguments. The return value of the *ToString* method is a string.

Just as you need a dot between *Console* (a class) and *WriteLine* (a method in that class), you need a dot between an integer variable and the *ToString* method. You can even call the *ToString* method for an integer literal:

```
S = 279.ToString();
```

As you'll discover, the *ToString* method has very high stature in the .NET Framework. You can use *ToString* with any variable or object of any type, and you'll always get some kind of text representation of the object.

Now let's go the other way and convert a string to an integer. Let's begin with a string that contains a text representation of an integer:

```
S = "57";
```

You may want to convert this string to an integer. Fortunately, the string contains only digits! But once again, you can't use an assignment statement if the types are different:

```
int I = S;    // Won't work!
```

This time you'll get the compiler message:

```
Cannot implicitly convert type 'string' to 'int'
```

The attempted cast

```
int I = (int) S;    // Still won't work!
```

generates the compiler message:

```
Cannot convert type 'string' to 'int'
```

You may wonder if there's a method of the *String* class similar to *ToString* that converts the strings to integers:

```
I = S.ToInt();    // Doesn't exist!
```

There is not. But you're on the right track. You'll recall that *int* is an alias for the *System.Int32* structure. That structure declares a method named *Parse* that performs exactly the conversion we want:

```
I = Int32.Parse(S);
```

The return value of *Int32.Parse* is an *int*. The string argument to *Parse* must contain a sequence of digits, optionally preceded by a negative sign. There can be white space on either side of the number. For example, this will work:

```
I = Int32.Parse("   -572   ");
```

If the string contains non-numeric characters, or if there's a space between the minus sign and the digits, *Parse* will raise an exception. *Parse* will also raise an exception if the number is too large to fit in an *int*.

Let's do a little contrast-and-compare on the two methods for converting between integers and strings:

```
S = I.ToString();
I = Int32.Parse(S);
```

Both the *ToString* method and the *Parse* method are members of the *System.Int32* structure, but there is something fundamentally very different about these two methods.

Look what's to the left of the period: to the left of *ToString* is the variable *I*. The *ToString* method applies to a particular integer. It converts that integer into a string. But to the left of *Parse* is not a variable, but a structure name—the *Int32* structure. The *Parse* method doesn't apply to a particular integer. It actually creates an integer.

The difference between *ToString* and *Parse* is this:

■   *ToString* is an *instance* method.

■   *Int32.Parse* is a *static* method.

ToString is an *instance* method. What that means is that the method applies to a particular integer, in other words, to an instance of the *Int32* structure. You must have an integer handy—either a variable or a literal or perhaps the return value of a method—to call the *ToString* method of the *Int32* structure.

Int32.Parse is a *static* method. You use this method by specifying the *Int32* structure to the left of the method name. You don't need to have an integer to call *Int32.Parse*. The method creates an integer.

You've already encountered other static methods. *Console.Write* and *Console.WriteLine* are static methods as is *Main*. You've also encountered some static fields—the *MinValue* and *MaxValue* fields of the integer structures. You must preface these fields with the name of the structure. However, the *Length* property of the *String* class is an instance property. You apply it to a particular string.

As you'll recall, the C# data type *int* is an alias for *System.Int32*. That little fact implies you can substitute *int* for *System.Int32* or (if you have a *using* directive for *System*) you can substitute *int* for *Int32*. Instead of calling

```
I = Int32.Parse(S);
```

you can call

```
I = int.Parse(S);
```

The two statements are the same, although the second one admittedly looks a little peculiar to me. I prefer using the actual class or structure name when calling static methods.

All the integer structures have a *ToString* method, and they all have a *Parse* method. To use the *Parse* method with integers other than the 32-bit signed variety, use the appropriate structure or type name, for example

```
ushort US = UInt16.Parse(S);
```

or

```
ushort US = ushort.Parse(S);
```

When using the versions of *Parse* from the unsigned integer structures, the presence of a negative sign in the string will raise an exception.

In the Operator Precedence and Associativity table on the inside back cover of this book, method calls are symbolized by *f(x)* and are part of the Primary category at the very top of the table. The Primary category also includes *x.y*, called the *dot* operator, which is the period that connects a class and a method, or an object and a method, or anything like that.

Let's examine how precedence and associativity work with multiple method calls. For example, suppose you want to convert a string to an integer and then back to a string all in one statement. Here it is:

```
string S2 = Int32.Parse(S).ToString();
```

To the right of the equal sign are two periods and two method calls, which have equal precedence and are associated left to right. That means that *Int32* and *Parse* are combined first and are interpreted as a structure and a static method in that structure. The *Parse* method name is followed by parentheses with the string argument, so that method is called. The result is an integer. So now the statement has been reduced to the following:

```
string S2 = 45.ToString();
```

Now it's a simple integer combined with the *ToString* method, which converts it to a string.

Let's go the other way. Let's convert an integer to a string and then back to an integer in one statement. Here's the statement:

```
int I2 = Int32.Parse(I.ToString());
```

This is a *nested* method call, one method that is an argument to another method. In this case, the *Parse* method seems to come first, but it can't be called until its argument is evaluated. That means that the *ToString* call is executed first, reducing the statement to the following:

```
int I2 = Int32.Parse("45");
```

The *System* namespace also includes a class named *Convert* that I'm very fond of. *Convert* is full of static methods that convert all the basic types into each other. Here's an alternative method for converting a string to an integer:

```
I = Convert.ToInt32(S);
```

The documentation of the *Convert* class indicates that the method makes use of the *Int32.Parse* method. Exactly the same restrictions apply to the allowable characters in the string. Here's a static alternative to the *ToString* instance method of the *Int32* structure:

```
S = Convert.ToString(I);
```

The *Convert* class also provides overloads to these methods that let you work with number bases other than decimal. These overloads require two arguments that you separate with a comma. For example, the call

```
I = Convert.ToInt32(S, 16);
```

assumes that the string contains hexadecimal digits, for example, "A578B2". You can set the second argument to 2, 8, 10, or 16, in which case the string must contain only characters associated with that number base. If the second argument is 2, the string must contain only 0s and 1s.

Similarly,

```
S = Convert.ToString(I, 16);
```

converts the integer to its hexadecimal representation. Again, the second argument can be 2, 8, 10, or 16.

The *Parse* method of the *Int32* structure also has an overload that lets you be more specific about the string, but in a much different way. I'll discuss that overload in Chapter 29. The *ToString* method of the *Int32* structure also allows more precise specification of the formatting. I'll discuss these options more in Chapter 16.

12

Console Input

Displaying program output to the user, which our C# programs have done since Chapter 5, is only half the job of handling user I/O. Programs must also frequently obtain input from the user. In graphical user interfaces, such input takes many forms, such as buttons, text-entry fields, and scroll bars, although in most systems, user input ultimately comes from either the keyboard or the mouse.

In the .NET console environment, user input is always text typed from the keyboard. Generally, console programs will display a *prompt* asking the user for some input. The user types a response and the program attempts to figure out what the user meant.

The *Console* class provides two static methods for reading input: *Console.Read* and *Console.ReadLine*. These are somewhat opposite of console output methods. The *Write* and *WriteLine* methods require arguments (in all but one case) and have no return value. The *Read* and *ReadLine* methods have no arguments but provide return values.

When your program calls either *Console.Read* or *Console.ReadLine*, the method doesn't return control to your program until the user presses the Enter key. The *Console.ReadLine* method is by far the easier of the two methods to use. You first declare a *string* variable to store the text the user types:

```
string Input;
```

You then call *Console.ReadLine*, assigning the return value to the *string* variable:

```
Input = Console.ReadLine();
```

Or, you can declare the string and initialize it with the return value from *Console.ReadLine*:

```
string Input = Console.ReadLine();
```

Often programmers use the same string variable with multiple *Console.Read-Line* calls. Such a technique is possible only if you're able to complete the processing of one string before you obtain the next.

Here's a little program that displays a prompt and reads some text from the keyboard:

ReadConsoleAndDisplay.cs

```
// ----------------------------------------------------------------
// ReadConsoleAndDisplay.cs from "Programming in the Key of C#"
// ----------------------------------------------------------------
using System;

class ReadConsoleAndDisplay
{
    static void Main()
    {
        Console.Write("Type something and press Enter: ");
        string Input = Console.ReadLine();
        Console.WriteLine("Here's what you typed: " + Input);
    }
}
```

Notice that the first statement is *Console.Write* rather than *Console.WriteLine*. I used *Console.Write* because I wanted the cursor to come to rest one space after the colon of the prompt. When the user presses Enter, the *Console.ReadLine* method causes the cursor to drop to the beginning of a new line. At that point the *Console.ReadLine* call returns control to the program. You learned in Chapter 9 that the Unicode character set contains codes for carriage return and line feed. These codes are *not* part of the returned string.

As you know, *Console.Write* and *Console.WriteLine* convert integers to strings on their way to the console. *Console.ReadLine* provides no such luxury. If you want to obtain an integer from the user, you must convert it yourself using *Int32.Parse*:

ReadNumberFromConsole.cs

```
// ----------------------------------------------------------------
// ReadNumberFromConsole.cs from "Programming in the Key of C#"
// ----------------------------------------------------------------
using System;

class ReadNumberFromConsole
{
    static void Main()
    {
        string S;
        int I;
```

```
        Console.Write("Enter a number: ");
        S = Console.ReadLine();
        I = Int32.Parse(S);
        Console.WriteLine("You entered the number " + I);
    }
}
```

Let's focus on the two assignment statements in this program. The first of these two statements sets *S* to the value returned from *Console.ReadLine*. The second passes the *S* variable to the *Int32.Parse* method, which returns a number. You can dispense with the *S* variable and combine the calls to *Console.ReadLine* and *Int32.Parse* in one statement:

```
i = Int32.Parse(Console.ReadLine());
```

As we saw in the previous chapter, the compiler has no problem interpreting nested method calls. When the compiler examines the argument of the *Int32.Parse* call, it sees that it's a *Console.ReadLine* call. The *ReadLine* method is called first, and the return value is passed to *Parse*.

Now that we know how to get numbers from the user, let's rewrite that little movie ticket program so that it's closer to something that might be found in the real world:

TicketCalc.cs

```
// --------------------------------------------------
// TicketCalc.cs from "Programming in the Key of C#"
// --------------------------------------------------
using System;

class TicketCalc
{
    static void Main()
    {
        int AdultPrice = 10, ChildPrice = 7;

        Console.Write("Enter number of adult tickets: ");
        int AdultTkts = Int32.Parse(Console.ReadLine());

        Console.Write("Enter number of child tickets: ");
        int ChildTkts = Int32.Parse(Console.ReadLine());

        int TotalCost = AdultTkts * AdultPrice + ChildTkts * ChildPrice;
        Console.WriteLine("The total cost is $" + TotalCost);
    }
}
```

The program asks the user for the number of tickets desired, but the ticket costs remain stored in the program. It wouldn't make sense to ask the user how much the tickets are. That's something the program controls.

I hope you're inquisitive enough to try typing something other than a number into the TicketCalc program. As I mentioned in the last chapter, when *Parse* encounters a string containing non-numeric characters, it raises an exception. The TicketCalc program also won't complain if you enter a negative number. A real-life program would have to protect itself against both of these eventualities.

For the programmer, input is always more difficult than output. Always, always, always. Even for people, talking is easier than comprehending others, as is most obvious when learning a foreign language. There's no real control over input, and a computer program is stuck with what it gets.

For example, a program may display the prompt:

```
Enter a number between 0 and 100:
```

And then the user types:

```
7Q
```

Well, yes, the left pinkie was probably aiming for the 1 or 2 key and missed. But the program has to deal with what the user actually typed. Only sophisticated word processing programs can—or should—automatically convert typed words such as "teh" into "the."

Any program that handles user input will probably spend a considerable amount of energy performing jobs that come under the category of *validity checking*. Strategies vary for dealing with errant user input. One approach is to check each character as it's being typed on the keyboard and reject any character that's not allowed. For example, if a user typed "7Q," such a program wouldn't even display the Q on the screen and would alert the user with a beep. Unfortunately, the .NET console doesn't allow such techniques. Instead, a program using the console has to wait until the user types an entire line of text and presses the Enter key. Only then can the program begin examining what the user has typed. If the input isn't adequate, there's really no solution but to ask the user to try again.

13

Constants

The TicketCalc program that concludes the preceding chapter contains four variables: two of them are initialized and the other two are entered by the user. In this chapter, I want to examine the roles these two pairs of numbers play and how you might want to treat them a little differently.

The TicketCalc program could have been shortened a bit by not declaring the *AdultPrice* and *ChildPrice* variables at all and simply calculating *TotalCost* like this:

```
TotalCost = AdultTkts * 10 + ChildTkts * 7;
```

There's nothing really wrong with this code. But it's not quite as clear as the earlier code because the 10 and 7 no longer have names—they're just numbers. A comment might help to clarify what they are, of course, but without a comment, a few months or a year from now, someone may look at this code and say, "What are these two numbers?" Maybe that someone will even be you! Not being able to read and comprehend your own code is a very disconcerting experience.

On the other hand, we don't want to give the user the opportunity to type in the price of the tickets:

```
Console.Write("Enter price of adult ticket: ");
int AdultPrice = Int32.Parse(Console.ReadLine());
```

I'm sure most users would be honest if given the opportunity to set their own ticket prices, but one or two may type in something less than a fair price.

No, for now we probably want the ticket prices to be *hard coded*, that is, to be set to specific values in the program source code. Hard coding the values isn't entirely the best solution. Whenever the ticket prices change, you have to *open up* the code, which means you have to locate the source code file, load it into an editor, make the changes, and recompile it. If everything you need for this job is on your computer, that's not a huge problem. But the source code may not be easily available. Changing the executable may require more work than just recompiling it. You may have to put together a new installation program or distribute the new program to other computers.

Later on in this book, you'll see how to use disk files—a good place to store and change the ticket prices (or similar items) without recompiling the code. Until then, you can do everybody a favor by putting these variable declarations up at the top of your code where they're easily locatable. It's best if the program can be opened and modified—either by yourself or someone else—with as little damage as possible.

Suppose you look at the program one day and you see the two declaration statements at the top of the program:

```
int AdultPrice = 10;
int ChildPrice = 7;
```

However, later in the code, sometime before the final calculation of *TotalCost*, you see another couple of statements:

```
AdultPrice = 12;
ChildPrice = 9;
```

What can this change of the ticket prices mean? Is it a mistake? Did somebody open up the code to change the ticket price and add these statements rather than change the declaration? It's a mystery (particularly since the programmer who changed the code also forgot to add a comment).

In a program like this one, *AdultPrice* and *ChildPrice* really shouldn't be variables at all! They should have one value apiece, and that value should remain constant for the duration of the program. In other words, *AdultPrice* and *ChildPrice* should be *constants*, not variables.

You can declare constants using the keyword *const* preceding the type:

```
const int AdultPrice = 10;
const int ChildPrice = 7;
```

When you use the *const* keyword in a declaration, it becomes incorrect to speak of *AdultPrice* and *ChildPrice* as variables. They cannot vary. They are not variables. They are constants.

What does the *const* do for you that a variable does not? Any time after the declaration statement, any attempt to change the constant results in a compile error. If you try to include the statement

```
AdultPrice = 12;
```

later in the program, the C# compiler will display the message:

```
The left-hand side of an assignment must be a variable, property,
  or indexer.
```

And *AdultPrice* is none of these. In particular, *AdultPrice* is not a variable; it's a constant. When you see a compile error like this one, you need to ask yourself: am I declaring something a constant that shouldn't be because it later needs to be changed in the program? Or—and this is the case in this example—am I properly declaring something a constant and then later making a mistake trying to assign it a value?

When you declare a constant, you must provide a value. The following code

```
const int AdultPrice;    // compile error!
```

results in the compile error:

```
A const field requires a value to be provided.
```

Any variable that has the same value for the duration of a program is an excellent candidate for a constant. Not only do constants help programmers avoid making errors (such as modifying a value that shouldn't change), they also improve the program's performance. The compiler doesn't have to generate all the code that stores the constant on the stack, and then retrieve the constant whenever it's used. The compiler can just stick the constant's value right in any expressions that use the constant. When you use constants to store *AdultPrice* and *ChildPrice*, the compiler ends up treating the calculation of *TotalCost* just like the statement at the beginning of this chapter.

You can use expressions rather than literals when you declare constants:

```
const int AdultPrice = 10;
const int ChildPrice = 3 * AdultPrice / 4;
```

The multiplication and division result in *ChildPrice* being set to ¾ of *Adult-Price*, truncated to the next lowest integer. You can now change both values proportionally just by changing *AdultPrice*. In this case, *AdultPrice* must be declared before *ChildPrice*. If you use an expression to set a constant's value, the expression cannot contain variables! It must consist of other constants or numeric literals.

In Chapter 7, I showed you how a statement like

```
SecondsOfPleasure = 86400 * VacationDays;
```

is much improved if you replace the numeric literal with a descriptive name. That name was declared as a variable in Chapter 7 but a constant is better in this case:

```
const int SecondsPerDay = 86400;
```

A statement using that constant is certainly more readable:

```
SecondsOfPleasure = SecondsPerDay * VacationDays;
```

But there's an even better approach. You can declare the constant with an explicit calculation of its value:

```
const int SecondsPerDay = 24 * 60 * 60;
```

Now there's no question that *SecondsPerDay* is the correct value. The C# compiler evaluates that expression at compile time so this apparent multiplication doesn't affect the performance of the program when it's running.

The values of constants must be available when the program is compiled. For example, you can declare a particular string prompt as a constant:

```
const string Prompt = "Enter your age: ";
```

Because *Prompt* is a *const*, *Prompt* can't be assigned any other string. But you cannot set a string constant like this:

```
const string Response = Console.ReadLine();    // No good!
```

The *ReadLine* call occurs at runtime, not at compile time. You can only set a constant to a value available at compile time.

Of course, I've been assuming all along that the ticket price is always a whole number of dollars. What do you do when it's not?

One approach is to initialize the two constants as 100 times the ticket price:

```
const int AdultPrice = 1175;
const int ChildPrice = 850;
```

In other words, all the calculated amounts are in cents rather than dollars. After calculating *TotalCost*, you display it like so:

```
Console.WriteLine("Total cost = $" + TotalCost / 100 +
                            "." + TotalCost % 100);
```

I sometimes use indentation to make similar pieces of code line up. Notice that the whole dollar amount is displayed by dividing *TotalCost* by 100. Integer division (which is performed by the / operator) truncates the value to a whole number, exactly what we want here. The *WriteLine* statement next displays a period, followed by the cents. The cents are calculated using the modulus or remainder operator (%), which calculates the remainder of dividing *TotalCost* by 100.

This may seem like a perverse way to take dollars and cents into account, but it's not as odd as it seems. Regardless what method you use to handle decimal amounts, what takes place inside the computer is always integer arithmetic. Still, though, it's always nice to use variable types that take care of decimal arithmetic for you.

14

Decimals

Some programming languages foster an attitude that the programmer should be able to use variables without ever worrying about the underlying data type. The original BASIC (developed in 1964 at Dartmouth) was one such language. It's interesting that as BASIC evolved over the years, one of the necessary improvements in the language involved giving the programmer more control over data types.

I think it's good for programmers to be active in choosing data types for their variables. You'll find, for example, that many variables in your programs need take on only integral values. Declaring such variables as integers improves the performance of your program.

However, for those numbers that are not integers (that is, for what mathematicians refer to as *real* numbers), C# gives you two alternative data types, called floating point and *decimal*. Floating point is supported in a similar way by virtually every programming language invented or modernized in the past couple of decades. The C# implementation of floating point is inherited from C and C++. The *decimal* data type is new with C#, although it resembles data types in some other programming languages.

If you need to declare a variable for real numbers, you must decide which of the two options to use. For most scientific or engineering applications, you'll want to use floating point. The storage of floating-point numbers is based on scientific notation; consequently, floating point is ideal for very large or very small numbers.

The flexibility of the floating-point data type is offset by a very peculiar drawback: As I'll demonstrate in the next chapter, the floating-point standard doesn't allow the exact representation of most numbers. The error is very small, and it can usually be ignored for most scientific or engineering applications, but it sometimes causes problems in some calculations.

That's where the *decimal* data type comes to the rescue. The *decimal* data type isn't quite as flexible as the floating point, but it stores exact values. One huge application of *decimal* in the real world is for programs that must deal with that ubiquitous thing called *money.*

The C# *decimal* data type is an alias for the .NET structure *System.Decimal.* You declare a *decimal* variable like so:

```
decimal EurosInMyPocket;
```

If you're carrying a whole amount of euros (no cents), you can assign an integer literal to the *decimal* variable:

```
EurosInMyPocket = 45;
```

In this assignment statement, the integer literal is implicitly converted to *decimal.* If you also have some cents in your pocket, you'll probably want to assign a decimal literal to the *decimal* variable like this:

```
EurosInMyPocket = 45.72;    // Won't quite work.
```

But that won't work. To avoid confusing the C# compiler, you must append an *M* or *m* to any decimal literal. I prefer the lowercase option:

```
EurosInMyPocket = 45.72m;    // This will work just fine.
```

The *m* may or may not be easy to remember because it's the fifth letter of the word *decimal* and the first letter of the word *money.*

If you're very wealthy, you can also express the number in scientific notation:

```
EurosUnderMyMattress = 2.573450e4m;
```

Notice the little *e* embedded in the number to separate the two parts of the number. The first part is called the mantissa and the second part is the exponent. You can use an uppercase *E* if you want. The actual value is 2.573450×10^4, or 25,734.50. You can optionally specify a negative sign for the mantissa and the exponent:

```
decimal SmallAmount = -123e-10m;
```

That number is -123×10^{-10}, or −.0000000123.

Let's rewrite the program to calculate total ticket costs using decimal values for the ticket prices.

TicketCalcWithDecimal.cs

```
// -----------------------------------------------------------
// TicketCalcWithDecimal.cs from "Programming in the Key of C#"
// -----------------------------------------------------------
using System;

class TicketCalcWithDecimal
{
    static void Main()
    {
        const decimal AdultPrice = 12.50m, ChildPrice = 8.25m;

        Console.Write("Enter number of adult tickets: ");
        int AdultTkts = Int32.Parse(Console.ReadLine());

        Console.Write("Enter number of child tickets: ");
        int ChildTkts = Int32.Parse(Console.ReadLine());

        decimal TotalCost = AdultTkts * AdultPrice + ChildTkts * ChildPrice;
        Console.WriteLine("The total cost is $" + TotalCost);
    }
}
```

As you can see, you can freely mix *decimal* numbers and integer numbers in the same expression. C# implicitly converts any integer to a *decimal* value for the calculation. Any calculation between *decimal* values and integers results in a *decimal* value.

However, C# won't implicitly convert a decimal into an integer:

```
decimal TotalMoney = 54.25m;
int NumberOfWholeDollars = TotalMoney;    // Compile error!
```

The C# compiler prohibits this conversion because it's likely that it's an accident on your part. During a conversion from *decimal* to integer, information may be lost—exactly 25 cents in this example.

If you *really* want to convert the decimal into an integer, C# requires that you perform an explicit conversion. One way to perform this conversion is to use the *ToInt32* method of the *Decimal* structure. *ToInt32* is an instance method that you can use on any *decimal* literal or variable:

```
NumberOfWholeDollars = TotalMoney.ToInt32();
```

Or you can use the static *ToInt32* method of the *Convert* class:

```
NumberOfWholeDollars = Convert.ToInt32(TotalMoney);
```

The easiest approach, as usual, is casting:

```
NumberOfWholeDollars = (int) TotalMoney;
```

You can use similar methods for converting to other types of integers. In all three cases, the *decimal* number is truncated for the conversion. The result is the next integer closest to zero (for example, −54.25m is truncated to −54). Any of these conversions could raise an exception if the integral part of the *decimal* value is too large for the integer.

Suppose you're working with some population statistics and you've declared the following variables:

```
int NumberOfChildren;
int NumberOfFamilies;
decimal AverageChildrenPerFamily;
```

The third variable is calculated by dividing *NumberOfChildren* by *NumberOf-Families*. Your first attempt at such a calculation might look like this:

```
AverageChildrenPerFamily = NumberOfChildren / NumberOfFamilies;
```

But this won't give you an exact result. Because the two variables involved in the division are integers, the result is an integer. If *NumberOfChildren* were 55 and *NumberOfFamilies* were 10, *AverageChildrenPerFamily* would be assigned 5. What you really want is 5.5. To get that value, cast one of the integer variables to a *decimal*:

```
AverageChildrenPerFamily = (decimal) NumberOfChildren / NumberOfFamilies;
```

In this example, it doesn't matter which one you cast. In the Operator Precedence and Associativity chart on the inside back cover of this book, casting is represented by *(type)* and it has the highest precedence, which means that it happens before the division. Because the division involves a *decimal* and an *int*, C# will implicitly convert the *int* to a *decimal* for the division. What you don't want to do is cast the result of the division:

```
AverageChildrenPerFamily =
    (decimal) (NumberOfChildren / NumberOfFamilies);    // Don't do this!
```

This statement is perfectly legal, but it doesn't do what you probably want. The integer division (and truncation) occurs first because it's in parentheses.

As you know, C# uses 32 bits (or 4 bytes) to store *int* or *uint* variables and 64 bits (8 bytes) to store *long* or *ulong* variables. For *decimal* variables, 128 bits (16 bytes) are required. To understand the range of numbers you can store in decimal variables, you'll want to know how the 128 bits are used.

■ First, 96 bits of the *decimal* value are used to store an integer that can range from 0 through 79,228,162,514,264,337,593,543,950,335. That's about 79 octillion in the United States or 79 quadrilliard by the European method.

■   Second, 5 bits are used for a *decimal scaling factor* that can range from 0 through 28. The decimal scaling factor indicates the number of decimal places of the number. For example, if the integer part is 1,576,878,984 and the scaling factor is 4, then the actual number is 157,687.8984.

■   Finally, 1 bit is used for the sign. If the bit is 1, then the number is negative.

That's a total of 102 bits. Of the 128 bits used for storing a decimal value, 26 bits are unused. That may seem like a waste, but it's really more efficient for 32-bit and 64-bit processors to work with 128-bit values rather than something between 64 bits and 128 bits.

Decimal numbers can range from −79,228,162,514,264,337,593,543,950,335 to 79,228,162,514,264,337,593,543,950,335. These two values are available from the static *MinValue* and *MaxValue* fields of the *Decimal* structure. The smallest *decimal* number greater than zero is 0.0000000000000000000000000001, or 10^{-28}, which is also the minimum amount that two *decimal* numbers can differ by. Dividing that number by 2 results in 0. Attempting to calculate a number greater than the maximum or lower than the minimum results in an overflow exception.

When working with dollars, euros, and other currency, it's often necessary to round results of calculations. For example, 5 percent of 25.77 is 1.2885, but in some circumstances that should be rounded to 1.29. The *Decimal* structure contains several static methods for performing rounding. Because the methods are static, you preface the method name with the structure name *Decimal*. The decimal value you're converting is an argument to the method. The expression

```
Decimal.Truncate(Value)
```

is similar to the integer conversions shown earlier, but the method returns a *decimal* value. The expression

```
Decimal.Floor(Value)
```

returns a decimal value that is equal to the next lowest integer. Both *Truncate* and *Floor* return the same value of positive decimal numbers. For negative decimal numbers, −25.645, for example, *Truncate* returns −25 while *Floor* returns −26. The *Truncate* method is sometimes described as "rounding toward zero" while the *Floor* method is "rounding toward negative infinity."

If you want to round to the closest integer—or the closest decimal number with a specific number of decimal places—use

```
Decimal.Round(Value, Digits)
```

The second argument is an *int* indicating the number of digits to round. Here's an example:

```
Result = 25.77m * .05m;
Rounded = Decimal.Round(Result, 2);
```

The *Result* variable equals 1.2885; the *Rounded* variable equals 1.29. The second argument of the *Round* method can range from 0 through 28.

For numbers exactly midway between two potential rounded values, *Round* implements a convention called *banker's rounding* or *round to even*. The result is the closest *even* number. For example, both 8.335 and 8.345 round to 8.34 (rather than 8.33 or 8.35) because the last digit of 8.34 is even.

Some applications may call for rounding to the next highest integer for midway values. For example, 8.335 would round to 8.34 and 8.345 would round to 8.35. You can easily implement such a rounding scheme like so:

```
Rounded = Decimal.Truncate(Value * 100 + 0.5m) / 100;
```

You use 100 as a multiplier and divider to round to two decimal places. In general, use 10 to the number of decimal places to which you need to round.

I've already emphasized the importance of giving your variables descriptive names. Some programmers also like to indicate the variable *type* in the name. It helps sometimes if you're looking at code involving a bunch of variable names to see just by the variable name which ones are integers, decimals, strings, and so forth. Such variable names may even have helped in this chapter and some earlier chapters where I showed conversions between different types of variables.

One popular naming convention is called Hungarian Notation, named after legendary Microsoft programmer Charles Simonyi, who was born in Budapest and originated the notation in his doctoral thesis. Hungarian Notation was popularized by the Microsoft Windows application-programming interface (API), which used it extensively.

Since then, Hungarian Notation has become quite controversial in the programming world. Do a Google search on "Hungarian Notation" to get a little taste of the pros and cons.

In its simplest form, Hungarian Notation involves a lowercase prefix on the variable name that indicates the type of the variable. For the variable types introduced so far (excluding those that are not CLS compliant), I'd like to use the following prefixes:

Type	Prefix
byte	*by*
short	*s*
int	*i*
long	*l*
decimal	*m*
string	*str*

For example, whenever you see a variable named *iConcertoDuration*, you'll know it's an *int*. A variable name *strComposerName* is a *string*. The *m* prefix for *decimal* is the same as the letter that must be appended to a numeric literal to indicate that it's a *decimal* value.

Sometimes, in code examples that deal only with a single integer and a single string, I'll use the Hungarian Notation alone: *i* for the integer variable and *str* for the string variable.

I'll begin using Hungarian Notation immediately. Whenever a new variable type comes along, I'll let you know its prefix. Usually they will be obvious.

15

Floating Point

When programming scientific or engineering applications, generally you want as much flexibility as possible in expressing very large or very small numbers. The C# *decimal* data type is limited to only 28 places to the left or right of the decimal point. Because of this limitation, *decimal* is insufficient to represent, for example, the mass of the Sun in kilograms (about 2×10^{30}) or the mass of an electron in kilograms (about 9×10^{-31}).

What turns out to be not very important in scientific or engineering applications is exactness. Indeed, excessive accuracy can be unwarranted and deceptive. For example, suppose you want to multiply 27.38 and 0.08945. The original numbers are accurate only to four significant digits. The value indicated as 27.38 could be a measurement that in actuality is somewhere in the range of 27.375 to 27.385. The precision of the original numbers implies that the result should have four significant digits as well. Using the calculated product of 2.449141 implies a precision that doesn't really exist in the original numbers. You should use 2.449 instead.

For many years, scientists and engineers performed many calculations using slide rules, which have a precision of approximately three or four decimal digits. These days, scientists and engineers use *floating point* in their computing applications, which is very similar to expressing numbers in scientific notation. In C# (as in C), there are two floating-point types, called *float* and *double*, which may raise the question, "Double what?"

Until relatively recently, computers and programming languages handled floating point in many incompatible ways. In 1985, the Institute of Electrical and Electronics Engineers (IEEE) established the *IEEE Standard for Binary Floating-Point Arithmetic*, ANSI/IEEE Std 754-1985. The standard defines two basic floating-point formats, named *single precision*, which requires 4 bytes, and *double precision*, which requires 8 bytes.

In the .NET Framework, the two structures that support these two formats are named *System.Single* and *System.Double*, but the data type names that C# has inherited from C are *float* and *double*. The following table summarizes the C# and .NET types, and provides some other information about *float* and *double*.

C# Type	.NET Type	Significand	Exponent
float	*System.Single*	23 bits (7 digits)	8 bits (-45 to 38)
double	*System.Double*	52 bits (15–16 digits)	11 bits (-324 to 308)

The two columns at the right show how the 32 bits of the *float* and the 64 bits of the *double* are apportioned into a *significand* (also called a *mantissa*) and an *exponent*. An additional bit indicates the sign of the significand. In a number such as

$$8.364 \times 10^{-24}$$

8.364 is the significand. The use of 23 bits for the significand in the *float* data type implies a precision of about 7 decimal digits. (Ten bits are approximately equivalent to 3 decimal digits because 2^{10} is approximately equal to 10^3.) The exponent is stored as a power of 2 rather than 10. The *float* data type uses 8 bits for the exponent. Because of the way floating-point numbers are stored, the equivalent decimal exponent can range from −45 to 38.

I'll be using Hungarian Notation prefixes of *f* for *float* and *d* for *double*. To declare a variable of type *float*, use

```
float f;
```

You can assign an integer literal to a *float* in either the declaration statement or an assignment statement:

```
f = 123456789;
```

However, such an integer will lose a couple digits of precision in the conversion. If you print out the value of *f* using *Console.WriteLine*, you'll see

```
1.234568E+08
```

It's basically the same number, but with only seven digits of precision. Precision is lost but the magnitude is the same.

You can also assign a *float* variable a numeric literal with a decimal point, as in:

```
f = 45.384f;
```

or in scientific notation, as here:

```
f = -34.78e-14f;
```

In either case, a lowercase or an uppercase *F* must be appended to the number to indicate a *float*. The letter that separates the significand from the exponent in scientific notation can be either a lowercase or an uppercase *E*.

Here's how to declare and initialize a *double*:

```
double d = 456.374584;
```

No suffix is required on the literal, but you can include a lowercase or an uppercase *D* if you want to indicate a *double*. In other words, numeric literals with decimal points or in scientific notation are assumed to be *double* by default.

Many programmers themselves use *double* by default and don't even bother with *float*. Because floating-point operations are generally carried out by a dedicated math coprocessor unit in the computer's microprocessor, there is no performance advantage of *float* over *double*. For many applications running on today's machines, the memory difference is negligible.

If necessary, C# will implicitly convert any integral type to *float* or *double* (or, as we learned in Chapter 14, to *decimal*). Some precision may be lost, but the magnitude of the number will be preserved. In addition, C# will implicitly convert a *float* to a *double*.

C# will *not* implicitly convert a *float* to any numeric type except a *double*. C# also will *not* implicitly convert a *double* or a *decimal* to each other or to any other numeric type. If you want such conversions, you'll have to cast. The following chart shows the implicit conversions among the numeric types:

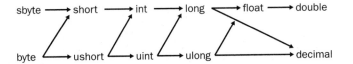

One interesting aspect of floating point defined by the IEEE standard makes floating point very different from the other numeric types: operations involving floating-point values never raise exceptions. Never.

Here's some code that would raise a zero-divide exception for integers or *decimal* values:

```
double dNumerator = 55;
double dDenominator = 0;
double dQuotient = dNumerator / dDenomiator;
```

As a result of this operation, the variable *dQuotient* takes on a special value, indicated by a special combination of bits that are precisely defined by the IEEE standard. That special combination of bits represents the value *infinity*. In fact, if you were to display that variable using

```
Console.WriteLine(dQuotient);
```

you'd see the word

```
Infinity
```

If you change *dNumerator* to −55, *Console.WriteLine* displays

```
-Infinity
```

If you change *dNumerator* to 0, then you have division of 0 by 0, and *Console.WriteLine* displays

```
NaN
```

That stands for "not a number" and is pronounced "nan." A NaN also results from floating-point overflow or underflow.

The *Float* and *Double* structures include three static fields named *PositiveInfinity*, *NegativeInfinity*, and *NaN* that provide these values explicitly. You can even perform calculations with these special values. For example, if you divide 1 by *Double.PositiveInfinity*, you'll get 0. (However, *Double.PositiveInfinity* divided by itself is NaN rather than 1.)

In Chapter 22, I'll show you how to detect and deal with these special floating-point values. For now, just be aware that you may see these values when you're working with floating point.

Floating point is a natural choice when you need to multiply and divide a combination of large and small numbers but you want to reduce your worry about whether any intermediate results will cause overflow errors. Here's a program that calculates the number of inches that light travels in 1 nanosecond. (The result may surprise you.)

NanoSecond.cs

```
// ----------------------------------------------------
// NanoSecond.cs from "Programming in the Key of C#"
// ----------------------------------------------------
using System;

class NanoSecond
{
    static void Main()
    {
        const double CinMilesPerSecond = 186E3;
        const double FeetPerMile = 5280;
        const double InchesPerFeet = 12;
        const double SecondsPerNanoSecond = 1E-9;

        double InchesPerNanoSecond =
            CinMilesPerSecond * FeetPerMile *
            InchesPerFeet * SecondsPerNanoSecond;

        Console.WriteLine("In one nanosecond light travels " +
            InchesPerNanoSecond + " inches.");
    }
}
```

When rounded to the nearest inch, it's an interesting fact to remember and gives you a good idea of how short a nanosecond really is.

If you'll be using C# for scientific or engineering applications, you'll undoubtedly need to calculate exponents, logarithms, and trigonometric functions. All that cool stuff can be found in the *Math* class, a class in the *System* namespace that (like *Console*) consists almost entirely of static methods.

For example, to do exponentiation in C# you use the *Pow* ("power") method:

```
dResult = Math.Pow(dBase, dPower);
```

You pass two *double* arguments to the method separated by a comma. Arguments that are not *double* are implicitly converted to *double*. (The arguments cannot be *decimal* values, which are not implicitly convertible to *double*. You'll have to provide an explicit cast if you want to use *decimal* values with *Pow*.) The return value is also a *double*. The expression

```
Math.Pow(5, 3)
```

equals 5 to the third power or 125. To take a square root, you can use *Pow* with a power of 0.5:

```
dResult = Math.Pow(dNumber, 0.5);
```

Or you can use the *Sqrt* ("square root") method:

```
dResult = Math.Sqrt(dNumber);
```

Here's a little program that calculates the hypotenuse of a right triangle. From the Pythagorean theorem, you know that the hypotenuse of a right triangle is the square root of the sum of the squares of the other two sides. The argument to *Math.Sqrt* is the sum of two calls to *Math.Pow*:

HypotenuseCalc.cs

```
// ------------------------------------------------------
// HypotenuseCalc.cs from "Programming in the Key of C#"
// ------------------------------------------------------
using System;

class HypotenuseCalc
{
    static void Main()
    {
        Console.Write("Enter first side: ");
        double dSide1 = Double.Parse(Console.ReadLine());

        Console.Write("Enter second side: ");
        double dSide2 = Double.Parse(Console.ReadLine());
```

```
        double dResult = Math.Sqrt(Math.Pow(dSide1, 2) + Math.Pow(dSide2, 2));
        Console.WriteLine("The hypotenuse is {0}", dResult);
    }
}
```

The *Math* class also contains two constant fields, which are simply handy numbers that you can use in your program. The field *Math.PI* is the numeric value of π, while *Math.E* is the constant e.

While floating point is indispensable for certain applications, it's not right for everything. Floating point is abused when it is overused. Classical BASIC was one of the worst offenders. For many years, BASIC implementations would store every numeric variable—unless used in a context where integers were obviously more appropriate—as floating point. But even in programming languages that allowed the programmer to choose appropriate variable types, programmers often found an ease in working with floating point (No overflow! No underflow!) that led them to use it more extensively than it probably should have been. I know because I've been there. A couple of decades ago, I programmed extensively in PL/I and floating point was my default data type.

Programmers with lots of experience with floating point are familiar with common quirks. A number that should be 23.5, for example, might seem to be stored as 23.50001 or 23.49999. That latter one is a real problem because it's actually closer to 23 than 24. If you try to round it to the nearest integer, you'll get 23.

These days, floating point doesn't seem to behave quite as badly. Someone has apparently been working on improving floating-point calculations, but it's still possible to get a quirky result every now and then. Try this:

```
Console.WriteLine(9.666e-7f);
```

Shouldn't *WriteLine* be displaying the exact number it's given?

You should also be aware of other aspects of floating point that can cause problems. Consider the following code:

```
float f1 = 1234567;
float f2 = 0.1234567f;
float f3 = f1 + f2;
```

The *float* data type is only capable of storing about seven significant digits, so the result of this addition is 1234567. The *f2* variable is basically ignored. If you need more than seven significant digits, use *double*. (But then, don't expect more than 16 significant digits.)

It often comes as a shock to many people that the IEEE standard doesn't allow most numbers to be stored exactly, and that's the reason for the occasional anomaly. Part of this is due to the precision of the significand. The *float* representations of 16,777,216 and 16,777,217 are the same, for example. But most smaller numbers are also subject to some degree of approximation. The number 12.34, for example, when stored as a *float*, is essentially stored as the integer 12,939,428 divided by 2^{20} (or 1,048,576). That's only *approximately* equal to 12.34. The same number stored as a *double* is 6,946,802,425,218,990 divided by 2^{49} (or 562,949,953,421,312). Yes, that's very, very close to 12.34, but it's not exact.

The same number stored as a *decimal*, on the other hand, is essentially stored as the integer 1234 divided by 10^2. Now that's exact, and that's why you should use *decimal* whenever you want to store and calculate nonintegral numbers exactly.

16

Fancy Formatting

As you know, if *m* is a *decimal*, the expression

```
m.ToString()
```

converts the number to a string. However, you have some flexibility in the way you can use *ToString*. For numeric data types, it's also possible to pass an argument to *ToString* that controls the appearance—what programmers refer to as *format*—of the displayed number. The optional argument to *ToString* is itself a string. For example,

```
m.ToString("G")
```

is identical to *ToString* without an argument. The G stands for *general* formatting. To specify a different format, you can use uppercase or lowercase C, D, E, F, G, N, P, R, or X, which are described in the following table:

Letter	Meaning	Description
C	Currency	A currency sign is displayed. Thousands are separated.
D	Decimal	(integer only) The number may be padded with zeros at the left.
E	Exponential	The number is displayed in scientific notation.
F	Fixed point	The number is not displayed in scientific notation.
G	General	Exponential or floating point, whichever is more concise.
N	Number	The same as F, but thousands are separated.
P	Percent	The number is multiplied by 100, a percent sign is displayed, and thousands are separated.
R	Roundtrip	(floating point only) Creates strings that can be converted back to numbers of the same value using *Parse*.
X	Hexadecimal	(integer only) The number is displayed in hexadecimal.

As an example of using one of the nine formatting specifications with *ToString*, if a decimal *m* stores the number 0.123, the expression

```
m.ToString("P")
```

will create the string "12.3 %".

The *C* formatting specification causes a currency symbol to be displayed. The currency symbol is not necessarily a dollar sign. In situations like this, the .NET Framework uses something appropriate for the user's locale, and that depends on the Regional and Language Options set in the user's Control Panel. If your program needs to specifically display amounts in dollars or pounds or euros or any other type of currency, don't use *C* formatting. Specify the symbol exactly, as shown here:

```
"$" + m.ToString("N")
```

Or, for euros:

```
"\u20A0" + m.ToString("N")
```

Whether commas or spaces are used in separating thousands is also governed by the Regional And Language Options.

You can optionally follow the letter with a number, for example:

```
m.ToString("P5")
```

The number has a different meaning depending on the letter used. Here's a table that describes how the *ToString* methods uses that number:

Letter	Meaning	Effect of Number
C	Currency	Number of decimal places displayed (default is 2).
D	Decimal	Desired character width of result, padded with zeroes if necessary.
E	Exponential	Number of places after the decimal point (default is 6).
F	Fixed point	Number of decimal places displayed (default is 2).
G	General	Desired character width of result.
N	Number	Number of decimal places displayed (default is 2).
P	Percent	Number of decimal places displayed (default is 2).
R	Roundtrip	Ignored.
X	Hexadecimal	Desired character width of result, padded with zeroes if necessary.

Here's a little program that displays a decimal variable with all the formatting specifications allowed for decimal:

NumericFormatting.cs

```
// ----------------------------------------------------------
// NumericFormatting.cs from "Programming in the Key of C#"
// ----------------------------------------------------------
using System;

class NumericFormatting
{
    static void Main()
    {
        decimal m = 12345.345m;

        Console.WriteLine("Currency formatting: " + m.ToString("C2"));
        Console.WriteLine("Exponential formatting: " + m.ToString("E2"));
        Console.WriteLine("Fixed-point formatting: " + m.ToString("F2"));
        Console.WriteLine("General formatting: " + m.ToString("G2"));
        Console.WriteLine("Number formatting: " + m.ToString("N2"));
        Console.WriteLine("Percent formatting: " + m.ToString("P2"));
    }
}
```

For a user in the United States, the default regional options cause the program to display the following lines of text:

```
Currency formatting: $12,345.35
Exponential formatting: 1.23E+004
Fixed-point formatting: 12345.35
General formatting: 1.2E+04
Number formatting: 12,345.35
Percent formatting: 1,234,534.50 %
```

As you can see, the *ToString* method sometimes rounds the number before converting it to a string. However, *ToString* uses somewhat different rounding rules than the rules used by the *Round* method. Values exactly between two rounded values are rounded up. In the NumericFormatting program, the number 12345.345 is rounded to 12345.35 rather than 12345.34. If these rounding results don't work for you, round the number using one of the *Round* methods *before* you display it.

Here's a conversion to hexadecimal using the integer 12345:

```
i.ToString("X8")
```

ToString creates the string 00003039. If you indicate a number less than 4 in this example, the resultant string will have four characters. These formatting specifications never cause numbers to be truncated because of insufficient column width. The worst that can happen with formatting is that precision will be lost. For example:

```
i.ToString("E2")
```

results in the string "1.23E+004" because you've specified only two decimal places.

When displaying multiple numbers with the *Console.WriteLine* method, we've been using string concatenation, like this:

```
Console.WriteLine("The sum of " + A + " and " + B + " is " + (A + B));
```

If you want to control the formatting of any of these values, you can use the *ToString* method to convert the numbers to strings before concatenation:

```
Console.WriteLine("The sum of " + A.ToString("E4") +
                  " and " + B.ToString("E4") +
                  " is " + (A + B).ToString("E4"));
```

You'll probably agree that this looks rather messy and not very readable.

The *Write* and *WriteLine* methods support an alternative to displaying text and multiple numbers that is based on the concept of a *formatting string* with *placeholders* where the values of variables are to appear. Here's an equivalent of the first of the two *WriteLine* calls I just showed you:

```
Console.WriteLine("The sum of {0} and {1} is {2}", A, B, A + B);
```

This is yet another overload of the *WriteLine* method. Four arguments are shown here. The first argument is the formatting string that basically contains the text we want to display. In this string are the numbers 0, 1, and 2 enclosed in curly brackets. These numbers in brackets are placeholders. When *WriteLine* displays the string, the second argument to *WriteLine* (the variable *A* in this example) is inserted at the position {0}, the third argument (*B*) is inserted at {1}, and the fourth argument (*A* + *B*) at {2}. The arguments could be numeric variables, string variables, or any other type of variable or literal.

If you want to display curly brackets as part of your formatting string, use two curly brackets together.

The placeholders don't have to be in numeric order in the formatting string, but the numeric order must correspond to the order of the subsequent arguments. Here's an equivalent:

```
Console.WriteLine("The sum of {2} and {1} is {0}", A + B, B, A);
```

The only real rule is that the number of arguments after the formatting string must be greater than or equal to the highest number you use in a placeholder minus 1. There's no problem if you have more arguments than the placeholders would indicate:

```
Console.WriteLine("The sum of {2} and {1} is {0}", A + B, B, A, C);
```

Notice the extra *C* variable at the end. It's ignored in this *WriteLine* call. You can also skip placeholder numbers if you want:

```
Console.WriteLine("The sum of {0} and {1} is {3}", A, B, C, A + B);
```

In this case, the variable *C* is not displayed because it would correspond to a placeholder of {2}. You can also reuse placeholders to display a number multiple times.

```
Console.WriteLine("The answer is {0} and nothing but {0}", A);
```

But this statement is a problem and would raise an exception:

```
Console.WriteLine("The sum of {0} and {1} is {3}", A, B, A + B);
```

The highest placeholder number is 3, which would require four arguments following the formatting string.

Here's the *WriteLine* statement I showed you earlier using *String* concatenation and explicit calls to *ToString* to format the numbers more to our liking:

```
Console.WriteLine("The sum of " + A.ToString("E4") +
                " and " + B.ToString("E4") +
                " is " + (A + B).ToString("E4"));
```

You could write this statement using a formatting string like so:

```
Console.WriteLine("The sum of {0} and {1} is {2}",
                A.ToString("E4"), B.ToString("E4"),
                (A + B).ToString("E4"));
```

Still a mess. But check this out: you can include the numeric formatting specifications as part of the formatting string. All the explicit *ToString* calls are gone:

```
Console.WriteLine("The sum of {0:E4} and {1:E4} is {2:E4}", A, B, A + B);
```

The placeholder number is simply followed by a colon and then the short formatting specification string that you'd normally pass to *ToString*. In practice, this approach to formatting numbers is much more common than using *ToString*, for obvious reasons.

In most cases, you really can't predict the character width of displayed numbers. Depending on its value, an *int* could require anywhere from 1 to 10 characters (if the number is positive), 11 characters (if it's negative), or 14 characters if thousands are separated. Formatting doesn't introduce extra space. If you do something like this:

```
Console.WriteLine("{0}{1}{2}{3}", A, B, C, D);
```

the numbers will be jammed up against each other and you won't be able to read them. It's fairly easy to prevent this problem by leaving some space between the placeholders:

```
Console.WriteLine("{0} {1} {2} {3}", A, B, C, D);
```

Sometimes you'll have several similar *WriteLine* statements (or one *WriteLine* statement that's executed multiple times with different variable values), and you'll want everything arranged in nice, neat columns. To indicate a character width for the displayed variable, you can include that width—called a *field width*—in the placeholder string. Separate the placeholder number and the field width with a comma:

```
Console.WriteLine("{0,10}{1,15}{2,10}{3,20}", mA, strB, iC, mD);
```

The first number is displayed in a field 10 characters wide. The number is right justified in that field. The second variable (a string) is right justified in a field 15 characters wide. Here's how the total line might look:

```
    85.748         banana        98            93713.74
```

Use a negative field width if you want the variable to be left justified in the field. In this next example, the string is displayed first and is left justified to begin in the left margin:

```
Console.WriteLine("{0,-15}{1,10}{2,10}{3,20}", strB, mA, iC, mD);
```

The output looks like this:

```
banana            85.748        98            93713.74
```

Your console display probably has a width of 80 characters (a standard value that originated with the number of character columns on IBM punch cards), so it's traditional to restrict the entire formatting string and field widths to something fewer than 80 characters. However, if the numbers require more space than the field width, they will be given that space.

Finally, you can combine everything you've learned in this chapter by using both field widths and format specifications in the formatting string:

```
Console.WriteLine("{0,-15}{1,10:C2}{2,10:X5}{3,20:E3}", strB, mA, iC, mD);
```

The output looks like this:

```
banana            $85.75     00062         9.371E4
```

Within limits, this same *WriteLine* call could handle a multitude of different variable values and everything would line up in nice neat columns.

17

Methods and Fields

There will come a time when you will need a method that doesn't yet exist. Perhaps it's a method that you thought might have been included in a class in the .NET Framework, but you searched around and couldn't find it. Or maybe your program requires something special that's just not common enough to be included in the .NET Framework.

Suppose you need to calculate hypotenuses of right triangles, for example. From the Pythagorean theorem, you know that the hypotenuse of a right triangle is the square root of the sum of the squares of the other two sides. As I demonstrated in the HypotenuseCalc program in Chapter 15, you can calculate a hypotenuse using two methods from the *Math* class:

```
double dResult = Math.Sqrt(Math.Pow(dSide1, 2) + Math.Pow(dSide2, 2));
```

If your program needs to calculate quite a few hypotenuses, you might feel tempted to copy and paste the code into your program each place you need to perform the calculation. But that's not a good solution. The statement you're pasting involves two variables named *dSide1* and *dSide2*, so if you need to calculate a hypotenuse based on variables named *dBase* and *dHeight*, you'd need to make changes in the code anyway. And what if you later discover a more efficient way of performing the calculation? You'd probably want to take advantage of this more efficient approach by changing all the pasted calculations.

In fact, there *is* a more efficient hypotenuse calculation than that shown in the HypotenuseCalc program. Rather than use the *Math.Pow* method to square a number, like

```
Math.Pow(dNumber, 2)
```

a better approach is simply to multiply the number by itself:

```
dNumber * dNumber
```

Although these two expressions may seem equivalent to a human, they are not equivalent to a computer. In practice, the *Math.Pow* method uses a generalized power algorithm, which is considerably more complex than the multiplication. An informal test reveals the multiplication to be about 40 to 50 times faster than the *Math.Pow* method when the second argument is 2. If your program does very many squares, that time difference could start to make an impact.

Even if you like writing code, you should always try to write the minimum amount of code possible, and that includes copying and pasting. In general, the less code you write, the fewer bugs you'll create.

If your program needs to perform many hypotenuse calculations, it's an excellent candidate for a custom method.

A method is a little algorithmic machine—a factory of sorts in which raw materials go in and a finished product comes out. If the method is designed and programmed well enough, it becomes a *black box*. Nobody cares what goes on inside the box, as long as what comes out is correct, the box works efficiently, and it doesn't make any funny noises.

There are generally two challenges in writing a method. The most obvious is coding the algorithm that the method will perform. But the other challenge comes first, and that is defining the method's interface. What goes into the method and what comes out?

Although you've seen examples of multiple arguments going into a method, what you've seen coming out of the method is only *one* thing: the method's return value. A method has zero or more parameters and one return value (which may be *void*, to indicate no return value).

For the *Hypotenuse* method, the input and output are pretty simple. The method will have two parameters for the two sides of the triangle, and the method will return the hypotenuse. Just as you can call the *Math.Pow* method like

```
dResult = System.Math.Pow(dBase, dExponent);
```

or (if the *System* namespace has been included in a *using* directive) like

```
dResult = Math.Pow(dBase, dExponent);
```

you'll be able to call your *Hypotenuse* method like this:

```
dResult = Hypotenuse(dSide1, dSide2);
```

Our first version of the *Hypotenuse* method won't need a namespace or a class name because it's going right in the same class as the *Main* method that will be using *Hypotenuse*.

Here's an example of the typical type of class we've been declaring:

```
class MyClass
{
    static void Main()
    {
        // The body of Main
    }
}
```

If you want to add another method to this class, you must put it inside the curly brackets associated with the class but not inside the curly brackets associated with *Main*. Here are your two options:

```
class MyClass
{
    // The new method can go here.

    static void Main()
    {
        // The body of Main
    }

    // Or the new method can go here.
}
```

One restriction: the method can't have the same name as the class. (Actually it can, but then it's a very special type of method, which I'll discuss in Chapter 33.)

C# doesn't care whether you put the new method before or after *Main*. But the positioning of *Main* might make a difference to you in how you think about your programs. Some programmers like to start off writing methods that perform the low-level jobs (such as *Hypotenuse*) and then finally, at the very end of the program, write a *Main* method that uses all the methods declared earlier. This is called *bottom-up* programming, and it's often associated with the Pascal programming language. Pascal tended to impose this sort of structure because the program couldn't call methods until after they were declared. But you can write bottom-up programming in any language.

Other programmers prefer a top-down structure, in which *Main* comes first in the program and other methods that it uses appear in a hierarchy below it. That's generally the structure I like to use.

Let's declare our *Hypotenuse* method. Just as with *Main*, the method declaration begins with the keyword *static*:

```
static
```

As you might have gotten a sense of in Chapter 11, *static* indicates a method that doesn't apply to a particular instance of a class or structure.

Next comes the type of the value that the method returns. The *Hypotenuse* method returns a *double*:

```
static double
```

The method name is next followed by a left parenthesis:

```
static double Hypotenuse(
```

At this point, the method declaration should look quite similar to the *Main* method we've been using since Chapter 3. The *Main* method doesn't return a value, so the return type is *void*. The *Main* method also doesn't have anything in its parentheses.

We want to pass two arguments to the *Hypotenuse* method. From the method's perspective, these two arguments are *parameters*. The first parameter is a *double* that we'll call *d1*. The type and the name of the first parameter follow the left parenthesis:

```
static double Hypotenuse(double d1
```

The second parameter is also a *double*, and we'll call it *d2*. The two parameters are separated by a comma and terminated with a right parenthesis:

```
static double Hypotenuse(double d1, double d2)
```

Just as with *Main*, the method must have a body that's enclosed within a pair of curly brackets:

```
static double Hypotenuse(double d1, double d2)
{
    // The method body goes here.
}
```

Very often, methods declare their own variables. In this case, we want a variable to store the hypotenuse of the triangle, which we'll call *dResult*. We can also include a calculation of *dResult* based on the two parameters:

```
static double Hypotenuse(double d1, double d2)
{
    double dResult;

    dResult = Math.Sqrt(d1 * d1 + d2 * d2);

    // The rest of the method body goes here.
}
```

Of course, the assignment statement could have been written as an initialization in the declaration statement, so let's do it that way in the next version.

The method must return the value of *dResult*. To return something from a method, you use the keyword *return* with the value the method returns:

```
static double Hypotenuse(double d1, double d2)
{
    double dResult = Math.Sqrt(d1 * d1 + d2 * d2);

    return dResult;
}
```

The *return* statement also terminates the execution of the method. For that reason, the *return* statement is usually the *last* statement of the method. However, in more complex situations, a method can have multiple *return* statements.

Here's a complete program that includes a declaration of the *Hypotenuse* method and uses this method in *Main*.

CalculationWithSeparateMethod.cs

```
// ----------------------------------------------------------------
// CalculationWithSeparateMethod.cs from "Programming in the Key of C#"
// ----------------------------------------------------------------
using System;

class CalculationWithSeparateMethod
{
    static void Main()
    {
        Console.Write("Enter first side: ");
        double dSide1 = Convert.ToDouble(Console.ReadLine());

        Console.Write("Enter second side: ");
        double dSide2 = Convert.ToDouble(Console.ReadLine());

        double dResult = Hypotenuse(dSide1, dSide2);
        Console.WriteLine("The hypotenuse is " + dResult);
    }
    static double Hypotenuse(double d1, double d2)
    {
        double dResult = Math.Sqrt(d1 * d1 + d2 * d2);

        return dResult;
    }
}
```

Look at the class declaration, the two method declarations, and how the curly brackets define the structure of this program. Both methods are included in the class because they are within the curly brackets that are part of the class declaration. But the two methods are separate from each other. The body of each method is indicated by the curly brackets that are part of each method's declaration.

Because *Hypotenuse* is in the same class as *Main*, code in *Main* can call *Hypotenuse* simply by specifying the method name:

```
double dResult = Hypotenuse(dSide1, dSide2);
```

If you want, you can also preface *Hypotenuse* with the class name:

```
double dResult = CalculationWithSeparateMethod.Hypotenuse(dSide1, dSide2);
```

Fortunately, most classes that contain commonly used methods don't have names as long as this one.

Let's follow through the sequence of execution in this program. Everything proceeds normally until the initialization of *dResult*. The initialization of *dResult* involves a call to the *Hypotenuse* method passing the two arguments *dSide1* and *dSide2*. At that point, execution jumps to the *Hypotenuse* method. Within the *Hypotenuse* method, the two parameters *d1* and *d2* are assigned the values *dSide1* and *dSide2*. The *Hypotenuse* method performs its calculation. The *return* statement terminates the execution of the *Hypotenuse* method. At this point, the *Hypotenuse* call in *Main* has returned the value that is assigned to *dResult*, as shown here:

```
// ----------------------------------------------------------------------
// CalculationWithSeparateMethod.cs from "Programming in the Key of C#"
// ----------------------------------------------------------------------
using System;

class CalculationWithSeparateMethod
{
    static void Main()
    {
        Console.Write("Enter first side: ");
        double dSide1 = Convert.ToDouble(Console.ReadLine());

        Console.Write("Enter second side: ");
        double dSide2 = Convert.ToDouble(Console.ReadLine());

        double dResult = Hypotenuse(dSide1, dSide2);
        Console.WriteLine("The hypotenuse is " + dResult);
    }
    static double Hypotenuse(double d1, double d2)

    {
        double dResult = Math.Sqrt(d1 * d1 + d2 * d2);

        return dResult;
    }
}
```

Both *Main* and *Hypotenuse* contain a variable named *dResult*. Despite having the same name, these are two separate and unique variables because they are declared in two different methods. The program would work just the same if one or both of these two variables were named something else. Some programmers might give the variable returned from *Hypotenuse* a name similar to the method, such as *dHypotenuse*. The *Main* method could do without its *dResult* variable and call *Hypotenuse* right in the final *Console.WriteLine* call:

```
Console.WriteLine("The hypotenuse is " + Hypotenuse(dSide1, dSide2));
```

Variables declared inside a method—such as the variables *dSide1*, *dSide2*, and both occurrences of *dResult*—are known as *local variables*. Local variables are restricted to the method in which they are declared. Local variables are also said to have a *scope* or *visibility* that is limited to the method. Because *dSide1* and *dSide2* are local to *Main*, the *Hypotenuse* method cannot refer to those *dSide1* and *dSide2* variables. They are not visible outside of *Main*. The method also governs the *lifetime* of any local variables. When a method ends, the stack memory storing the local variables in that method is freed.

Until the CalculationWithSeparateMethod program, all the variables we've declared have been local variables. But the *Hypotenuse* method contains two variables, *d1* and *d2*, that are known as parameters. Strictly speaking, parameters are not local variables, although their visibility, scope, and lifetime are limited to the method in which they appear.

Even experienced programmers can be a bit confused about distinguishing between the words *argument* and *parameter*. The words are sometimes used interchangeably, and although I've tried to keep the meanings distinct when writing this book, I've sometimes struggled with deciding which term is correct in a particular context.

Just as one country's emigrant is another country's immigrant, the value of an argument that is passed to a method becomes the value of a parameter that is used inside the method. A parameter is a variable that takes on a value only when the method is called. The parameter takes on the value of the argument passed to the method.

Like local variables, parameters are visible only in the method in which they are declared. The parameters to the *Hypotenuse* method could have been named *dSide1* and *dSide2*, and they would not have conflicted with the two local variables in *Main*. However, I was afraid you might think that the parameters had to have the same names as the arguments. They obviously do not.

If a method indicates that it returns a value—which means there's a data type in front of the method name in the method declaration—the method must have a *return* statement. *Main* doesn't need a *return* statement because it doesn't return anything. But if you wanted to put a *return* statement at the bottom of *Main*, it would look like this:

```
return;
```

In such a case, the *return* statement simply terminates execution of the method.

If you're debugging or experimenting, you might have some code at the top of *Main* that you want to test and some other code toward the bottom of *Main* that you don't want to run for the time being. You could comment out the code you didn't want to run, or you could just put a *return* statement in *Main* right before that code. The compiler will give you the warning message

```
Unreachable code detected
```

because the code following the *return* statement won't be executed. But it's only a warning message, and the program can be compiled and run. Later on, that warning message may be a good reminder to remove the early *return* statement so the program can run normally.

Often programmers put parentheses around the value that a method returns:

```
return (dResult);
```

But such parentheses are never necessary. The *return* statement can be an expression rather than a variable. In fact, you can eliminate the *dResult* variable entirely from the *Hypotenuse* method:

```
static double Hypotenuse(double d1, double d2)
{
    return Math.Sqrt(d1 * d1 + d2 * d2);
}
```

Whenever you write a snippet of code that looks like it might be useful beyond the program you're currently writing, think about how you might *encapsulate* it in a method. Think about how you can *generalize* the method and *isolate* it in a black box. What should guide your behavior most is the idea of *reusable* code, code that can perform in a variety of programs. The less code, the fewer bugs.

What if you needed this *Hypotenuse* method in another program? Because the calculation has been isolated in its own method, it's much safer to copy and paste. If you must copy and paste, copy and paste whole methods that are self-contained and tested. With any luck—and particularly if you've documented the method well—you won't have to worry about the actual code inside the method.

But there are better approaches. In the next two programs in this chapter, I'm going to show how you can progressively isolate the *Hypotenuse* method so that it becomes increasingly accessible to other programs that may need to use it. The first step will be to move the *Hypotenuse* method to its own class, and the second step will be to move that class to its own source code file.

So far, our programs have had the following general structure:

```
using System;

class MyClass
{
    // Main and possibly other methods in the class
}
```

A single source code file has contained a single class. Until this chapter, that class has had a single method named *Main*.

Just as a class can have multiple methods, a C# source code file can contain multiple classes. It doesn't matter whether you put the new class before or after the existing class in the source code file:

```
using System;

// The new class can go here.

class MyClass
{
    // Main and possibly other methods in the class
}

// Or it can go here.
```

Actually, the new class can also be declared *inside* the existing class, but that's something that's not done very often, and only if the new class is of value solely to the existing class.

If a source code file has multiple classes, I prefer that the class containing *Main* be the first class in the file. The overall structure should look like this:

```
using System;

class MyClass
{
    // Main and possibly other methods in the class
}
class NewClass
{
    // Methods in the class
}
```

Here's a new, complete program that has two classes.

CalculationWithSeparateClass.cs

```
// -------------------------------------------------------------
// CalculationWithSeparateClass.cs from "Programming in the Key of C#"
// -------------------------------------------------------------
using System;

class CalculationWithSeparateClass
{
    static void Main()
    {
        Console.Write("Enter first side: ");
        double dSide1 = Convert.ToDouble(Console.ReadLine());

        Console.Write("Enter second side: ");
        double dSide2 = Convert.ToDouble(Console.ReadLine());

        double dResult = HandyCalcs.Hypotenuse(dSide1, dSide2);
        Console.WriteLine("The hypotenuse is " + dResult);
    }
}

class HandyCalcs
{
    public static double Hypotenuse(double d1, double d2)
    {
        return Math.Sqrt(d1 * d1 + d2 * d2);
    }
}
```

The new class is named *HandyCalcs* and might include a multitude of methods that perform various types of related calculations. For now, just one method suffices to demonstrate how this works.

The *Hypotenuse* method in *HandyCalcs* must be available to other methods outside the class. For that reason, the declaration of the method must include the *public* keyword:

```
public static double Hypotenuse(double d1, double d2)
```

It doesn't matter whether *public* or *static* comes first. These are both termed *method modifiers*, and they can appear in any order. But they must come before the return type of the method, which in this case is *double*.

The *public* keyword is one of a class of modifiers called *access modifiers* that also includes *private*, *protected*, *internal*, and *protected internal*. These last three I'll discuss later in this book. The *private* access modifier is the default when you don't specify one of the others. That's why you haven't seen it so far. The *private* modifier means that the method is available only in the class in which it's declared; the *public* modifier means that the method can be called from other classes.

The other significant change in the program is the manner in which *Hypotenuse* is called. When the *Hypotenuse* method was in the same class as *Main*, you could call it just by specifying the method name:

```
double dResult = Hypotenuse(dSide1, dSide2);
```

But now, because the method is in a different class, the class name must precede the method name:

```
double dResult = HandyCalcs.Hypotenuse(dSide1, dSide2);
```

Now it looks more like the calls to other static methods that we've been using since Chapter 5.

What about the namespace? As you know, all the classes in the .NET Framework are organized into namespaces, including the *System* namespace that has many of the essential basic classes. But when classes are declared without a namespace (as these are), they become part of a global namespace. In essence, these classes have no namespace.

I mentioned earlier that we're going to isolate the *Hypotenuse* method in two progressive steps. The next step is to move the *HandyCalcs* class to its own file. By isolating a class in its own file, the class becomes available to a variety of programs that might need to use it.

The Java programming language has an interesting requirement that each class must be in its own source code file with the same name as the class. C# requires no such thing, but I think the Java approach is an excellent programming practice regardless. I often violate the rule, and there's no reason why you can't either, but having one class per file is a very good way to organize your source code.

If you're running Visual C# .NET or Key of C#, create a new project named CalculationWithSeparateFile and a file CalculationWithSeparateFile.cs. This file has the following code.

CalculationWithSeparateFile.cs
```
// -----------------------------------------------------------------
// CalculationWithSeparateFile.cs from "Programming in the Key of C#"
// -----------------------------------------------------------------
using System;

class CalculationWithSeparateFile
{
    static void Main()
```

```
    {
        Console.Write("Enter first side: ");
        double dSide1 = Convert.ToDouble(Console.ReadLine());

        Console.Write("Enter second side: ");
        double dSide2 = Convert.ToDouble(Console.ReadLine());

        double dResult = HandyCalcs.Hypotenuse(dSide1, dSide2);
        Console.WriteLine("The hypotenuse is " + dResult);
    }
}
```

This program is basically the same as the previous program but without the *HandyCalcs* class. You won't be able to compile this program by itself because there's no *HandyCalcs* class in the project or in the *System* namespace.

Let's now add another file to the project. If you're using Visual C# .NET, select Add New Item from the Project menu. Select Local Project Items at the left of the dialog box and Code File at the right. Type in the name HandyCalcs.cs. In Key of C#, select Add New Source Code File from the Project menu and enter the name HandyCalcs.cs in the dialog box. In either case, the HandyCalcs.cs file looks like this:

HandyCalcs.cs

```
// -------------------------------------------------
// HandyCalcs.cs from "Programming in the Key of C#"
// -------------------------------------------------
using System;

class HandyCalcs
{
    public static double Hypotenuse(double d1, double d2)
    {
        return Math.Sqrt(d1 * d1 + d2 * d2);
    }
}
```

Both files need a *using* directive because they both make reference to a class in the *System* namespace, but otherwise, the original file has just been broken into two.

You can now compile the program, which will run the same as the previous version.

Now let's see if we can write a second program that uses the same *HandyCalcs* class. In Visual C# .NET or Key of C#, you'll want to create a new project named, for example, AnotherProgram. Let's create a file named AnotherProgram.cs that should look pretty familiar by now.

AnotherProgram.cs
```
// -------------------------------------------------------
// AnotherProgram.cs from "Programming in the Key of C#"
// -------------------------------------------------------
using System;

class AnotherProgram
{
    static void Main()
    {
        Console.Write("Enter first side: ");
        double dSide1 = Convert.ToDouble(Console.ReadLine());

        Console.Write("Enter second side: ");
        double dSide2 = Convert.ToDouble(Console.ReadLine());

        double dResult = HandyCalcs.Hypotenuse(dSide1, dSide2);
        Console.WriteLine("The hypotenuse is " + dResult);
    }
}
```

Here's the important part: you don't want this project to contain another *new* file. You want it to contain the *existing* HandyCalcs.cs file. This requires a special approach. In Visual C# .NET, select Add Existing Item from the Project menu. Navigate to the existing HandyCalcs.cs file. Then, using the little arrow at the right of the Open button, select Link File. This prevents the file from being copied. On the right, you'll see this file identified with a special icon that contains a little arrow, indicating that the file is linked. In Key of C#, select Link To Existing Source Code File from the Project menu and navigate to HandyCalcs.cs.

Now you have two programs using the same *HandyCalcs* class. If you want to modify that class—by enhancing it, adding more methods, or fixing some bugs—you only have to fiddle with the one file. You then recompile every program that uses the file, and the programs will be using the new version. (Of course, it's always possible that changing *HandyCalcs* will *break* one of the programs that use it, which means the program won't run right anymore, but that's a whole different problem.) Any program that uses *HandyCalcs* can itself be changed and recompiled without affecting other programs that use *HandyCalcs*.

There's actually another step we can take, which is to put the *HandyCalcs* class in a dynamic-link library (DLL). In that way, *HandyCalcs* becomes almost exactly like the classes in the .NET Framework. A program using *HandyCalcs* wouldn't have to contain the *HandyCalcs* code because the code would be pre-compiled in the DLL. I'll show you how to put a class in a DLL in Chapter 39.

As a programmer, you will be dealing with immediate and specific programming problems, but you should also be thinking of ways to generalize and reuse your code. For example, a particular programming job might require that you replace all occurrences of "Visual Basic" with "C#" in a specific text document. A generalized search-and-replace method wouldn't be that much more difficult to write and would potentially be useful in other programming jobs. Even if you enjoy coding, you don't want to be writing the same code over and over again.

Sometimes you can anticipate a particular need in a programming job and first write a class that you eventually will be using in the context of the larger program. Suppose you're beginning a project in which you'll be needing to do a lot of trigonometry. (Despite the popular presumption that you'll "never need" high school mathematics in real life, computer graphics programming, among other applications, makes extensive use of trigonometry.) If you've explored the *Math* class in the *System* namespace, you'll have discovered a collection of methods named *Sin*, *Cos*, and *Tan*, as well as inverse trigonometric functions. These seem to be exactly what you need, but maybe not. Perhaps you're not happy that all the trigonometric functions in the *Math* class work in units of radians rather than degrees. (One radian is the angle subtended by an arc equal in length to the radius. There are thus 2π radians in 360 degrees.)

If you much prefer to work with angles rather than radians, you need to adjust the arguments to the trigonometric methods. For example, if *dDegrees* is an angle in degrees, you can call the *Math.Sin* method like this:

```
dResult = Math.Sin(Math.PI * dDegrees / 180);
```

But do you want to include that conversion in every trigonometric method your program calls? Probably not. So, even before starting work on the program that will use these trigonometric functions, you can create a class that's similar to the *Math* class, and that uses the *Math* class, but lets you specify angles in degrees.

Here's a first shot at such a class. Although this class will eventually be used by a larger program, I've included a *Main* method for testing purposes. This is a common technique. Once the class is more or less debugged, the *Main* method can be removed.

Trig1.cs
```
// ------------------------------------------------
// Trig1.cs from "Programming in the Key of C#"
// ------------------------------------------------
using System;

class Trig1
{
    static void Main()
    {
        Console.WriteLine("The Sin of 45 degrees is " + Trig1.Sin(45));
        Console.WriteLine("The Cos of 45 degrees is " + Trig1.Cos(45));
        Console.WriteLine("The Tan of 45 degrees is " + Trig1.Tan(45));
    }
    public static double Sin(double dAngle)
    {
        return Math.Sin(Math.PI * dAngle / 180);
    }
    public static double Cos(double dAngle)
    {
        return Math.Cos(Math.PI * dAngle / 180);
    }
    public static double Tan(double dAngle)
    {
        return Math.Tan(Math.PI * dAngle / 180);
    }
}
```

Despite the fact that these methods are not yet being called from another class, I've included the *public* modifier in anticipation of that day. Also, even though *Main* is right in the class with the methods, the methods are called from *Main* with the class name attached to the method. *Main* could very easily be in another class in another file. I'm just trying to streamline the process here.

Notice that each of the three public methods has a similar type of calculation to convert angles to radians. If I were to include angle versions of the inverse trigonometric functions, those would have a similar conversion from radians to angles.

It seems fairly trivial in this case, but you'll frequently encounter situations where more than one method in a class uses similar code. That should be like a trigger for you, the programmer, to consolidate the duplicated code in one place.

One solution might be another method:

```
static double DegreesToRadians(double dDegrees)
{
    return Math.PI * dDegrees / 180;
}
```

Then the other methods might look something like this:

```
public static double Sin(double dAngle)
{
    return Math.Sin(DegreesToRadians(dAngle));
}
```

Notice that the *DegreesToRadians* method doesn't have the *public* modifier, which means that it's *private* to the class. It would be your decision whether or not to make the method public. You should really make public only those methods that would be useful to other classes. Other programmers might someday be using this class, and by declaring too many elements in it public, you risk the danger of making the class seem more complex than it is.

But I don't like the *DegreesToRadians* method. There's some overhead involved in method calls, and it seems a waste to have a method call just to perform a little multiplication. I'd prefer declaring a multiplicative factor that converts degrees to radians:

```
double dFactor = Math.PI / 180;
```

The calculation of the sine function would look like this:

```
return Math.Sin(dFactor * dAngle);
```

But where should *dFactor* be declared? Certainly not in the *Sin* method. That would make it local to *Sin*. The same factor would then have to be declared in *Cos* and *Tan* as well, and that would defeat the whole purpose.

What would make most sense is to declare *dFactor* as a *field*. We've encountered fields before. The *Math* class has two fields named *PI* and *E* that store important constants, one of which we've been using here to convert from angles to radians. You declare a field in the class but outside of all the methods in the class. The field is then available to all the methods in the class. A class (perhaps named *Trig2*) that contained such a field could start off like this:

```
class Trig2
{
    static double dFactor = Math.PI / 180;
```

Often fields are declared at the top of a class so they visually stick out and don't get lost among the methods. Like the methods, *dFactor* is declared with the *static* modifier because the field is associated with the class rather than an instance of the class. I haven't used the *public* modifier with *dFactor* because other classes don't need access to this field.

Although other classes can't access *dFactor* at all, methods in *Trig2* can both read and alter the *dFactor* field. It really should be a constant. Simply replace *static* with *const* to make the field read-only. Any field that is declared with *const* is implicitly *static* as well. "Even though constants are considered static members, a *constant-declaration* neither requires nor allows a *static* modifier" (*C# Language Specification*, §10.3). Here's how it would look:

```
class Trig2
{
    const double dFactor = Math.PI / 180;
```

While we're at it, let's fix something I don't like about the *Math* class. I can never remember whether it's the *PI* field or the *Pi* field. Let's add two public constants to the *Trig2* class that let us use either *Trig2.PI* or *Trig2.Pi*. Here's the complete *Trig2* class with three fields and a *Main* method to test the code.

Trig2.cs
```
// --------------------------------------------
// Trig2.cs from "Programming in the Key of C#"
// --------------------------------------------
using System;

class Trig2
{
    public const double PI = Math.PI;
    public const double Pi = PI;
    const double dFactor = PI / 180;

    static void Main()
    {
        Console.WriteLine("The Sin of 45 degrees is " + Trig2.Sin(45));
        Console.WriteLine("The Cos of 45 degrees is " + Trig2.Cos(45));
        Console.WriteLine("The Tan of 45 degrees is " + Trig2.Tan(45));
    }
    public static double Sin(double dAngle)
    {
        return Math.Sin(dFactor * dAngle);
    }
    public static double Cos(double dAngle)
    {
        return Math.Cos(dFactor * dAngle);
    }
    public static double Tan(double dAngle)
    {
        return Math.Tan(dFactor * dAngle);
    }
}
```

Notice that the initializations of the fields *Pi* and *dFactor* both refer to the *PI* field initialized from *Math.PI*.

18

Arrays

"Thirty days hath September, April, June, and November…" That's one way to remember it. The other way is to write a program. Perhaps the program could begin by displaying the prompt

```
Enter the month (1 for January... 12 for December):
```

After the user responds, the program would display something like this:

```
That month has 30 days.
```

Without really knowing how such a program would work, you might begin by declaring some constants anyway:

```
const int iDaysInJanuary = 31;
const int iDaysInFebruary =
```

Uh oh. Now what? Some years February has 28 days, and some years it has 29. Well, for now let's just forget about leap years, OK? Continue:

```
const int iDaysInFebruary = 28;
const int iDaysInMarch = 31;
const int iDaysInApril = 30;
```

But wait. Before you get too far, maybe you really *should* consider how this program is going to work. After the program prompts for the month, it's going to have a number indicating the month, for example, 6 for June. How do you then use that number to display the *iDaysInJune* constant? With what you've learned so far in this book, it's not obvious at all.

These constants that we're declaring—they're all related in a way. They all indicate the number of days in a particular month.

It's often very convenient to store a bunch of related numbers in a single variable—a very special variable that's known as an *array*. An array stores multiple values of a specific type. These multiple values are known as *elements* of the array. You refer to each element using a number, called an *index*. An array is perfect for this application. It can have 12 elements for the 12 months, and the index used to access these elements would be the number entered by the user. Here's how you might visualize such a 12-element array containing the number of days in each month:

31	28	31	30	31	30	31	31	30	31	30	31

You've seen that C# (like C before it) uses curly brackets for class declarations, method declarations, and blocks. C and C# use parentheses for methods, casting, and overriding precedence rules. For arrays, you'll be using *square* brackets: [and]. Almost always, square brackets mean an array is present.

The process of declaring, creating, and initializing an array generally involves three steps.

Step 1: Declare the array. All the elements of an array are the same type, which is called the *element type* of the array. In our example, the array elements are integers. If you wanted to declare an ordinary integer variable, you'd begin with the keyword *int*. To declare an array of integer values, you use the element type of the array followed by a pair of square brackets:

```
int[]
```

You follow that by the name you want to use for the array. I like to use a Hungarian Notation prefix of *a* for arrays, followed by a second prefix indicating the element type:

```
int[] aiDaysInMonth;
```

We say that *aiDaysInMonth* is an array of *int*, or an *int* array. What this declaration does is declare *aiDaysInMonth* as an array of integers. The actual elements of the array aren't yet specified. In fact, you haven't even specified the number of elements in the array (which is referred to as the *length* of the array).

Once you have declared *aiDaysInMonth* as an array of integers, you *cannot* assign a value to the array like this:

```
aiDaysInMonth = 31;    // Won't work
```

This is not an integer variable. It is an array variable.

Step 2: Allocate memory for the array by specifying the number of elements in the array. In our example, the array has 12 elements:

```
aiDaysInMonth = new int[12];
```

This is known as *creating* the array. An array is a reference type. The actual array—that is, all the elements of the array—is stored in the heap. The keyword *new* performs a very special function here by causing memory to be allocated from the heap, in this case, 48 bytes. That's 12 elements of 4 bytes each. Again, notice the square brackets. Here they indicate the size of the array. The *new* expression returns a reference to the memory allocated from the heap. If the array is a local variable, the reference is stored on the stack.

At this point, you have an array of 12 *int* values. Memory allocated from the heap is automatically set to 0, so each element of the array is automatically initialized to 0. Here's how you might visualize the array after this step:

| 0 | 0 | 0 | 0 | 0 | 0 | 0 | 0 | 0 | 0 | 0 | 0 |

Step 3: You can now start working with the individual array elements. You refer to the 12 elements of the array using the array name and an index in square brackets. These indices begin with 0. For example,

```
aiDaysInMonth[0]
```

refers to the first element, which would correspond to the number of days in January. Again, notice the square brackets. Here you use them for setting or referencing the elements of the array.

You use an indexed array name in the same way as you use a regular variable, for example, on the left side of an assignment statement:

```
aiDaysInMonth[0] = 31;     // Number of days in January
```

Now the array looks like this:

| 31 | 0 | 0 | 0 | 0 | 0 | 0 | 0 | 0 | 0 | 0 | 0 |

You can later display this value:

```
Console.WriteLine("The number of days in January is " + aiDaysInMonth[0]);
```

Likewise,

```
aiDaysInMonth[11]
```

refers to the last element, which is the number of days in December.

Array indices begin with 0, a characteristic referred to as *zero-based indexing*:

Index:	0	1	2	3	4	5	6	7	8	9	10	11
Value:	31	0	0	0	0	0	0	0	0	0	0	0

This type of indexing is certainly one of the most confusing aspects of working with arrays for new programmers. Historically, zero-based indexing made perfect sense, because in C the indices really indicate memory offsets from the beginning of the array to the particular element, and the first element is stored at the very beginning, which is an offset of zero.

But it may take you awhile to get accustomed to zero-based indexing. Array indices always range from zero through the number of elements *minus one*. If the array has 12 elements, any attempt to reference

```
aiDaysInMonth[12]
```

will raise an exception. You'll also raise an exception if you attempt to index an array using negative integers.

In a program such as the one we've been contemplating, step 3 would probably involve setting all the elements of the array to their appropriate values. Here's one way to do it:

```
aiDaysInMonth[0] = 31;     // January
aiDaysInMonth[1] = 28;
aiDaysInMonth[2] = 31;
aiDaysInMonth[3] = 30;
aiDaysInMonth[4] = 31;
aiDaysInMonth[5] = 30;
aiDaysInMonth[6] = 31;
aiDaysInMonth[7] = 31;
aiDaysInMonth[8] = 30;
aiDaysInMonth[9] = 31;
aiDaysInMonth[10] = 30;
aiDaysInMonth[11] = 31;    // December
```

That's the *long* way of doing it. There are certainly shortcuts and some variations on the theme.

First, you can combine steps 1 and 2 by allocating memory for the array at the same time you declare it:

```
int[] aiDaysInMonth = new int[12];
```

This syntax is similar to initializing a non-array variable when it's declared. In this case, *aiDaysInMonth* is initialized to an array of 12 elements, with every element initialized to 0.

You can combine steps 2 and 3 by initializing the elements of the array when you allocate memory for it:

```
aiDaysInMonth = new int[12] { 31, 28, 31, 30, 31, 30,
                             31, 31, 30, 31, 30, 31 } ;
```

This is a shortcut you'll want to take advantage of whenever possible, that is, whenever you're creating an array where you know the value of each element ahead of time.

If you initialize the array elements, you must have the same number of initializers as the length of the array. Here it's 12. There must be 12 numbers in the curly brackets or the compiler will complain. Because the specified array length is redundant, you can leave it out if you're initializing the array elements:

```
aiDaysInMonth = new int[] { 31, 28, 31, 30, 31, 30,
                            31, 31, 30, 31, 30, 31 } ;
```

Notice the empty brackets.

All three steps can be combined in a declaration that looks like this:

```
int[] aiDaysInMonth = new int[12] { 31, 28, 31, 30, 31, 30,
                                     31, 31, 30, 31, 30, 31 } ;
```

Or it can be slightly shortened like this:

```
int[] aiDaysInMonth = new int[] { 31, 28, 31, 30, 31, 30,
                                  31, 31, 30, 31, 30, 31 } ;
```

Now the array is declared, memory is allocated, and the elements are initialized, all in one shot. In this particular case, you're allowed to eliminate the part of the statement that explicitly allocates memory for the array. The equal sign can be followed immediately with the curly brackets containing the initial element values:

```
int[] aiDaysInMonth = { 31, 28, 31, 30, 31, 30,
                        31, 31, 30, 31, 30, 31 } ;
```

Regardless of the absence of the *new* expression, memory is still being allocated from the heap. You're allowed to eliminate the *new* expressions only when you're initializing the elements of the array in the declaration statement.

In general, the three steps must be performed in sequence: You need to declare the type of the array first, then allocate memory of it, and then reference the actual elements. I've shown examples of referencing the array elements using integer literals:

```
aiDaysInMonth[11] = 31;
```

But you can also index an array using any integer expression:

```
Console.WriteLine(aiDaysInMonth[iMonth]);
```

In this example, the value of *iMonth* must range from 0 through 11 or an exception will be raised.

Now let's take a look at a complete program.

DaysInMonth.cs

```
// ---------------------------------------------------
// DaysInMonth.cs from "Programming in the Key of C#"
// ---------------------------------------------------
using System;

class DaysInMonth
{
    static void Main()
    {
        int[] aiDaysInMonth = { 31, 28, 31, 30, 31, 30,
                                31, 31, 30, 31, 30, 31 };

        Console.Write
            ("Enter the month (1 for January... 12 for December): ");
        int iMonth = Int32.Parse(Console.ReadLine());
        Console.WriteLine("That month has {0} days.",
                          aiDaysInMonth[iMonth - 1]);
    }
}
```

The prompt asks the user to enter 1 for January, 2 for February, and so forth. The program could just as easily have asked the user to type 0 for January, 1 for February, and so on, to be consistent with the zero-based indexing of the array. But the program is making it easier for the user. That's the primary consideration. Always lean toward ease of use rather than programmer convenience. You're smarter than they are (or you think you are, anyway).

Assuming that the user types in a good value, the value of *iMonth* is in the range from 1 through 12. But the valid array indices are 0 through 11. For that reason, *iDaysInMonth* must be indexed with one less than *iMonth*:

```
Console.WriteLine("That month has {0} days.", iDaysInMonth[iMonth - 1]);
```

The indexing of *iDaysInMonth* is the crucial part of this statement. The program won't work right without the −1.

Does the program really say "That month"? Why not give the user some feedback by displaying the actual name of the month?

You can declare and initialize arrays of strings just as easily as arrays of integers. Here's a better version of the program that displays the month name.

DaysAndNameOfMonth.cs

```
// --------------------------------------------------------
// DaysAndNameOfMonth.cs from "Programming in the Key of C#"
// --------------------------------------------------------
using System;

class DaysAndNameOfMonth
{
    static void Main()
    {
        string[] astrMonthName = { "January", "February", "March",
                                   "April", "May", "June", "July",
                                   "August", "September", "October",
                                   "November", "December" };

        int[] aiDaysInMonth = { 31, 28, 31, 30, 31, 30,
                                31, 31, 30, 31, 30, 31 };

        Console.Write
            ("Enter the month (1 for January... 12 for December): ");
        int iMonth = Int32.Parse(Console.ReadLine());
        Console.WriteLine("{0} has {1} days.", astrMonthName[iMonth - 1],
                                          aiDaysInMonth[iMonth - 1]);
    }
}
```

The two arrays in this program have the same number of elements and are indexed the same way in the *Console.WriteLine* call. They are, in a sense, *parallel* arrays, and the most important rule about parallel arrays is to keep them parallel. If one array has 11 initializers rather than 12, there's going to be a problem.

I want you to run one of these programs and type in a bogus month number, like 0 (in which case the array is indexed with –1) or 13 (indexing the array with 12). You'll get an error dialog box asking whether you want to debug using the selected debugger. When you click No, you'll see this message:

```
Unhandled Exception: System.IndexOutOfRangeException: Index was
    outside the bounds of the array.
```

Eventually, you'll learn how your program itself can detect exceptions. But I'd like you to know what would happen if this program were written in C or C++ rather than C#. These languages do not implement any check of array indices (what is technically termed *array bounds checking*). The C or C++ program would simply try to access the array with the improper index and display what is technically termed *garbage*. What's worse is when a C or C++ program *sets* an array element using an index that's out of bounds. Some other variable could easily be altered in the process!

The lack of array bounds checking is one of the features of C and C++ that allows compilers for these languages to generate such fast, efficient executables. That's part of what made these languages so popular in the final decades of the last century. But the bugs that can result from out-of-bounds indexing are no longer tolerable. We rely on software too much to use languages that don't cooperate in helping us create bug-free code.

Arrays are *reference types*. Memory for the array elements is allocated from the heap. Almost always, this allocation takes place at the *new* expression. (The only exception is when you leave out the *new* expression when you're initializing array elements in the array declaration. The memory is allocated regardless, just as if the *new* statement were present.) The *new* expression returns a reference to the allocated memory in the heap. That's what the array variable itself stores: a reference to the heap.

Consider the following sequence of simple code involving integers:

```
int i1 = 55;
int i2 = i1;
i1 = 0;
```

What does *i2* equal? Obviously, it equals 55, which is the value it was assigned in the second statement. The latter assignment of *i1* obviously has no effect on *i2*.

Now let's look at some similar code but using arrays of integers:

```
int[] ai1 = new int[3] { 33, 55, 77 };
int[] ai2 = ai1;
ai1[1] = 0;
```

What does *ai2[1]* equal? The correct answer requires that you understand what happens in the second statement. The variable *ai1* is a reference to the memory allocated in the heap for the array. The second statement assigns this same reference to *ai2*. Now *ai1* and *ai2* reference the same block of memory in the heap. The following diagram uses a fictitious number stored on the stack to symbolize a reference to the heap:

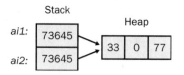

Both array variables reference the same array! Any change to any element of *ai1* changes the corresponding element in *ai2*, and vice versa. In this example, the element *ai2[1]* equals 0.

When thinking about code involving arrays, it's helpful to keep in mind the role of the *new* keyword. A *new* expression causes memory to be allocated from the heap. With just a few exceptions, a *new* expression is explicitly required to allocate *any* memory from the heap. (Many of the exceptions involve strings; when you add two strings, for example, heap memory must be allocated to store the result, but the addition doesn't require an explicit *new* expression. Also, when you initialize array elements in a declaration statement, you can leave out the *new* expression.) There's only one *new* expression in this sequence of statements:

```
int[] ai1 = new int[3] { 33, 55, 77 };
int[] ai2 = ai1;
ai1[1] = 0;
```

That means there's only one array allocated. The second statement does *not* cause an additional block of memory to be allocated from the heap, and it does *not* copy all the elements from *ai1* to *ai2*. The assignment statement only causes the reference to be copied.

Suppose you declare an array of *double* and allocate memory for 100 elements:

```
double[] adArray = new double[100];
```

As usual, memory is allocated from the heap for the 100 elements and (like all heap memory) the elements are initialized to 0:

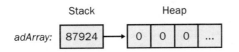

Your program uses this array normally. But later on in the program, you use that same array variable for an array of a different number of elements, or perhaps the same number:

```
adArray = new double[100];
```

This is a second *new* expression, which means that more memory is allocated from the heap. This is a whole new array. The original 100 elements are *not* copied over to the new array:

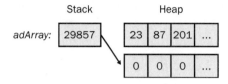

What happens to the original array allocated in the heap? If there are no other references to it, it becomes eligible for garbage collection. Eventually (and certainly as the program terminates) the memory is freed. But it's not clear from these two statements that there are no other references to the original array. You could have copied the reference to the original array to another array:

```
double[] adAnother = adArray;
```

Because the first array can still be referenced by *adAnother*, it's not eligible for garbage collection. You can remove a reference to the array by simply setting the array variable to *null*:

```
adAnother = null;
```

It's possible to declare multiple array variables in a single declaration statement:

```
decimal[] amSales, amCommissions, amBonuses;
```

These three variables are all *decimal* arrays. You could also allocate memory for all these arrays, or only some of them:

```
decimal[] amSales = new decimal[6], amCommissions,
        amBonuses = new decimal[10];
```

You could also initialize elements of these arrays, but at that point the statement would start getting much too long and messy. For purposes of clarity, it would probably be best to use separate declarations.

Understanding array creation and initialization is sometimes clarified if you look at it in terms of expressions. The expression

```
new string[4]
```

allocates memory for an array of four strings and returns a reference to that memory. If the element type were a value type (such as *int* or *decimal*), each element would be initialized to 0. Because the element type here is a reference type (specifically *string*), each element is initialized to *null*.

Here's another expression:

```
new string[] {"North", "East", "South", "West"}
```

That expression allocates memory for an array of four strings. Each element of the array is another reference to an area in the heap where each string is stored.

And here's an interesting expression:

```
new string[] {"North", "East", "South", "West"} [2]
```

It's the same as the previous expression except that it also includes an array index at the end. If you check the Operator Precedence and Associativity table on the inside back cover of this book, you'll see that the keyword *new* and array indexing (indicated by *a[x]*) have the same precedence and are associated from left to right. The index essentially chooses one of the elements of the array. This expression evaluates to the string "South".

This means that if you need to use a little array just once, you don't need to declare an array variable. Here's a statement that displays one of the four compass points based on the variable *i*:

```
Console.Write(new string[] {"North", "East", "South", "West"} [i]);
```

As you know from Chapter 10, when a method begins executing, space on the stack is allocated for all the local variables in the method. For an array, the amount of space needed on the stack is the size of a reference. If the declaration of the array also includes element initialization, the compiler generates code that allocates memory from the heap and initializes all the element values in the array one by one.

If the array is declared in *Main*, the array creation and initialization occur once when the program starts up. But suppose the array is in another method. Here's a little method that calculates a day-of-year value based on the one-based month and day (ignoring leap years):

```
static int DayOfYear(int iMonth, int iDay)
{
    int[] aiCumulativeDays = { 0, 31, 59, 90, 120, 151,
                               181, 212, 243, 273, 304, 334 };

    return aiCumulativeDays[iMonth - 1] + iDay;
}
```

For example, the expression

```
DayOfYear(5, 10)
```

returns the day of year value for May 10th, which is 130.

A program might be going through a file and calling this method hundreds or thousands or even millions of times. Each and every time the *DayOfYear* method is called, the array must be allocated from the heap and initialized. After the method exits, the block of memory allocated from the heap is no longer referenced and becomes eligible for garbage collection. That whole process seems like a waste for an array that essentially stores constant values. However, you can't declare an array using *const*. Constants can be set only to values available at compile time. An array requires a *new* operation, and *new* operations occur at run time.

The general rule is that you should keep code local to where it's being used—not only arrays but any kind of variable. By this rule, an array that is used only in one method should be declared in that method. However, if you need to access an array with constant values in a method that is frequently called while a program is running, you should move the array out of the method and make it a *static* field. An array declared as a *static* field is initialized only once during the course of the program. If you want to keep the array visually close to the method that uses it, you can do so:

```
class SomeClass
{
    // Possibly some fields

    static void Main()
    {
        // Body of Main
    }

    // Possibly other methods

    static int[] aiCumulativeDays = { 0, 31, 59, 90, 120, 151,
                                  181, 212, 243, 273, 304, 334 };

    static int DayOfYear(int iMonth, int iDay)
    {
        return aiCumulativeDays[iMonth - 1] + iDay;
    }

    // Possibly other methods
}
```

Fields don't have to be declared at the top of the class.

This is not to say that all arrays should be fields. An array that is filled dynamically at run time can certainly be local to a method. If the array is used in multiple methods, it can be passed as an argument to other methods. But an array that is central to the functionality of a program and is used by many methods (for example, the arrays of names and addresses used in an address book program) should probably be a field.

You can't declare an array as *const* because the *new* expression is evaluated at run time. Nor is there any way to protect the elements of an array from being changed by a program that uses the array. In other words, the array elements cannot be made read-only.

All arrays are treated as if they are instances of the *Array* class in the *System* namespace. This class contains several static methods that let you sort or search arrays. I'll have an example in the OperatorTest program in Chapter 38.

The *Array* class also contains a couple of useful properties that you can use with arrays. The *Length* property indicates the total number of elements in the array. For example, the expression

```
astrMonthName.Length
```

equals the integer 12 for the array declared earlier. That's the number of elements in that array. As you'll recall, the *String* class also has a property named *Length*. That property returns the number of characters of the string. Be careful when you have an array of strings! Notice that *astrMonthName* is indexed in this expression:

```
astrMonthName[1].Length
```

The expression first obtains the second element of *astrMonthName* (the word "February") and then obtains the number of characters in that string (which is 8). Array indexing and the dot operator are both in the Primary category of the Operator Precedence and Associativity table, so the two operations have equal precedence and are associated left to right.

The second useful property of the *Array* class is *Rank*, which returns the number of *dimensions* of the array. For all the arrays described so far, *Rank* returns 1 because all the arrays have had a single dimension. It is also possible to make multidimensional (or *rectangular*) arrays. For example, if you were writing a chess program, you'd probably have an array to represent the chessboard. This could be an array of 64 elements, but it might be easier to work with if it were a two-dimensional array of 8-by-8 elements.

Here's a declaration of a one-dimensional array of integers:

```
int[] aiOneDim;
```

And here's a declaration of a two-dimensional array:

```
int[,] aiTwoDim;
```

Notice the comma in the square brackets. A three-dimensional array is declared like so:

```
int[,,] aiThreeDim;
```

And so on.

You create the arrays using statements like these:

```
aiOneDim = new int[15];
aiTwoDim = new int[3, 6];
aiThreeDim = new int[8, 5, 3];
```

Or you could include the *new* expression in the declaration. The total number of elements in each of these arrays (the array's length) is equal to the product of the sizes of each dimension. For example, *aiThreeDim* has a total of 120 elements; that's the number returned by the *Length* property.

You reference the elements of a multidimensional array using indices separated by commas:

```
aiThreeDim[i, j, k] = 265;
```

The variable *i* must be in the range 0 through 7, *j* must be 0 through 4, and *k* must be 0 through 2.

For a multidimensional array, the *Length* property returns the total number of elements in the array. If you need the number of elements in a particular dimension, you can use the *GetLength* method of the *Array* class. The argument is a zero-based dimension. For example,

```
aiThreeDim.GetLength(1)
```

returns the size of the second dimension of *aiThreeDim*, which is 5.

Interestingly enough, multidimensional arrays seem to be *less* common in object-oriented programming than in traditional procedural programming. As you'll eventually discover, what's more common in object-oriented programming are single-dimensional arrays of objects, where the objects themselves encapsulate multiple items. But some "real-life" examples of multidimensional arrays do exist. If you were unfortunate enough to be working on a program involving United States senators, for example, the following array would help store their names:

```
string[,] astrSenators = new string[50, 2];
```

That's 50 states and 2 senators each.

Initializing the elements of multidimensional arrays requires a precise use of curly brackets. Here's another three-dimensional array that's a bit smaller than the previous ones:

```
int[,,] ai3D = new int[3,2,4] {{{8, 3, 4, 2}, {7, 4, 1, 2}},
                               {{2, 7, 3, 6}, {5, 1, 9, 0}},
                               {{0, 4, 9, 7}, {3, 9, 8, 5}}};
```

The first four initialization values are *ai3D[0,0,0]* through *ai3D[0,0,3]*, the second four values are *ai3D[0,1,0]* through *ai3D[0,1,3]*, and so forth. The last four values are *ai3D[2,1,0]* through *ai3D[2,1,3]*. The *Rank* property of this array returns 3. The *Length* property returns 24. You can also shorten the array initialization to

```
int[,,] ai3D = new int[,,] {{{8, 3, 4, 2}, {7, 4, 1, 2}},
                            {{2, 7, 3, 6}, {5, 1, 9, 0}},
                            {{0, 4, 9, 7}, {3, 9, 8, 5}}};
```

without explicitly specifying the number of elements in each dimension, or you can leave out the *new* expression entirely:

```
int[,,] ai3D = {{{8, 3, 4, 2}, {7, 4, 1, 2}},
                {{2, 7, 3, 6}, {5, 1, 9, 0}},
                {{0, 4, 9, 7}, {3, 9, 8, 5}}};
```

C# also supports arrays of arrays; that is, elements of the array can themselves be arrays. These are referred to as *jagged* arrays because the size of the second dimension (and possibly subsequent dimensions) is not constant. The size of each dimension depends on the indexing of the previous dimensions.

For example, suppose you want to declare an array for storing all the names of everyone in your four closest friends' families. These families range in size from two to eight people. You can certainly declare a normal two-dimensional array sufficient for the largest family:

```
string[,] astrNormal = new string[4,8];
```

But that approach wastes some space. Not all of your four friends' families have eight people. (And if the wasted space of this example seems meager, how about an array similar to the *astrSenators* array but for members of the House of Representatives? Depending on the state, the number of representatives ranges from 1 to 53.)

Because a jagged array is essentially an array of arrays, creating the array requires multiple *new* expressions. Here's the declaration and the first *new* expression for the array that stores your four friends' family members:

```
string[][] astrJagged = new string[4][];
```

Next you need four additional *new* statements for each of the four families:

```
astrJagged[0] = new string[5];
astrJagged[1] = new string[2];
astrJagged[2] = new string[8];
astrJagged[3] = new string[4];
```

Each of these *new* expressions indicates the number of members in that family. The family sizes range from two to eight.

At this point, you can access *astrJagged[0][0]* through *astrJagged[0][4]* for the five members of the first family. The two members of the second family are stored in *astrJagged[1][0]* and *astrJagged[1][1]*. And so forth.

An assignment statement such as

```
astrJagged[3] = new string[4];
```

can also include initializations for that family:

```
astrJagged[3] = new string[4] { "Jack", "Diane", "Bobby", "Sally" };
```

or

```
astrJagged[3] = new string[] { "Jack", "Diane", "Bobby", "Sally" };
```

You can also initialize the whole array in the original declaration. The initialization includes all the *new* expressions:

```
string[][] astrJagged = new string[4][]
            { new string[] { "Jill", "Alice", "Billy", "Judy", "Sammy"},
            new string[] { "James", "Ellen" },
            new string[] { "Steve", "Sue", "Bernie", "Rich",
                        "Chris", "Erika", "Michelle", "Alyssa" },
            new string[] { "Jack", "Diane", "Bobby", "Sally" }};
```

Because this is a declaration, the first *new* expression can be eliminated, but the rest are required.

So far in this book, you've encountered two types of variables that require memory to be allocated from the heap: strings and arrays, which are instances of the *System.String* and *System.Array* classes. Classes are reference types, and instances of classes are always stored in the heap. With few exceptions, a *new* expression is explicitly required to allocate heap memory. As you'll discover, you'll also be using *new* expressions to create instances of other classes. (An example is coming up shortly.)

Most of the C# basic types (such as *int* and *decimal*) are not reference types. They are value types. The *int* and *decimal* keywords are aliases for the *System.Int32* and *System.Decimal* structures. Although value types are stored on the stack and don't require heap memory, you can use a *new* expression with value types. The *new* expression doesn't cause any memory to be allocated from the heap. Instead, the *new* expression merely initializes the object in some way. For example, here's an alternative declaration of an integer:

```
int i = new int();
```

You can tell this isn't an array because no square brackets are involved. The parentheses make this *new* expression look more like a method call, and that's pretty much what it is. It's a call to a special method called a *constructor* that is responsible for initializing the object. (Don't worry if this concept seems a little vague right now; you'll have plenty of time to get accustomed to it.)

In the case of a value type like *int*, the *new* expression initializes the integer object by setting it to 0. You can get the same effect like this:

```
int i = 0;
```

What you can't do, however, is declare a constant using a *new* expression:

```
const int i = new int();    // Not allowed!
```

Because the *new* expression generally involves allocating memory from the heap, it occurs at run time, not compile time. Constants must be set to values that are known at compile time. Some of the classes you've encountered so far, such as *Console* and *Math*, have consisted solely of static methods and fields. You've also seen how you can create your own classes containing static methods and fields. Most classes, however, are different. Most classes need to retain some information, and for that they use the heap. To use most classes, you must create an instance of the class using a *new* expression.

In the next example program, I'll be using a class from the *System* namespace named *Random*. This class generates random numbers. *Random* is a class. It's a reference type.

In computer programs, random numbers are usually generated from something called a *pseudo-random sequence*. The random number generator begins with a *seed*, which is simply a number. A complex formula is applied to the seed to produce another number, and then the same formula is applied to that number to get a third number, and so forth. The formula is devised so that these generated numbers satisfy statistical tests for randomness. However, the pseudo-random sequence is entirely deterministic because it depends solely on the seed. If you need to reproduce the same sequence of numbers, you can do so simply by using the same seed. The use of a pseudo-random sequence allows applications that require random numbers (such as a simulation of some sort) to repeatedly produce the same results, if that is desired.

By default, the *Random* class chooses a seed for you based on the system clock. The determination of the seed occurs when you create an object of the *Random* class:

```
Random rand = new Random();
```

The variable *rand* is declared as an object (or instance) of type *Random*. I like to give objects a lowercase name (or a lowercase prefix) somewhat reminiscent of the object name.

If you were to simply declare *rand* without the *new* statement, as in

```
Random rand;
```

then *rand* would be uninitialized. No memory has yet been allocated from the heap for the object. The assignment statement

```
rand = new Random();
```

allocates memory from the heap, chooses a seed, and stores the seed in the heap memory.

The *Random* class supports several instance methods for generating random numbers from this object. Because they are instance methods, they apply to an object of type *Random* rather than the *Random* class itself. For example, the method call

```
rand.NextDouble()
```

returns a new random *double* between 0.0 and 1.0 every time it's called. You could scale and adjust that *double* to whatever you need for your application. If your program required random numbers that ranged between 0.25 and 1.75, you could adjust the result of *NextDouble* like this:

```
1.5 * rand.NextDouble + 0.25
```

Often applications need random integers. The *Next* method provides them. It exists in three different forms. First, there's a version with no arguments:

```
rand.Next()
```

that returns a positive integer that can range from 0 through *Int32.MaxValue* (which equals 2,147,483,647). The call

```
rand.Next(iMaxValue)
```

returns a positive integer ranging from 0 to *iMaxValue* minus 1. If the argument to *Next* is an array's *Length* property, the return value is suitable for indexing the array. For example, suppose you have an array named *arr*. This expression selects a random element of the array:

```
arr[rand.Next(arr.Length)]
```

The array is indexed by the return value from *Next*, which has an argument equal to the array length. Finally, the method call

```
rand.Next(iMinValue, iMaxValue)
```

returns a random number in the range *iMinValue* to *iMaxValue* minus 1. I would bet that the last *Next* method is implemented like this:

```
public int Next(int iMinValue, int iMaxValue)
{
    return iMinValue + Next(iMaxValue - iMinValue);
}
```

That is, it uses the version of the *Next* method with one argument.

Let's write a program that composes haikus. Haikus are three-line poems that have five, seven, and five syllables per line. The following program declares and initializes a two-dimensional string array that contains words with which to construct the poem.

Haiku.cs
```
// ----------------------------------------------
// Haiku.cs from "Programming in the Key of C#"
// ----------------------------------------------
using System;
```

```
class Haiku
{
    static void Main()
    {
        string[,] astr = {
            { "scent", "bliss", "strut", "foot", "shade" },
            { "ox", "nerd", "pie", "skull", "bike" },
            { "transcends", "wrestles", "merges",
                "sidesteps", "exalts" },
            { "poetry", "restlessness", "ruthlessness",
                "itchiness", "comedy" },
            { "life", "death", "pain", "joy", "code" },
            { "graceful", "ugly", "dancing", "hefty", "furry" },
            { "dawn", "end", "blast", "lunch", "crunch" }};

        Random rand = new Random();
        int iMax = astr.GetLength(1);

        Console.WriteLine("The {0} of the {1}",
                    astr[0, rand.Next(iMax)],
                    astr[1, rand.Next(iMax)]);
        Console.WriteLine("{0} {1} of {2}",
                    astr[2, rand.Next(iMax)],
                    astr[3, rand.Next(iMax)],
                    astr[4, rand.Next(iMax)]);
        Console.WriteLine("til the {0} {1}.",
                    astr[5, rand.Next(iMax)],
                    astr[6, rand.Next(iMax)]);
    }
}
```

The size of the first dimension is seven, for the total of seven placeholders needed when the poem is displayed by the three *Console.WriteLine* calls. The size of the second dimension is five. There are five possibilities for each placeholder. The *iMax* value obtains the size of that second dimension and uses it for the seven calls to the *Next* method of the *Random* class. The *iMax* variable helps generalize the code: The array could be expanded to have more possibilities than just five without affecting the rest of the program. The return value of *Next* indexes the second dimension of the array. Here's a typical display:

```
The strut of the pie
wrestles ruthlessness of life
'til the ugly lunch.
```

If you understand the haikus this program composes, maybe it's time to stop coding and get some sleep.

19

Booleans

In much of real life, truth can be an elusive concept. In computer programs, truth is often easier to nail down. Is a particular integer greater than 100? Is a text string identical to the string "Schubert"?

To help the programmer answer such questions, C# supports a data type called *bool* (rhymes with "cool"), which is four-fifths of the last name of George Boole (1815–1864), the nineteenth century English mathematician who invented a form of symbolic logic that has come to be known as Boolean algebra. Possibly because Boole used common arithmetic symbols such as + and · for unconventional uses, Bertrand Russell is reputed to have said that "Pure mathematics was discovered by Boole."

Boolean algebra got a big boost in 1938 when, in his master's thesis from MIT, Claude Elwood Shannon (1916–2001) demonstrated how electrical relays could be wired to solve Boolean expressions, thus providing a practical theory for logic circuitry in digital computers.

In C#, you declare a *bool* like this:

```
bool IsRaining;
```

You can refer to such a variable as *bool*, which is a C# keyword, or *Boolean*, which is the generic term. Just as *int* is an alias for *System.Int32* and *string* is an alias for *System.String*, the keyword *bool* is an alias for *System.Boolean*. Usually the variable name will suggest that it's a Boolean, but I'll often use a Hungarian Notation 'b' prefix to indicate a Boolean variable.

You may be familiar with thinking about a Boolean as being 0 and 1. But you can't do this:

```
IsRaining = 0;    // Won't work!
```

It's an error to assign an integer to a Boolean. Instead, you must use one of the two special Boolean literals, which are the keywords *true* and *false*.

```
IsRaining = true;
```

You can also initialize a Boolean variable when it's declared:

```
bool IsSnowing = false;
```

The keywords *true* and *false* must be spelled in lowercase. You can also declare constant Booleans:

```
const bool AllMenAreMortal = true;
```

Despite your wish to the contrary, the program cannot later set *AllMenAreMortal* to another value.

You'll recall that a numeric expression is an expression that evaluates to a number. A *Boolean expression* is an expression that evaluates to a *bool*. But you can't use any of the normal arithmetic operators (+, −, *, /, and %) with Booleans. Instead, C# supports a collection of three *logical* operators that correspond to the Boolean operations AND, OR, and XOR (also known as exclusive OR).

In C#, as in C, you perform a logical AND operation using the ampersand, which commonly means "and" in English shorthand. The Boolean expression

```
IsRaining & IsSnowing
```

is *true* only if both *IsRaining* and *IsSnowing* are *true*. You can use such an expression in a statement like this:

```
bool MixedRainAndSnow = IsRaining & IsSnowing;
```

Here's a little table that shows the result of an AND operation between Boolean variables or expressions:

& (AND)	false	true
false	false	false
true	false	true

The second Boolean operator is OR, which in C# (as in C) is represented by the terribly neglected vertical bar character. On U.S. keyboards, the vertical bar is the upper-shift of the backslash. The expression

```
IsRaining | IsSnowing
```

is *true* if either *IsRaining* or *IsSnowing* or both are *true*. You might help yourself remember the OR symbol if you think the vertical bar looks something like an *oar*. Here's how you might use the OR operation in a complete statement:

```
bool IsPrecipitating = IsRaining | IsSnowing;
```

And again, here's a table showing the result of the OR operation:

| (OR)	false	true
false	false	true
true	true	true

The third logical operation is the Exclusive OR, commonly abbreviated XOR. For the XOR operation, all C-family languages use the *caret* (also known as the *circumflex* or *hat*), which is the upper-shift 6 on U.S. keyboards. A result of an XOR expression is *true* if either of the two operands is *true*, but not both:

^ (XOR)	false	true
false	false	true
true	true	false

Another way to think about an XOR operation is that the result is *true* if the values of the two operands are different.

For example, suppose you had two Boolean variables named *Particle1* and *Particle2* that represented the electrical charge on a particle—*true* for positive and *false* for negative. You could then calculate whether the particles are attracted to each other using the XOR operator:

```
bool Attraction = Particle1 ^ Particle2;
```

Perhaps you can associate the caret symbol with the XOR operation in your mind by noting that the caret looks like the bottom half of the X in XOR.

The AND, OR, and XOR operations are all binary operations. C# also defines a unary operation for Booleans, which corresponds to the logical operation NOT. The exclamation point is called the *logical negation* operator:

```
Short = !Tall;
```

If *Tall* is *false*, then *Short* is assigned *true*. If *Tall* is *true*, then *Short* is assigned *false*. The exclamation point is called the *bang* in some UNIX circles, but primarily in connection with obsolete e-mail addresses. In C# programming, you can refer to the operation as *not*, as in "Short gets not Tall."

If you didn't have the XOR operation, you could simulate it with AND, OR, and NOT. The following

```
C = (A | B) & !(A & B);
```

is the same as:

```
C = A ^ B;
```

Notice that the first expression has a couple of parentheses. According to the table of Operator Precedence and Associativity on the inside back cover of this book, NOT is grouped with the other unary operators and has a very high precedence. AND is much further down in the table, followed by XOR and then OR. Because these particular precedence rules are rarely remembered, the prudent programmer uses parentheses for clarification.

You can also use AND, OR, and XOR in compound assignment statements. For example, the statement

```
bToggle = bToggle ^ true;
```

is more economically written as:

```
bToggle ^= true;
```

This statement always changes the value of *bToggle*. If *bToggle* is *true*, the statement sets it to *false*; if *bToggle* is *false*, the statement sets it to *true*.

You can also create arrays of Booleans:

```
bool[] abRainDay = new bool[31];
```

As you may recall, memory for arrays is always allocated from the heap, and heap memory is always initialized to 0. For arrays of numeric variables, this means that every element of the array is initialized to 0. For arrays of strings, every element is initialized to *null*. For arrays of Booleans, every element is initialized to *false*.

As with every class and structure in the .NET Framework, *System.Boolean* has a *ToString* method. This *ToString* method returns the words *True* or *False*, which is also what *Console.WriteLine* displays when you pass it a Boolean variable. (The C# keywords are *true* and *false* in lowercase.) The *System.Boolean* structure also supports a static *Parse* method that accepts a string argument:

```
bool b = Boolean.Parse(str);
```

The *Parse* method performs a case-insensitive comparison of the string argument with the words *true* and *false*, ignoring any preceding or trailing white space.

The *Convert* class also provides methods to convert between Booleans and other data types. When converting from a number to a Boolean,

```
bool b = Convert.ToBoolean(mValue);
```

zero values convert to *false*, and non-zero values convert to *true*. When converting from a Boolean to a number,

```
decimal mValue = Convert.ToDecimal(b);
```

the value 1 is returned if *b* is *true*, and the value 0 is returned if *b* is *false*.

Although it would be fairly unusual, you could write entire programs using only Boolean variables and maybe some string variables. Let's do so.

Suppose you go to the local animal shelter in search of a cat to take home.[*] You say, "I want a male cat, neutered, either white or tan; or a female cat, neutered, any color but white; or I'll take any cat you have as long as it's black."

This is a little too much for the people at the animal shelter, but fortunately you've written a little C# program that helps with the logic.

AnimalShelter.cs
```
// ---------------------------------------------------
// AnimalShelter.cs from "Programming in the Key of C#"
// ---------------------------------------------------
using System;

class AnimalShelter
{
    static void Main()
    {
        bool bMale, bNeutered, bBlack, bWhite, bTan, bAcceptable;

        Console.Write("Is the cat male? Type true or false: ");
        bMale = Boolean.Parse(Console.ReadLine());

        Console.Write("Is the cat neutered? Type true or false: ");
        bNeutered = Boolean.Parse(Console.ReadLine());

        Console.Write("Is the cat black? Type true or false: ");
        bBlack = Boolean.Parse(Console.ReadLine());

        Console.Write("Is the cat white? Type true or false: ");
        bWhite = Boolean.Parse(Console.ReadLine());

        Console.Write("Is the cat tan? Type true or false: ");
        bTan = Boolean.Parse(Console.ReadLine());

        bAcceptable = (bMale & bNeutered & (bWhite | bTan)) |
                      (!bMale & bNeutered & !bWhite) |
                      bBlack;

        Console.WriteLine("Acceptable: " + bAcceptable);
    }
}
```

---

[*] This example is from my book *Code: The Hidden Language of Computer Hardware and Software*. In chapters 10 and 11 of that book I show how to build machines using switches, relays, and logic gates to solve this same problem.

The program asks a series of questions and requests that the user enter *true* or *false*. The *Boolean.Parse* method converts those answers into *bool* variables. (The color is problematic. The program declares the Boolean variables *bBlack*, *bWhite*, and *bTan*. At most, only one of these should be *true*, yet there's nothing to prevent the user from indicating that more than one is *true*. That little problem will be fixed in Chapter 21.) Finally, the program sets the *bAcceptable* variable based on your stringent criteria converted into Boolean algebra.

When you use Boolean expressions, it helps to know a couple of shortcuts, and in particular, De Morgan's Theorem, which is named after British mathematician Augustus De Morgan (1806–1871) who, among other achievements, was math tutor to Augusta Ada, Countess of Lovelace, née Byron (1815–1852). In 1843, Ada translated into English an Italian article about the Analytical Engine of Charles Babbage (1792–1871) and also added some notes to the translation, including what is credited with being the first computer program (albeit for a machine that was never built). See how everything fits together?

De Morgan stated his famous theorem like this: "The contrary of an aggregate is the compound of the contraries of the aggregants: the contrary of a compound is the aggregate of the contraries of the components."[*]

The *aggregate* is De Morgan's OR and the *compound* is De Morgan's AND. Symbolically, De Morgan's Laws state that

!(A | B) equals !A & !B

and

!(A & B) equals !A | !B

Earlier, I showed the following assignment:

```
IsPrecipitating = IsRaining | IsSnowing;
```

If you'd rather have a variable called *PleasantWeather*, you could express it as either the negation of the *IsPrecipitating* expression

```
PleasantWeather = !(IsRaining | IsSnowing);
```

or you can use De Morgan's Theorem to express it a little differently:

```
PleasantWeather = !IsRaining & !IsSnowing;
```

This second formulation may make more sense to you in English: "It's not raining and it's not snowing."

---

[*] De Morgan, Augustus. *On the Syllogism and Other Logical Writings*. London, England: Routledge & Kegan Paul, 1966, p. 119.

20

Characters and Strings

Unlike C#, the C programming language does not have a *string* data type. Instead, C supports a data type called the *char*, which represents one lowly character, such as B, x, or *. Strings in C are actually arrays of characters.

C# also has a *char* data type (corresponding to the *String.Char* structure in the .NET Framework), but the name is where the similarity ends. In C# you can create a string *from* an array of characters, and you can convert a string *to* an array of characters, but it's not proper to say that a C# string *is* an array of characters. A string is its own data type.

Another difference: all programming languages use numbers to represent characters, but in C a *char* is a numeric data type much like *int*, *short*, and *long*; in C you can even declare variables as *signed char* or *unsigned char*. In most C implementations, a *char* is 8 bits wide and represents a character in the ASCII character set. In C#, a *char* is 16 bits wide and represents a Unicode character. Although you can certainly convert between characters and numbers in C#, strictly speaking, *char* variables in C# are *not* numbers.

As I mentioned in Chapter 9, Unicode is documented on the Web site *http://www.unicode.org*. In particular, pages accessible from *http://www.unicode.org/charts* contain all the Unicode characters and their numeric equivalents.

Pronunciation of the word *char* varies. Some programmers pronounce it as in "Don't let the fire char the broccoli," but I prefer pronouncing it like the first syllable of "character"—more like "care."

As you know, a string literal is zero or more characters inside double quotes. You use single quotes to indicate a single character literal. Here's how you can declare and initialize a *char* variable:

```
char ch = 'Z';
```

I'll be using *ch* as the Hungarian Notation prefix for characters. You can also specify an escape sequence in the single quotes:

```
ch = '\b';
```

You learned in Chapter 9 that a backslash followed by a 'b' is the ASCII and Unicode representation of the backspace. You can specify a single Unicode character using a backslash followed by an uppercase or lowercase 'U' or 'X' followed by the hexadecimal code for that character:

```
ch = '\u00B0';
```

That's the degree sign. If you need to store the single quote character itself, preface it with a backslash:

```
ch = '\'';
```

You can convert between numbers and characters by casting. For example, here's another way you can get the Unicode character for the degree sign:

```
ch = (char) 0x00B0;
```

or

```
ch = (char) 176;
```

What's the value of *i* after this assignment statement?

```
i = (int) '7';
```

Watch out! It's not 7. It's 55, which is the ASCII and Unicode code for the character '7'.

C# will also perform implicit conversions from character to numeric types if you use a character in an arithmetical expression involving numbers or other characters. For example, the expression

```
'a' + 5
```

is the number 102 because the ASCII and Unicode code for 'a' is 97. C# will also convert characters to strings for concatenation with other strings. The expression

```
"a" + 'b'
```

is the string "ab" but the expression

```
'a' + 'b'
```

is the number 195.

Back in Chapter 11, I discussed the *Length* property of the *String* class, which indicates the number of characters in the string. The *String* class has a second property that the .NET Framework documentation says is named *Chars*. You'll also see the statement "In C#, this property is the indexer for the *String* class." What that statement means is that you don't really refer to the *Chars* property. As far as C# is concerned, the *String* class doesn't even have a property named *Chars*. This property is an *indexer*, and what it really does is let you index the string like an array.

For example, let's begin with a string:

```
string str = "hello, world";
```

Here's a statement that indexes the string variable as if it were an array and assigns the result to the *char* variable named *ch*:

```
ch = str[0];
```

After this statement, *ch* will contain the character 'h'. Similarly:

```
ch = str[11];
```

Now *ch* is the character 'd'. Any index less than 0 or greater than 11 will raise an exception at runtime.

You'll get a compile error if you attempt to use the string indexer on the left side of an equal sign:

```
str[0] = 'H';    // Compile error
```

The indexer for strings is read-only. In fact, once a string is created in a program, you cannot alter it. Strings in C# are said to be *immutable*. If you need to change a string in a program, you really need to write code that creates a new string that's the same as the old string but with the changes you want. Some methods that appear to modify a string actually return a new string containing the modification.

You can also index a string literal. For example, if *i* is an integer with a value from 0 through 25, the following expression is the single character corresponding to that number:

```
"ABCDEFGHIJKLMNOPQRSTUVWXYZ"[i]
```

But you can do that job more efficiently like this:

```
(char) ((int) 'A' + i)
```

Uppercase A (which has the code 65 in Unicode) is first converted to an integer, then *i* is added, and the result is converted back to a *char*.

Don't confuse indexing a string with indexing an *array* of strings. Here's a little array of strings:

```
string[] astr = { "Bach", "Beethoven", "Brahms" };
```

The expression *astr[1]* is the string "Beethoven." You can also use the string indexer on this element. The expression *astr[1][6]* is the letter 'v', which is the seventh character of the second string. Remember, indexing associates left to right.

Don't confuse the two *Length* properties, either! The expression *astr.Length* equals 3 because the array contains three elements. The expression *astr[1].Length* equals 9 because the string "Beethoven" contains nine characters. Indexing and the dot operator have equal precedence and associate left to right.

In Chapter 18 I showed you how you can initialize an *int* variable using a *new* expression and a constructor:

```
int i = new int();
```

This is called a *parameterless* constructor because, well, it has no parameters. You *cannot* create a *string* object in the same way:

```
string str = new string();    // Won't work!
```

The *String* class doesn't support a parameterless constructor. What it does support, however, are several other constructors that take arguments. These constructors allow you to create string variables from characters.

Although you can index a string as if it were an array of characters, it's not really proper to say that a C# string *is* an array of characters. Here's an actual array of characters:

```
char[] ach = { 'h', 'e', 'l', 'l', 'o' };
```

And here's a string constructor that converts that array of characters into a string:

```
string str = new string(ach);
```

The *String* class has a method that does the reverse by turning a string into an array of characters:

```
char[] ach2 = str.ToCharArray();
```

You might find it easier to declare and initialize an array of characters using the *ToCharArray* method applied to a string literal:

```
char[] ach = "hello".ToCharArray();
```

Suppose you want to create a string with 21 @ signs. You can do it like this with some careful counting:

```
string str = "@@@@@@@@@@@@@@@@@@@@@";
```

Or you can use this string constructor with two arguments:

```
string str = new string('@', 21);
```

The big advantage with the constructor is that the second argument can be a variable. Here's a program that displays part of a table of contents of a book:

TableOfContents.cs

```csharp
// ----------------------------------------------------
// TableOfContents.cs from "Programming in the Key of C#"
// ----------------------------------------------------
using System;

class TableOfContents
{
    static string[] astrChapter = { "You the Programmer",
                "First Assignments", "Declarations of Purpose",
                "Edit, Compile, Run", "Console Output" };
    static int[] aiPageNumber = { 3, 10, 16, 24, 29 };

    static void Main()
    {
        DisplayLine(0);
        DisplayLine(1);
        DisplayLine(2);
        DisplayLine(3);
        DisplayLine(4);
    }
    static void DisplayLine(int i)
    {
        const int iWidth = 60;
        string strDots = new string('.',
            iWidth - (i + 1).ToString().Length
                - astrChapter[i].Length
                - aiPageNumber[i].ToString().Length);

        Console.WriteLine("{0}. {1}{2}{3}",
            i + 1, astrChapter[i], strDots, aiPageNumber[i]);
    }
}
```

The program declares three fields: an array of five chapter names, an array of five page numbers, and a constant that indicates the desired total character width of the output. The crucial code occurs in the string constructor used to initialize *strDots*. The first argument is the period character. The second argument is the desired total width minus the character width of the chapter number, minus the character width of the chapter name, and minus the character width of the page number when converted to a string. Here's the result:

```
1. You the Programmer.........................................3
2. First Assignments........................................10
3. Declarations of Purpose..................................16
4. Edit, Compile, Run.......................................24
5. Console Output...........................................29
```

The *DisplayLine* method contains the code to print a single line. The parameter is the zero-based chapter number, which is also used as the index to the two arrays. The *Main* method simply calls the *DisplayLine* method five times. I'll show you better ways of performing repetitive operations in Chapter 24.

Because characters and strings are so much a part of human communication, the *Char* structure and *String* class have many methods that assist you in working with these data types. I'll discuss a few of the most important methods, and let you explore the rest on your own.

Your program may need to figure out exactly what kind of character it's looking at. The *Char* structure has a number of static methods that return Booleans indicating the basic category of the character. For example,

```
Char.IsDigit(ch)
```

returns *true* if the character represents a digit from '0' through '9'. The method also has an overload that accepts a string and an index. This overload

```
Char.IsDigit(str, i)
```

returns *true* if *str[i]* is a character that represents a digit from '0' through '9'. If you were dealing only with ASCII, the determination of whether a character is a digit or not is fairly trivial: the 10 digits are represented by character codes 48 through 57. But Unicode has other character codes that represent digits, and *IsDigit* returns *true* for those as well.

Similar to the *IsDigit* method of the *Char* structure are *IsLetter, IsLetterOrDigit, IsLower* (referring to lowercase), *IsUpper, IsNumber* (which includes fractions as well as digits), *IsPunctuation, IsWhiteSpace,* and a couple of others.

Strings are immutable. Once you create a string you cannot change it. But you can create new strings that are based on existing strings. The *String* class provides a multitude of methods that let you do just this.

Suppose you had a string variable named *str* and you wanted to convert all the characters in that string to lower case. Here's an instance method that does the job:

```
string str2 = str.ToLower();
```

The *ToLower* method applies to a particular string instance and returns a new string, which here is stored in the variable *str2*. If you no longer need the string with mixed case, you can assign the return value of *ToLower* to the original string variable:

```
str = str.ToLower();
```

This code doesn't violate the rule about strings being immutable. The original string is discarded when the new string is assigned to the *str* variable. The *String* class also has a *ToUpper* method.

The *SubString* method is popular. This method extracts part of an existing string and assigns it to a new string:

```
string str2 = str.SubString(iStartIndex, iNumberOfCharacters);
```

For example, if *str* stores the string "concerto for orchestra," the expression

```
str.SubString(6, 9)
```

is the string "to for or."

You can also perform case-sensitive searches in a string for particular characters or substrings. The *AnyIndexOf* method searches for any one of several characters. The corresponding methods *LastIndexOf* and *LastIndexOfAny* perform the same type of searches but begin at the end of the string.

Several methods in the *String* class allow you to compare two strings. You can use these methods for both *searching* (something an online telephone directory might do, for example) or for *sorting* a collection of strings alphabetically. You don't yet have the programming tools to use the methods (those are coming in Part III), but let's take a brief look at them anyway.

Some of these string-comparison methods are static; others are instance methods. One returns a *bool*; others return an *int*. Some perform *numeric* comparisons, which means that they compare the character codes; others perform *lexical* comparisons, which I'll describe in more detail shortly. Here's a little table that summarizes the string-comparison methods:

Method	Static / Instance	Returns	Comparison Type
Equals	Both	*bool*	Numeric (case sensitive)
Compare	Static	*int*	Lexical (optionally case insensitive)
CompareTo	Instance	*int*	Lexical (case insensitive)
CompareOrdinal	Static	*int*	Numeric

The integer return values are useful for sorting strings. Here's the simplest version of the *Compare* method:

```
i = String.Compare(str1, str2);
```

The *int* return value is:

- negative if *str1* < *str2*
- 0 if *str1* equals *str2*
- positive if *str1* > *str2*

What does it mean for one string to be less than or greater than another string? It depends. A numeric comparison is based on the numeric character codes. Here's how a few select characters are sorted numerically:

D < E < F < d < e < f < È < É < Ê < Ë < è < é < ê < ë

If you're sorting strings alphabetically, this last example is probably not what you want. You probably want a lexical comparison:

d < D < e < E < é < É < è < È < ê < Ê < ë < Ë < f < F

Lexical comparisons are also mostly case insensitive. For example, the string "New Jersey" is considered less than "new York" despite the lowercase 'n' in the second string. But when two strings are identical except for case, lowercase letters are considered less than uppercase letters, that is, "the" is less than "The." However, "Them" is less than "then."

In other words, a lexical comparison is usually case sensitive only when a method must decide whether or not to return 0; otherwise, it's case insensitive.

The *Compare* method gives you an option. Here's how you elect to ignore case:

```
i = String.Compare(str1, str2, true);
```

This option is more useful for searching for a string rather than sorting strings. This third argument affects the return value only when two strings are the same except for case. Two strings that differ only by case will cause this *Compare* call to return 0.

The last method I want to talk about from the *String* class is the static method *String.Format*, which is a method that you already know how to use. The first argument is a formatting string that contains placeholders for variables. The optional second and subsequent arguments are variables corresponding to the placeholders. In other words, it's exactly like using *Console.WriteLine* with a formatting string. The big difference is that *String.Format* returns a string rather than displaying anything.

```
str = String.Format("{0} + {1} = {2}", A, B, A + B);
```

In fact, this is the method that *Console.WriteLine* uses when the first argument is a formatting string. *WriteLine* calls *String.Format* and then simply displays the string to the console.

We have now reached an important milestone. The *C# Language Specification*, §4.1.3, lists 13 simple value types: *sbyte, byte, short, ushort, int, uint, long, ulong, char, float, double, bool*, and *decimal*. You have now encountered all of them, as well as the *string* and *array* reference types, and we are ready to explore other aspects of C# programming.

Part III
Ifs and Loops

Preludio III.

Vivace. (♩.=92.)

```
int i = 2;
if (strNote(1) == '#')
    iNote++;
```

21

Comparisons

The AnimalShelter program in Chapter 19 demonstrated that it's possible for a program to deal entirely with Boolean variables. But such a program is quite uncommon. More frequently a program determines the values of Boolean expressions based on the values of numeric or string variables. You *test* or *compare* the numeric or string variable with another variable or a literal to create a Boolean.

You can create a Boolean expression using one of the four *relational* operators or one of the two *equality* operators:

Operator	Meaning
<	Less than
>	Greater than
<=	Less than or equal to
>=	Greater than or equal to
==	Equal to
!=	Not equal to

For example, if *iScore* is an integer, this is a Boolean expression:

```
iScore >= 75
```

The expression is *true* if *iScore* is greater than or equal to 75 and *false* otherwise. The operators that consist of two symbols must be written in the correct order, with the equal sign on the right; this order is the same order that you usually pronounce the phrase "greater than or equal to" or "less than or equal to" or "not equal to." The two operands on either side of the operator must be the same type or implicitly convertible to the same type.

Let's try to get clear about the difference between numeric expressions and Boolean expressions. Differentiating those expressions is sometimes confusing because Boolean expressions often contain numbers and numeric variables. Suppose you have an integer named *iAge*, which stores someone's age:

```
int iAge;
```

And then the program sets *iAge* to a particular value:

```
iAge = 18;
```

Here's an expression (not a complete statement) involving the variable *iAge*:

```
iAge + 5
```

As we know by now, this expression is a *numeric* expression because it evaluates to a number. However, the expression

```
iAge >= 16
```

is a *Boolean* expression because it evaluates to a Boolean. The result of this Boolean expression will be *true* if *iAge* is greater than or equal to 16 (which it happens to be in this example). If you declare a Boolean variable like so:

```
bool bOldEnoughToDrive;
```

then you could set the Boolean variable from the Boolean expression:

```
bOldEnoughToDrive = (iAge >= 16);
```

The parentheses are not necessary. The relational and equality operators have higher precedence than the assignment operator.

What you *cannot* do is set a numeric variable from a Boolean expression:

```
iAge = (iAge >= 16);      // Won't work!
```

Nor can you set a Boolean variable from a numeric expression:

```
bOldEnoughToDrive = (iAge + 5);      // Won't work either!
```

Here's a short program that declares both an integer and a Boolean variable.

OldEnough.cs

```
// ----------------------------------------------------
// OldEnough.cs from "Programming in the Key of C#"
// ----------------------------------------------------
using System;

class OldEnough
{
    static void Main()
    {
        Console.Write("Enter your age: ");
```

```
      int iAge = Int32.Parse(Console.ReadLine());
      bool bOldEnoughToDrive = iAge >= 16;
      Console.WriteLine("It is " + bOldEnoughToDrive +
                  " that you are old enough to drive.");

   }

}
```

There is sometimes confusion between the assignment operator, which is one equal sign, and the equality operator, which is two equal signs.

Note   Traditionally, programming languages have usually attempted to distinguish between the assignment operator and the equality operator, but sometimes in odd ways. In ALGOL and Pascal, the symbol := was used for assignment so that = could be used for testing equality. In FORTRAN, = was used for assignment and .EQ. for equality. In COBOL, = was used for testing equality, but keywords such as *MOVE*, *ADD/TO*, and *MULTIPLY/BY* were required for arithmetic operations and assignment. BASIC was an exception. It used the same operator for both assignment and equality, but the syntax was so strict there could be no possible confusion. In early versions of BASIC, the assignment statement had to begin with the BASIC keyword *LET*.

The assignment operator sets the variable on the left of the operator to the value of the expression on the right. This is an assignment statement:

```
iMarbles = 19;
```

The double equal sign is the equality operator. This is a Boolean expression:

```
iMarbles == 0
```

The expression is *true* if the value of *iMarbles* is currently equal to 0. Here's a statement that uses both the assignment operator and the equality operator:

```
bool bBucketIsEmpty = iMarbles == 0;
```

The Boolean variable is *true* if the integer is equal to 0.

Unlike C#, the C programming language doesn't have a *bool* data type, but C does have Boolean expressions. Relational and equality operators in C return an integer 1 or 0 to mean true or false. In C, you'd write the previous statement like this:

```
int iBucketIsEmpty = iMarbles == 0;    // Legal C statement
```

Unfortunately, accidentally typing a single equal sign for the equality operand creates a statement that's syntactically correct but probably not what you want:

```
int iBucketIsEmpty = iMarbles = 0;    // Buggy C statement
```

In this statement, *iMarbles* is set to 0, and *iBucketIsEmpty* is also set to 0, meaning false.

By introducing a *bool* data type, C# has made it much more difficult to mistype an equality operator. The statement

```
bool bBucketIsEmpty = iMarbles = 0;    // Illegal C# statement
```

won't pass the compiler because you're trying to assign an integer (*iMarbles*) to a Boolean (*bBucketIsEmpty*).

Here's another statement that uses both an assignment and an equality operator:

```
bool bCompletelyHappy = iHappinessIndex == 100;
```

And here's one that uses the assignment and the inequality operator:

```
bool bSomewhatHappy = iHappinessIndex != 0;
```

If you need to test whether a *float* and a *double* value equal infinity or NaN, don't compare the values with the *PositiveInfinity*, *NegativeInfinity*, and *NaN* fields in the *Single* and *Double* structures. Use the *IsInfinity*, *IsPositiveInfinity*, *IsNegativeInfinity*, and *IsNaN* methods instead. The bit patterns that denote infinity and NaN in floating point numbers are not unique.

You should exercise caution regardless when comparing *float* and *double* values and particularly when using the equality or inequality operations. As discussed in Chapter 15, floating-point numbers are not stored precisely, so comparing floating point numbers may not work well. If you need to compare two floating-point variables, you may want to round them first to the same number of decimal places.

The two equality operators == and != (but not the comparison operators, which include the less than and greater than signs) also work with characters and strings. The Boolean expression

```
str == "Franz Schubert"
```

is *true* only if *str* has 14 characters and the characters exactly match (case and all) the 14 characters of the string literal. The equality operator is the equivalent of the *Equals* method of the *String* class discussed in the last chapter.

Here's a revised version of the AnimalShelter program that corrects the flaw in the earlier program that let you type conflicting answers to questions about the cat's color. This version requests that you type in the cat's color directly (in lowercase, please). The Booleans are calculated from the inputted color string.

AnimalShelterWithCompare.cs

```
// -----------------------------------------------------------
// AnimalShelterWithCompare.cs from "Programming in the Key of C#"
// -----------------------------------------------------------
using System;

class AnimalShelterWithCompare
{
    static void Main()
    {
        bool bMale, bNeutered, bBlack, bWhite, bTan, bAcceptable;

        Console.Write("Is the cat male? Type true or false: ");
        bMale = Convert.ToBoolean(Console.ReadLine());

        Console.Write("Is the cat neutered? Type true or false: ");
        bNeutered = Convert.ToBoolean(Console.ReadLine());

        Console.Write("Enter cat color. Type black, white, tan, etc: ");
        string strColor = Console.ReadLine();

        bBlack = strColor == "black";
        bWhite = strColor == "white";
        bTan = strColor == "tan";

        bAcceptable = (bMale & bNeutered & (bWhite | bTan)) |
                      (!bMale & bNeutered & !bWhite) |
                      bBlack;

        Console.WriteLine("Acceptable: " + bAcceptable);
    }
}
```

If you want to make the program more flexible and allow the user to type the cat's color in lowercase or uppercase, you have a couple of options. The first idea that might occur to you is to use the case-insensitive version of *String.Compare* for each of the three statements that perform comparisons:

```
bBlack = String.Compare(strColor, "black", true) == 0;
```

Because *Compare* returns an integer, the return value must be compared with 0 to create a Boolean to assign to *bBlack*. You'd have similar statements for *bWhite* and *bTan*.

A better approach is to perform a little pre-compare processing on the user input. Change the call containing *ReadLine* from

```
string strColor = Console.ReadLine();
```

to

```
string strColor = Console.ReadLine().ToLower();
```

The *ToLower* call converts the user input to lowercase. While you're at it, another instance method of the *String* class named *Trim* removes any white space from the beginning or end of the string:

```
string strColor = Console.ReadLine().ToLower().Trim();
```

Otherwise, if the user typed "tan" with a space at the beginning or end, the program wouldn't set *bTan* to *true* and the implied color would be something else.

The equality operators (but not the comparison operators) also work on Booleans:

```
bWeAreCompatible = bYouLikeMahler == bILikeMahler;
```

The *bWeAreCompatible* Boolean will be set to *true* only if *bYouLikeMahler* and *bILikeMahler* are equal—that is, they're both *true* or both *false*.

But I beg you *not* to use the equality operands with Booleans because you can easily make a mistake by dropping one of the equal signs in the equality operand:

```
bWeAreCompatible = bYouLikeMahler = bILikeMahler;
```

This statement is perfectly legal, but it first sets *bYouLikeMahler* to the value of *bILikeMahler*, and then sets *bWeAreCompatible* to the same value. Unless you're in the habit of imposing your tastes in music on other people, that's probably not what you want.

Rather than using == and != with Booleans, use the XOR operator. The XOR operator is equivalent to !=, which is why the XOR is sometimes referred to as an inequality operator. Instead of ==, you can use the XOR operator and negate the result.

```
bWeAreCompatible = !(bYouLikeMahler ^ bILikeMahler);
```

When I first introduced Booleans, I mentioned that you might be in the habit of associating Booleans with the numeric values 0 and 1, and I also discussed a couple of static methods in the *Convert* class that let you convert between Booleans and integers in this way. Here's the first method:

```
Convert.ToBoolean(iValue)
```

This method returns *false* if *iValue* equals zero and *true* otherwise. You can use any type of numeric value in the *ToBoolean* method. You can also go the other way:

```
Convert.ToInt32(bValue)
```

The method returns 1 if *bValue* is *true* and 0 if *bValue* is *false*. Such a conversion lets you use a Boolean in an arithmetic expression, as I'll demonstrate in the next chapter.

22

Making Decisions

Despite the fact that you're less than halfway through your C# book, your manager asks you to write a program that calculates monthly sales commissions for your company. The calculation is fairly easy—commissions are simply 12.5 percent of sales—but your manager wants a program to do it. She wants to type in a monthly sales figure and let the program calculate and display the commission.

Here's your first shot at the program.

FirstCommissionCalc.cs

```
// -----------------------------------------------------------
// FirstCommissionCalc.cs from "Programming in the Key of C#"
// -----------------------------------------------------------
using System;

class FirstCommissionCalc
{
    static void Main()
    {
        decimal mSales, mCommission;

        Console.Write("Enter sales: ");
        mSales = Decimal.Parse(Console.ReadLine());
        mCommission = 0.125m * mSales;
        Console.WriteLine("The commission is " + mCommission);
    }
}
```

After you've spent all day working on this gorgeous program, your manager says, "Oh, I forgot to mention: We have something new. Anybody who has monthly sales over $10,000 gets a $1,000 bonus."

Well, that's something a little different now, isn't it? The program is pretty easy when everybody gets the same percentage, but this bonus is a *sometimes* thing.

After pondering this problem for a while, you're pretty sure that somewhere in the program you need the Boolean expression

```
mSales > 10000
```

That expression is *true* if the salesperson is to receive a bonus and *false* otherwise. But how can the Boolean expression be used in an arithmetical calculation? You remember the *Convert.ToInt32* method, which converts a Boolean into an integer. Let's try using that method with the Boolean expression

```
Convert.ToInt32(mSales > 10000)
```

Now we have an expression that equals 1 if sales are greater than $10,000 and 0 otherwise. That's almost it! If the bonus were $1, you'd be dancing around the room already. Because the bonus is actually $1,000, you need to multiply the result of the *Convert.ToInt32* call by 1,000:

```
1000 * Convert.ToInt32(mSales > 10000)
```

Now we have an expression that equals 1,000 if *mSales* is greater than 10,000, and 0 otherwise. Let's include a new variable (named *mBonus*) in the program and include this calculation.

CommissionCalcWithBonus.cs

```
// -------------------------------------------------------------
// CommissionCalcWithBonus.cs from "Programming in the Key of C#"
// -------------------------------------------------------------
using System;

class CommissionCalcWithBonus
{
    static void Main()
    {
        decimal mSales, mCommission, mBonus;

        Console.Write("Enter sales: ");
        mSales = Decimal.Parse(Console.ReadLine());
        mCommission = 0.125m * mSales;
        mBonus = 1000 * Convert.ToInt32(mSales > 10000);
        mCommission += mBonus;

        Console.WriteLine("The commission is " + mCommission);
    }
}
```

The program calculates *mBonus* based on the Boolean expression and the *Convert.ToInt32* method, and then adds *mBonus* to *mCommision*.

This approach to calculating the bonus is certainly clever, but it's also a bit obscure. Someone reading this program might take awhile to realize what's going on. Moreover, when confronted with problems like this one, you can't always solve them by converting Booleans to integers. Suppose you wanted to display a special message if the salesperson were getting a bonus. You'd need another way to do it.

A better approach is the *if* statement, which is a versatile solution to tasks that require decisions to be made. The *if* statement lets your program *conditionally* execute a statement or group of statements based on the value of a Boolean variable or expression. The *if* statement is the primary *selection* statement in C#, which means that it lets you selectively alter the program flow—and that's one of the basic differences between programming and merely calculating.

The *if* statement begins with the keyword *if*. The *if* keyword must be followed by a Boolean expression enclosed in parentheses:

```
if (mSales > 10000)
```

Very often the Boolean expression in the *if* statement involves a comparison of some sort, but the parentheses can contain simply a Boolean variable or constant:

```
if (bIsRaining)
```

You can even put a Boolean literal in there:

```
if (true)
```

But this is much less common.

The *if* statement continues with a matching pair of curly brackets:

```
if (mSales > 10000)
{
    // Other statements go here.
}
```

Some programmers prefer to put the first curly bracket on the same line as the *if* keyword, after the right parenthesis. Virtually all programmers indent the statements inside the curly brackets.

A group of statements enclosed by curly brackets is referred to as a *block*. Any statements in the *if* block are executed only if the Boolean expression evaluates as *true*. If the Boolean expression evaluates as *false*, the statements inside the block are simply skipped. The following code shows the equivalent of those earlier statements that added the bonus amount to the commission.

```
if (mSales > 10000)
{
    mBonus = 1000;
    mCommission += mBonus;
}
```

Although there are certainly more lines of code here than in the earlier solution, if you add up the number of characters, this code is actually quite a bit shorter.

The use of the *if* statement is also—and here's the crucial point—much clearer. You can practically read it aloud: "If sales are greater than ten thousand, then the bonus equals one thousand…"

Here's a complete program that implements the *if* statement.

CommissionCalcWithIf.cs
```
// ----------------------------------------------------------------
// CommissionCalcWithIf.cs from "Programming in the Key of C#"
// ----------------------------------------------------------------
using System;

class CommissionCalcWithIf
{
    static void Main()
    {
        decimal mSales, mCommission, mBonus;

        Console.Write("Enter sales: ");
        mSales = Decimal.Parse(Console.ReadLine());
        mCommission = 0.125m * mSales;

        if (mSales > 10000)
        {
            mBonus = 1000;
            mCommission += mBonus;
        }
        Console.WriteLine("The commission is " + mCommission);
    }
}
```

Although this program has a Boolean expression, it doesn't have any Boolean variables. It's not uncommon for programs to have no Boolean variables, but it's extremely rare for all but very small programs to have no Boolean expressions.

Let's experiment with some variations of the *if* statement. First, notice that the program uses the *mBonus* variable only within the *if* statement. In such a situation, the declaration of the *mBonus* variable can be removed from the top of *Main* and moved instead to the block:

```
if (mSales > 10000)
{
    decimal mBonus;

    mBonus = 1000;
    mCommission += mBonus;
}
```

If there are variables that are required only within the block, it's often clearer if they're declared in the block.

Of course, since *mBonus* is assigned right after it's declared, you can consolidate those two statements by initializing *mBonus* when you declare it:

```
if (mSales > 10000)
{
    decimal mBonus = 1000;
    mCommission += mBonus;
}
```

And you really don't even need the *mBonus* variable in this case. You could simply add 1,000 to the *mCommission* value. But I want to make a point here: A variable (or constant) declared *inside* a block cannot be used *outside* the block. A variable is said to be *visible* only within the block in which it is declared. It's also said that the *scope* of the variable is restricted to the block in which it is declared. That's the same rule as with methods that I discussed in Chapter 17. The body of a method is considered to be a block, so every block within the method is a *subblock* (or *child* block) of the method block.

Suppose you try to use a variable outside the block in which it's declared:

```
if (mSales > 10000)
{
    decimal mBonus = 1000;
    mCommission += mBonus;
}
mBonus = 0;    // Won't work.
```

You'll get a message from the compiler saying that the name *mBonus* doesn't exist; that is, it's not declared. Within a block, you can use variables declared *outside* the block, as you can see from the use of *mCommission*, but as usual, the variable must be declared before it's used.

Although *mBonus* isn't visible outside the block, that doesn't mean it has no effect on what you can do outside the block. For example, you may try to redeclare *mBonus* outside the block:

```
if (mSales > 10000)
{
    decimal mBonus = 1000;
```

```
        mCommission += mBonus;
}
decimal mBonus = 0;      // Also won't work.
```

Although it might seem reasonable that you should be allowed to declare such a variable outside the block, the C# compiler objects. You'll get this message:

```
A local variable named 'mBonus' cannot be declared in this scope
 because it would give a different meaning to 'mBonus', which is
 already used in a 'child' scope to denote something else
```

Suppose you try something a little different. Suppose you declare *mBonus* sometime before the *if* statement and then try to redeclare *mBonus* inside the *if* block:

```
decimal mBonus = 0;

if (mSales > 10000)
{
    decimal mBonus = 1000;      // Now the error's here.
    mCommission += mBonus;
}
```

Now you'll get an error message for the second declaration of *mBonus*:

```
A local variable named 'mBonus' cannot be declared in this scope
 because it would give a different meaning to 'mBonus', which is already
 used in a 'parent or current' scope to denote something else
```

I'm dwelling on this issue because C and C++ *do* allow you to redeclare variables inside a block. This feature resulted in many obscure bugs over the decades, and the designers of C# decided simply to prohibit redeclaration of variables in nested blocks. You can, however, use the same variable in two blocks that have a *sibling* relationship to each other; that is, they are both children of the same block.

I haven't shown you the entire syntax of the *if* statement yet. Often the *if* statement also includes the keyword *else* followed by another block. Here's the general syntax:

```
if (bExpression)
{
    // Statements executed if bExpression is true.
}
else
{
    // Statements executed if bExpression is false.
}
```

This is all part of the same *if* statement. There's no such thing as an *"else* statement." (The *C# Language Specification*, §8.7.1, refers to the second half of the *if* statement as the *"else* part.") There's only one Boolean expression in an *if* statement, and that follows the *if* keyword. The keyword *else* is followed by another block.

In the calculation of commissions, you can use the *else* part to set *mBonus* to 0. Here's an alternative commission calculation.

CommissionCalcWithIfAndElse.cs

```
// -------------------------------------------------------------------
// CommissionCalcWithIfAndElse.cs from "Programming in the Key of C#"
// -------------------------------------------------------------------
using System;

class CommissionCalcWithIfAndElse
{
    static void Main()
    {
        decimal mSales, mCommission, mBonus;

        Console.Write("Enter sales: ");
        mSales = Decimal.Parse(Console.ReadLine());
        mCommission = 0.125m * mSales;

        if (mSales > 10000)
        {
            mBonus = 1000;
        }
        else
        {
            mBonus = 0;
        }
        mCommission += mBonus;

        Console.WriteLine("The commission is " + mCommission);
    }
}
```

Notice that *mBonus* is added to commissions *following* the *if* statement. The statement is executed regardless of the value of *mSales*, but in those cases in which sales are not greater than $10,000, the bonus is 0. Another option: You could remove this statement that calculates the normal commission

```
mCommission = 0.125m * mSales;
```

and combine both calculations in a single statement following the *if* statement:

```
mCommission = 0.125m * mSales + mBonus;
```

Yet another approach: You could initialize *mBonus* when it's declared:

```
decimal mSales, mCommission, mBonus = 0;
```

A bonus of 0 is the default, or normal, case. Now you can have an *if* statement without an *else* part but still keep the final commission calculation outside the *if* statement:

```
if (mSales > 10000)
{
    mBonus = 1000;
}
mCommission += mBonus;
```

You may be starting to get annoyed that I'm showing different approaches to this problem without saying which one is best! That's because none of them are really any better or worse than the alternatives. However, I *do* prefer setting *mBonus* explicitly to 0 in the default case. Doing so anticipates future changes. Your manager may someday say that everybody who doesn't get a bonus of $1,000 gets a bonus of $50. It's easier to change the number 0 to 50 rather than to add some code.

The big rule is this: If you find that you have identical statements in the *if* block and the *else* block, you should probably try to move those common statements outside the *if* statement. For example, suppose you don't declare *mBonus* along with *mSales* and *mCommission* at the top of *Main*. Instead, you decide to declare and initialize *mBonus* in both the *if* and *else* blocks. That's certainly allowed because the two blocks are sibling blocks. However, you'll also need to calculate the final commission value in the two blocks:

```
if (mSales > 10000)
{
    decimal mBonus = 1000;
    mCommission += mBonus;
}
else
{
    decimal mBonus = 0;
    mCommission *= mBonus;
}
```

This code is getting a bit dangerous. You're repeating identical statements, and there's a very good chance that they are not as identical as you mean them to be. Look closely at the second calculation of *mCommission*. The asterisk rather than the plus sign is a bug.

Here's probably the worst way to do it:

```
if (mSales > 10000)    // Worst way!
{
    mCommission = 0.125m * mSales;
    mBonus = 1000;
    mCommission += mBonus;
}
else
{
    mCommission = 0.125m * mSales;
    mBonus = 0;
    mCommission += mBonus;
}
```

This code is free of bugs and probably runs just as efficiently as anything else you've seen in this chapter. But there's no reason for identical statements to be in both the *if* and *else* blocks.

There's another reason for keeping the statements in the *if* statement to a minimum. If the block has only one statement, you can remove the curly brackets:

```
if (mSales > 10000)
    mBonus = 1000;
else
    mBonus = 0;
```

It's very common for programmers to eliminate the curly brackets if only a single statement is involved. But the curly brackets are never wrong, and they never hurt. Even if you don't need the curly brackets, they often help to clarify the code and plan for the future. Countless times in my programming life, I've had to add a second statement in an unbracketed *if* or *else* part, and it would just be easier if the curly brackets were already there.

Curly brackets also help prevent errors. Take a look at this interesting snippet of code:

```
if (A < 50)
    B = 75;
    C = 100;
```

Don't be misled by the deceptive indentation! Only variable *B* is affected by the *if* statement. The variable *C* will be set to 100 regardless. If you really want *C* to be affected by the *if* statement, include both statements in a block:

```
if (A < 50)
{
    B = 75;
    C = 100;
}
```

The *C# Language Specification*, §8, calls the type of statement that follows the Boolean expression or the *else* keyword an *embedded* statement. It's a category that includes the *empty statement* (simply a semicolon), a block, or another *if* statement. One interesting restriction is that you can't declare a variable in a nonblocked *if* or *else* part. Here's an example:

```
if (mSales > 10000)
    decimal mBonus;    // Not allowed!
```

The declaration is not allowed because the scope of *mBonus* is restricted to the single declaration statement. Even if *mBonus* were initialized

```
if (mSales > 10000)
    decimal mBonus = 1000;    // Not allowed!
```

the *mBonus* variable couldn't be used for anything because no other statements could refer to it.

Meanwhile, your commission-calculation program is a big hit with your manager. She's using your program to calculate all the monthly commissions for all the salespeople. Several months pass, and you continue to bask in your glory. And then it happens. Catastrophe. A salesperson has submitted a formal complaint: "I had $10,000 in sales. How come I didn't get a bonus?"

You look into this case and discover that the salesperson had *exactly* $10,000 in sales. Your program is giving a bonus only if the sales are *greater* than $10,000. After checking with your manager (who will naturally swear "*Of course* I made it clear that a bonus is paid if sales are exactly $10,000") you decide not to argue about it. Just fix the program and treat it as a learning experience. The fix is easy:

```
if (mSales >= 10000)
```

But there's an important lesson here: *Most people aren't as precise as computer programs need to be.* Human language is sloppy. We accept that. But sloppy computer programs are often wrong.

The second lesson is equally important: After you write a program, you must test to make sure it's working right. And when you test the program, always check the *boundaries*, the *edges*, the areas where you know the program is supposed to do something a little differently. Test the program for sales of $9,999.99, $10,000.00, and $10,000.01, for example. If you had done that, you might have wondered if the results were correct, and you might have checked with your manager at the time.

The final lesson is this: *Always get program specifications in writing.* When your manager says "Yes I did," you'll want to have written proof of "No you didn't."

After more months of using the program, your manager decides on another change: Now every salesperson who has sales over $25,000 ("and that includes sales of *exactly* $25,000") gets a $2,000 bonus. Here's an approach that uses three *if* statements with no *else* parts:

```
if (mSales < 10000)
    mBonus = 0;

if (mSales >= 10000 & mSales < 25000)
    mBonus = 1000;

if (mSales >= 25000)
    mBonus = 2000;
```

The three Boolean expressions have been carefully defined to be mutually exclusive. The second *if* statement accounts for those salespersons who have sales greater than or equal to $10,000 but less than $25,000.

Another approach is to set *mBonus* to 0, probably in the declaration statement, and then bump up the value of *mBonus* depending on *mSales*:

```
if (mSales >= 10000)
    mBonus += 1000;

if (mSales >= 25000)
    mBonus += 1000;
```

These two *if* statements are *not* mutually exclusive. Salespersons who made $25,000 or over in sales satisfy both *if* conditions, thus accumulating a bonus of $2,000. It works but it's probably a bit vague and dangerous.

Here's an approach that nests one *if* statement inside another:

```
if (mSales >= 25000)
{
    mBonus = 2000;
}
else
{
    if (mSales >= 10000)
    {
        mBonus = 1000;
    }
    else
    {
        mBonus = 0;
    }
}
```

The outermost *else* part is executed only if *mSales* is less than $25,000. A second *if* statement compares *mSales* with $10,000 to determine whether the bonus should be $1,000 or nothing.

I indicated earlier that there is no such thing as an "*else* statement." The *if* statement can comprise both an *if* part and an *else* part. I also said that if only one statement is enclosed in an *if* or *else* part, the curly brackets could be removed. Let's remove the curly brackets of the outermost *else* clause:

```
if (mSales >= 25000)
{
    mBonus = 2000;
}
else
    if (mSales >= 10000)
    {
        mBonus = 1000;
    }
    else
    {
        mBonus = 0;
    }
```

This is perfectly legitimate code that obeys all the syntax and indentation rules for *if* statements. But it would look funny to any seasoned C-family programmer. In cases like this—which actually occur quite frequently—it's common to fiddle around a bit with the indentation, like this:

```
if (mSales >= 25000)
{
    mBonus = 2000;
}
else if (mSales >= 10000)
{
    mBonus = 1000;
}
else
{
    mBonus = 0;
}
```

No other changes have been made beyond a little shifting. The second *if* keyword has been moved up to follow the first *else*, and the rest of the second *if* statement has been lined up with the first *if* statement. The result looks like—and actually is—a series of mutually exclusive sequential comparisons that is much easier to read than the nested *if* statement it really is.

Now that we have only one statement in each block, we can remove all the curly brackets:

```
if (mSales >= 25000)
    mBonus = 2000;

else if (mSales >= 10000)
    mBonus = 1000;

else
    mBonus = 0;
```

This piece of code has two *if* statements, each of which includes an *else* part. I mentioned earlier that it's incorrect to refer to an "*else* statement." It's also incorrect to refer to an "*else if* statement." Such a thing does not exist in C#.

Here's another way of performing the same logic:

```
if (mSales < 10000)
    mBonus = 0;

else if (mSales < 25000)
    mBonus = 1000;

else
    mBonus = 2000;
```

Here the order goes the other way, from lowest sales (and bonus) to highest. You can use either approach.

What you probably *don't* want to do is start the first *if* statement somewhere in the middle, as shown here:

```
if (mSales >= 10000)
{
    if (mSales >= 25000)
    {
        mBonus = 2000;
    }
    else
    {
        mBonus = 1000;
    }
}
else
{
    mBonus = 0;
}
```

There's nothing logically wrong with this code. You could even remove all the curly brackets and it would work just fine. But because there are two *if* parts in a row and two *else* parts in a row, the *if* and *else* parts can't be shifted around in a nice neat linear way. The code is confusing. Anybody trying to wind his or her way through the logic would soon get lost.

Take a look at this code:

```
if (mSales >= 10000)
    mBonus = 1000;

if (mSales >= 25000)
    mBonus += 1000;

else
    mBonus = 0;
```

It looks like the programmer was using a technique I showed earlier, where persons with sales of $25,000 or over satisfied two *if* statements that resulted in a total bonus of $2,000. But what about that last *else* part? Exactly what *if* statement is that *else* a part of?

The rule (in the *C# Language Specification*, § 8.7.1) is, "An *else* part is associated with the lexically nearest preceding *if* statement that is allowed by the syntax." But that's not what we want. Everyone who doesn't satisfy the second *if* statement (which compares *mSales* with 25,000) has his or her bonus set to 0. The programmer should have used brackets to make the code correct:

```
if (mSales >= 10000)
{
    mBonus = 1000;

    if (mSales >= 25000)
        mBonus += 1000;
}
else
    mBonus = 0;
```

Now the *else* part is associated with the first *if* statement. The embedded *if* statement has no *else* part.

It sometimes happens that you've written out your Boolean expression in the *if* statement, and then you see you've done it backwards. You actually want the *else* part to execute if the Boolean expression is *true*. There's no need to start shifting around your code. Simply surround the Boolean expression with parentheses and put a logical negation operator (!) in front. You may then see that you can simplify the expression somewhat using De Morgan's Laws, as mentioned in Chapter 19.

Here's something I've done once or twice:

```
if (bDoIt = true)
{
    ...
}
```

Do you see the problem? I wanted the *if* statement to test if *bDoIt* were *true*, but I accidentally used the assignment operator rather than the equality operator. The expression sets *bDoIt* to *true*, and the *if* block is executed based on that new value of *bDoIt*. The statement is syntactically correct but logically wrong. As usual, it's best to keep it simple:

```
if (bDoIt)
{
    ...
}
```

Sometimes programmers get so accustomed to using *if* and *else* that they use them when an alternative is actually easier. Here's a correct determination of leap years. A year is a leap year if it's equally divisible by 4 unless it's equally divisible by 100, except if it's also equally divisible by 400:

```
if (iYear % 4 == 0 & (iYear % 100 != 0 | iYear % 400 == 0))
{
    bIsLeapYear = true;
}
else
{
    bIsLeapYear = false;
}
```

The modulus (or remainder) operator is useful for testing divisibility. If the result of the operation is 0, the left operand is equally divisible by the right operand.

That *if* statement is correct, but why bother using an *if* statement to set a Boolean variable? Simply set the variable from the Boolean expression:

```
bIsLeapYear = iYear % 4 == 0 & (iYear % 100 != 0 | iYear % 400 == 0);
```

In the next chapter, you'll see a slightly better way to perform this logic.

23

The Conditional Operators

Suppose you're writing a program that determines whether the number of cookies you have in your house is sufficient to feed a certain number of guests under the assumption that each guest will have three cookies. Such a program might have some code that looks like this:

```
if (iCookies / iGuests < 3)
{
    BakeMoreCookies();
}
```

I'm a little curious myself about what the *BakeMoreCookies* method actually does; perhaps it controls an automatic oven and a robot cook.

But what if there were *no* guests on a particular day? If *iGuests* equals 0, then we have a zero-divide problem. Also, if there aren't any guests, we don't want the code in the block to be executed. One approach might be to test for *iGuests* being greater than 0 in the *if* statement:

```
if (iGuests > 0 & iCookies / iGuests < 3)
{
    BakeMoreCookies();
}
```

Well, we're getting closer, but it's not quite ready yet. Even if *iGuests* equals 0, the division will still be performed, and a divide-by-zero exception will be raised. What you really want to do is prevent the division from taking place if *iGuests* is 0. Here's an approach that separates the Boolean expression into two pieces in a nested *if* statement.

```
if (iGuests > 0)
{
    if (iCookies / iGuests < 3)
```

```
    {
        BakeMoreCookies();
    }
}
```

This will work. If *iGuests* equals 0, then the second *if* statement isn't executed.

But another approach is to use the *conditional-AND* operator, an operator designed specifically for situations such as this. The normal AND operator is an ampersand (&). The conditional-AND operator is two ampersands (&&):

```
if (iGuests > 0 && iCookies / iGuests < 3)
{
    BakeMoreCookies();
}
```

The conditional-AND operator is very similar to the normal AND operator except that the Boolean expression on the right of the operator isn't evaluated if it doesn't *need* to be evaluated.

Suppose *iGuests* equals 0. Let's parse the *if* statement pretending that we're the computer. Compare *iGuests* with 0. That comparison returns *false*. The next operand is a conditional-AND. Since the expression to the left of the AND operand is *false*, it doesn't matter what's on the right of the operand. The result of the entire Boolean expression will never be *true*. It's not even necessary to evaluate the expression to the right of the AND operand, and so it's ignored. If *iGuests* is 0, the division won't occur.

Here's a generalized expression involving two Boolean expressions and the normal AND operand:

```
bExpression1 & bExpression2
```

Both expressions are always evaluated. Here's the conditional-AND:

```
bExpression1 && bExpression2
```

If *bExpression1* is *false*, then *bExpression2* is not evaluated.

Similar to the conditional-AND is the conditional-OR, which is two vertical bars (||):

```
if (iGuests == 0 || iCookies / iGuests >= 3)
{
    StopTheCookieMachine();
}
```

This is simply the same logic turned inside out. Cookie production must be halted if there are no guests or if there are at least three cookies per guest. If the Boolean expression to the left of the conditional-OR is *true*, then the expression on the right doesn't have to be evaluated because the overall expression will be *true* regardless.

Here's the conditional-AND again:

```
bExpression1 && bExpression2
```

If *bExpression1* is *false*, then *bExpression2* is not evaluated. And here's the conditional-OR:

```
bExpression1 || bExpression2
```

If *bExpression1* is *true*, then *bExpression2* is not evaluated. There's no such thing as a conditional-XOR because the result of an XOR is never predictable based on just one of the operands.

Many C# programmers, and particularly those with backgrounds in C or C++, tend to use the conditional-OR and conditional-AND in preference to the normal OR and AND, if only to prevent code from being executed unnecessarily. Here's the statement from the end of the last chapter rewritten to use the conditional operators:

```
bIsLeapYear = iYear % 4 == 0 && (iYear % 100 != 0 || iYear % 400 == 0);
```

If *iYear* is not divisible by 4, then it's never a leap year, and nothing to the right of the && operator needs to be evaluated.

C# also supports an oddity inherited from C called the *conditional expression*, which makes use of the *conditional operator*. So far, you've seen unary operators, which have one operand, and binary operators, which have two operands. The conditional operator is the only *ternary* operator in C#. The three operands are separated by a question mark and a colon. Here's what it looks like:

```
bExpression ? A : B
```

A and *B* must be expressions of the same type (or implicitly convertible into the same type). If *bExpression* is *true*, then the result of the conditional expression is *A*. If *bExpression* is *false*, then the result of the expression is *B*. Here's an example:

```
bIsLeapYear ? 29 : 28
```

The result of this conditional expression equals 29 if *bIsLeapYear* is *true* and 28 if *bIsLeapYear* is *false*. You can use this conditional expression in an assignment statement:

```
iFebruaryDays = bIsLeapYear ? 29 : 28;
```

The advantage of the conditional operator is that it's considerably shorter than the alternative:

```
if (bIsLeapYear)
    iFebruaryDays = 29;
else
    iFebruaryDays = 28;
```

Here's the bonus calculation from the last chapter rewritten in a conditional expression:

```
mBonus = mSales >= 10000 ? 1000 : 0;
```

The conditional operator has the lowest priority of all operators except for assignment. The highest-priority operation in this statement is the comparison of *mSales* with 10000. No parentheses are required. Even so, some programmers would feel more comfortable highlighting the conditional expression with a pair of parentheses, like so:

```
mBonus = (mSales >= 10000 ? 1000 : 0);
```

Or even two pairs:

```
mBonus = ((mSales >= 10000) ? 1000 : 0);
```

I like using the conditional operator in *WriteLine* calls, essentially to convert Boolean expressions into plain English. Here's a possible final statement for one of the AnimalShelter programs:

```
Console.WriteLine("This cat is " + (bAcceptable ? "" : "not ") + "acceptable");
```

If *bAcceptable* is true, then the result of the conditional operation is the string "not "; otherwise, it's the empty string. The inner set of parentheses is required.

Although the conditional operator achieves a certain economy, it is easily abused, particularly when multiple conditional expressions are nested. Here's a complete calculation of *iDaysInMonth* based on *iMonth* (1 through 12) and *bIsleapYear*:

```
iDaysInMonth = iMonth == 4 || iMonth == 6 ||
                  iMonth == 9 || iMonth == 11 ? 30 :
                      iMonth != 2 ? 31 : bLeapYear ? 29 : 28;
```

This statement is virtually unreadable.

24

The *While* Loop

Programming is really all about repetition. Rarely do we write programs that are run only once. Most are run many times, each time doing basically the same thing but with enough variation to make the results consistently valuable. Often within a program itself, there is much repetition, again with a bit of variation, and that's what we'll begin to explore in this chapter. The *C# Language Specification*, §8.8, calls statements that perform repetitions *iteration* statements, but programmers commonly refer to them as *loops*.

The rent on your new apartment is $1,200 a month. You are told that it will probably increase 5 percent a year. What will the rent be for the next 10 years? Here's one way to figure it out.

RentCalc.cs

```
// ------------------------------------------------
// RentCalc.cs from "Programming in the Key of C#"
// ------------------------------------------------
using System;

class RentCalc
{
    static void Main()
    {
        decimal mRent = 1200, mIncrease = 5.0m;

        Console.WriteLine("My rent in 2004 is {0}", mRent);
        Console.WriteLine("My rent in 2005 will be {0}",
                        mRent *= (1 + mIncrease / 100));
        Console.WriteLine("My rent in 2006 will be {0}",
                        mRent *= (1 + mIncrease / 100));
        Console.WriteLine("My rent in 2007 will be {0}",
                        mRent *= (1 + mIncrease / 100));
```

```
        Console.WriteLine("My rent in 2008 will be {0}",
                        mRent *= (1 + mIncrease / 100));
        Console.WriteLine("My rent in 2009 will be {0}",
                        mRent *= (1 + mIncrease / 100));
        Console.WriteLine("My rent in 2010 will be {0}",
                        mRent *= (1 + mIncrease / 100));
        Console.WriteLine("My rent in 2011 will be {0}",
                        mRent *= (1 + mIncrease / 100));
        Console.WriteLine("My rent in 2012 will be {0}",
                        mRent *= (1 + mIncrease / 100));
        Console.WriteLine("My rent in 2013 will be {0}",
                        mRent *= (1 + mIncrease / 100));
        Console.WriteLine("My rent in 2014 will be {0}",
                        mRent *= (1 + mIncrease / 100));
    }
}
```

Isn't copy and paste wonderful? To keep the number of statements down, I also found it helpful to consolidate all the math in the *WriteLine* statement by using a compound assignment statement. Each statement raises the value of *mRent*. After I wrote the statement for 2005, I simply copied it nine times and then changed the year that the *WriteLine* statement displayed. Here's the result:

```
My rent in 2004 is 1200
My rent in 2005 will be 1260
My rent in 2006 will be 1323
My rent in 2007 will be 1389.15
My rent in 2008 will be 1458.6075
My rent in 2009 will be 1531.537875
My rent in 2010 will be 1608.11476875
My rent in 2011 will be 1688.5205071875
My rent in 2012 will be 1772.946532546875
My rent in 2013 will be 1861.59385917421875
My rent in 2014 will be 1954.6735521329296875
```

Except for the runaway decimal places, it seems to work fine. But I'm sure you'll agree that this program lacks a certain elegance. It wouldn't be so bad for just a few years. But the more years you want to calculate, the worse it gets. You wouldn't want pages and pages of almost identical code. What if you discovered a little error *after* you pasted and altered all those statements?

While such a *brute force* solution may work with some problems, it's usually much easier to use a loop. The simplest loop in C# is the *while* statement. It looks a lot like a simple *if* statement without an *else* clause. The keyword *while* is followed by a Boolean expression in parentheses. A pair of curly brackets encloses one or more statements:

```
while (bExpression)
{
    // Other statements
}
```

Rather than curly brackets, you can use one of the other embedded statements shown in the *C# Language Specification, §8*, but including the curly brackets anyway is never incorrect.

Here's the difference between the *if* and *while* statements: The *if* statement executes the statements in the curly brackets only once—and only if the Boolean expression is *true*. The *while* statement repeatedly executes the statements in the curly brackets as long as the Boolean expression is *true*. The repetition stops when *bExpression* becomes *false*.

Suppose you've initialized the variable *i* to the value 55. Here's an *if* statement:

```
if (i < 100)
{
    Console.WriteLine(i);
}
```

The result is

```
55
```

Now here's the *while* statement:

```
while (i < 100)
{
    Console.WriteLine(i);
}
```

In this case, the result is

```
55
55
55
55
55
55
55
55
```

and so forth. A loop that runs forever is known as an *infinite loop*, but generally you'll want to terminate an infinite loop long before the end of time by ending the program. You can end the program by clicking the close button on the console window or by typing Ctrl+C. On the MS-DOS command line, Ctrl+C usually interrupts a program and causes it to prematurely end.

There are certainly applications for infinite loops, but in most cases, code inside the curly brackets changes the variable that is referred to in the Boolean expression.

CountUntil100.cs

```
// ------------------------------------------------------
// CountUntil100.cs from "Programming in the Key of C#"
// ------------------------------------------------------
using System;

class CountUntil100
{
    static void Main()
    {
        int i = 0;

        while (i < 100)
        {
            Console.WriteLine(i);
            i++;
        }
        Console.WriteLine("Final value of i equals " + i);
    }
}
```

Because *i* is less than 100 when the flow of execution first encounters this *while* statement, the statements inside the curly brackets will be executed. The code inside the curly brackets displays the value of *i* and then increments the variable. The flow of execution loops back around to the Boolean expression. Is *i* still less than 100? If so, the code inside the curly brackets executes again. Each time through is known as an *iteration*. The program output begins like this:

```
0
1
2
```

Eventually you'll see the output

```
97
98
99
```

After 99 is displayed, the value of *i* is incremented to 100. The flow of execution loops back to the Boolean expression. Is *i* less than 100? No, now it's not. Execution of the program continues with the code after the *while* statement. The value of *i* at that point is 100, as the program shows:

```
Final value of i equals 100
```

If *i* is initialized to 100 (or anything above 100) in the CountUntil100 program, the statements inside the curly brackets won't be executed at all.

Here's a little variation on the loop in CountUntil100:

```
while (i < 100)
{
    i++;
    Console.WriteLine(i);
}
```

Because *i* is incremented before the *WriteLine* call, this loop displays the numbers 1 through 100. The loop doesn't immediately stop at the point where *i* is incremented to 100. After the *WriteLine* call, execution loops to the top, and only then is the Boolean expression checked again.

If there's only one statement in the curly brackets, you don't need the curly brackets. The single statement in the *while* loop could be an *if* statement or another *while* statement or any embedded statement as defined in the *C# Language Specification*, §8.

Here's a *while* statement that avoids the curly brackets by incrementing *i* in the *Console.WriteLine* call:

```
while (i < 100)
    Console.WriteLine(i++);
```

The postfix increment has the effect of changing the variable *after* it's displayed, just as in the first version of the program. The program displays 0 through 99. If you use the prefix increment

```
while (i < 100)
    Console.WriteLine(++i);
```

the variable is incremented before it's displayed. The program displays 1 through 100.

You can also increment *i* in the Boolean expression. For example,

```
while (i++ < 100)
    Console.WriteLine(i);
```

The postfix operator causes *i* to be incremented after it's used in the Boolean expression but before its display by *WriteLine*. The program displays 1 through 100. Here's the prefix version:

```
while (++i < 100)
    Console.WriteLine(i);
```

Now the program displays 1 through 99. After displaying 99, *i* is incremented to 100. The Boolean expression returns *false* and execution continues with the next statement.

I'm emphasizing these differences because the bulk of a *while* statement generally works just fine. The troublesome areas are usually the numbers on the edge that govern where the *while* begins and ends. Consider carefully where and how you're incrementing the variable you're testing in the Boolean expression. You also have the option of using a <= operator rather than a < in the above examples to display one additional number at the end of the loop.

Now let's rewrite the rent calculation using a *while* loop. While we're at it, let's also make an attempt to display the results in nice, neat columns. The program starts off by declaring a few variables and then uses two *Console.WriteLine* statements to display column headings.

RentCalcWithWhile.cs

```
// ------------------------------------------------------------
// RentCalcWithWhile.cs from "Programming in the Key of C#"
// ------------------------------------------------------------
using System;

class RentCalcWithWhile
{
    static void Main()
    {
        int iYear = 2004, iFinalYear = 2014;
        decimal mRent = 1200, mIncrease = 5.0m;

        Console.WriteLine("Year        Rent");
        Console.WriteLine("----        ----");

        while (iYear <= iFinalYear)
        {
            Console.WriteLine("{0,-8}{1,10:C2}", iYear, mRent);
            mRent *= (1 + mIncrease / 100);
            mRent = Decimal.Round(mRent, 2);
            iYear++;
        }
    }
}
```

The calculation is also a little different. After displaying the year and rent, the program calculates the rent for the next year and rounds it to two decimal places, which is probably more in accordance with the calculation in real rent hikes.

In displaying the results, I decided to go for a tabular format. The year is left justified in a field 8 characters wide. The program displays the rent as a currency with two decimal places in a field 10 characters wide. Prior to the *while* statement, two *WriteLine* calls display column headers. Here's the result:

```
Year          Rent
----          ----
2004       $1,200.00
2005       $1,260.00
2006       $1,323.00
2007       $1,389.15
2008       $1,458.61
2009       $1,531.54
2010       $1,608.12
2011       $1,688.53
2012       $1,772.96
2013       $1,861.61
2014       $1,954.69
```

Beautiful. What's important to consider is that I was able to progressively fine-tune the program—get the formatting just the way I wanted it, round the result to two decimal places—without doing a copy and 10 pastes every time I made a little change.

When the RentCalcWithWhile program displays the last line of output for the year 2014, it then increases both the *mRent* and *iYear* variables in preparation for the next loop. That increase of *mRent* is an unnecessary calculation because it's never used. In this particular example, that's not a big deal, but it could be a problem in some larger programs.

If you look at the output of the program, it's pretty easy to satisfy yourself that the program needs 11 calls to *WriteLine* to display the rent for the years 2004 through 2014. But the program needs to perform only 10 calculations, which are the rent hikes between those years. One solution is to have an extra *WriteLine* statement outside the loop:

```
while (iYear < iFinalYear)
{
    Console.WriteLine("{0,-8}{1,10:C2}", iYear, mRent);
    mRent *= (1 + mInterest / 100);
    mRent = Decimal.Round(mRent, 2);
```

```
    iYear++;
}
Console.WriteLine("{0,-8}{1,10:C2}", iYear, mRent);
```

Notice that I also changed the Boolean expression from a <= to a < so that the code inside the loop executes for the final time for the year 2013. The *WriteLine* statement at the bottom of the loop displays the results for 2014 that have already been calculated inside the loop.

A variation (perhaps more common) is to first display the initial year and rent, and then go into the loop for the rent increases. Now the calculation occurs at the beginning of the loop, with the *WriteLine* call at the loop bottom:

```
Console.WriteLine("{0,-8}{1,10:C2}", iYear, mRent);

while (iYear < iFinalYear)
{
    iYear++;
    mRent *= (1 + mInterest / 100);
    mRent = Decimal.Round(mRent, 2);
    Console.WriteLine("{0,-8}{1,10:C2}", iYear, mRent);
}
```

Neither of these two solutions is ideal because they both involve two versions of an identical *WriteLine* call. Change one and you'll have to change the other.

If we really want to make 11 *WriteLine* calls in the loop but perform only 10 calculations in the same loop, we must somehow exit the loop in the middle. You can exit in the middle of a *while* loop using a statement called *break*. The *break* statement always looks the same:

```
break;
```

The entire statement is the keyword *break* followed by a semicolon. The statement causes an exit from a *while* loop and continues execution with the next statement after the loop. Almost always, the *break* statement is part of an *if* statement:

```
if (iYear == iFinalYear)
    break;
```

Here's a version of the rent calculation that uses a *break* statement to prevent an extra unnecessary calculation. Notice that the Boolean expression in the *while* loop is now simply *true*. Without a *break* statement, this would be an infinite loop.

RentCalcWithBreak.cs

```
// --------------------------------------------------------
// RentCalcWithBreak.cs from "Programming in the Key of C#"
// --------------------------------------------------------
using System;

class RentCalcWithBreak
{
    static void Main()
    {
        int iYear = 2004, iFinalYear = 2014;
        decimal mRent = 1200, mIncrease = 5.0m;

        Console.WriteLine("Year            Rent");
        Console.WriteLine("----            ----");

        while (true)
        {
            Console.WriteLine("{0,-8}{1,10:C2}", iYear, mRent);

            if (iYear == iFinalYear)
                break;

            mRent *= (1 + mIncrease / 100);
            mRent = Decimal.Round(mRent, 2);
            iYear++;
        }
    }
}
```

Although the *break* statement sure is handy in some applications, some programmers don't care for it because it resembles a much-disparaged statement called the *goto* (see Chapter 27). In fact, the *C# Language Specification*, §8.9, classifies *break* as one of several *jump* statements. The *break* statement upsets the normal repetitive structure of the *while* loop, so you should probably use it only as a last resort.

Another of the C# jump statements is *continue*, which like *break* is often found in a *while* loop and often triggered by an *if* statement. The *continue* statement causes the remainder of the statements in the loop to be skipped. Execution continues with the next iteration.

For example, suppose you know that your local Rent Control Board never allows a rent increase in any year that ends in 0. In other words, the rent for the year 2010 will be the same as the year 2009. Let's go back to the original *while* loop in RentCalcWithWhile:

```
while (iYear <= iFinalYear)
{
    Console.WriteLine("{0,-8}{1,10:C2}", iYear, mRent);
    mRent *= (1 + mIncrease / 100);
    mRent = Decimal.Round(mRent, 2);
    iYear++;
}
```

One way you can fix this code for the magic year of 2010 is with an *if* statement:

```
while (iYear <= iFinalYear)
{
    Console.WriteLine("{0,-8}{1,10:C2}", iYear, mRent);

    if (iYear != 2009)
    {
        mRent *= (1 + mIncrease / 100);
        mRent = Decimal.Round(mRent, 2);
    }
    iYear++;
}
```

The rent increase doesn't occur between the years 2009 and 2010, so the *if* statement blocks any increase after the year 2009 is displayed. You can also do it with an *if* statement and a *continue*:

```
while (iYear <= iFinalYear)
{
    Console.WriteLine("{0,-8}{1,10:C2}", iYear, mRent);
    iYear++;

    if (iYear == 2010)
        continue;

    mRent *= (1 + mIncrease / 100);
    mRent = Decimal.Round(mRent, 2);
}
```

I've moved the increment of *iYear* up in the loop and followed it by an *if* statement. If the new year is 2010, then the *continue* statement causes execution to continue with the next iteration of the loop. The final two statements in the loop are skipped in that case.

A variation of the *while* loop is the *do* loop. Here's the general form of the *while* loop:

```
while (bExpression)
{
    // Body of while loop
}
```

Here's the *do* loop, which also involves the *while* keyword:

```
do
{
    // Body of do loop
}
while (bExpression);
```

Notice the semicolon at the very end. You can use the *break* and *continue* statements in *do* loops as well as in *while* loops.

As the structure of the *do* loop implies, the Boolean expression is evaluated and checked at the conclusion of the loop rather than the beginning. Regardless of the Boolean expression, the body of the *do* loop always executes *at least once*.

The *do* loop is useful in programs that ask for input from the user. Here's a simple little adding machine program.

AddingMachine.cs

```
// ----------------------------------------------------------
// AddingMachine.cs from "Programming in the Key of C#"
// ----------------------------------------------------------
using System;

class AddingMachine
{
    static void Main()
    {
        string strAnswer;

        do
        {
            Console.Write("Enter first number: ");
            double d1 = Double.Parse(Console.ReadLine());
            Console.Write("Enter second number: ");
            double d2 = Double.Parse(Console.ReadLine());
            Console.WriteLine("The sum is {0}", d1 + d2);

            Console.Write("Do you want to do another? (y/n) ");
            strAnswer = Console.ReadLine() .Trim();
        }
        while (strAnswer.Length > 0 && strAnswer.ToLower()[0] == 'y');
    }
}
```

Because *strAnswer* is used in the Boolean expression after the *while* keyword, it could not be declared inside the block.

The key part of this program occurs near the bottom of the *do* loop. A prompt asks whether the user wants to perform another calculation, and then *strAnswer* stores the answer. The Boolean expression in the *do* statement first tests if the *Length* property of the string is greater than 0. If it is, the *strAnswer* is converted to lowercase and the first character of the string is compared to the character 'y'. Only if the first character of the string is equal to 'y' does execution continue at the top of the loop.

The comparison of *strAnswer.Length* with zero protects the program if the user simply presses Enter in response to the question. If the user presses Enter, *Console.ReadLine* returns the empty string, and attempting to index the first character would raise an exception. The program continues if the user types any response beginning with a lowercase or an uppercase 'y', even if it's preceded by some white space.

Of course, the program could still terminate with a run-time error if the user types something other than a proper number in response to the first two prompts. We'll tackle handling program exceptions in the next chapter.

Here's something I've done once or twice:

```
while (i < 100)
{
    // Other statements
}
while (i < 101);
```

I probably thought I was writing a *while* statement when I started, but by the time I got to the bottom, I thought I was writing a *do* statement. There are actually two *while* statements here. The first looks like this:

```
while (i < 100)
{
    // Other statements
}
```

The second *while* statement has a body that consists of the empty statement, otherwise known as the semicolon:

```
while (i < 101);
```

Because *i* is probably equal to 100 after the first *while* loop finishes, the second *while* is an infinite loop. The program will seem to *hang*. It will just seem to sit there with no output being displayed.

Whenever a console program hangs, just press Ctrl+C to terminate the program. Then take a close look at your source code and try to find an infinite loop. If it's not evident right away, insert a few *WriteLine* calls displaying text like "About to enter the while loop" and "Finished with the while loop" so you can monitor the progress of the program as it's executing. This is how you narrow down the possibilities. If necessary, you can use the debugger built into Visual C# .NET to trace through every step of your code. But I like to exhaust other forms of debugging before resorting to the Visual C# .NET debugger.

It's common to use loops in conjunction with arrays. Suppose you're lucky enough to be working on a program involving the planets of the solar system. Your first job: Demonstrate the validity of the Third Law of Johannes Kepler (1571–1630), which states that for any group of bodies (such as the planets) revolving in orbit around a common body (such as the sun), the squares of the periods of revolution are directly proportional to the cubes of their mean distances from the body they orbit, or

$$\text{Period}^2 \sim \text{Distance}^3$$

Here's a program that declares three parallel arrays containing the planet names, their period of revolution around the sun in earth years, and their distance from the sun in Astronomical Units (where Earth is 1).

KeplersThirdLaw.cs

```
// -------------------------------------------------
// KeplersThirdLaw.cs from "Programming in the Key of C#
// -------------------------------------------------
using System;

class KeplersThirdLaw
{
    static void Main()
    {
        string[] astrPlanet = { "Mercury", "Venus", "Earth",
                                "Mars", "Jupiter", "Saturn",
                                "Uranus", "Neptune", "Pluto" };

        // Periods of revolution around the sun
        //     are in earth years.

        double[] adPeriod = { 0.2409, 0.6152, 1.000,
                              1.881, 11.86, 29.65,
                              83.67, 163.9, 247.7 } ;

        // Mean distances from the sun are in
        //     Astronomical Units where Earth is 1.

        double[] adDistance = { 0.3871, 0.7233, 1.000,
                                1.524, 5.202, 9.581,
                                19.13, 29.95, 39.44 };
```

```
// All data for epoch July 20, 2003 from
//      "Observer's Handbook 2003" (Royal
//      Astronomical Society of Canada), page 21.

int i = 0;

while (i < astrPlanet.Length)
{
    double dRatio = Math.Pow(adPeriod[i], 2) /
                    Math.Pow(adDistance[i], 3);

    Console.WriteLine("{0,-10}: {1,7:F3}",
                    astrPlanet[i], dRatio);
    i++;
}
}
}
```

The declarations are followed by code that performs the calculations. An integer *i* is used for indexing the three arrays. The *while* loop compares *i* with the *Length* property of the first array and increments *i* at the end of the loop. Within the loop, the program also calculates *dRatio* as the ratio of the square of the period to the cube of the distance and displays the value along with the planet name. As you can see, Kepler was really on the ball with his Third Law:

```
Mercury      1.000
Venus        1.000
Earth        1.000
Mars         1.000
Jupiter      0.999
Saturn       1.000
Uranus       1.000
Neptune      1.000
Pluto        1.000
```

The general structure of the *while* loop in KeplersThirdLaw—initialize an array index variable to 0, compare it with the length of the array, and increment it at the bottom of the *while* loop—are pretty standard for working with arrays. In fact, you'll discover in Chapter 26 an alternative to the *while* loop for jobs just like this one.

25

Catching Exceptions

You've been encountering run-time exceptions since Chapter 6, when you ran a program that attempted to divide an integer by 0. Exceptions are identified by classes, such as the *DivideByZeroException* class; most of the basic exception classes are declared in the *System* namespace, and some are listed in the *C# Language Specification*, §16.4.

If overflow checking is enabled, an overflow raises an *OverflowException*. Many programs in this book use *Parse* methods to convert strings to numeric values. If the string contains non-numeric characters, a *FormatException* is raised. If *null* is substituted for the string argument in *Parse* (or if the string variable equals *null*), an *ArgumentNullException* is raised. If you try to index an array outside its bounds or a string beyond its length, you'll cause an *IndexOutOfRangeException* to be raised. The .NET Framework documentation always indicates precisely what exceptions each method can raise.

I've used the verb *raise* in the previous paragraph and earlier chapters to describe how an invalid operation or a method call causes an exception to occur. The *C# Language Specification* uses the word *throw*, which is also a C# keyword, but which I think is more obscure until you discover how exceptions are raised. Starting now, I'll use both words interchangeably.

To a user, an exception means simply that your program has crashed. Bombed. Toasted. Gone down in flames. Ascended to the great bit bucket in the sky. Fortunately, it won't bring Windows down with it. (This isn't the '90s, you know.) You don't want users to see your program crash. You don't even want them to know that you're capable of writing imperfect code. What's most advantageous is for your program to *gracefully recover* from any exceptions that may be thrown. To gracefully recover, your program must *catch* the exception, do something with it, and continue on its merry way.

Throwing and catching exceptions are all part of *structured exception handling*, which is considered to be the modern approach to dealing with problems that can arise during program run time. Consider the *Decimal.Parse* method. This method requires a *string* argument and returns a *decimal*. But what if the string contains letters or other non-numeric characters? In the olden days, such a method might simply ignore non-numeric characters! Or it might have *two* return values, the other being a Boolean that indicated whether the conversion went smoothly. But such techniques were never implemented consistently. With structured exception handling, *Decimal.Parse* throws an exception, essentially saying, "I can't deal with this input, and now it's your problem."

Your program can either let the exception be reported to the user or handle the exception itself. If the latter option is more appealing to you, use the *try* statement. The simplest form of the *try* statement begins with the keyword *try* followed by a pair of curly brackets that enclose a statement that may throw an exception. This is followed by a *catch* clause, which is another block that deals with the exception.

For example, suppose your program reads string input from the user and converts it to a *double* using the following statement:

```
double dValue = Double.Parse(Console.ReadLine());
```

To catch any exceptions that may be thrown by *Parse*, you can replace the statement with the following:

```
double dValue;

try
{
    dValue = Double.Parse(Console.ReadLine());
}
catch
{
    Console.WriteLine("You typed an invalid number.");
    dValue = Double.NaN;
}
```

Notice first that I've separated the declaration of *dValue* and its assignment. If *dValue* were declared in the *try* block, it wouldn't be available outside the *try* block, and couldn't be referred to inside the *catch* block.

If *Double.Parse* succeeds in converting the input string into a *double*, execution continues at the next statement following the *catch* block. If *Parse* throws an exception, then the *catch* block catches it. The code in the *catch* block is executed, and then normal execution resumes with the code following the *catch* block. This particular *catch* block displays a message and then sets *dValue* to NaN. Presumably the code that follows the *catch* block recognizes that *dValue* equals NaN and requests that the user reenter the value.

In a real-life program that reads numeric values from the user, you'll probably put the *try* and *catch* blocks in a *do* loop and keep asking the user to reenter the values until they pass *Parse*. Here's a program that contains a method to do precisely that.

InputDoubles.cs

```
// -----------------------------------------------------
// InputDoubles.cs from "Programming in the Key of C#"
// -----------------------------------------------------
using System;

class InputDoubles
{
    static void Main()
    {
        double dBase = GetDouble("Enter the base: ");
        double dExp = GetDouble("Enter the exponent: ");
        Console.WriteLine("{0} to the power of {1} is {2}",
                    dBase, dExp, Math.Pow(dBase, dExp));
    }
    static double GetDouble(string strPrompt)
    {
        double dValue = Double.NaN;

        do
        {
            Console.Write(strPrompt);

            try
            {
                dValue = Double.Parse(Console.ReadLine());
            }
            catch
            {
                Console.WriteLine();
                Console.WriteLine("You typed an invalid number!");
                Console.WriteLine("Please try again.");
                Console.WriteLine();
            }
        }
        while (Double.IsNaN(dValue));

        return dValue;
    }
}
```

The *GetDouble* method has a *string* parameter and returns a *double*. The method begins by declaring *dValue* and initializing it to NaN. The *do* loop follows. It begins by displaying the string parameter as a prompt and then attempts to convert the input string to a *double*.

If an exception is raised, the method displays a message to the user. At the bottom of the *do* loop, the static *Double.IsNaN* method returns *true*, so execution continues at the top of the *do* loop: The prompt is displayed again.

If *Parse* successfully returns a value, execution continues after the *catch* block. *Double.IsNaN* returns *false*, and the method returns *dValue*.

Although the method sure adds a lot of bulk to the basic *Parse* call, it compensates in part by making *Main* much simpler. And, of course, the user never gets the opportunity to see your program take a nosedive.

It's important to recognize that if *Parse* throws an exception, the *Parse* method doesn't actually return to the program the way it normally does. Execution proceeds from somewhere deep inside the *Parse* method directly to the *catch* clause. If you don't initialize *dValue* to NaN, then *dValue* will be uninitialized when the *catch* clause executes.

If you're working with values of type *decimal* rather than *double*, you don't have the convenience of using NaN to denote that a valid value hasn't yet been typed. You could instead initialize the *decimal* to the minimum possible value (*Decimal.MinValue*) under the assumption that the user would never have occasion to type in such a number, and then compare *mValue* (as it would be called) with that value:

```
while (mValue != Decimal.MinValue);
```

Or you could initialize a Boolean named *bGotValidValue* to *false* and only set it to *true* following the *Parse* call in the *try* block:

```
try
{
    dValue = Double.Parse(Console.ReadLine());
    bGotValidValue = true;
}
```

You then use that value at the bottom of the *do* loop:

```
while (!bGotValidValue);
```

The *catch* clause in the InputDoubles program is known as a *general catch* clause. It will catch any exception raised in the *try* block. You can instead indicate that a *catch* clause apply only to a specific type of exception. For example, here's a little variation of the basic *try* statement that includes a specific *catch* clause.

```
try
{
    // Statement or statements to try
}
catch (Exception exc)
{
    // Error processing
}
```

The *catch* keyword is followed by parentheses and a variable declaration that makes it look a bit like a parameter list to a method. *Exception* is a class that's declared in the *System* namespace, and *exc* (you can name it anything you want) is declared to be an object of type *Exception*. Within the *catch* block, you can use this *Exception* object to obtain more information about the error. You display the *Message* property of the object like so:

```
Console.WriteLine(exc.Message);
```

For the program shown earlier in this chapter, this *Message* property will be either

```
Input string was not in a correct format.
```

if the user types letters (for example) rather than numbers, or

```
Value was either too large or too small for a Double.
```

This error can be raised if the number is typed in scientific notation with too large or too small an exponent. You may prefer displaying messages like these to the user instead of making up your own.

If you pass the *Exception* object directly to *WriteLine* as

```
Console.WriteLine(exc);
```

you'll effectively call the *ToString* method of the *Exception* class. You'll get the same detailed text about the exception that you've been seeing all along.

Although the *catch* clause with the *Exception* object is classified as a specific *catch* clause, it's really just as generalized as the general *catch* clause. That's because all the different exception classes (*DivideByZeroException*, *OverflowException*, and so forth) are defined in a hierarchy with the *Exception* class at the top. All the other exceptions are said to *inherit* from *Exception*. You'll get a much better idea of the concept of inheritance in Part IV of this book. For now, you can think of the *Exception* class as representing any type of exception. Other classes that inherit from *Exception* are more specific.

The *Parse* method of the *Double* class can raise one of three exceptions: *FormatException* (for typing letters), *OverflowException* (if the number is too large or too small), or *ArgumentNullException* (if the argument to *Parse* is *null*).

Here's how you can get very specific in the way you handle each of these exceptions:

```
try
{
    dValue = Double.Parse(Console.ReadLine());
}
catch (FormatException exc)
{
    // Handle format exceptions
}
catch (OverflowException exc)
{
    // Handle overflow exceptions
}
catch (ArgumentNullException exc)
{
    // Handle null argument exceptions
}
catch (Exception exc)
{
    // Handle all other exceptions
}
```

The *catch* clauses are examined in sequence for the first one that matches the exception. The final *catch* clause can be a general clause with no parameter. At any rate, if you're examining individual types of exceptions, you should always include a general *catch* clause or a *catch* clause using *Exception* at the end to get all the exceptions not handled individually.

   In this particular example using *Double.Parse*, the final *catch* clause should never be executed because all the possible exceptions that *Parse* can raise are handled individually. Nor should the *ArgumentNullException* clause be raised because *Console.ReadLine* never returns *null*. But including non-functional *catch* clauses never hurts, even if you simply insert the statement

```
Console.WriteLine("This statement should never be executed.");
```

in the clause. It's surprising how often you'll see such a message when developing a new program!

   There's a third clause, called the *finally* clause, that you can use in the *try* statement. The *finally* clause comes after all the *catch* clauses, like this:

```
finally
{
    // Statements in finally block
}
```

The statements in the *finally* clause are guaranteed to execute following the execution of the *try* clause (if no exception is thrown) or the relevant *catch* clause. The *finally* clause puzzled me the first time I encountered it. Why is it necessary? If an exception does not occur in the *try* clause, execution continues normally with the code following the *catch* clause. If an exception occurs, execution jumps to the *catch* clause and then to the code following the *catch* clause. If I want code to be executed after *try* and *catch*, why can't I simply put it after the *catch* clause? Why should I use a *finally* clause?

The solution to this puzzle is simple: It's possible for a *try* or *catch* clause to contain a *return* statement to return control to the calling method or (if the method is *Main*) to terminate the program. In that case, the statements following the last *catch* clause of the *try* statement would *not* be executed. That's where the *finally* clause helps out. If the *try* or *catch* clause includes a *return* statement, the statements in the *finally* clause are guaranteed to execute anyway. (It's also possible to prematurely exit a *try* or *catch* clause with a *goto* statement, which I'll describe in Chapter 27, or a *throw* statement, which I'll describe shortly. Code in the *finally* clause executes in these cases as well.)

You would generally use a *finally* clause for cleaning up. If, for example, your program is writing to a file when the exception occurs, the *finally* clause might close the file and perhaps delete the file so as not to leave it in an incomplete state.

It's also possible to have a *finally* clause without a *catch* clause. Here are the three possible configurations of the *try* statement:

- *try* clause, one or more *catch* clauses
- *try* clause, one or more *catch* clauses, *finally* clause
- *try* clause, *finally* clause

In the last configuration, the program doesn't catch the error. The user is notified with a dialog box, and the program is terminated. But before the program terminates, the code in the *finally* clause is executed.

Now that you know how to catch exceptions, you should also know how to *throw* them. If you're writing a method that might encounter problems of various sorts, generally you'll want the method to throw an exception to notify the code calling the method of these problems. The *throw* statement can be as simple as

```
throw;
```

But this simple form of the *throw* statement can be used only in a *catch* block to rethrow the exception.

If you're not rethrowing an exception, you must supply an argument in the *throw* statement. This argument is an instance of the *Exception* class or any class that is descended from the *Exception* class, even classes that you create yourself:

```
throw new Exception();
```

The *new* expression includes an *Exception* constructor that creates an instance of the *Exception* class. But you really shouldn't use an instance of the *Exception* class in your *throw* statements because it doesn't tell you what kind of exception it is! Use one of the more specific exceptions. Very often you'll find a descendent of *Exception* in the *System* namespace that comes close to what you need. For example, if your method has a *string* parameter and the method can't work if a *null* argument is passed, you'll probably have code that looks like this:

```
if (strInput == null)
    throw new ArgumentNullException();
```

It's also possible to pass a *string* argument to the *ArgumentNullException* constructor. Such an argument might indicate the particular method parameter that caused the problem:

```
if (strInput == null)
    throw new ArgumentNullException("Input String")
```

That string you pass to the constructor will become part of the exception message available in a *catch* clause that deals with this exception.

Let me emphasize again that as soon as the *throw* statement executes, the method is finished. No further code will be executed. It makes no sense to have an *else* clause with such an *if* statement:

```
if (strInput == null)
    throw new ArgumentNullException();
else
{
    // Do stuff if exception is not thrown.
}
```

You can simply follow the *if* statement containing the *throw* statement with the other code:

```
if (strInput == null)
    throw new ArgumentNullException();

// Do stuff if exception is not thrown.
```

Let's write a *Parse* method for integers. To keep it relatively simple, negative signs won't be allowed. Like the normal *Parse* methods, *MyParse* throws three types of exceptions: an *ArgumentNullException* if the argument is null, a *FormatException* if the string contains any characters that aren't digits, or an *OverflowException* if the number won't fit in an *int*.

MethodWithThrows.cs

```
// ------------------------------------------------------------
// MethodWithThrows.cs from "Programming in the Key of C#"
// ------------------------------------------------------------
using System;

class MethodWithThrows
{
    static void Main()
    {
        int iInput;

        Console.Write("Enter an unsigned integer: ");

        try
        {
            iInput = MyParse(Console.ReadLine());
            Console.WriteLine("You entered {0}", iInput);
        }
        catch (Exception exc)
        {
            Console.WriteLine(exc.Message);
        }
    }
    static int MyParse(string str)
    {
        int iResult = 0, i = 0;

        // If argument is null, throw an exception.

        if (str == null)
            throw new ArgumentNullException();

        // Get rid of white space.

        str = str.Trim();

        // Check if there's at least one character.

        if (str.Length == 0)
            throw new FormatException();

        // Loop through all the characters in the string.
```

```
        while (i < str.Length)
        {
            // If the next character's not a digit, throw exception.

            if (!Char.IsDigit(str, i))
                throw new FormatException();

            // Accumulate the next digit (notice "checked").

            iResult = checked(10 * iResult + (int) str[i] - (int) '0');

            i++;
        }
        return iResult;
    }
}
```

The *MyParse* method first trims off the white space and then uses a *while* statement to loop through all the characters in the string. If a character passes the *IsDigit* test, the method multiplies the *iResult* by 10 and adds the new digit converted from Unicode to its numeric value. *MyParse* doesn't explicitly throw an *OverflowException*; instead, it performs the calculation in a *checked* statement to generate the normal *OverflowException*. The *Main* method lets you experiment with *MyParse* and catches any exceptions it may throw.

26

For and *Foreach*

When you've been programming for a while, you'll start to recognize certain patterns of code that tend to show up a lot. Here's a code pattern that we've already seen a few times:

```
i = 0;

while (i < iRepetitions)
{
    // Do something here with variable i.

    i++;
}
```

Very often *iRepetitions* is the length of a string (as in the *MyParse* method of the MethodWithThrows program from the last chapter) or the length of an array (such as KeplersThirdLaw program of Chapter 24). The value of *iRepetitions* indicates the number of times the code in the loop is executed. The *i* variable is often initialized to 0 so that it's suitable for indexing an array or string starting at the beginning. The Boolean expression in the *while* statement often uses < rather than <= so that values of *i* range from 0 through (*iRepetitions* −1), again appropriate for indexing an array or string.

This pattern of code is so common that there's a special statement that encompasses all these operations called the *for* statement. Here's the exact equivalent of the chunk of code shown above:

```
for (i = 0; i < iRepetitions; i++)
{
    // Do something here with variable i.
}
```

The actual savings in typing isn't much, but the *for* statement consolidates all the pertinent information about *i*—its initial value, its maximum value, and how it's increased—all in one spot. If you're like most programmers, you'll probably use the *for* loop more than the *while* or *do* loop—even when the *while* or *do* would be simpler!

The *for* statement has a unique syntax unlike anything else in C#, so it's important to take some time to study it. Although the most common form of the *for* statement involves a single variable that is initialized, tested, and incremented, more complex varieties of the *for* statement are possible. Like the *while* loop, a *for* loop can include a *break* statement to exit the loop or a *continue* statement to skip the rest of the loop and perform the next iteration.

The *for* statement begins with the word *for* followed by parentheses. Inside the parentheses are three expressions separated by semicolons. This is the only use of semicolons in C# other than a statement separator! The three expressions are called the *initializer*, the *condition*, and the *iterator*.

The first expression in the *for* statement is the *initializer*. This expression is executed just once before the loop commences. Generally, you'll use a simple assignment statement such as the one shown earlier. But you can include multiple assignment statements separated by commas:

```
for (i = 0, j = 17; …
```

If present, the second expression, the *condition*, must be a Boolean expression. This Boolean expression is evaluated before each iteration of the loop, including the first iteration. If the Boolean expression is *true*, the statements inside the curly brackets are executed. If *false*, execution continues with the statement following the right curly bracket. If you set the middle clause to *false*, the statements in the *for* loop are never executed:

```
for (i = 0; false; i++)
{
    // Statements never executed.
}
```

The third clause is the *iterator*. This is generally an expression that is executed at the end of each iteration. As with the *initializer*, you can include multiple expressions separated by commas:

```
for (i = 0, j = 100; i < j; i++, j -= 5)
{
    // Do something with i and j.
}
```

This *for* statement initializes two variables, includes a Boolean expression involving both variables, and alters both variables at the end of each iteration.

The initializer and the iterator can be *statement expressions* as defined in the *C# Language Specification*, §8.6, which includes assignment statements, increments or decrements, invocation expressions (that is, method calls), or creations of objects. Multiple statement expressions must be separated by commas.

You don't have to crowd everything into a single *for* statement. If you'd prefer, you could move some of those statements elsewhere. This next code is an exact equivalent of the previous *for* statement that might look a bit clearer:

```
j = 100;

for (i = 0; i < j; i++)
{
    // Do something with i and j.

    j -= 5;
}
```

The initializer, condition, and iterator expressions are all optional, but the semicolons are not. Here's a *for* statement with nothing but semicolons:

```
for (;;)
{
    // Do something.
}
```

That statement is equivalent to the classical infinite loop:

```
while (true)
{
    // Do something.
}
```

You have one additional option with the *initializer*. You can make it a single declaration statement. The first *for* loop I showed you looked like this:

```
for (i = 0; i < iRepetitions; i++)
{
    // Do something here with variable i.
}
```

It was assumed, of course, that *i* was declared as an integer earlier in the program. However, if you're only going to be using the variable in the loop, the *for* statement allows you to declare the variable right in the initializer:

```
for (int i = 0; i < iRepetitions; i++)
{
    // Do something here with variable i.
}
```

Notice the *int* keyword right after the left parenthesis. If you declare the variable in the *for* statement (and it's a very popular technique), *i* cannot have been declared earlier in the parent scope. The variable is available only inside the loop, and it's not visible outside the loop. You can, however, declare and use the same variable name in other loops.

You can initialize multiple variables in the *for* loop:

```
for (int i = 0, j = 0; …
```

But it's an either/or situation. If you declare one or more variables of the same type, you can't do anything else in the initializer. You can't initialize one and declare another:

```
for (i = 0, int j = 7; …     // Won't work!
```

Nor can you declare variables of two different types:

```
for (int i = 0, decimal m = 7; …    // Won't work!
```

The *for* loop is very common when working with arrays. Suppose *astr* is an array of strings. Here's a *for* loop to display them all:

```
for (int i = 0; i < astr.Length; i++)
{
    Console.WriteLine(astr[i]);
}
```

In this loop the variable *i* ranges from 0 up to and including (*astr.Length* − 1), exactly what you want. Because this loop contains only a single statement, you don't need the curly brackets:

```
for (int i = 0; i < astr.Length; i++)
    Console.WriteLine(astr[i]);
```

Sometimes you'll need to use the loop variable after the loop has finished. In these cases, you'll want to declare the variable before the *for* statement:

```
int i;

for (i = 0; i < iRepetitions; i++)
{
    // Statements in the loop
}
```

After the loop has finished, what does *i* equal? Normally it equals *iRepetitions*. However, if the loop were terminated prematurely with a *break* statement, it would be something less than *iRepetitions*. In fact, comparing the value of *i* with *iRepetitions* after the loop is the customary way to determine if a *for* statement has concluded normally or exited with a *break*.

Because the *for* loop is so often used for accessing array elements, programmers get into the habit of initializing the loop variable to 0 and comparing it to the length of the array (which equals the number of repetitions of the loop) using the less than (<) operator. If you ask a veteran C or C++ programmer to write some C# code that lists the numbers from 1 through 100, you might get the following:

```
for (int i = 0; i < 100; i++)
    Console.WriteLine(i + 1);
```

The variable *i* actually ranges from 0 through 99, but the *WriteLine* statement displays *i* plus 1. Because such a *for* loop looks so familiar to the veteran programmer, that code is easier to comprehend at first look than the more direct solution:

```
for (int i = 1; i <= 100; i++)
    Console.WriteLine(i);
```

And then there's the smarty who'll do it like this:

```
for (int i = 0; i < 100; Console.WriteLine(++i));
```

I mentioned that the initializer or iterator can be method calls. Here the iterator is a call to *Console.WriteLine* displaying the incremented value of *i*. The body of this *for* statement is called an *empty statement* (see the *C# Language Specification*, §8.3) and consists solely of the semicolon, which you'll notice following the last right parenthesis.

It's very common for *if* statements to be nested in the bodies of *for* statements. Suppose you had an array *astr* that you wanted to display in three columns with a width of 20 characters each. Here's the code:

```
for (int i = 0; i < astr.Length; i++)
{
    Console.Write("{0,-20}", astr[i]);
    if (i % 3 == 2)
        Console.WriteLine();
}
```

The *Console.Write* call displays the string but does not skip to the next line. The *if* statement uses the remainder operator with a divisor of 3 and compares the result with 2. This code executes the *Console.WriteLine* call only if *i* equals 2, 5, 8, 11, and so forth. You can also do this job using *if* with an *else* clause:

```
for (int i = 0; i < astr.Length; i++)
{
    if (i % 3 == 2)
        Console.WriteLine("{0,-20}", astr[i]);
    else
        Console.Write("{0,-20}", astr[i]);
}
```

That's a bit bulkier, but you can remove the curly brackets because they contain only one statement:

```
for (int i = 0; i < astr.Length; i++)
    if (i % 3 == 2)
        Console.WriteLine("{0,-20}", astr[i]);
    else
        Console.Write("{0,-20}", astr[i]);
```

Earlier in this chapter, I showed an example of a *for* loop that seemed to involve *two* variables. You may wonder when such *for* loops would be used. Often it's necessary to index two or more arrays in a single loop, perhaps to copy some selected elements from one array into another.

For example, suppose it occurs to you one day that many of your friends seem to have the letter 'Z' in their names. Maybe it's a coincidence, or perhaps you feel some affinity to people with names containing 'Z'. Fortunately, you already have an array named *astrMyFriends* containing the names of your 31 closest friends. You can use a simple *for* loop with one variable declared in the initializer to simply count up the number of your friends with 'Z' in their names:

```
char[] achSearch = {'z', 'Z'};
int iNamesWithZees = 0;

for (int i = 0; i < astrMyFriends.Length; i++)
    if (astrMyFriends[i].IndexOfAny(achSearch) != -1)
        iNamesWithZees++;
```

The code initializes *iNamesWithZees* to 0 and uses it to count up the number of names containing 'z' or 'Z'. The actual search is performed using the *IndexOfAny* method from the *String* class. The argument to *IndexOfAny* must be an array of characters, which is the *achSearch* array. If none of those characters are in the string, *IndexOfAny* returns –1. If *IndexOfAny* does not return –1, *iNamesWithZees* is incremented.

After the loop has ended, the value of *iNamesWithZees* is the number of names containing 'z' or 'Z'. That's why *iNamesWithZees* was not declared in the *for* statement; if it were, it wouldn't be available after the *for* statement concluded. Suppose you also want to copy these names with 'z' or 'Z' into another array. You already know the size of that array. It's the value of *iNamesWithZees*. Here's the complete program:

ZeeNames.cs
```
// ---------------------------------------------------
// ZeeNames.cs from "Programming in the Key of C#"
// ---------------------------------------------------
using System;
```

```
class ZeeNames
{
    static void Main()
    {
        string[] astrMyFriends =
        {
            "Hazem Abolrous", "Wanida Benshoof", "Suzana De Canuto",
            "Terry Clayton", "Brenda Diaz", "Terri Lee Duffy",
            "Maciej Dusza", "Charles Fitzgerald", "Guy Gilbert",
            "Jossef Goldberg", "Greg Guzik", "Annette Hill",
            "George Jiang", "Tengiz Kharatishvili",
            "Rebecca Laszlo", "Yan Li", "Jose Lugo",
            "Sandra I. Martinez", "Ben Miller", "Zheng Mu",
            "Merav Netz", "Deborah Poe", "Amy Rusko",
            "Vadim Sazanovich", "David So", "Rachel B. Valdez",
            "Raja D. Venugopal", "Paul West", "Robert Zare",
            "Kimberly B. Zimmerman", "Karen Zimprich"
        };
        int iNamesWithZees = 0;
        char[] achSearch = {'z', 'Z'};

        // First, count up the names with 'z' or 'Z' in them.

        for (int i = 0; i < astrMyFriends.Length; i++)
            if (astrMyFriends[i].IndexOfAny(achSearch) != -1)
                iNamesWithZees++;

        // Next, declare an array of that size

        string[] astrMyFriendsWithZees = new string[iNamesWithZees];

        // Transfer the names from one array to another

        for (int i = 0, j = 0; i < astrMyFriends.Length; i++)
            if (astrMyFriends[i].IndexOfAny(achSearch) != -1)
                astrMyFriendsWithZees[j++] = astrMyFriends[i];

        // Display some statistical information

        Console.WriteLine("Of my {0} friends, {1} " +
                          "have a name with 'Z' in it:",
                          astrMyFriends.Length, iNamesWithZees);

        // Display the new array

        for (int i = 0; i < astrMyFriendsWithZees.Length; i++)
            Console.WriteLine(astrMyFriendsWithZees[i]);
    }
}
```

There are three *for* loops in this program. The first I've already discussed—it just counts up the names. The program then declares an array named *astrMyFriendsWithZees* of that size. It's the next *for* loop that declares two variables in the initializer. The first variable, *i*, is used to index *astrMyFriends* normally. The *j* variable is also initialized to 0 and indexes *astrMyFriendsWithZees*. Notice that the iterator statement in the *for* loop only increments *i*. Code in the *for* loop increments *j* only when a name is copied to *astrMyFriendsWithZees*.

The final *for* loop in the program just prints out the contents of the second array.

You may find that this program has a little too much repeated code. Both the first and second *for* loops call the *IndexOfAny* method, and that really doesn't seem necessary. Is there a better way to do this job? Perhaps. You could begin by declaring an array (let's call it *astrTemp* because it will perform an intermediary or temporary role in this program) the same size as *astrMyFriends*:

```
string[] astrTemp = new string[astrMyFriends.Length];
```

You then copy the names to *astrTemp* as you're counting the names containing the letter 'Z':

```
for (int i = 0; i < astrMyFriends.Length; i++)
    if (astrMyFriends[i].IndexOfAny(achSearch) != -1)
        astrTemp[iNamesWithZees++] = astrMyFriends[i];
```

You can't declare the *iNamesWithZees* variable in the *for* loop because you'll be using it outside the loop. After the loop has concluded, you have all the names containing 'z' or 'Z' stored in the *astrTemp* array, but the array is the same size as *astrMyFriends*. The value *astrTemp.Length* doesn't really give you any information. A number of the elements contain *null* values. You'll probably want to declare a third array to store just these names. The size of this array must be *iNamesWithZees*:

```
string[] astrMyFriendsWithZees = new string[iNamesWithZees];
```

You can then simply copy the elements from *astrTemp* to *astrMyFriendsWithZees*. Notice that the *condition* part of the *for* statement is based on *iNamesWithZees*:

```
for (int i = 0; i < iNamesWithZees; i++)
    astrMyFriendsWithZees[i] = astrTemp[i];
```

The complete alternative approach is shown in the project ZeeNamesAlternative included with the companion content. You may prefer this code because the second *for* loop is simpler than in the ZeeNames program. But using this code comes at a cost of declaring the *astrTemp* array that's only used for temporary storage.

The problem that causes the code bulk in both ZeeNames programs is that you can't use an array until you've created it, and to create it you must know its size. Once that size is set, you can't change it without creating a new array.

A possible solution is to use the *ArrayList* class of the *System.Collections*. An *ArrayList* object is like an array but with a flexible size. You use the *Add* method to add elements to an *ArrayList* object and the *Remove* method to remove elements. The *Count* property indicates the number of elements in the *ArrayList* object. You can index the *ArrayList* object like an array or convert the collection elements into an array. I'll be using an *ArrayList* object in Chapter 41.

It's common for loops to be nested, that is, for one *for* loop to be within another. You'll probably need nested loops to work with a multidimensional array. You also need nested loops if you want to implement one of the classical programming algorithms called the *Sieve of Eratosthenes*, which is a relatively simple way to generate prime numbers. As you'll recall, prime numbers are those numbers that are equally divisible only by 1 and themselves. The first prime number is 2, which is the only even prime.

Eratosthenes (276–196 BCE) was an Alexandrian astronomer, geometrician, and poet. He served as superintendent of the legendary library at Alexandria, and once performed an accurate measurement of the circumference of the earth based on the comparison of shadows cast at different latitudes on the summer solstice.

The sieve of Eratosthenes begins by imagining a string of consecutive integers beginning at 2:

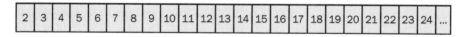

Examine these numbers one by one. Two is a prime, so any multiple of 2 is *not* a prime. You can thus eliminate any multiple of 2 from the list of primes:

Three is a prime, so any multiple of 3 is not a prime. Eliminate them:

The next prime is 5, so the next step would be to eliminate all multiples of 5. But for the few numbers we have here, we're done. The numbers that remain are primes.

In a program that implements the sieve, you use a Boolean array. The size of the array is based on the maximum number you want to check. For example, you may want to find all prime numbers up to 10,000. That would be the size of the array. The program begins by setting all the elements of the Boolean array to *true*. Based on the sieve logic, the program sets any element determined not to be a prime to *false*. At the program's end, only those elements that are still *true* are the prime numbers.

The SieveOfEratosthenes program shown here declares the array *abIsPrime* to store Boolean values—*false* if the number is not a prime and *true* if it is. To keep confusion to a minimum, I decided to avoid indexing discrepancies. For example, *abIsPrime[i]* is *true* if *i* is a prime number, not *(i + 1)*. For this reason, when the program asks for a maximum integer to check, and the program stores this value as *iMax*, the program declares an array of that size plus one so that *abArray[iMax]* is a valid element of the array.

SieveOfEratosthenes.cs

```
// -----------------------------------------------------------
// SieveOfEratosthenes.cs from "Programming in the Key of C#"
// -----------------------------------------------------------
using System;

class SieveOfEratosthenes
{
    static void Main()
    {
        Console.Write("Enter a maximum integer to check: ");
        int iMax = Int32.Parse(Console.ReadLine());
        bool[] abIsPrime = new bool[iMax + 1];

        // Initialize the array to true.

        for (int i = 0; i <= iMax; i++)
            abIsPrime[i] = true;

        // Perform the sieve.

        for (int i = 2; i * i <= iMax; i++)
            if (abIsPrime[i])
                for (int j = 2; j <= iMax / i; j++)
                    abIsPrime[i * j] = false;

        // Display the prime numbers.

        for (int i = 2; i <= iMax; i++)
            if (abIsPrime[i])
                Console.Write("{0} ", i);
    }
}
```

The first *for* loop simply sets all the elements of the array to *true*. Notice that the condition uses a <= operator rather than < because *iMax* is the maximum index.

The next section of the program involves nested *for* loops, which we can refer to as the *outer* loop and the *inner* loop. This is the actual sieve. The outer loop first sets *i* to 2. The *abIsPrime[2]* element is *true*, so the inner loop now kicks in, setting the following elements to *false*: *abIsPrime[2 * 2]*, *abIsPrime[2 * 3]*, *abIsPrime[2 * 4]* and so forth. Those are the numbers divisible by 2.

The outer loop next sets *i* equal to 3. Again, *abIsPrime[3]* is *true*, so the inner loop sets the following elements to *false*: *abIsPrime[3 * 2]*, *abIsPrime[3 * 3]*, *abIsPrime[3 * 4]*, and so forth. When the outer loop sets *i* equal to 4, *abIsPrime[4]* is *false*, so the inner loop is skipped.

Take a look at the two condition expressions of the inner and outer loops. For the inner loop, the condition is

```
j <= iMax / i
```

Within that loop, the *abIsPrime* array is indexed by the product of *i* and *j*. Limiting *j* to *iMax* divided by *i* prevents the index from exceeding *iMax*. The outer loop has a condition expression of

```
i * i < iMax
```

In other words, *i* never gets higher than the square root of *iMax*. Any nonprime less than or equal to *iMax* has at least two non-trivial divisors, only one of which can be greater than the square root of *iMax*. (If they were both greater than the square root of *iMax*, their product would be greater than *iMax*.) And that case was already handled in the inner loop.

The program concludes by displaying all the prime numbers (with a space between them) using *Write* rather than *WriteLine*. Notice that the *Write* statement doesn't display the array elements, which are either *false* or *true*. Instead, the *Write* statement displays the index of the array whenever the element is *true*.

It's possible for this program to be simplified in a few ways. Suppose the array were named *abIsNotPrime*. Some of the program logic would have to be changed. The two *if* statements would require an exclamation point:

```
if (!abIsNotPrime[i])
```

And you'd need to change the statement in the inner loop of the sieve:

```
abIsNotPrime[i * j] = true;
```

But the entire first *for* loop could be eliminated. The program doesn't need to initialize all the elements to *false* because that happens when memory for the array is allocated from the heap.

It's also possible to reduce the size of the array by one or two elements by indexing it differently. The value *abIsPrime[0]* could refer to the number 1, or even 2, because we know that 1 is not a prime. Some programmers even chop the array size in half because they know that all even numbers (except 2) aren't prime, so why bother having array elements for those?

If you really, really, really want to make the sieve as efficient as possible, you may want to eliminate this multiplication in the inner loop:

```
for (int j = 2; j <= iMax / i; j++)
    abIsPrime[i * j] = false;
```

In the computer's microprocessor, multiplications take longer than additions. What this *for* statement does is calculate indexes of 2 * *i*, 3 * *i*, 4 * *i*, and so forth. You can do the same thing with this loop:

```
for (int j = i + i; j <= iMax; j += i)
    abIsPrime[j] = false;
```

Notice that *j* is initialized to *i + i*, which is the same as *2 * i*. That's the first index. The iterator increases *j* not by 1, but by *i*, thus resulting in *3 * i*, *4 * i*, and so forth, exactly what we want. The condition statement now compares *j* with *iMax* rather than *iMax* divided by *i*. An informal test reveals that this non-multiplying version shaves about 20 percent from the total calculation time of the nested loops.

As you've seen, it's often common to use a *for* loop to access the elements of an array. Here's an example that sums up all the elements of a *decimal* array named *amArray*:

```
decimal mTotal = 0;

for (int i = 0; i < amArray.Length; i++)
{
    mTotal += amArray[i];
}
```

If all you need to do is access all the elements of an array, an easier way to do it is to use a statement called *foreach*. The *foreach* statement also involves the *in* keyword:

```
decimal mTotal = 0;

foreach (decimal m in amArray)
{
    mTotal += m
}
```

The *foreach* keyword must be followed by a left parenthesis, then a variable type (in this case *decimal*) that matches the type of the array you're accessing. The type must be followed by an identifier (here I've named it *m*) called the *iteration variable*. The iteration variable is valid only within the loop. In the *foreach* statement, the iteration variable is followed by the keyword *in*, the name of the array, and a right parenthesis.

For each iteration of the *foreach* loop, the iteration variable is set to the next element of the array. The *foreach* loop gives you access to all the array elements in order, but what you don't have is an index. You could simulate an array index just by initializing an integer variable to 0 and incrementing it in the *foreach* loop, but if you need to do that, you might as well use *for* rather than *foreach*. (Well, maybe not. The *foreach* has a performance benefit that I'll discuss shortly.)

The iteration variable is read-only. It cannot appear on the left side of an assignment statement. You cannot change the elements of the array using the iteration variable. You cannot, for example, use the *foreach* statement to initialize the elements of an array.

Because the iteration variable is read-only, you can't substitute a *foreach* statement for the first *for* statement in the SieveOfEratosthenes program. Because you don't have access to an array index, you can't replace the last *for* statement of that program with a *foreach* statement. And the nested *for* statements are just too complex to be replaced with *foreach* statements.

What's interesting, however, is that *foreach* works with a lot more than just arrays. As with the *for* statement, you can use it with strings. Here's a statement that displays all the characters of a string named *str*, one character per line:

```
foreach (char ch in str)
    Console.WriteLine(ch);
```

The *foreach* statement also works with any class that is a *collection* type, which is an object that stores other objects. Technically, a collection type "implements the *System.IEnumerable* interface" (*C# Language Specification*, §8.8.4).

The *C# Language Specification* is not quite correct here: *IEnumerable* is actually declared in the *System.Collections* namespace. It's declared as an *interface*, which is a C# keyword. I'll discuss C# interfaces in more detail in Chapter 38. For now, just take a look at the documentation of *IEnumerable* to see the long list of classes in the .NET Framework that implement the interface. For example, if you'll be using C# to write applications that run under Windows, you can loop through all the controls (such as buttons, text boxes, and so forth) that appear on a form (such as a dialog box) using a *foreach* statement:

```
foreach (Control ctrl in frm.Controls)
{
    // Do something with each control
}
```

When dealing with collections other than simple arrays and strings, *foreach* has some distinct performance benefits when compared with *for*. To get a little taste of the difference, consider the following program that has a method named *MyFriends* that creates, initializes, and returns the *astrMyFriends* array used earlier:

ForAndForEach.cs

```
// ------------------------------------------------------
// ForAndForEach.cs from "Programming in the Key of C#"
// ------------------------------------------------------
using System;

class ForAndForEach
{
    static void Main()
    {
        int iNamesWithZees = 0;
        char[] achSearch = {'z', 'Z'};

        Console.WriteLine("Looping through MyFriends using a for loop:");

        for (int i = 0; i < MyFriends().Length; i++)
            if (MyFriends()[i].IndexOfAny(achSearch) != -1)
                iNamesWithZees++;

        Console.WriteLine();
        Console.WriteLine("Names with Z's: " + iNamesWithZees);

        iNamesWithZees = 0;

        Console.WriteLine("Looping through MyFriends using foreach:");

        foreach (string str in MyFriends())
            if (str.IndexOfAny(achSearch) != -1)
                iNamesWithZees++;

        Console.WriteLine();
        Console.WriteLine("Names with Z's: " + iNamesWithZees);
    }
    static string[] MyFriends()
    {
        Console.Write("*");

        return new string[]
        {
            "Hazem Abolrous", "Wanida Benshoof", "Suzana De Canuto",
            "Terry Clayton", "Brenda Diaz", "Terri Lee Duffy",
```

```
                    "Maciej Dusza", "Charles Fitzgerald", "Guy Gilbert",
                    "Jossef Goldberg", "Greg Guzik", "Annette Hill",
                    "George Jiang", "Tengiz Kharatishvili",
                    "Rebecca Laszlo", "Yan Li", "Jose Lugo",
                    "Sandra I. Martinez", "Ben Miller", "Zheng Mu",
                    "Merav Netz", "Deborah Poe", "Amy Rusko",
                    "Vadim Sazanovich", "David So", "Rachel B. Valdez",
                    "Raja D. Venugopal", "Paul West", "Robert Zare",
                    "Kimberly B. Zimmerman", "Karen Zimprich"
                };
        }
    }
```

The *Main* method uses both *for* and *foreach* loops to count up the names containing the letter Z. To demonstrate the difference, the *MyFriends* method displays an asterisk every time it's called. Here's the program output:

```
Looping through MyFriends using a for loop:
**************************************************************
Names with Z's: 16
Looping through MyFriends using foreach:
*
Names with Z's: 16
```

The *for* loop calls *MyFriends* twice for every iteration of the loop, the first time to determine if the loop variable has exceeded the length of the array, and the second time to access a particular element of the array. The *foreach* loop, however, calls the method just once. After it obtains the entire array, it loops through each element.

The *for* and *foreach* loops really represent entirely different philosophies in working with collections. The *for* statement can actually modify or recreate an array as it's looping through its elements; the *foreach* statement essentially takes a snapshot of the array (or other collection) at the time of the *foreach* statement. Which statement is more appropriate for your application is something only you can decide.

27

The Infamous *Goto*

What distinguishes a computer program from a simple list of calculations is the ability to change the flow of execution based on the values of variables. The *if*, *while*, *do*, *for*, and *foreach* statements all help the programmer write code that performs conditional or repetitive instructions. In machine code programming, the techniques for controlling flow of execution are generally more limited. You can compare numbers, which set certain *flags* in the microprocessor, and then you can *jump* or *branch* to a particular instruction (actually, a particular memory address where the instruction is stored) based on the setting of a flag.

When high-level programming languages were first being invented in the 1950s and 1960s, it wasn't quite clear what was important and what wasn't, what was good and what was bad. Many people were locked into the paradigm of machine code and designed high-level statements that imitated the machine code branch instructions. These were often called *Go To* statements, and they simply caused the flow of execution to jump from one part of the program to another. *Go To* statements were valuable tools, and programmers used them with abandon, even when alternatives (such as *while* and *for*) became available.

In 1968, Dutch-born computer scientist Edsger W. Dijkstra (1930–2002) wrote a paper for the *Communications of the ACM* (Association for Computing Machinery) entitled "Go To Statement Considered Harmful" that began

> *For a number of years I have been familiar with the observation*
> *that the quality of programmers is a decreasing function of the*
> *density of* go to *statements in the programs they produce. More*

recently I discovered why the use of the go to *statement has such disastrous effects, and I became convinced that the* go to *statement should be abolished from all "higher level" programming languages (i.e., everything except, perhaps, plain machine code).*[*]

Very simply, the *Go To* statement did not lend itself to writing comprehensible code. The *Go To* was the primary cause of *spaghetti code*, in which the flow of execution could be determined *only* by a computer. The entanglements of hops, leaps, and jumps were beyond the analysis of mere humans.

The elimination of the *Go To* from the programmer's mindset (if not from the actual programming languages) was an important step in the road to *structured* and *block-oriented* programming. Today, programmers trained in the wake of Dijkstra's assault on the *Go To* sometimes go for years without using one.

Still, however, the *Go To* is sometimes useful, and it's included in C# with the *goto* keyword. As with most modern languages, the *goto* statement requires a label, which is an identifier followed by a colon:

```
TopOfLoop:
```

The *goto* statement references that label:

```
goto TopOfLoop;
```

Here's a little bit of code that uses a *goto* where a *while*, *do*, or *for* might be more appropriate:

```
int i = 0;

TopOfLoop:
    Console.WriteLine(i);
i++;
if (i < 100)
    goto TopOfLoop;
```

And, despite my better judgment, here's the prime number sieve program written with *goto* statements rather than *for* loops.

---

[*] The complete paper is available at *http://www.acm.org/classics/oct95*. Other information and papers by Dijkstra can be found at *http://www.cs.utexas.edu/users/EWD*.

SieveWithGoto.cs

```
// ------------------------------------------------------------
// SieveOfEratosthenes.cs from "Programming in the Key of C#"
// ------------------------------------------------------------
using System;

class SieveOfEratosthenes
{
    static void Main()
    {
        Console.Write("Enter a maximum integer to check: ");
        int iMax = Int32.Parse(Console.ReadLine());
        bool[] abIsPrime = new bool[iMax + 1];
        int i, j;

        // Initialize the array to true.

        i = 0;
    Initialize:
        abIsPrime[i] = true;
        i++;
        if (i <= iMax) goto Initialize;

        // Perform the sieve.

        i = 2;
    NextBase:
        if (!abIsPrime[i]) goto SkipLoop;
        j = 2;
    NextMultiplier:
        abIsPrime[i * j] = false;
        j++;
        if (j <= iMax / i) goto NextMultiplier;
    SkipLoop:
        i++;
        if (i * i < iMax) goto NextBase;

        // Display the prime numbers.

        i = 2;
    Display:
        if (!abIsPrime[i]) goto SkipDisplay;
        Console.Write("{0} ", i);
    SkipDisplay:
        i++;
        if (i <= iMax) goto Display;
    }
}
```

I've also restricted my use of block structure. The only statement I've allowed myself with an *if* statement is a *goto*. Despite the fact that the functionality of the *goto* statement is more intuitively obvious than the *for* statement, I'm sure you'll agree that the actual flow of execution is more difficult to interpret.

A label has a scope just like a variable. "The scope of a label is the block in which the label is declared, including any nested blocks" (*C# Language Specification*, §8.4). You can't jump into a block, which means you can't jump into an *if* or *while* or *try* statement. You can jump out of these blocks, but not into them.

Programmers today generally use *goto* statements only in extreme circumstances. The classic example involves code deep inside multiple nested *for* or *while* statements. Maybe you're reading a file, and suddenly the file ends prematurely. The "right" way to get out of the nested *for* statements is with a series of *break* statements. But that might be messy. A simple

```
goto CriticalErrorNoMoreFile;
```

statement might be the best solution. (But consider throwing an exception instead.)

The *goto* statement is so rare these days that there's no consensus about how the label should be indented. Visual C# .NET indents the single statement that follows the label, as shown in the SieveWithGoto.cs listing. But that looks wrong to me. If you're using the *goto* in one or two extreme cases, it might make more sense to move the label to the left margin so it stands out—conspicuously if not exactly proudly.

Normally, after telling you to avoid the *goto* whenever possible, I'd be finished with the entire subject of the *goto* statement. But I'm not. It may come as a surprise to veteran C or C++ programmers that C# has resurrected the *goto* statement for use in a somewhat different context: the *switch* statement, as you'll see in the next chapter.

28

Switch and Case

Let's write a little calculator program. The program will prompt the user for two numbers (storing them in *dNum1* and *dNum2*) and then prompt for an arithmetic operator:

```
Console.Write("Enter the operation (+, -, *, /, %): ");
string strOp = Console.ReadLine();
```

At this point, you have a string variable named *strOp* that contains a single character that is one of the five C# arithmetic operations. Or maybe not. Maybe the user didn't follow instructions and typed something else. But here's how you can combine five nested if statements into a nice ordered list of comparisons:

```
if (strOp == "+")
    dResult = dNum1 + dNum2;

else if (strOp == "-")
    dResult = dNum1 - dNum2;

else if (strOp == "*")
    dResult = dNum1 * dNum2;

else if (strOp == "/")
    dResult = dNum1 / dNum2;

else if (strOp == "%")
    dResult = dNum1 % dNum2;

else
{
    Console.WriteLine("Incorrect operation");
    dResult = Double.NaN;
}
```

Notice that the last *else* at the bottom takes care of the possibility that the user didn't enter a correct operation. The program displays a terse message and sets the *dResult* variable to NaN (not a number).

Whenever you have a long list of *if* and *else* clauses comparing a single variable with a number of possibilities, you can use an alternative that's a bit cleaner and clearer. It's called the *switch* statement, and it also involves the keywords *case* and *break*:

```
switch (strOp)
{
case "+":
    dResult = dNum1 + dNum2;
    break;

case "-":
    dResult = dNum1 - dNum2;
    break;

case "*":
    dResult = dNum1 * dNum2;
    break;

case "/":
    dResult = dNum1 / dNum2;
    break;

case "%":
    dResult = dNum1 % dNum2;
    break;

default:
    Console.Writeline("Incorrect operation");
    dResult = Double.NaN;
    break;
}
```

The *switch* statement begins with the keyword *switch* and a variable (or an expression) in parentheses. I'm using a *string* variable in this example, but you can also use any integral type, *char*, or an enumeration (which I'll discuss in the next chapter). You can't use a floating-point or *decimal* variable in a *switch* statement. Following the variable in parentheses, the rest of the *switch* statement is enclosed in a pair of curly brackets. The curly brackets are always required.

Within the curly brackets are multiple *switch sections* (as the C# Language Specification, §8.7.2, calls them). These sections generally consist of the keyword *case* followed by a constant and a colon. (That's called a *switch label*.) Very often the constant is a string or a numeric literal, but it could be any constant expression. Within a single *switch* statement, these constants must be unique. If the variable equals the constant, then the code in the *switch* section is executed. No curly brackets are required to enclose the code in each section.

A *switch* statement can have one section labeled *default*. The code in this section is executed only if there's no match with the other sections. The *default* section is not required, and it doesn't have to be the last section, but it's usually placed last to mimic the final *else* clause in a series of nested *if* statements.

Generally, you'll terminate the code in each *switch* section with a *break* statement. The *break* statement causes program flow to hop out of the *switch* statement and continue with the next statement following the *switch* statement. (That's the next statement after the right curly bracket that encloses all the *switch* sections.)

Here's the complete Calculator program. It puts the whole *switch* statement in a *do* loop to implement a better technique for handling incorrect operations.

Calculator.cs

```
// ----------------------------------------------------
// Calculator.cs from "Programming in the Key of C#"
// ----------------------------------------------------
using System;

class Calculator
{
    static void Main()
    {
        double dNum1, dNum2, dResult = 0;
        bool bGotOperation;

        Console.Write("Enter first number: ");
        dNum1 = Double.Parse(Console.ReadLine());

        Console.Write("Enter second number: ");
        dNum2 = Double.Parse(Console.ReadLine());

        do
        {
            Console.Write("Enter the operation (+, -, *, /, %): ");
            string strOp = Console.ReadLine().Trim();
            bGotOperation = true;

            switch (strOp)
            {
            case "+":
                dResult = dNum1 + dNum2;
                break;
```

```
        case "-":
            dResult = dNum1 - dNum2;
            break;

        case "*":
            dResult = dNum1 * dNum2;
            break;

        case "/":
            dResult = dNum1 / dNum2;
            break;

        case "%":
            dResult = dNum1 % dNum2;
            break;

        default:
            Console.WriteLine("Operation {0} is not valid", strOp);
            bGotOperation = false;
            break;
        }
    }
    while (!bGotOperation);

    Console.WriteLine("The result is " + dResult);
    }
}
```

Each section in the *switch* statement begins with the keyword *case* (or *default*) and ends with a *break*. That's the normal way to do it. But there are a few alternatives.

First, let me show you what you *can't* do. You can't leave out a *break* statement and expect program flow to continue from one section to the next:

```
switch (strInstruction)
{
    case "AddFour":
        x += 2;
    case "AddTwo":
        x += 2;
    default:
        Console.WriteLine(x);
        break;
}
```

This looks like something you might want to do. It's called a *fall through*, and it's perfectly legal in C and C++, but it's not legal in C#. As veteran C and C++ programmers can attest, there's just too much danger of forgetting a *break* statement and inadvertently making a fall through.

However, there are ways other than *break* to terminate a *switch* section. The last statement in a *switch* section can be any statement that unconditionally leaves the *switch* statement, such as *return* or *throw* or *goto*. But the rule is actually just a bit more flexible than that. The real rule is simply that you can't allow a fall through. You must prevent the flow of execution dropping from one *switch* section into another. For example, the *C# Language Specification*, §8.6.2, shows a *switch* section that concludes with a *while (true)* statement to create an infinite loop! In a real-life program, something in that infinite loop would have to get out of the loop in some way (such as a *return*, *goto*, or *throw*, or perhaps a call to the method *Environment.Exit*, which terminates a program). An infinite loop that ends a *switch* section cannot contain a *break* statement, however. That would violate the no-fall-through rule.

What you *can* do is use multiple *switch* labels with a single *switch* section. For example, suppose you want to allow the user of the Calculation program to use a lowercase or an uppercase *X* for multiplication. Here's the new *switch* section for multiplication:

```
case "*":
case "x":
case "X":
    dResult = dNum1 * dNum2;
    break;
```

This piece of code doesn't violate the no-fall-through rule because it's considered a single *switch* section. It's allowed because the programmer's intention is obvious.

If you want to jump from one *switch* section to another, C# allows you to do that as well, and it's a bit more flexible than the old fall-through routine. It's a special form of the *goto* statement:

```
switch (strInstruction)
{
    case "AddFour":
        x += 2;
        goto "AddTwo";

    case "AddTwo":
        x += 2;
        goto default;
```

```
default:
    Console.WriteLine(x);
    break;
}
```

The *goto* statement must reference one of the *case* constants or *default*. Using *goto* is more flexible than fall through because you can jump to any *switch* section from the end of any other *switch* section.

The *C# Language Specification*, §8, orders statements into several categories. The selection statements are *if* and *switch*. These statements control the flow of execution based on comparisons or other Boolean operations. The iteration statements are *while*, *do*, *for*, and *foreach*. These are the loops. The jump statements are *return*, *break*, *continue*, *throw*, and *goto*. The jump statements transfer program flow from one place to another. Along with assignment and declaration statements, these statements constitute your basic tools for writing code.

29

Bits and Enumerations

As you know, +, -, *, /, and % are all arithmetic operators that you can use with numeric operands (integers, decimals, and floating points). With Boolean operands, you use the logical operators &, |, ^, &&, and ||. You can't use the arithmetic operators with Boolean operands.

But you can use the Boolean operators &, |, and ^ with integers. Here's a little program that demonstrates it.

BitOperations.cs

```
// --------------------------------------------------------
// BitOperations.cs from "Programming in the Key of C#"
// --------------------------------------------------------
using System;

class BitOperations
{
    static void Main()
    {
        int i1 = 0x1357;    // Bits: 0001-0011-0101-0111
        int i2 = 0x2468;    // Bits: 0010-0100-0110-1000

        Console.WriteLine("And: {0,8:X}\nOr:  {1,8:X}\nXor: {2,8:X}",
                          i1 & i2, i1 | i2, i1 ^ i2);
    }
}
```

Two integers are initialized with numbers in a hexadecimal format, and the *WriteLine* statement displays the results in hexadecimal. Here they are:

```
And:      40
Or:     377F
Xor:    373F
```

When used with integers, these operands are called *bitwise* AND, OR, and XOR operators. They perform Boolean operations on individual bits. Written in bits, *i1* and *i2* are

```
0001-0011-0101-0111
0010-0100-0110-1000
```

On a bit-by-bit basis, perform an AND operation between the two operands. The result is 1 only if both bits are 1. The result is

```
0000-0000-0100-0000
```

or 0x0040. Likewise, you can manually perform OR and XOR operations to verify that the program is working correctly.

These bitwise operations work on *int*, *uint*, *long*, and *ulong* only; you can't use them with 8-bit or 16-bit integers or with the nonintegral numeric types. You can't use the conditional logical operations && and || with integers, but you can use the compound assignment statements &=, |=, and ^=. You can't mix integers and Booleans in a single expression involving one of the operands. This expression won't work:

```
iNumber | bValue    // Not allowed!
```

Both operands must be integers or Booleans.

As I mentioned in Chapter 21, the C programming language doesn't have a Boolean data type. C and C++ programmers instead use integers to represent Boolean values: a 1 means true and a 0 means false. In C and C++, performing a bitwise logical operation is equivalent to performing a Boolean operation.

But that's only part of the reason why these operations exist. In days when memory was scarce and expensive, programmers often tried to pack a lot of information into a small amount of space. A 32-bit integer can store a number, or—if you work with the individual bits—it can store 32 Boolean values, or sixteen 2-bit values, or eight 4-bit values, or any combination that adds up to 32 bits.

Putting a bunch of different pieces of information into a single integer is sometimes known as *packing*; disassembling an integer back into the separate pieces is known as *unpacking*.

These days, bit packing is most prevalent in file formats that store compressed data. If you'll be programming encoders or decoders for graphics image files (such as JPEG or PNG) or movie files (MPEG or AVI) or sound files (like MP3), you'll need a good facility with bit operations.

As I'll discuss toward the end of this chapter, bitwise logical operators also play a part in *enumerations*, which are used extensively in the .NET Framework.

When working with bits, it's sometimes convenient to refer to their state—that is, whether the bit is equal to 1 or 0—using the words *set* (meaning 1) and *clear* (meaning 0). Sometimes the word *reset* is used instead of clear, but I'll avoid that usage. The words *set* and *clear* are also used as verbs when a bit is being changed from one state to another.

It's also convenient to refer to bits by number. Traditionally, bits are numbered starting with the least significant bit, which is assigned the number 0. In a 32-bit integer, the most significant bit (which is the sign bit in an *int*) is assigned the number 31. Here's the number 55 showing the numbering of the bits:

31	30	29	28	27	26	25	24	23	22	21	20	19	18	17	16	15	14	13	12	11	10	9	8	7	6	5	4	3	2	1	0
0	0	0	0	0	0	0	0	0	0	0	0	0	0	0	0	0	0	0	0	0	0	0	0	0	0	1	1	0	1	1	1

This numbering is convenient because an integer with only the *n*th bit set is equal to 2^n. Here are some examples:

The decimal number 1 has only the 0 bit set.
The number 2 has only the 1 bit set. The binary representation of 2 is 10.
4 has only the 2 bit set: 100
8 has only the 3 bit set: 1000
16 or 0x10 has only the 4 bit set: 1-0000
32 or 0x20 has only the 5 bit set: 10-0000
64 or 0x40 has only the 6 bit set: 100-0000.
128 or 0x80 has only the 7 bit set: 1000-0000
256 or 0x100 has only the 8 bit set: 1-0000-0000

Using hexadecimal is often convenient when working with bits because counting the bits is easier. There are 4 bits per hexadecimal digit:

Decimal	Binary	Hexadecimal	Decimal	Binary	Hexadecimal
0	0000	0	8	1000	8
1	0001	1	9	1001	9
2	0010	2	10	1010	A
3	0011	3	11	1011	B
4	0100	4	12	1100	C
5	0101	5	13	1101	D
6	0110	6	14	1110	E
7	0111	7	15	1111	F

Let's suppose you're working with a file that uses 32-bit integers to store some information about people. (So we don't run into problems later, let's suppose that only the lower 31 bits of these integers are used for storing information. The sign bit is always 0.) In these integers, bit number 6 indicates the sex. The bit is 1 for female and 0 for male:

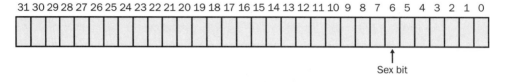

In your program, you store these integers in the variable *iPersonData*. Here's how you can assign a Boolean variable in your program based on the value of the sex bit:

```
bIsFemale = (iPersonData & 0x40) != 0;
```

Such a calculation is sometimes called *testing* the bit. You perform a bitwise AND between the integer and a value (here it's 0x40) with only the bit set that you want to test. If bit 6 in *iPersonData* is set, then the AND expression equals 0x40. If not, then the AND expression equals 0. The AND expression essentially isolates the bit by eliminating all the other bits. The result of the AND expression is compared with 0 to yield a Boolean. The AND expression must be enclosed in parentheses because it has a lower precedence than the equality operands.

You can also go the other way. Suppose you're putting together an *iPersonData* integer from information you have in your program. Here's how you set bit number 6 if *bIsFemale* is *true*:

```
if (bIsFemale)
    iPersonData |= 0x40;
```

The compound assignment statement performs an OR operation of *iPersonData* with the value 0x40. You can alternatively use the conditional operand:

```
iPersonData |= bIsFemale ? 0x40 : 0;
```

Bit number 5 in *iPersonData* might be the "retired" bit. When a person retires, your program can set that bit:

```
iPersonData |= 0x20;
```

But what happens when a person who has been retired returns to work? Bit number 5 must now be cleared. Here's one way to do it:

```
iPersonData &= 0x7FFFFFDF;
```

This statement performs an AND operation with *iPersonData* and a number that is mostly just 1 bits. Wherever a 1 bit appears in that number, the corresponding bit in *iPersonData* remains unchanged. Notice that the second digit from the right is a hexadecimal D (which has the bit pattern 1101). When the AND operation occurs between bit number 5 in *iPersonData* and that 0 bit, the result is 0. The "retired" bit is cleared. (Also notice that the leftmost digit of that long hexadecimal number is a 7—the bit pattern 0111. If we were working with unsigned integers, that leftmost digit could be an F—the bit pattern 1111. But setting that digit to an F creates an *unsigned* integer literal, which can't be implicitly converted to an *int*. Early on, I said that the sign bit in *iPersonData* was not used, so there's no harm in using a 7 for this digit.)

Rather than specifying an integer literal with all the 1 bits sets, as

```
iPersonData &= 0x7FFFFFDF;
```

you can instead use the *bitwise complement* operator, which is the tilde (~). The bitwise complement is a unary operator that flips the states of all bits. The 0's becomes 1's, and the 1's become 0's. That's exactly what we want here:

```
iPersonData &= ~0x20;
```

That statement clears bit number 5. For comparison,

```
iPersonData |= 0x20;
```

sets bit number 5 and

```
iPersonData ^= 0x20;
```

flips the bit. It changes a 1 bit to a 0, or a 0 bit to a 1. None of these operations affects any other bit.

The bitwise complement is very close to the unary minus operator. As I discussed in Chapter 8, an integer stored in 2's complement is negated by flipping all the bits (that's the bitwise complement) and adding 1. Don't confuse the bitwise complement with the logical negation, which is the exclamation point. The logical negation works only with Boolean values, and changes *true* to *false* and *false* to *true*.

Suppose *iPersonData* stores some other information about a person. For example, the person's age is stored in bits 8 through 14:

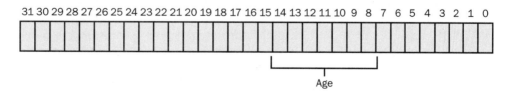

Those 7 bits are sufficient to represent ages up to 127. How would you extract these bits to store the age in a variable named *iAge*?

First, let's look at the expression

```
(iPersonData & 0x7F00)
```

In a context like this, the 0x7F00 constant is sometimes called a *mask*. It successfully eliminates everything except the 7 bits we want to look at, but unfortunately these bits are still somewhere in the middle of the result. For example, if the encoded age is 63, the result of that AND expression is 0x3F00, or 16,128 in decimal.

You can turn this number into something usable with a division, and specifically, a division by a power of two. That power is the number of bits at the right you want to ignore. In this case, there are 8 bits on the right you want to ignore, so you divide by 2^8 or 256:

```
iAge = (iPersonData & 0x7F00) / 256;
```

But there's a better way to perform operations like this, and that's by using *shift* operations. The operator >> shifts all the bits in an integer right by a specified number of bits. For example, if a particular integer has the following bits set:

31	30	29	28	27	26	25	24	23	22	21	20	19	18	17	16	15	14	13	12	11	10	9	8	7	6	5	4	3	2	1	0
0	0	0	0	0	0	0	0	0	0	0	0	0	0	0	0	0	1	0	0	1	1	0	1	0	0	1	1	0	1	1	1

then shifting the integer right by 8 bits results in the following:

31	30	29	28	27	26	25	24	23	22	21	20	19	18	17	16	15	14	13	12	11	10	9	8	7	6	5	4	3	2	1	0
0	0	0	0	0	0	0	0	0	0	0	0	0	0	0	0	0	0	0	0	0	0	0	0	0	1	0	0	1	1	0	1

The original rightmost 8 bits are lost in this operation.

Here's the code to shift the age bits right 8 bits:

```
iAge = (iPersonData & 0x7F00) >> 8;
```

Using the shift rather than the division has several advantages: The code is certainly clearer. The shift indicates the number of bits to shift and doesn't involve a power of two that may be somewhat more obscure. The shift is also considerably more efficient. Shift instructions implemented in microprocessors are much faster than divisions. (In fact, most compilers will detect if an expression involves a multiplication or division by a power of two and substitute a shift instruction instead.)

You can alternatively perform the shift before the mask:

```
iAge = iPersonData >> 8 & 0x7F;
```

Notice that the AND operation is with 0x7F rather than 0x7F00. Also, you don't need the parentheses because the shift has higher precedence than the bitwise logical operations.

Suppose you need to set bits 8 through 13 in *iPersonData* based on the value of *iAge*. You can use a left shift for that:

```
iPersonData |= iAge << 8;    // Possibly problematic
```

In this statement, you're first shifting *iAge* left 8 bits, essentially *multiplying* the value by 256. The OR operation merges that value into *iPersonData* without affecting anything else.

So why did I indicate that the statement was "possibly problematic"? Suppose some other age were already encoded in *iPersonData*. Any bits already set would continue to be set. What you probably want to do first is clear bits 8 through 13 before setting the new age:

```
iPersonData &= ~(0x7F << 8);
iPersonData |= iAge << 8;
```

The first statement shifts the value 0x7F left 8 bits and then performs a bitwise complement. The result is the number 0xFFFF80FF. The logical AND operation keeps all the bits intact except those in positions 8 through 13. Those are cleared.

A few details about the shift operations. The left side of the operand—the number that gets shifted—can be only an *int*, a *uint*, a *long*, or a *ulong*. The value on the right side of the operand (which is referred to as the *count*) must be an *int*. Because it doesn't make much sense to shift a 32-bit integer more than 31 bits, only the lowest 5 bits of the count are used. When shifting a *long* or a *ulong*, only the lowest 6 bits of the count value are used. A shift value of 0 has no effect on the left operand.

C# also allows left shift and right shift compound assignment operators. The shift count goes to the right of the equal sign. The statement

```
i <<= 4;
```

shifts the value of *i* left 4 bits and stores the result back in *i*.

There's a special rule involving shifting signed integers right. When an *int* or a *long* is shifted right, the sign bit is shifted into lower bits, but the sign bit itself remains the same. For example, suppose you start with an integer that equals 65,536:

```
int i = 0x10000;
```

Here are the bits:

```
31 30 29 28 27 26 25 24 23 22 21 20 19 18 17 16 15 14 13 12 11 10 9 8 7 6 5 4 3 2 1 0
 0  0  0  0  0  0  0  0  0  0  0  0  0  0  0  1  0  0  0  0  0  0 0 0 0 0 0 0 0 0 0 0
```

You can shift it left 15 bits like this:

```
i <<= 15;
```

The 1 bit shifts into the high spot:

```
31 30 29 28 27 26 25 24 23 22 21 20 19 18 17 16 15 14 13 12 11 10 9 8 7 6 5 4 3 2 1 0
 1  0  0  0  0  0  0  0  0  0  0  0  0  0  0  0  0  0  0  0  0  0 0 0 0 0 0 0 0 0 0 0
```

The result is 0x80000000 or - 2,147,483,648. Now shift the variable right 15 bits:

```
i >>= 15;
```

As the variable is shifted right, the sign bit remains set:

```
31 30 29 28 27 26 25 24 23 22 21 20 19 18 17 16 15 14 13 12 11 10 9 8 7 6 5 4 3 2 1 0
 1  1  1  1  1  1  1  1  1  1  1  1  1  1  1  1  0  0  0  0  0  0 0 0 0 0 0 0 0 0 0 0
```

The final result is 0xFFFF0000 or - 65,536.

The right shift for signed integers is called an *arithmetic* shift because the sign of the integer is preserved. All other shifts are *logical* shifts, which means that the sign bit is treated as any other bit. In particular, an *int* or a *long* shifted left could change from negative to positive or from positive to negative, as we've just seen. Shifting never raises an overflow condition. All this information is succinctly summarized in the *C# Language Specification*, §7.8.

In some cases, you need to deal with bit positions that are themselves stored in variables. For example, suppose the variable *iBit* is a bit position. You want to know whether that bit is set in *iValue*. Here's an expression involving *iValue* and *iBit*:

```
iValue & (1 << iBit)
```

This expression is nonzero if the *iBit* bit is set. Notice that 1 is shifted left *iBit* positions. If *iBit* equals 0, the value 1 is not shifted at all, which is correct. You're then testing the bit in position 0. You can also use the expression

```
(iValue >> iBit) & 1
```

Suppose you need to store a lot of stuff in a file, including dates. A date is a year, a month, and a day, and today we'd feel few qualms if we used an integer or even text for each of the three items. But if you examine the actual values, a day never exceeds 31, so you really only need to devote 5 bits for the day. Similarly, you need 4 bits for the month and 11 or 12 bits for the year (depending on whether you want to store dates of 2048 and later).

Here's a program that packs a date (a year, a month, and a day) into a single integer. It doesn't do any validity checking and retains the common 1-based nature of the day and month.

DatePack.cs

```csharp
// ----------------------------------------------------
// DatePack.cs from "Programming in the Key of C#"
// ----------------------------------------------------
using System;

class DatePack
{
    static void Main()
    {
        Console.Write("Enter the year: ");
        int iYear = Int32.Parse(Console.ReadLine());

        Console.Write("Enter the month: ");
        int iMonth = Int32.Parse(Console.ReadLine());

        Console.Write("Enter the day: ");
        int iDay = Int32.Parse(Console.ReadLine());

        // Pack the date.

        int iDate = (iYear << 9) | (iMonth << 5) | iDay;

        Console.WriteLine("Packed date: {0:X}", iDate);

        // Unpack the date.

        iYear = iDate >> 9;
        iMonth = (iDate >> 5) & 0xF;
        iDay = iDate & 0x1F;

        Console.WriteLine("Year: {0} Month: {1} Day: {2}",
                          iYear, iMonth, iDay);
    }
}
```

You might encounter bitwise operations in a particular programming application (for example, dealing with file formats that store compressed data), or you might decide that bitwise operations are appropriate in a particular programming job. You might also encounter bitwise operations when you're working with the .NET Framework, for example, when doing Web or Windows programming. In the .NET Framework, bitwise operations are disguised somewhat; you'll probably encounter them mostly when working with *enumerations*.

Enumerations are basically collections of integral constants; although some enumerations involve the use of bitwise operations, not all of them do so. Enumerations can help you write bug-free and simpler programs in two ways.

First, enumerations help you make sure that method arguments are exactly what they're supposed to be. For example, suppose you want to write a method that determines if a particular day of the week is a weekend. If the integer 0 represents Sunday, 1 represents Monday, and so forth, here's how you might write such a method:

```
public bool IsWeekEnd(int iDayOfWeek)
{
    return iDayOfWeek == 0 || iDayOfWeek == 6;
}
```

This method returns *true* if the parameter equals 0 (Sunday) or 6 (Saturday). The problem with such a method is that the C# compiler will allow *any* integer to be passed as an argument to the method. For example, this expression would be perfectly valid:

```
IsWeekEnd(iMonth)
```

But it's probably wrong. As you can surmise from the variable name, the *iMonth* variable passed as an argument to *IsWeekEnd* is probably not an integer representing a day of week. You can avoid such errors by using an enumeration. Declaring an enumeration is very similar to declaring a series of constants. Here's how you might declare a *DayOfWeek* enumeration:

```
enum DayOfWeek
{
    Sunday,
    Monday,
    Tuesday,
    Wednesday,
    Thursday,
    Friday,
    Saturday
}
```

The keyword *enum* is followed by an identifier. The enumeration body is enclosed in a set of curly brackets. The enumeration members inside the curly brackets are separated by commas.

Members of the enumeration are assigned consecutive constant values beginning at 0. You refer to each member by the enumeration name (*DayOf-Week*) followed by a period and the member name. For example, *DayOf-Week.Sunday* is equivalent to 0, *DayOfWeek.Monday* is equivalent to 1, and so forth. The member cannot be specified by itself. It must be preceded by the enumeration name. It's possible to declare an enumeration inside a class, just like a method or a field, but it's more common to declare an enumeration external to any class or structure. If you need a *DayOfWeek* enumeration in one of your programs, you don't need to declare it yourself. This particular enumeration happens to be already declared in the *System* namespace of the .NET Framework, and you can use it in any programs that you write.

You can use the enumeration like other data types. If you need a particular variable to represent the day of the week, you can declare it as a variable of type *DayOfWeek* like so:

```
DayOfWeek dw;
```

Normally you can only assign this variable a member of the *DayOfWeek* enumeration:

```
dw = DayOfWeek.Friday;
```

But you can cast an integer to an enumeration member:

```
dw = (DayOfWeek) 3
```

Or you can cast an enumeration member into an integer:

```
(int) DayOfWeek.Wednesday
```

Here's a better *IsWeekEnd* method that uses the *DayOfWeek* enumeration:

```
public bool IsWeekEnd(DayOfWeek dw)
{
    return dw == DayOfWeek.Sunday || dw == DayOfWeek.Saturday;
}
```

This method must be called with a *DayOfWeek* member:

```
IsWeekEnd(DayOfWeek.Monday)
```

or with a *DayOfWeek* variable such as the *dw* variable declared earlier:

```
IsWeekEnd(dw)
```

or with an integer explicitly cast to a *DayOfWeek* value:

```
IsWeekEnd((DayOfWeek) iDayOfWeek)
```

There's much less chance of passing an invalid argument to this method.

Enumerations are supported by the *Enum* class declared in the *System* namespace. The *Enum* class has *ToString* and *Parse* methods that you can use with enumerations. Although *Enum* is a class, enumerations themselves are value types, and they always have an underlying integral type, which by default is *int*. You can specify the integral type in the enumeration declaration:

```
enum DayOfWeek: ushort
```

Although the enumeration members are normally assigned values beginning with 0, you can override that by specifying a value of any or all members. For example,

```
enum DayOfWeek
{
    Sunday,
    Monday,
    Tuesday,
    Wednesday = 8,
    Thursday,
    Friday,
    Saturday
}
```

In this case, *DayOfWeek.Tuesday* is equivalent to 2, *DayOfWeek.Wednesday* is equivalent to 8, *DayOfWeek.Thursday* is equivalent to 9, and so forth.

I mentioned earlier that there are *two* ways that enumerations can improve your programs. The second way involves the bitwise OR operator. Because enumerations are basically integers, you can use the bitwise operations on enumeration members. That turns out to be very useful when a method requires a lot of Boolean information. For example, here's another enumeration as it's probably declared in the *System.Globalization* namespace. (I say *probably* because I haven't seen the source code of the .NET Framework.)

```
public enum NumberStyles
{
    None = 0,
    AllowLeadingWhite = 0x0001,
    AllowTrailingWhite = 0x0002,
    AllowLeadingSign = 0x0004,
    Integer = AllowLeadingWhite | AllowTrailingWhite | AllowLeadingSign,
    AllowTrailingSign = 0x0008,
    AllowParentheses = 0x0010,
```

```
    AllowDecimalPoint = 0x0020,
    AllowThousands = 0x0040,
    Number = Integer | AllowTrailingSign | AllowDecimalPoint | AllowThousands,
    AllowExponent = 0x0080,
    Float = Integer | AllowDecimalPoint | AllowExponent,
    AllowCurrencySymbol = 0x0100,
    Currency = Integer | AllowTrailingSign | AllowParentheses |
                    AllowDecimalPoint | AllowThousands | AllowCurrencySymbol,
    Any = AllowCurrency | AllowExponent,
    AllowHexSpecifier = 0x0200,
    HexNumber = AllowHexSpecifier | AllowLeadingWhite | AllowTrailingWhite
}
```

Many of these members are declared as individual bits. These are often known as *flags*. Other members are combinations of these individual bits. You can use this enumeration in overloads of the *Parse* methods of all the numeric types. These overloads have a second parameter that is declared to be of type *NumberStyles*. This parameter lets you specify that *Parse* allow or disallow text that contains certain categories of characters.

For example, suppose you want to turn some text into a *decimal*. You want to allow white space before or after the number, and you want to allow decimal points, but you don't want to allow negative signs, thousands separators, or anything else. Use the bitwise OR operator to combine the appropriate members of the *NumberStyles* enumeration, like this:

```
decimal mValue = Decimal.Parse(str, NumberStyles.AllowLeadingWhite |
        NumberStyles.AllowTrailingWhite | NumberStyles.AllowDecimalPoint);
```

Imagine if *Parse* had individual Boolean parameters for all the various options. That would be 10 Boolean parameters! Combining all these options into one parameter wouldn't be possible without packing and unpacking bits.

30

Parameters and Arguments

This tiny program illustrates an important fact about the inability of methods to change variables that are passed to them as arguments:

```
ValueParameters.cs
// -------------------------------------------------------
// ValueParameters.cs from "Programming in the Key of C#"
// -------------------------------------------------------
using System;

class ValueParameters
{
    static void Main()
    {
        int i = 0;
        ChangeInteger(i);
        Console.WriteLine(i);
    }
    static void ChangeInteger(int i)
    {
        i = 55;
    }
}
```

The *Main* method in this program calls the *ChangeInteger* method, passing to the method an integer initialized to zero. *Main* then displays the integer. Despite the fact that *ChangeInteger* sets its parameter to 55, the program displays the result:

0

In the normal case, when one method calls another, the arguments passed to the method are essentially *copied* and become local variables to the method. A method often uses these parameters in some way, but it can also change the variables without causing any change to the originals. The purpose of methods is usually not to change the arguments that are passed to them but rather to do something with the arguments and perhaps to return a value. As the name of the previous program suggests, method parameters declared in the normal way are called *value parameters*.

There are times, however, when you *do* want to change the original variables passed as arguments to a method. The classic example involves swapping the values of two variables, for example, *i1* and *i2*. To swap two variables, you need a third variable that you use for temporarily storing the value of one variable before you set it to the other variable:

```
int iTemp = i1;
i1 = i2;
i2 = iTemp;
```

At first, putting this code in a little method seems easy:

```
static void Swap(int i1, int i2)
{
    int iTemp = i1;
    i1 = i2;
    i2 = iTemp;
}
```

But if you tried to call this method, like so:

```
Swap(iMyAge, iYourAge);
```

you would discover that the variables *iMyAge* and *iYourAge* were not swapped.

To write a *Swap* method that does what you want it to do, you need to declare the parameters as *reference parameters*. To do this, you use the *ref* keyword in front of the type of each value parameter:

```
static void Swap(ref int i1, ref int i2)
{
    int iTemp = i1;
    i1 = i2;
    i2 = iTemp;
}
```

What the *ref* keyword does is quite drastic. Instead of the method receiving a copy of each argument passed to the method, it now receives a *reference* to each argument. The method then has the ability to change the original variable. Fortunately, aside from specifying the *ref* keyword, you don't have to worry about the complications involved in how the method uses these references, or even what these references *are* precisely.

Here's a complete program that declares and uses this *Swap* method:

ReferenceParameters.cs
```
// ------------------------------------------------------------
// ReferenceParameters.cs from "Programming in the Key of C#"
// ------------------------------------------------------------
using System;

class ReferenceParameters
{
    static void Main()
    {
        int iMyAge = 50

        Console.Write("Enter your age: ");
        int iYourAge = Int32.Parse(Console.ReadLine());

        Console.WriteLine("My age: {0} Your age: {1}", iMyAge, iYourAge);
        Swap(ref iMyAge, ref iYourAge);
        Console.WriteLine("My age: {0} Your age: {1}", iMyAge, iYourAge);
    }
    static void Swap(ref int i1, ref int i2)
    {
        int iTemp = i1;
        i1 = i2;
        i2 = iTemp;
    }
}
```

Notice that *Main* also had to use the *ref* keyword when calling the *Swap* method:

```
Swap(ref iMyAge, ref iYourAge);
```

You can mix value parameters and reference parameters in the same method. You just have to be consistent when declaring the method and calling the method.

A similar keyword to *ref* is *out*, which you use to declare *output parameters*. You generally use output parameters when you need to write a method that returns more than one result. Here's an example of a method that implements the formulas to determine the three angles of an oblique triangle based on the three sides:

OutputParameters.cs

```
// ----------------------------------------------------------
// OutputParameters.cs from "Programming in the Key of C#"
// ----------------------------------------------------------
using System;

class OutputParameters
{
    static void Main()
    {
        double dSide1 = 50, dSide2 = 60, dSide3 = 100;
        double dAngle1, dAngle2, dAngle3;

        TriangleAngles(dSide1, dSide2, dSide3,
                    out dAngle1, out dAngle2, out dAngle3);

        Console.WriteLine("{0} + {1} + {2} = {3}",
                    dAngle1, dAngle2, dAngle3,
                    dAngle1 + dAngle2 + dAngle3);
    }
    static void TriangleAngles(double A, double B, double C,
            out double alpha, out double beta, out double gamma)
    {
        alpha = Math.Acos((B * B + C * C - A * A) / (2 * B * C));
        beta  = Math.Acos((A * A + C * C - B * B) / (2 * A * C));
        gamma = Math.Acos((A * A + B * B - C * C) / (2 * A * B));
    }
}
```

The names of the parameters to the *TriangleAngles* method are those used in the book from which I copied the formulas. The three sides are *A*, *B*, and *C*. The opposite angles are *alpha*, *beta*, and *gamma*.

Remember that the *Math* class does all trigonometric calculations using radians. The *Console.WriteLine* method displays the values of all three angles and also displays the sum to check whether the program is working properly; the sum is equal to π radians, which is 180°.

Reference parameters and output parameters are very similar. In fact, *ref* and *out* are implemented in intermediate language (IL) in exactly the same way. In C#, however, a *ref* argument must be set to some value before the method is called. The idea is that the method has the ability to both use the *ref* parameter and to alter it. An *out* argument can be uninitialized when a method is called, but the method is required to set the value of any *out* parameter.

In summary, a *ref* argument must be set before the method is called; an *out* parameter must be set by the method.

Methods with reference and output parameters in the .NET Framework are fairly rare, but the *Double* structure has a method named *TryParse* that has an output parameter. As you know, the *Parse* method throws an exception if you pass a string that contains improper characters. The *TryParse* method does not raise an exception. Instead, its Boolean return value is *true* if the method was successful in converting the string to a *double* and *false* if it encountered a problem. Because the return value is a Boolean, the actual *double* that the method creates from the string must be an output parameter. Here's a program that demonstrates its use.

TryParseDemo.cs

```
// ------------------------------------------------------
// TryParseDemo.cs from "Programming in the Key of C#"
// ------------------------------------------------------
using System;
using System.Globalization;

class TryParseDemo
{
    static void Main()
    {
        double dResult;

        Console.Write("Enter a double: ");
        string strInput = Console.ReadLine();
        bool bSuccess = Double.TryParse(strInput, NumberStyles.Any,
                                        null, out dResult);

        if (bSuccess)
            Console.WriteLine("You typed " + dResult);
        else
            Console.WriteLine("The string was an invalid double.");
    }
}
```

TryParse has four parameters. The second parameter is any combination of *NumberStyles* members combined with the bitwise OR operation. The third parameter is optional; you can use it to force *TryParse* to use thousands separators and currency signs associated with other regions of the world. The fourth parameter is an output parameter that returns the *double* value.

I said earlier that normal value parameters (those declared without *ref* or *out*) can be altered by the method without affecting the original variables passed as arguments to the method; however, that's not entirely true. If the parameter is itself a reference type, the method can make changes to the original object.

One such reference type is an array. The following program is very similar to the ValueParameters program at the beginning of this chapter except that it uses an array of integers rather than just an integer.

ArrayValueParameter.cs

```
// -----------------------------------------------------------
// ArrayValueParameter.cs from "Programming in the Key of C#"
// -----------------------------------------------------------
using System;

class ArrayValueParameter
{
    static void Main()
    {
        int[] aiNumbers = new int[5];
        ChangeArray(aiNumbers);
        Console.WriteLine(aiNumbers[0]);
    }
    static void ChangeArray(int[] ai)
    {
        ai[0] = 55;
        ai = null;
    }
}
```

The *Main* method creates an integer array with five elements. As usual, the array elements are automatically initialized to 0. The entire array is passed to the *ChangeArray* method. *ChangeArray* sets the first element of the array to 0, and also sets the array itself to *null*. When you run this program you get the output

55

which means that *ChangeArray* really did change the array without the benefit of the *ref* keyword. But *ChangeArray* also sets *ai* to *null*. That seems to have no effect on the original *aiNumbers* array; otherwise the *Console.WriteLine* call would raise an exception.

When *Main* calls *ChangeArray*, a copy is made of *aiNumbers*. But *aiNumbers* is a reference. It refers to the area of memory in the heap where the array is stored. Any copy of *aiNumbers* is simply another reference to the same area of memory! That means that *ChangeArray* can change the elements of the array. However, when *ChangeArray* sets its parameter to *null*, only the copy of the reference is affected.

If the parameter to *ChangeArray* had been declared as *ref*, then the parameter would be a reference to another reference. The last statement of the *ChangeArray* method would have set the original array to *null*, and the *Console.WriteLine* call would have failed.

I'll have more to say about this issue in Chapter 34. How a method can change an object is one of the differences between classes and structures.

As you've discovered in using classes and methods declared in the .NET Framework, a class can contain multiple methods that have the same name but different parameters. These are known as *overloads* of the method. Each method has a unique *signature*, which is the number of parameters and their types, including any *ref* or *out* modifiers. The return type does not contribute to the signature. In other words, you can't have two methods that differ only by return type. Examples of methods that have many overloads are *Console.Write-Line* and just about any method in the *Convert* class.

The C# compiler matches a method call to the correct overload based on the number and types of the arguments. In some cases, implicit conversions must be performed, and some ambiguity might exist regarding which method is actually best matched to the method call. The *C# Language Specification*, §7.4.2, discusses overload resolution, which is how the compiler determines which overload is invoked when a method is called.

You might be working with a program in which it's handy to have a method that calculates the average of two numbers:

```
static decimal Average(decimal m1, decimal m2)
{
    return (m1 + m2) / 2;
}
```

You might then discover that your program sometimes requires averaging three numbers rather than just two. To accommodate those cases, you can declare an additional method that is also named *Average*:

```
static decimal Average(decimal m1, decimal m2, decimal m3)
{
    return (m1 + m2 + m3) / 3;
}
```

And if you then discover you sometimes need to average four decimal numbers, you could declare another overload:

```
static decimal Average(decimal m1, decimal m2, decimal m3, decimal m4)
{
    return (Average(m1, m2) + Average(m3, m4)) / 2;
}
```

This overload makes use of the *Average* method with two arguments.

You could go on and on like this. But once you realize that you need *Average* methods with five, six, or even seven or eight arguments, you might wonder whether a more generalized approach is available. If the multiple *decimal* values were stored in an array, you could write a generalized *Average* method that works with *decimal* arrays of any size:

```
static decimal Average(decimal[] amValues)
{
    decimal mTotal = 0;

    foreach(decimal mValue in amValues)
        mTotal += mValue;

    return mTotal / amValues.Length;
}
```

Calling this method with an array of decimal values is easy:

```
mAverage = Average(amData);
```

But it's also fairly easy to create a decimal array right in the method call and to initialize the array with any number of decimal literals or variables. Here's an example in which *Average* is called with three decimal literals and two decimal variables:

```
mAverage = Average(new decimal[] { 35.4m, mRadius, 24.2m, 76.8m, mZed });
```

Declaring a method with an array parameter is a good way to generalize the method for dealing with an indeterminate number of variables. But C# provides a somewhat easier way of calling a method that implements an array parameter.

You first need to include the keyword *params* before the array type in the parameter list:

```
static decimal Average(params decimal[] amValues)
{
    decimal mTotal = 0;

    foreach(decimal mValue in amValues)
        mTotal += mValue;

    return mTotal / amValues.Length;
}
```

The only difference is the *params* keyword. The method is otherwise exactly the same as the one shown previously. Such a parameter is known as a *parameter array*.

When the method is declared with *params*, you can still call the method using an array:

```
mAverage = Average(amData);
```

But you no longer need to explicitly create an array when you wish to take the average of a bunch of discrete values or variables. Earlier I showed you how to create this array:

```
mAverage = Average(new decimal[] { 35.4m, mRadius, 24.2m, 76.8m, mZed });
```

When the method parameter is declared with the *params* keyword, you can pass the values directly:

```
mAverage = Average(35.4m, mRadius, 24.2m, 76.8m, mZed);
```

Passing the values directly is the big difference that *params* makes. The array is still created behind the scenes because that's how the *Average* method gets the values; however, you don't have to include the array-creation code in the method call.

There are several restrictions on using parameter arrays: The array parameter must have a single dimension only. If there are multiple parameters to the method, only one of the parameters can be a *params* parameter, and it must be the last parameter in the parameter list.

We've already encountered methods in the .NET Framework that use a parameters array. The *String.Format* method has a generalized form where the first parameter is a formatting string, followed by any number of arguments:

```
public static string Format(string format, params object[] args)
```

The same syntax is also used in the *Console.WriteLine* method:

```
public static void WriteLine(string format, params object[] args)
```

In most cases, there's a one-to-one correspondence between the parameters listed in the method declaration and the arguments passed to the method when the method is called. This direct correspondence probably explains why the words *parameter* and *argument* are frequently interchanged. But when you use the *params* keyword, it's possible for multiple arguments to be consolidated into a single parameter.

If you use a parameters array as I did in an overload of the *Average* method, don't delete all the overloads you created earlier that have two, three, or four arguments. If you call *Average* with three arguments:

```
Average(35.4m, 29.55m, 67.2m)
```

the compiler will select the overload with three parameters rather than go to the trouble of creating an array. The array construction takes time and memory, and the method with three explicit parameters is more efficient.

As you saw earlier, the *Average* method with four parameters performed its calculation by twice calling the *Average* method with two parameters. That's certainly allowed.

A method can also call *itself*. Such a method is called a *recursive* method. Obviously a method can't call itself indefinitely, which would be similar to an infinite loop. There must be some way for the recursive calls to stop.

The classic example is a factorial calculation. A factorial is symbolized by the exclamation point. For positive integers, the factorial calculation is calculated by multiplying all integers from 1 through the number:

N! equals $1 \times 2 \times 3 \times 4 \times \ldots \times N$

Thus, 5! equals 120. Zero factorial is also defined to equal 1. You can also express the factorial calculation as

N! equals $N \times (N - 1)!$

and that's the key to writing a factorial method recursively. (You can also write a factorial calculation using a *for* loop.) Here's the program.

RecursiveMethod.cs

```
// ----------------------------------------------------
// RecursiveMethod.cs from "Programming in the Key of C#"
// ----------------------------------------------------
using System;

class RecursiveMethod
{
    static void Main()
    {
        Console.Write("Enter a long integer: ");
        long lInput = Int64.Parse(Console.ReadLine());

        Console.WriteLine("{0} factorial is {1}",
                        lInput, Factorial(lInput));
    }
    static long Factorial(long lNum)
    {
        if (lNum < 0)
            throw new ArgumentOutOfRangeException();

        else if (lNum < 2)
            return 1;

        else
            return checked(lNum * Factorial(lNum - 1));
    }
}
```

The *Factorial* method doesn't allow negative parameters and returns 1 if the parameter is 0 or 1. Otherwise, it multiplies the parameter by the value returned from calling the method with the argument minus 1.

I've put the multiplication in a *checked* statement because factorials can get very big very quickly, and it makes no sense to allow overflow. The value of 21! is too large to fit in a *long*. You may find it interesting to plug a larger number (such as 100) into this program. When the exception is displayed on the console, you'll get a list of statements showing what method calls were involved at the time of the exception. This list is known as a *stack trace*. Aside from storing local variables, the stack also stores information necessary to execute the *return* statement. When a program prematurely terminates, the stack contains information about all the nested method calls that may have been in effect. For the RecursiveMethod program, the stack trace is largely a list of identical method calls—all involving *Factorial*.

You may want to input an even larger number into the RecursiveMethod program (such as 10,000 if you're compiling in Debug mode or 40,000 in Release mode). I've gotten the simple message

```
Unhandled Exception:
   Exception.ToString() failed.
```

that appears to me to indicate that the string containing the stack trace list was too long to process.

In years gone by, recursive methods (or functions or procedures as they're called in other languages) were limited by the size of the program stack. Because stack memory is required for each recursive call, using up all the stack memory was a distinct possibility. These days, stacks are much larger, but you still may encounter a *StackOverflowException*. Try removing the *checked* statement in RecursiveMethod and typing in 50,000. Recursive calls would be limited even more if the method declared local variables because all the local variables in all the recursive calls would be saved on the stack.

If you look at the table of Operator Precedence and Associativity on the inside back cover of this book, you'll find that you've encountered all the operators except *typeof*, *sizeof*, *is*, and *as*. I'm not going to discuss *sizeof* in this book, but the others are all connected with creating and using objects of various types.

It's now time to plunge into object-oriented programming.

Part IV

Objects

Preludio III.

Vivace. (♩· = 92.)

```
int i = 2;
if (strNote(1) == '#')
    iNote++;
```

31

Encapsulating Data

Objects are basically data. The term wasn't used back in the days when the only pieces of data in programs were numbers and text. It seems a bit pompous to call a mere integer an object (although integers surely qualify). The term became truly useful only when techniques evolved in programming languages to consolidate and encapsulate different pieces of data in useful and flexible ways.

It's important to understand the difference between classes, structures, and objects. In C#, an object is an instance of a structure or a class. Several structures and classes in the .NET Framework represent the basic data types in C#: *System.Boolean*, *System.Byte*, *System.Char*, *System.Int16*, *System.Int32*, *System.Int64*, and *System.String*. These structures and classes exist regardless of any programs you write. Your programs create instances of these structures and classes by declaring variables and constants. These variables and constants are objects. So are numeric and string literals. Objects don't really come into existence until your program actually runs.

Although the basic C# types are indispensable, many real-world applications supplement these basic types with types that are more sophisticated and interesting. We've already had a few encounters with some such classes and objects. The Haiku program in Chapter 18 used a class named *System.Random* to create an object named *rand* that generated random numbers. The *SystemException* classes and their descendents store information about program exceptions. In both cases, the keyword *new* was required to create the object—an instance of the class.

Not all classes are used for creating objects. The *System.Console* and *System.Math* class contain only static methods and fields. These methods and fields are associated with the classes themselves rather than any instances of the class. In fact, you cannot create objects from these classes. A statement like

```
Console cons = new Console();   // Not allowed
```

will not pass the compiler. It is said that these classes cannot be *instantiated*. Several programs in Chapter 17 demonstrated how you can create your own classes containing solely static methods and fields. But a class or structure designed to be instantiated must contain at least one *instance* field.

Suppose you're working on a program that has to deal with dates in the form of months, days, and years. Many computer programs need to work with dates in some way, and dates can involve some messy calculations. You could store a date as three integers:

```
int iYear, iMonth, iDay;
```

But it would be much more convenient to deal with a date as a single entity rather than three discrete variables.

The idea that it's *more convenient* to deal with a date as an entity in itself is an initial impetus behind object-oriented programming. The first step in such a process is to *generalize*, and with dates this is fairly obvious. A generalized date is a year, month, and day. A specific date is July 20, 1969. Such a specific date is only one possible instance of the *Date* class (or whatever we choose to call it). Eventually, you'll be able to deal with dates with as much ease as integers and strings. All the messy code and data involved will be hidden away in a class that you can treat as a black box.

If you've been exploring the .NET Framework, you may have discovered a structure named *DateTime* in the *System* namespace, which you use to represent a particular date and time. *DateTime* is a very useful and very important structure, and you should eventually explore it on your own. But for now, perhaps you don't need all the bells and whistles in *DateTime*, or perhaps you'd just prefer to use something you know inside and out. At any rate, let's create a new structure named *Date*. By the time you explore *DateTime*, you'll have some real insights into what's inside, and you'll have a much better appreciation for it.

Traditionally—even before the era of classes and objects—programming languages allowed multiple variables to be consolidated in entities sometimes referred to as *programmer-defined* data types, or *compound* data types, but very often named *structures*. This declaration of a structure would be familiar to C programmers:

```
struct Date
{
    int iYear;
    int iMonth;
    int iDay;
}
```

You follow the *struct* keyword by the structure name, which is an identifier that you make up. The body of the structure is enclosed in curly brackets. This particular structure has three members, all of which are fields.

Although that C-style structure is also valid in C#, it wouldn't be very useful. The structure fields need to be accessible from outside the structure, so they require the keyword *public*. Here's the first version of the C# *Date* structure:

```
struct Date
{
    public int iYear;
    public int iMonth;
    public int iDay;
}
```

You'll recall the use of the *public* keyword in Chapter 17, when I showed how to declare a class containing some static methods and fields. The use of *public* allows a member of a class or structure to be referenced from code outside the class or structure.

Just as importantly, the three fields in the *Date* structure do *not* include the *static* keyword. The absence of the *static* keyword means that these are *instance* fields rather than static fields. There is no *instance* keyword. Fields and methods are instance by default, which indicates the importance of instance fields to the C# language.

We've had frequent contact with both instance methods and static methods. The expression

```
iValue.ToString()
```

involves an instance method that applies to a particular integer—an instance of the *Int32* structure. The expression

```
Int32.Parse(str);
```

involves a static method. You refer to a static method by prefacing it with the structure name. You don't need an instance of the *Int32* structure to call *Parse*.

We've also had encounters with static fields, such as the *PI* field in the *Math* class. (Actually *PI* is a constant, but a constant field is also implicitly static.) You refer to that field using the name of the class followed by the field name:

```
Math.PI
```

Instance fields are different. You do *not* refer to these fields using the structure name. For example, you can't set the *iYear* field of the *Date* structure like this:

```
Date.iYear = 1969;    // Won't work.
```

To represent a particular date, you first need an instance of the *Date* structure, which you can get by declaring a variable of type *Date*:

```
Date dateMoonWalk;
```

When you declare a variable based on a structure, memory from the stack is set aside for the variable.

When naming instances of classes or structures, I like to use a Hungarian Notation prefix that's a lowercase version or abbreviation of the class or structure name. You can refer to the *dateMoonWalk* variable as "an object of type *Date*" or "an instance of the *Date* structure." You reference the structure fields using this variable name. You can set the fields like so:

```
dateMoonWalk.iYear = 1969;
```

Or reference them just as easily:

```
Console.WriteLine("The year of the first moon walk was " +
                  dateMoonWalk.iYear);
```

But before we get too far adrift, let's look at an actual complete program.

SimpleDateStructureProgram.cs

```
// ----------------------------------------------------------------
// SimpleDateStructureProgram.cs from "Programming in the Key of C#"
// ----------------------------------------------------------------
using System;

class SimpleDateStructureProgram
{
    static void Main()
    {
        Date dateMoonWalk;

        dateMoonWalk.iYear = 1969;
        dateMoonWalk.iMonth = 7;
        dateMoonWalk.iDay = 20;

        Console.WriteLine("Moon walk: {0}/{1}/{2}",
            dateMoonWalk.iMonth, dateMoonWalk.iDay, dateMoonWalk.iYear);
    }
}

struct Date
{
    public int iYear;
    public int iMonth;
    public int iDay;
}
```

The order of the class and the structure in the file doesn't matter. The *Date* structure could also just as easily have been declared in its own source code file. Once you develop a structure or class that might be reuseable, you'll want to move it in its own source-code file to make it available to other programs.

The code in the *SimpleDateStructureProgram* class implies some unstated *rules* about this particular *Date* structure. I've decided that the *iMonth* and *iDay* fields should be one-based rather than zero-based. An *iMonth* value of 1 is January, and a value of 12 is December. An *iDay* value of 1 is the first of the month. That's how people think of numeric dates. Zero values of *iMonth* and *iDay* are not allowed (although it's not quite clear yet how they will be prohibited).

I'm also going to set another rule that will come into play later: The *iYear* field shall refer to years in the common era of the Gregorian calendar. The Gregorian calendar was established by Pope Gregory XIII in 1582 and was eventually adopted by the rest of the Western world to replace the Julian calendar in use since the days of Julius Caesar. The Julian calendar has leap years every four years. The Gregorian calendar eliminates leap years in years divisible by 100, except those years that are also divisible by 400.

It's almost as easy to declare instances of the *Date* structure as it is to declare integers or strings. The declaration statement

```
Date dateMoonWalk;
```

could easily accommodate multiple objects:

```
Date dateApollo11Launch, dateMoonWalk, dateApollo11SplashDown;
```

However, it's not possible (not yet anyway) to set the *Date* object to a particular date by initializing it in the declaration statement.

What you *can* do, and what SimpleDateStructureProgram does not do, is to initialize a structure variable using a *new* expression, either right in the declaration statement

```
Date dateMoonWalk = new Date();
```

or after the declaration statement:

```
dateMoonWalk = new Date();
```

The keyword *new* is followed by the structure name and a pair of parentheses. The *new* expression causes all the fields of the structure to be initialized to 0. If the structure happened to have any fields that were reference types (*string*, for example), those fields would be initialized to *null*.

The *new* expression wasn't needed in SimpleDateStructureProgram because the program explicitly initialized all three fields of the structure before it accessed those fields in the *Console.WriteLine* statement. As our structures get more complex, the compiler can't always determine if a field has been initialized, and you'll start getting error messages about uninitialized fields. Get into the habit of using a *new* expression before using any structure variable. Often the *new* expression will appear right in the declaration statement.

Suppose you declare a *Date* object using the *new* expression and then display the values of the resultant fields:

```
Date dateWhatever = new Date();
Console.WriteLine("{0}/{1}/{2}", dateWhatever.iMonth,
                  dateWhatever.iDay, dateWhatever.iYear);
```

The date will be displayed as:

```
0/0/0
```

That's not a real date. It's an invalid month, an invalid day, and an invalid year. (There is no year 0 in the common era. The year before 1 A.D. is 1 B.C.) If at all possible, when you declare a structure, the value it gets by default using the *new* operator should be something *equivalent* to a 0. Under the rules that we've established for dates, a 0 date should be the first date in the common era, which is 1/1/1. Yes, it's important to solve this problem and, yes, we will solve it. But let's worry about it a bit later.

You can declare an array of *Date* structures also using the *new* operator:

```
Date[] adate = new Date[5];
```

When you declare an array of *Date* structures, it's as if each element of the array is created using a *new* expression, which means that all the fields of each of the five elements are initialized to 0. You can set and reference the fields of the third element (for example) using code like this:

```
adate[2].iYear = 1969;
adate[2].iMonth = 7;
adate[2].iDay = 20;

Console.WriteLine("{0}/{1}/{2}", adate[2].iMonth,
                  adate[2].iDay, adate[2].iYear);
```

You index the array variable using square brackets, and then refer to a field of that element with a period and the field name. In the Operator Precedence and Associativity table, both array indexing (symbolized by *a[x]* in the table) and the dot operator (*x.y*) are primary operators and associate from left to right.

Now let's look at basically the same program as SimpleDateStructureProgram, but this time we'll declare *Date* as a class rather than a structure:

SimpleDateClassProgram.cs

```
// --------------------------------------------------------------
// SimpleDateClassProgram.cs from "Programming in the Key of C#"
// --------------------------------------------------------------
using System;

class SimpleDateClassProgram
{
    static void Main()
    {
        Date dateMoonWalk = new Date();

        dateMoonWalk.iYear = 1969;
        dateMoonWalk.iMonth = 7;
        dateMoonWalk.iDay = 20;

        Console.WriteLine("Moon walk: {0}/{1}/{2}",
            dateMoonWalk.iMonth, dateMoonWalk.iDay, dateMoonWalk.iYear);
    }
}

class Date
{
    public int iYear;
    public int iMonth;
    public int iDay;
}
```

A class is a reference type. When you simply declare a variable using a class like this

```
Date dateMoonWalk;
```

then *dateMoonWalk* is considered to be uninitialized. It doesn't even equal *null*. No memory has been allocated from the heap. You can't assign anything to the fields because there is no memory to hold the values. Before you use *dateMoonWalk* at all you must use the *new* operator to declare a new instance of the *Date* class, either in an assignment statement:

```
dateMoonWalk = new Date();
```

or right in the declaration:

```
Date dateMoonWalk = new Date();
```

The *new* operator causes memory to be allocated for the instance, and then causes all the fields of the instance to be initialized to 0. Heap memory is always initialized to 0.

You can also declare an array of *Date* objects:

```
Date[] adate;
```

Memory has not yet been allocated for the array, and *adate* is considered to be uninitialized. To allocate memory for the array, you need to use the *new* expression either by itself

```
adate = new Date[5];
```

or right in the declaration:

```
Date[] adate = new Date[5];
```

If *Date* is a structure, then this statement causes memory to be allocated from the heap for five instances of the structure, and all the fields of each element are initialized to 0. If *Date* is a class, however, this statement causes memory to be allocated only for the array itself. Each element of the array is *null* because each element of the array is a reference. Before you use any element of the array, you must use the *new* operator for that element:

```
adate[0] = new Date();
```

That statement allocates memory from the heap for the first array element. You can allocate memory for each element of the array using a *for* loop:

```
for (int i = 0; i < adate.Length; i++)
    adate[i] = new Date();
```

You can't use *foreach* for this job because the array elements are read-only in the body of the *foreach* statement.

Here's another way to declare, create, and initialize an array of *Date* objects when *Date* is a class:

```
Date[] adate = new Date[5] { new Date(), new Date(), new Date(),
                            new Date(), new Date() };
```

Each of these six *new* expressions allocates memory from the heap. As usual, you can leave out the first *new* expression if you're initializing the array in the declaration statement.

Let's review some of the differences between classes and structures that contain instance fields. You can declare an object like this:

```
Date dateMoonWalk;
```

What happens depends on whether *Date* is a structure or a class. If *Date* is a structure, then the *dateMoonWalk* object is stored on the stack. The object has three instance fields of 4 bytes each, so the object requires 12 bytes on the stack. The fields are uninitialized. If *Date* is a class, then *dateMoonWalk* is a reference, perhaps a memory address that is 4 bytes in size on today's computers. This reference is stored on the stack and is also uninitialized.

You can assign an object a *null* reference

```
dateMoonWalk = null;
```

only if *Date* is a class. The object is no longer uninitialized, but its value indicates that it doesn't refer to anything.

You can also use the *new* operator with the object:

```
dateMoonWalk = new Date();
```

Again, what happens depends on whether *Date* is a structure or a class. If *Date* is a structure, then all the instance fields are initialized to 0 (if they are value types) or *null* (for reference types). If *Date* is a class, then memory is allocated from the heap of sufficient size to store the object. That's 12 bytes plus additional space to store information identifying the type of the object (the fact that it's an object of type *Date*). Heap memory is automatically initialized to 0, so all fields of the object are initialized to 0 or *null*.

If you all declare an array

```
Date[] adate;
```

then *adate* is a reference regardless of whether *Date* is a class or a structure. The reference is stored on the stack but it's uninitialized.

Arrays themselves are always stored in the heap. You use the *new* operator to create the array by allocating memory from the heap:

```
adate = new Date[27];
```

If *Date* is a structure, sufficient space is allocated from the heap to store 27 instances of the *Date* structure. Because heap memory is always initialized to 0, every field of every element is initialized to 0 or *null*. If *Date* is a class, space is allocated from the heap sufficient to store 27 references (probably 4 bytes for each). All 27 references are initialized to 0, which means that every element of the array equals *null*. Each element of the array must be allocated individually from the heap.

It should be fairly obvious that instances of a structure require less memory than instances of a class. Structures also involve less activity during initialization, particularly for arrays. Structures are often suitable for *light-weight objects*, particularly objects that are similar to numbers in some way. (A date certainly qualifies.) Whenever you need to declare a new class or structure whose instance fields require a fairly small amount of memory, you should probably use a structure unless you need something you can only do with a class. As you'll see, structures in C# have some distinct drawbacks.

So far, however, we haven't seen any real advantage to using the structure or a class rather than the three discrete variables. Those advantages will be evident soon.

32

Instance Methods

When working with dates, it's often convenient to calculate a day-of-year value that ranges from 1 through 365 (or 366 in leap years). Let's begin this job with a static method to determine whether a particular year is a leap year. You've seen this logic before, in Chapter 23.

```
static bool IsLeapYear(int iYear)
{
    return iYear % 4 == 0 && (iYear % 100 != 0 || iYear % 400 == 0);
}
```

Chapter 18 showed a static *DayOfYear* method that ignored leap years. That method used a static array named *aiCumulativeDays*:

```
static int[] aiCumulativeDays = { 0, 31, 59, 90, 120, 151,
                                  181, 212, 243, 273, 304, 334 };

static int DayOfYear(int iMonth, int iDay)
{
    return aiCumulativeDays[iMonth - 1] + iDay;
}
```

As I said in Chapter 18, it's best to declare initialized arrays as static fields rather than local variables. That way, the array is initialized only once instead of every time the method is called.

The leap year affects the day-of-year values only in March or later (that is, *iMonth* > 2), so the *DayOfYear* method is fairly easy to enhance for those situations. One approach is to use the conditional operator covered in Chapter 23:

```
static int DayOfYear(int iYear, int iMonth, int iDay)
{
    return aiCumulativeDays[iMonth - 1] + iDay +
        (iMonth > 2 && IsLeapYear(iYear) ? 1 : 0);
}
```

We'll be using a *DayOfYear* method in conjunction with the *Date* class (or structure). The *Date* class lets us create objects that represent entire dates. So let's revise *DayOfYear* so that it doesn't have three parameters. Let's declare *DayOf-Year* with just one parameter, which is an object of type *Date*:

```
static int DayOfYear(Date dateParam)
{
    return aiCumulativeDays[dateParam.iMonth - 1] + dateParam.iDay +
        (dateParam.iMonth > 2 && IsLeapYear(dateParam.iYear) ? 1 : 0);
}
```

The parameter to *DayOfYear* is declared just as if *Date* were one of the predefined simple types. The *dateParam* variable is an object of type *Date*. Within the body of *DayOfYear*, you need to refer to the three fields of the object by using *dateParam* and the field name separated by a period, just as if you were using fields of a *Date* object elsewhere.

Changing *DayOfYear* from a method that has three arguments to a method that has one certainly simplifies the parameter list, but it tends to make the rest of the method a bit bulkier than before. Don't worry—it'll shrink back down in size before the end of this chapter. For now, let's put the *IsLeapYear* and *Day OfYear* methods in a program and see how they work. This program is called StructureAndMethodsOne because it's the first of three steps in moving from traditional procedural programming to object-oriented programming. This program declares *Date* as a structure; nothing in this chapter depends on whether *Date* is a class or a structure.

StructureAndMethodsOne.cs

```
// -----------------------------------------------------------------
// StructureAndMethodsOne.cs from "Programming in the Key of C#"
// -----------------------------------------------------------------
using System;

class StructureAndMethodsOne
{
    static void Main()
    {
        Date dateMoonWalk = new Date();

        dateMoonWalk.iYear = 1969;
        dateMoonWalk.iMonth = 7;
        dateMoonWalk.iDay = 20;

        Console.WriteLine("Moon walk: {0}/{1}/{2} Day of Year: {3}",
            dateMoonWalk.iMonth, dateMoonWalk.iDay, dateMoonWalk.iYear,
            DayOfYear(dateMoonWalk));
    }
```

```
    static bool IsLeapYear(int iYear)
    {
        return iYear % 4 == 0 && (iYear % 100 != 0 || iYear % 400 == 0);
    }

    static int[] aiCumulativeDays = { 0, 31, 59, 90, 120, 151,
                                    181, 212, 243, 273, 304, 334 };

    static int DayOfYear(Date dateParam)
    {
        return aiCumulativeDays[dateParam.iMonth - 1] + dateParam.iDay +
            (dateParam.iMonth > 2 && IsLeapYear(dateParam.iYear) ? 1 : 0);
    }
}

struct Date
{
    public int iYear;
    public int iMonth;
    public int iDay;
}
```

Besides displaying the date, as programs in the preceding chapter did, this program also displays the day-of-year value by making the method call:

```
DayOfYear(dateMoonWalk)
```

There's nothing really wrong with the StructureAndMethodsOne program. It's similar to how you might do the job in a traditional procedural language like C. But one of the objectives of object-oriented languages is to write code that is reusable. We should be thinking that the *Date* class or structure might eventually be moved to its own file or perhaps a dynamic-link library so that it can be used by multiple programs. That means it would make more sense to move the method involving the *Date* structure right into the structure itself.

Putting code into a structure is not allowed in C. That's one way in which C tended to keep code and data separate. Object-oriented languages allow classes and structures to contain both code and data. Here's the new version.

StructureAndMethodsTwo.cs

```
// -----------------------------------------------------------
// StructureAndMethodsTwo.cs from "Programming in the Key of C#"
// -----------------------------------------------------------
using System;

class StructureAndMethodsTwo
{
```

```
    static void Main()
    {
        Date dateMoonWalk = new Date();

        dateMoonWalk.iYear = 1969;
        dateMoonWalk.iMonth = 7;
        dateMoonWalk.iDay = 20;

        Console.WriteLine("Moon walk: {0}/{1}/{2} Day of Year: {3}",
            dateMoonWalk.iMonth, dateMoonWalk.iDay, dateMoonWalk.iYear,
            Date.DayOfYear(dateMoonWalk));
    }
}

struct Date
{
    public int iYear;
    public int iMonth;
    public int iDay;

    public static bool IsLeapYear(int iYear)
    {
        return iYear % 4 == 0 && (iYear % 100 != 0 || iYear % 400 == 0);
    }

    static int[] aiCumulativeDays = { 0, 31, 59, 90, 120, 151,
                                181, 212, 243, 273, 304, 334 };

    public static int DayOfYear(Date dateParam)
    {
        return aiCumulativeDays[dateParam.iMonth - 1] + dateParam.iDay +
            (dateParam.iMonth > 2 && IsLeapYear(dateParam.iYear) ? 1 : 0);
    }
}
```

Let's look at the *Date* structure first. Basically, I just cut and pasted the two static methods and the static array into the structure. Because *DayOfYear* needs to be accessed from outside the *Date* structure, I gave it a *public* access modifier. I also gave a *public* modifier to the *IsLeapYear* method, perhaps anticipating that it might be of use as well. I left *aiCumulativeDays* the way it was. With no access modifier, it's *private* by default. I didn't think other classes would need access to the elements of that array.

You might notice that *IsLeapYear* has a parameter that's the same name as one of the fields. That's allowed. Within the method, *iYear* is assumed to refer to the parameter. We'll see in the next chapter how a method can differentiate between parameters and fields that have the same names.

The sole difference in *Main* is how it calls the *DayOfYear* method. When the *DayOfYear* method was in the same class as *Main*, *DayOfYear* could be called simply with the method name:

```
DayOfYear(dateMoonWalk)
```

Now that the static method is in the *Date* structure, the code in *Main* needs to preface the method name with the structure name:

```
Date.DayOfYear(dateMoonWalk)
```

The *DayOfYear* method can continue to refer to *IsLeapYear* with no prefaced structure name because it's in the same structure.

The next enhancement, you'll be pleased to know, makes the code a bit shorter. What I'm going to do is change *DayOfYear* from a static method to an instance method. The ability to do this is actually the primary reason why I wanted to move the *DayOfYear* method to the *Date* structure in the previous step.

Converting *DayOfYear* from static to instance involves a bit more than just removing the static modifier.

StructureAndMethodsThree.cs

```
// ---------------------------------------------------------------
// StructureAndMethodsThree.cs from "Programming in the Key of C#"
// ---------------------------------------------------------------
using System;

class StructureAndMethodsThree
{
    static void Main()
    {
        Date dateMoonWalk = new Date();

        dateMoonWalk.iYear = 1969;
        dateMoonWalk.iMonth = 7;
        dateMoonWalk.iDay = 20;

        Console.WriteLine("Moon walk: {0}/{1}/{2} Day of Year: {3}",
            dateMoonWalk.iMonth, dateMoonWalk.iDay, dateMoonWalk.iYear,
            dateMoonWalk.DayOfYear());
    }
}

struct Date
{
    public int iYear;
    public int iMonth;
    public int iDay;
```

```
public static bool IsLeapYear(int iYear)
{
    return iYear % 4 == 0 && (iYear % 100 != 0 || iYear % 400 == 0);
}

static int[] aiCumulativeDays = { 0, 31, 59, 90, 120, 151,
                                  181, 212, 243, 273, 304, 334 };

public int DayOfYear()
{
    return aiCumulativeDays[iMonth - 1] + iDay +
        (iMonth > 2 && IsLeapYear(iYear) ? 1 : 0);
}
}
```

The static version of *DayOfYear* in the previous program calculated a day-of-year value based on a *Date* parameter to the method. It needed to reference the three fields of the *Date* structure by using the parameter variable.

This instance version of *DayOfYear* has no parameter. Instead, it refers directly to the instance fields of the structure. Notice that the code has been simplified. Rather than *dateParam.iMonth*, it can now use simply *iMonth*. An instance method of a class or structure has access to the instance fields declared in that class or structure.

Look at *Main* now. Previously, *Main* had to call the static *DayOfYear* method by specifying the structure in which it is declared (*Date*) and passing an argument to the method:

```
Date.DayOfYear(dateMoonWalk)
```

This new version calls the parameterless *DayOfYear* method using the *Date* instance:

```
dateMoonWalk.DayOfYear()
```

The *DayOfYear* method basically needs the same information as before. With the static version, it was getting the information through the method parameter. The instance version of the method is always called based on an instance of the structure. It can simply access the structure fields.

You might also start getting a feel for a subtle change in perspective. In the previous version of the program, the *Main* method was asking the *DayOfYear* method in the *Date* structure to calculate a day-of-year value for a particular instance of *Date*. Now the *Main* method is asking the *Date* object to calculate its own day-of-year value.

I've kept *IsLeapYear* as a static method just for some variety and also because it could be useful to a program regardless of whether a *Date* object has been created.

This third version of the *Date* structure contains instance fields, a static field (the array), an instance method, and a static method. As you can see, instance methods can make use of static methods and static fields with no problem. Because the static fields and methods are in the same structure, the instance method simply refers to them by name.

However, you can't go the other way. A static method in a class or structure *cannot* use instance fields or instance methods in the same class or structure. A static method can't possibly access instance fields or call instance methods because an instance of the class doesn't even have to exist when a static method is called.

The first instance method you encountered in this book was the *ToString* method. As you discovered, it's possible for a program to pass any object to the *Console.WriteLine* method, and you'll get some text representation of the object. *Console.WriteLine* accomplishes this feat by directly or indirectly calling the object's *ToString* method.

Well, *Date* doesn't have a *ToString* method. Or does it? You may want to try inserting the statement

```
Console.WriteLine(dateMoonWalk.ToString());
```

or

```
Console.WriteLine(dateMoonWalk);
```

in one of the programs with a *Date* class or structure. Unfortunately, this *ToString* method is not quite as smart as we perhaps were hoping. What's displayed in this case is the string

```
Date
```

which is the name of the *Date* structure rather than the actual date referred to by the object. *Date* really *does* have a *ToString* method, but it's not doing anything very useful yet.

Every structure and every class in the .NET Framework has a *ToString* method, and every structure and every class that you declare in your programs has a *ToString* method.

The ubiquity of the *ToString* object is made possible through the magic of *inheritance*, which is one of the primary characteristics of object-oriented programming. Classes inherit from other classes. When one class inherits (or *derives*) from another class, the new class acquires all the nonprivate fields and methods of the class that it inherits from, and it can add its own fields and methods to the mix. The class that a new class derives from is called the *base* class, which is also a C# keyword.

One of the major differences between classes and structures involves inheritance. Classes can inherit from other classes, but a structure exists mostly in isolation. A structure can't explicitly inherit from anything else, and nothing can inherit from a structure.

All classes and structures in C# ultimately derive from the grand matriarch of the .NET Framework, *System.Object*. In C#, the keyword *object* is an alias for *System.Object*.

Another important class in the *System* namespace is *System.ValueType*, which inherits directly from *System.Object*. Although structures can't *explicitly* inherit from anything else, all structures implicitly derive from *System.ValueType*.

The techniques and implications of inheritance will become more apparent in the chapters ahead. For now, you should know that the *ToString* method exists in all classes and structures because the *System.Object* class includes a *ToString* method declared like so:

```
public virtual string ToString()
```

As implemented in *System.Object*, this *ToString* method simply returns the type of the object, which is the name of the class or structure used to create the object.

The *virtual* keyword means that any class or structure can provide a custom-made *ToString* method that supersedes the one declared in *System.Object*. This is known as *overriding* the method, and you do it using the *override* keyword. To provide a custom *ToString* method in any class or structure, you declare it like so:

```
public override string ToString()
```

Otherwise, the signature of the method and its accessibility (in this case, the fact that *ToString* is a public instance method with no parameters) must be the same.

The *virtual* and *override* keywords are closely related. A *virtual* method in one class can be superseded by an *override* method in a derived class. I'll have much more to say about virtual methods in Chapter 37.

Let's take a look at a new *Date* structure that includes a *ToString* method and a new private static array, this one containing the names of the months.

StructureWithToString.cs

```
// ------------------------------------------------------------
// StructureWithToString.cs from "Programming in the Key of C#"
// ------------------------------------------------------------
using System;

class StructureWithToString
{
    static void Main()
```

```
    {
        Date dateMoonWalk = new Date();

        dateMoonWalk.iYear = 1969;
        dateMoonWalk.iMonth = 7;
        dateMoonWalk.iDay = 20;

        Console.WriteLine("Moon walk: {0}, Day of Year: {1}",
            dateMoonWalk, dateMoonWalk.DayOfYear());
    }
}

struct Date
{
    public int iYear;
    public int iMonth;
    public int iDay;

    public static bool IsLeapYear(int iYear)
    {
        return iYear % 4 == 0 && (iYear % 100 != 0 || iYear % 400 == 0);
    }

    static int[] aiCumulativeDays = { 0, 31, 59, 90, 120, 151,
                                181, 212, 243, 273, 304, 334 };

    public int DayOfYear()
    {
        return aiCumulativeDays[iMonth - 1] + iDay +
            (iMonth > 2 && IsLeapYear(iYear) ? 1 : 0);
    }

    static string[] astrMonths = { "Jan", "Feb", "Mar", "Apr", "May", "Jun",
                                "Jul", "Aug", "Sep", "Oct", "Nov", "Dec"};

    public override string ToString()
    {
        return String.Format("{0} {1} {2}", iDay,
            astrMonths[iMonth - 1], iYear);
    }
}
```

Because *ToString* is an instance method, it can simply refer to the instance fields, much like *DayOfYear*. Many *ToString* implementations use *String.Format* to create and return a string rendition of the object. I decided to write *ToString* so that the string is displayed in the European fashion, with the day preceding the month. Rather than representing the month with a number, *ToString* uses English month name abbreviations to avoid any ambiguity.

Now *Main* can display the date just by passing an instance such as *date-MoonWalk* to *Console.WriteLine*. *Console.WriteLine* passes the object to *String.Format*, which calls the object's *ToString* method, which also calls *String.Format*.

But the problem with invalid dates is getting more critical. If you try the two statements

```
Date dt = new Date();
Console.WriteLine(dt);
```

the *ToString* method of *Date* will throw an exception because it will attempt to reference the *astrMonths* array with an index of –1. *DayOfYear* has a similar problem. That might suggest to you that *ToString* or *DayOfYear* is at fault and must be fixed. That's not so. The problem occurs much earlier, when *Date* allows an invalid date to be created in the first place. We must prevent that from happening.

33

Constructors

The expression

```
new Date()
```

creates a new object of type *Date*. If *Date* is a class, then memory is allocated from the heap at run time sufficient to store all the instance fields in the class. That memory is automatically initialized to 0, so all value-type fields are effectively set to 0, and all reference-type fields are set to *null*. If *Date* is a structure, the object is stored on the stack. The *new* expression causes all the fields to be explicitly initialized to 0 or *null*.

This behavior has been causing us problems. We want a newly created *Date* object to represent a date of 1/1/1, not the invalid date 0/0/0.

One way to fix this problem is to simply initialize the fields in the declaration statements:

```
class Date
{
    public int iYear = 1;
    public int iMonth = 1;
    public int iDay = 1;

    ...

}
```

Now during the *new* expression, all three fields are assigned values of 1. The default date is valid.

The problem with this little solution is that you can provide field initializers only in classes, and not in structures. If *Date* is a structure, then field initializers are not allowed, and all fields are automatically set to 0 or *null*.

This prohibition is part of the reduced overhead involved with structures. For an individual structure, it may not seem like much, but it really makes a difference when a program creates an array based on a structure type. It's much faster to allocate a block of heap memory that is initialized to 0 rather than a block in which individual fields must be set for all the elements. Keep in mind that arrays based on classes work a little differently: each element of the array is initialized to *null*. Each element of the array requires another *new* expression, and that's when memory is allocated for the element and the fields are initialized to the indicated values.

Another approach to object initialization is much more generalized. You can initialize fields and perform additional initialization in special methods known as *constructors*. Constructors are methods that are executed automatically when an object is created. Constructors have two characteristics that visually distinguish them from other methods in the class or structure: First, they have the same name as the class or structure in which they are declared, and second, they have no return type.

Take a look at the *new* expression again:

```
new Date()
```

Doesn't the right side of that expression look like a method call? Yes it does: it looks like a call to a method named *Date* with no arguments. And that's really what it is. Here's a skeleton of a *Date* class containing a constructor that initializes the three fields to 1:

```
class Date
{
    int iYear, iMonth, iDay;

    public Date()
    {
        iYear = 1;
        iMonth = 1;
        iDay = 1;
    }
    ...
}
```

If *Date* were a regular method, it would have a return type between the *public* keyword and the name of the method. A return type is not allowed for constructors.

A constructor with no parameters is known as a *parameterless* constructor. And here's another difference between classes and structures: You can't declare a parameterless constructor in a structure. (Again, this prohibition exists to speed up the creation of arrays involving structure types.) So now you see *two* ways you can initialize the fields to a valid date value in a class, but neither of these methods works in a structure.

In a class, you can initialize some fields in the declaration statements, and you initialize others in the constructor:

```
class Date
{
    public int iYear;
    public int iMonth = 4;
    public int iDay = 1;

    public Date()
    {
        iYear = 1;
        iMonth = 1;
    }
    ...
}
```

The initialization of the fields occurs before the code in the constructor executes. In this particular example, the *iMonth* field is first set to 4 in the field initializer, but it ends up being set to 1 by the constructor (although I would be confused by the intent of a programmer who would write such code). In this example, there's really no advantage or disadvantage to the two approaches to initializing the fields. By the time the initialization occurs, the memory has already been allocated for the object. The object already exists.

The constructor is required to be *public* if you want to allow code external to the class to create objects. Sometimes you don't. In Chapter 17, I showed you how to create classes named *HandyCalcs*, *Trig1*, and *Trig2* that contain nothing but static methods and fields. It wouldn't make much sense for a program to create an instance of the *Trig2* class like this:

```
Trig2 trg = new Trig2();
```

There's nothing a program can do with the *trg* object. But go back and try it! The *Trig2* class doesn't prevent instances of the class. What *Trig2* needs is a parameterless constructor that's declared as *private*:

```
private Trig2()
{
}
```

Because the body of this method is empty, some programmers would write the whole method declaration on a single line:

```
private Trig2() {}
```

Now a program can't create an instance of the *Trig2* class. And that's why collections of static methods and fields are classes and not structures. A class can prohibit instances of itself by including a private parameterless constructor. A structure can't include a parameterless constructor, either public or private.

Besides the parameterless constructor, it's also possible to declare constructors that include parameters. These can be very, very useful for object initialization.

For example, we have been creating and initializing a *Date* object like so:

```
Date dateMoonWalk = new Date();
dateMoonWalk.iYear = 1969;
dateMoonWalk.iMonth = 7;
dateMoonWalk.iDay = 20;
```

With a parametered constructor, we could trim this code down to a single declaration statement:

```
Date dateMoonWalk = new Date(1969, 7, 20);
```

Again, the expression at the right looks like a method call. At its simplest (that is, without any consistency checking), such a constructor might look like this:

```
class Date
{
    int iYear, iMonth, iDay;

    public Date(int iYearInit, int iMonthInit, int iDayInit)
    {
        iYear = iYearInit;
        iMonth = iMonthInit;
        iDay = iDayInit;
    }
    ...
}
```

You can declare a parametered constructor in either a class or a structure.

I gave the three parameters different names than the fields to avoid confusion. However, it's possible to use the *same* names for fields and method parameters. If you want to use the same names (and it's often easier than making up different names for essentially the same variables), here's what the constructor would look like:

```
public Date(int iYear, int iMonth, int iDay)
{
    this.iYear = iYear;
    this.iMonth = iMonth;
    this.iDay = iDay;
}
```

Within instance methods in a class or structure, the keyword *this* refers to the current object. If they wanted to, all the instance methods could refer to *this.iYear* rather than just *iYear*. In a constructor, *this* refers to the object just created and being initialized by the constructor.

Although constructors with parameters are very popular, they aren't quite as safe as assigning fields explicitly after the object is created. It's harder to mix up assignments than to mix up the arguments of a constructor call. (On the other hand, it's easier to forget an assignment statement than to forget an argument to a constructor.) The *Date* constructor shown above was declared with the year argument first, then the month and day. If the *Date* constructor is called with a different order of arguments, the date would be wrong. Give some thought to how the parameters are ordered. The most important should usually be first.

The *C# Language Specification*, §10.10.4, states, "If a class contains no instance constructor declarations, a default instance constructor is automatically provided." We know this because our previous *Date* classes had parameterless constructors even though they weren't explicitly declared in the class. But there's another implication here: If a class contains a constructor declaration—any constructor declaration—then a default constructor is *not* provided. Specifically, if you include a parametered constructor in your class, such as the *Date* constructor with the three parameters, then a parameterless constructor is no longer automatically provided. You'd be able to create a *Date* object like this:

```
Date dt = new Date(2005, 8, 29);
```

But you couldn't do it like this:

```
Date dt = new Date();    // Not allowed.
```

You'd get the following compile error:

```
No overload for method 'Date' takes '0' arguments
```

If you declare parametered constructors, you also need to explicitly include a parameterless constructor if you still want to allow objects to be created using a parameterless constructor. You may not. You may want to prevent objects from being created with a parameterless constructor. It's your choice.

With a structure, it doesn't matter if you declare a bunch of constructors with parameters or not. C# continues to provide a public parameterless constructor. There's an interesting advantage to that: You can always create an array of structure types because structures always have public parameterless constructors.

You can always create arrays of class types as well, but you may not get very far. For example, you know that you can't create an object of type *Console* because *Console* has no public constructor:

```
Console cons = new Console();    // Not allowed.
```

But, amazingly enough, you *can* create an *array* of *Console* objects:

```
Console[] acons = new Console[5];    // No problem!
```

That statement looks very bizarre, but remember: When you create an array based on a class type, each element is set to *null*. Trying to set those elements to anything else would be a problem.

Speaking of arrays, parameted constructors are particularly useful when you're declaring an array of initialized objects. Here's some code involved with explicitly initializing an array of just three *Date* objects:

```
Date[] adate = new Date[3];

adate[0] = new Date();
adate[0].iYear = 2004;
adate[0].iMonth = 2;
adate[0].iDay = 2;

adate[1] = new Date();
adate[1].iYear = 2004;
adate[1].iMonth = 8;
adate[1].iDay = 29;

adate[2] = new Date();
adate[2].iYear = 2004;
adate[2].iMonth = 10;
adate[2].iDay = 22;
```

If *Date* were a structure, the first *new* expression would be required but the other *new* expressions would not.

If *Date* has a parameted constructor, then each element of the array can be set in a single statement:

```
Date[] adate = new Date[3];

adate[0] = new Date(2004, 2, 2);
adate[1] = new Date(2004, 8, 29);
adate[2] = new Date(2004, 10, 22);
```

Or the three elements can be initialized during array creation:

```
Date[] adate = { new Date(2004, 2, 2), new Date(2004, 8, 29),
                 new Date(2004, 10, 22) };
```

Let's look at a complete program with a *Date* class that declares a parameterless constructor to set the fields to the first day of the common era and has a parametered constructor with full consistency checking.

ConsistencyChecking.cs

```
// -----------------------------------------------------------------
// ConsistencyChecking.cs from "Programming in the Key of C#"
// -----------------------------------------------------------------
using System;

class ConsistencyChecking
{
    static void Main()
    {
        Date dateMoonWalk = new Date(1969, 7, 20);

        Console.WriteLine("Moon walk: {0}, Day of Year: {1}",
            dateMoonWalk, dateMoonWalk.DayOfYear());
    }
}

class Date
{
    public int iYear;
    public int iMonth;
    public int iDay;

    // Parameterless constructor

    public Date()
    {
        iYear = 1;
        iMonth = 1;
        iDay = 1;
    }

    // Parametered constructor

    public Date(int iYear, int iMonth, int iDay)
    {
        if (iYear < 1)
            throw new ArgumentOutOfRangeException("Year");

        if (iMonth < 1 || iMonth > 12)
            throw new ArgumentOutOfRangeException("Month");

        if (iDay < 1 || iDay > 31)
            throw new ArgumentOutOfRangeException("Day");
```

```
        if (iDay == 31 && (iMonth == 4 || iMonth == 6 ||
            iMonth == 9 || iMonth == 11))
            throw new ArgumentOutOfRangeException("Day");

        if (iMonth == 2 && iDay > 29)
            throw new ArgumentOutOfRangeException("Day");

        if (iMonth == 2 && iDay == 29 && !IsLeapYear(iYear))
            throw new ArgumentOutOfRangeException("Day");

        this.iYear = iYear;
        this.iMonth = iMonth;
        this.iDay = iDay;
    }

    public static bool IsLeapYear(int iYear)
    {
        return iYear % 4 == 0 && (iYear % 100 != 0 || iYear % 400 == 0);
    }

    static int[] aiCumulativeDays - { 0, 31, 59, 90, 120, 151,
                                      181, 212, 243, 273, 304, 334 };

    public int DayOfYear()
    {
        return aiCumulativeDays[iMonth - 1] + iDay +
            (iMonth > 2 && IsLeapYear(iYear) ? 1 : 0);
    }

    static string[] astrMonths = { "Jan", "Feb", "Mar", "Apr", "May", "Jun",
                                   "Jul", "Aug", "Sep", "Oct", "Nov", "Dec"};

    public override string ToString()
    {
        return String.Format("{0} {1} {2}", iDay,
            astrMonths[iMonth - 1], iYear);
    }
}
}
```

A constructor has no return value. If a constructor encounters a problem and can't continue, it has no choice but to throw an exception. The parametered constructor in this class checks for consistency among the parameters and throws an instance of the *ArgumentOutOfRangeException* if there's a problem. To help in diagnosing the problem, the exception constructors are provided with arguments indicating whether the year, month, or day was the primary culprit.

Notice the constructor's use of the static *IsLeapYear* method. If *IsLeapYear* were an instance method, the constructor would still be able to use it, but not with the same results. At the time *IsLeapYear* is called in the constructor, the *iYear* field has not been explicitly set by the constructor. It would have the value it got when memory for the object was allocated from the heap, and that would be a value of 0. Be very, very careful when calling instance methods from constructors.

If a class or structure has multiple constructors, they can make use of each other, but in a very special way. For example, suppose you want to have an additional *Date* constructor that has just one parameter, which is a year:

```
Date dateNewYearsDay = new Date(2005);
```

You may want this constructor to make a *Date* object for January 1 of that year. You could implement such a constructor fairly simply:

```
public Date(int iYear)
{
    if (iYear < 1)
        throw new ArgumentOutOfRangeException("Year");

    this.iYear = iYear;
    iMonth = 1;
    iDay = 1;
}
```

But why bother duplicating code? Here's another approach:

```
public Date(int iYear): this(iYear, 1, 1)
{
}
```

Notice the colon following the parameter list. The colon is followed by something resembling a method call, but using the keyword *this* with three arguments. It's actually referring to the three-parameter constructor specifying a month and day of 1. This call from one constructor to another is called a *constructor initializer*, and it's the only way one constructor can directly use another constructor. If you need a more flexible way of sharing code among constructors, the constructors can call other methods (probably static methods) in the class.

In general, a compiled constructor executes the following code in this order:

- Assignment statements to set the instance fields to initialized values

- A call to the constructor initializer

- The actual code that you put in the constructor

If you have many constructors in your class, each of the compiled constructors will contain identical code to set the instance fields to their initialized values. In such a case, you may want to avoid initializing the fields in their declaration statements and initialize them instead in the parameterless constructor. The parametered constructors can execute the code in the parameterless constructor through a constructor initializer.

The opposite approach might make more sense for the *Date* class. The parameterless constructor can use the parametered constructor by including a constructor initializer:

```
public Date(): this(1, 1, 1)
{
}
```

If you don't explicitly provide a constructor initializer, the constructor calls the parameterless constructor in the base class, the class that your class derives from. I'll discuss this process more in Chapter 36.

A class can also include one *static* parameterless constructor, although static constructors are fairly uncommon in real-life programs. The declaration of the static constructor includes the *static* keyword but has no accessor modifier. The code in the static constructor is guaranteed to execute before any instance constructor and before any static member in the class is accessed. Even if you don't provide one, a static constructor is generated in intermediate language. The static constructor contains code to initialize static members, such as the two static arrays in the *Date* class.

If you need to initialize static fields in a manner that only code can accomplish, the static constructor is the place to do it.

34

Concepts of Equality

Let's take a one-chapter break from working with dates to explore some other issues with classes and structures.

Since Chapter 21, you've been working with the two equality operators,

```
A == B
```

and:

```
A != B
```

The first operation returns *true* if the two operands are equal; the second returns *false* if the two operands are equal. These operators work with all numeric types as well as *bool*, *char*, and *string*.

In Chapter 20, you also encountered the *Equals* instance method in the *String* class. *Equals* is one of a collection of methods in *String* that determine whether two strings are equal. *Equals*, like *ToString*, is a virtual method in the *Object* class and is inherited by every other class and structure; therefore, it's available in every class and structure in the .NET Framework, and also classes and structures that you declare yourself. *Equals* also works for the basic types. For example, if you declare a couple of integers:

```
int i1, i2;
```

and you set them equal to the same value:

```
i1 = 55;
i2 = 55;
```

the method call:

```
i1.Equals(i2)
```

returns *true*.

Let's explore how *Equals* works for a simple class and structure. The following program creates both a structure and a class, named *PointStruct* and *PointClass*, each containing only two public fields named *x* and *y*, perhaps to represent a two-dimensional coordinate point:

EqualsTest.cs

```
// --------------------------------------------------
// EqualsTest.cs from "Programming in the Key of C#"
// --------------------------------------------------
using System;

class EqualsTest
{
    static void Main()
    {
        PointStruct ps1 = new PointStruct();
        ps1.x = ps1.y = 55;

        PointStruct ps2 = new PointStruct();
        ps2.x = ps2.y = 55;

        PointClass pc1 = new PointClass();
        pc1.x = pc1.y = 55;

        PointClass pc2 = new PointClass();
        pc2.x = pc2.y = 55;

        Console.WriteLine("ps1.Equals(ps2) results in " + ps1.Equals(ps2));
        Console.WriteLine("ps1.Equals(pc1) results in " + ps1.Equals(pc1));
        Console.WriteLine("pc1.Equals(pc2) results in " + pc1.Equals(pc2));
        Console.WriteLine("pc1 == pc2 results in " + (pc1 == pc2));
        // Console.WriteLine("ps1 == ps2 results in " + (ps1 == ps2));
    }
}
struct PointStruct
{
    public int x, y;
}
class PointClass
{
    public int x, y;
}
```

The *Main* method creates two *PointStruct* objects and two *PointClass* objects and sets all the fields of all four objects to the value 55. *Main* concludes with several *WriteLine* statements that show the results of the *Equals* method and the equals operator:

```
ps1.Equals(ps2) results in True
ps1.Equals(pc1) results in False
pc1.Equals(pc2) results in False
pc1 == pc2 results in False
```

The first *Equals* call returns *true*; this result seems reasonable because the structure objects *ps1* and *ps2* have their fields set to identical values.

The second *Equals* call, which compares *ps1* and *pc1*, returns *false*, despite the fact that these objects' fields are the same. Perhaps comparing an instance of a class and an instance of a structure just doesn't make sense, despite how similar they seem to be.

But here's the real kicker: the third *Equals* call in which the two classes *pc1* and *pc2* are compared, returns *false*. The equals operator for these two objects also returns *false*. Why is this?

A class is a reference type. What are *pc1* and *pc2* really? They are references to memory blocks that have been allocated in the heap. Even though these two blocks contain identical information, *pc1* and *pc2* are separate and distinct. The references are not equal. For that reason, the *Equals* method in *Object* (which *PointClass* inherits) returns *false*.

The *ValueType* class overrides the *Equals* method. You'll recall that all structures implicitly derive from *ValueType*, so the overridden *Equals* method is the one that applies in all structures. *ValueType* implements its own idea of *Equals* to perform a different type of comparison. The *Equals* method of *Value-Type* compares all the fields in the two objects. If all the fields are equal, then *Equals* returns *true*. This is called a *bitwise* equality because all that the *Equals* method really needs to do is compare the total object as it's stored on the stack. All structures that you create inherit this revised version of *Equals*.

The equality operator works for objects created from classes:

```
pc1 == pc2
```

But if these are two different objects, the references are not equal and the expression returns *false*.

It might surprise you that the equality and inequality operators are not implemented for structure types. The compiler will not allow the expression:

```
ps1 == ps2
```

That's why the statement in EqualsTest.cs that contains this expression has been commented out.

If you want to create a structure that supports the equality and inequality operands, you'll have to implement these operations yourself (as I'll be demonstrating in Chapter 38).

The bitwise equality implemented in structures is probably closer to your intuitive notion of what equality means for simple variables. With something like a coordinate point, bitwise equality makes sense. Two coordinate points with the same x and y fields are certainly equal.

But suppose you were dealing with objects that represented people, with fields for the person's name, birth date, height, and weight. If two people have the same name, birth date, height, and weight, does that mean they're the same person? Not necessarily. (However, if these two objects had the same Social Security number, then they probably do represent the same person, and should be equal.) Similarly, if two graphical buttons have the same text and the same location on the screen, does that mean they're the same button? Not necessarily. It could mean that one button is sitting on top of the other button.

Whenever you create a class or structure, you should give some thought to the concept of equality. If your concept doesn't match the default implementation, then you can override the *Equals* method and implement your own equality and inequality operations.

Consider the *String* class. Even though *String* is a class, the *Equals* method and the equality operators implemented in *String* compare the string characters and not the references to the string. The type of equals test actually implemented in *String* is much more valuable to us.

A related difference between classes and structures involves assignment. You've been working with assignment since Chapter 2, and you probably think you have a good feel for it. Suppose you declare two integer variables:

```
int i1, i2;
```

and then you assign them different values:

```
i1 = 22;
i2 = 33;
```

Next, you assign the first integer the value of the second integer:

```
i1 = i2;
```

and give the second integer a new value:

```
i2 = 55;
```

What does *i1* equal?

Obviously, *i1* equals 33, the value it obtained when it was assigned the original value of *i2*. But as you discovered in Chapter 18 and again in the Array-

ValueParameter program in Chapter 30, assignment isn't always quite as intuitive if you're working with arrays. Arrays are reference types, so assigning one array variable to another results in two variables that reference the same area of the heap.

Let's see how assignment works with simple classes and structures. Here's the AssignmentTest program, which declares the same two simple structures and classes as the previous program:

AssignmentTest.cs

```
// ----------------------------------------------------------
// AssignmentTest.cs from "Programming in the Key of C#"
// ----------------------------------------------------------
using System;

class AssignmentTest
{
    static void Main()
    {
        PointStruct ps1 = new PointStruct();
        ps1.x = ps1.y = 22;

        PointStruct ps2 = new PointStruct();
        ps2.x = ps2.y = 33;

        ps1 = ps2;
        ps2.x = ps2.y = 55;

        Console.WriteLine("ps1 is ({0}, {1})", ps1.x, ps1.y);
        Console.WriteLine("ps2 is ({0}, {1})", ps2.x, ps2.y);
        Console.WriteLine("ps1.Equals(ps2) results in " + ps1.Equals(ps2));

        PointClass pc1 = new PointClass();
        pc1.x = pc1.y = 22;

        PointClass pc2 = new PointClass();
        pc2.x = pc2.y = 33;

        pc1 = pc2;
        pc2.x = pc2.y = 55;

        Console.WriteLine("pc1 is ({0}, {1})", pc1.x, pc1.y);
        Console.WriteLine("pc2 is ({0}, {1})", pc2.x, pc2.y);
        Console.WriteLine("pc1.Equals(pc2) results in " + pc1.Equals(pc2));
        Console.WriteLine("pc1 == pc2 results in " + (pc1 == pc2));
    }
}
```

```
struct PointStruct
{
    public int x, y;
}
class PointClass
{
    public int x, y;
}
```

Let's start by looking at the first half of *Main*. The code here exactly parallels the code I showed earlier for integers. The program assigns 22 to the two fields of *ps1*, and 33 to the two fields of *ps2*. The next statement is an assignment involving the two structure objects themselves rather than the fields of the structure:

```
ps1 = ps2;
```

The program then assigns 55 to the two fields of *ps2* and displays the two fields of *ps1*. As we might expect, the two fields of *ps1* are the same values originally assigned to *ps2*:

```
ps1 is (33, 33)
ps2 is (55, 55)
```

This code works exactly like the code with the two integers.

The second half of *Main* contains parallel code that performs the same operations using objects based on *PointClass* rather than *PointStruct*. The two fields of *pc1* get the values 22, and the two fields of *pc2* get the values 33. Next, the *pc2* object is assigned to the *pc1* object:

```
pc1 = pc2;
```

The program then assigns 55 to the two fields of *pc2*

```
pc2.x = pc2.y = 55;
```

and displays the two fields of *pc1*. If you can anticipate the result, you've gotten the hang of this. The result is:

```
pc1 is (55, 55)
pc2 is (55, 55)
```

What happened here? Why does *pc1* have values later assigned to *pc2?*

A class is a reference type. The *pc1* and *pc2* variables are references to memory blocks allocated in the heap. Following the assignment statement

```
pc1 = pc2;
```

both the *pc1* and *pc2* variables store the same reference, and hence refer to the same memory block. Whatever you do to the fields of *pc1* will also affect the fields of *pc2*; likewise, any changes to the fields of *pc2* affect *pc1*. The *pc1* reference equals the *pc2* reference, as the program demonstrates at the end.

Because *PointStruct* is a structure, the statement

```
PointStruct ps1 = new PointStruct();
```

does not result in any memory allocation from the heap. Regardless of the *new* expression, the *ps1* variable is stored on the stack. The *new* expression merely assures that all the fields of the structure are initialized to 0. In contrast, the statement

```
PointClass pc1 = new PointClass();
```

results in memory allocated from the heap. The value of *pc1* is the reference to that memory. Similarly,

```
PointClass pc2 = new PointClass();
```

results in another block of memory being allocated from the heap. Following the assignment statement

```
pc1 = pc2;
```

both variables are the same value and refer to the first block of memory allocated from the heap.

What happens to the second block of memory? It seems to be orphaned, and in fact, in this simple program, it is. No references to the memory block remain, so the program has no way to access that block ever again. That block becomes eligible for garbage collection. The system can free the block before the program terminates because the block is no longer needed.

Let's write a couple methods that change the fields of the *PointStruct* and *PointClass* objects:

MethodCallTest.cs

```
// ------------------------------------------------------------
// MethodCallTest.cs from "Programming in the Key of C#"
// ------------------------------------------------------------
using System;

class MethodCallTest
{
    static void Main()
    {
        PointStruct ps = new PointStruct();
        ps.x = ps.y = 22;
```

```
            Console.WriteLine("Before method: ps is ({0}, {1})", ps.x, ps.y);
            ChangeStructure(ps);
            Console.WriteLine("After method:  ps is ({0}, {1})", ps.x, ps.y);

            PointClass pc = new PointClass();
            pc.x = pc.y = 22;

            Console.WriteLine("Before method: pc is ({0}, {1})", pc.x, pc.y);
            ChangeClass(pc);
            Console.WriteLine("After method:  pc is ({0}, {1})", pc.x, pc.y);
        }
        static void ChangeStructure(PointStruct ps)
        {
            ps.x = ps.y = 33;
        }
        static void ChangeClass(PointClass pc)
        {
            pc.x = pc.y = 33;
        }
    }
    struct PointStruct
    {
        public int x, y;
    }
    class PointClass
    {
        public int x, y;
    }
```

In Chapter 30, we saw that a method can change elements of arrays that are passed to the method. The MethodCallTest program demonstrates that methods can change the fields of classes but not of structures. The program results are:

```
Before method: ps is (22, 22)
After method:  ps is (22, 22)
Before method: pc is (22, 22)
After method:  pc is (33, 33)
```

When a program passes an object to a method in preparation for a method call, what happens depends on whether the object is based on a structure or a class. If the object is a value type, a bitwise copy is made for use by the method. If the object is a reference type, the reference is copied for use by the method. The method can use this reference to change any field of the class. These changes affect the original object.

That equality, assignment, and method calls all work differently with objects created from structures and classes is certainly important to know. But underlying these differences is an equally important fact involving the *new* operator: A call to the *new* operator is required to create a new instance of a class, and the *new* operator initiates some very serious activity. The *new* operator allocates memory from the heap for the object and calls one of the class's constructors. For this reason, *new* operations don't arbitrarily occur behind the scenes. (Well, there are some exceptions, particularly involving strings.) For example:

```
PointClass pc1 = new PointClass();
PointClass pc2 = pc1;
```

There's only one *new* expression in this code, so only one instance of *PointClass* is involved here. Similarly, a *new* operation doesn't take place when an object is passed to a method. The method is working with the the same object passed to it. The following code is much different because it creates two distinct objects:

```
PointClass pc1 = new PointClass();
PointClass pc2 = new PointClass();
```

This whole issue becomes crucial when you start working with classes with constructors that do more than just initialize a few fields. Some classes that I'll discuss toward the end of this book have constructors that open disk files in preparation for reading and writing. You don't want the same file reopened if you happen to pass the object to a method. Some Windows Forms classes create user interface objects such as buttons or dialog boxes in their constructors. Again, you don't want multiple buttons or dialog boxes created just by passing the object to a method.

Creating a new instance of a class is often serious business, and that's why it doesn't happen without you, the programmer, knowing about it.

Creating a new instance of a structure is much less serious. This code involving a structure:

```
PointStruct ps1 = new PointStruct();
PointStruct ps2 = ps1;
```

is equivalent to code that has two *new* operators:

```
PointStruct ps1 = new PointStruct();
PointStruct ps2 = new PointStruct();
```

These two little blocks of code are equivalent because the parameterless constructor of a structure only initializes all the fields to 0 or *null*. And it never *can* do anything else. C# doesn't allow you to initialize the fields of a structure to non-zero values or to write your own parameterless constructor. That privilege is reserved for classes.

35

Fields and Properties

Despite all the consistency checking implemented in the *Date* constructor of the ConsistencyChecking program in Chapter 33, the class is still not safe from invalid dates. A program using the class can create a valid date by using one of the constructors and then set invalid dates simply by setting the fields:

```
Date dt = new Date(2005, 2, 2);
dt.iDay = 31;
```

Setting the fields is possible because the fields are public. If you don't want the fields in a class to be changed by programs using the class, you should make the fields private:

```
private int iYear;
private int iMonth;
private int iDay;
```

Or because private is the default, simply remove the access modifier entirely:

```
int iYear;
int iMonth;
int iDay;
```

That solves the invalid date problem, but at a cost. Code encountering a *Date* object can't even determine what date is represented by the object! A better solution is to make the fields public but also to mark them as read-only:

```
public readonly int iYear;
public readonly int iMonth;
public readonly int iDay;
```

The *readonly* modifier can be used only on fields. You can initialize a read-only field in the declaration:

```
public readonly int iYear = 1;
```

You can also set a read-only field in the constructor:

```
class Date
{
    public readonly int iYear;

    ...
    public Date(int iYear, iMonth, iDay)
    {

        ...
        this.iYear = iYear;

        ...
    }

    ...
}
```

But after the constructor finishes, a read-only field is fixed and cannot be changed. Using *readonly* on the fields essentially makes the *Date* object immutable. You set the value of the *Date* object at creation, and then you're stuck with it. That's not necessarily a bad thing. An immutable object may be exactly what you need in some cases. The *DateTime* structure in the .NET Framework is immutable.

Let's step back a moment and review the *modifiers* that you can use with fields and methods. The modifiers always appear before the type of the field or the return type of the method, but they can be in any order among themselves.

The access modifiers are *public* and *private*. (There are actually three more access modifiers—*protected*, *internal*, and *internal protected*—that I'll discuss later in this book.) These two modifiers are mutually exclusive and indicate whether a field or method is accessible from outside the class or whether its use is restricted to methods inside the class.

The *static* modifier indicates that the field or method is associated with the class rather than an instance of the class. You refer to a static field or method by prefacing it with the class name. You refer to an instance field or method by prefacing it with an object name. A static method cannot refer to an instance field and cannot call an instance method.

You can use *const* to create a constant. It's not quite correct to say that a constant is a field. (The *C# Language Specification* discusses them in two separate sections: §10.3 and §10.4. However, in the documentation of classes in the .NET Framework, constants are listed under the category of Fields.) As with local constants (that is, constants declared inside of methods), the value of a constant must be set in the declaration, and it must be available at compile time. The value of a constant cannot be changed by code. Although you cannot use the *static* keyword with constants, a constant is inherently static. That is, you refer to a constant with the class name rather than an instance of the class.

The *readonly* modifier is valid only with fields. The value of a read-only field must be set in the declaration or by a constructor. After the conclusion of the constructor, a read-only field cannot be modified.

The *static, const,* and *readonly* modifiers are somewhat related: A constant has only a single value regardless of the instance, so a constant is inherently static. A *readonly* field is generally an instance field, but after a constructor finishes execution, it becomes similar to a constant in that it cannot be changed.

There are times when you want to declare a constant, but the value is not available at compile time. This is the case if you're trying to set a constant using a *new* expression:

```
const Date dateSputnik = new Date(1957, 10, 4);    // Won't work!
```

Expressions using *new* can be executed only at run time. The *C# Language Specification,* §10.4.2.1, has the solution: Use *static readonly* rather than *const*:

```
static readonly Date dateSputnik = new Date(1957, 10, 4);
```

You may be satisfied with an immutable *Date* object with those *readonly* fields that cannot be changed after the constructor terminates. Or you may want a *Date* object that you can later change. If that is so, let's go for a different approach. Let's make the fields private, but let's also give a program the opportunity to change the fields on an existing *Date* object. You do this by providing public methods in the class that access and change the private fields. The methods that change the fields can also perform consistency checking.

Traditionally, such methods begin with the words *Set* and *Get.* Here's a possible public *SetYear* method to change a private *iYear* field:

```
public void SetYear(int iYear)
{
    if (iYear < 1)
        throw new ArgumentOutOfRangeException("Year");

    this.iYear = iYear;
}
```

The method is public. The field is private. There's actually a subtle problem with the *SetYear* method that I'll describe shortly. For now, I'm sure you get the general idea. The *GetYear* method is quite simple:

```
public int GetYear()
{
    return iYear;
}
```

Notice that the two methods are somewhat symmetrical. The *SetYear* method has a single *int* argument and returns nothing, indicated by the keyword *void*. The *GetYear* method has an empty parameter list but returns an *int* value. Likewise, you could also write *SetMonth*, *GetMonth*, *SetDay*, and *GetDay* methods.

Here's how you'd use the *Set* methods in some code if you prefer to set the date after the object has been created:

```
Date dateMoonWalk = new Date();

dateMoonWalk.SetYear(1969);
dateMoonWalk.SetMonth(7);
dateMoonWalk.SetDay(20);
```

Likewise, you can access the year, month, and day using the *GetYear*, *GetMonth*, and *GetDay* methods.

But like I said, that's the *traditional* approach. C# has another feature that's a little cleaner, a little easier, and a little prettier, and that's called the *property*.

Like methods, fields, and constants, properties are also members of classes and structures. We've already encountered some properties earlier in this book. The *Length* property of the *String* class indicates the length of the string. The *Array* class has a *Length* property and a *Rank* property. All these properties are read-only, but properties that you declare in your classes and structures don't have to be.

In use, properties look a lot like fields. Here's how you might set a *Date* object using three properties named *Year*, *Month*, and *Day*:

```
dateMoonWalk.Year = 1969;
dateMoonWalk.Month = 7;
dateMoonWalk.Day = 20;
```

It's unusual to use Hungarian Notation with property names. Similarly, you can access properties as if they were fields:

```
Console.WriteLine("The moon walk took place in " + dateMoonWalk.Year);
```

This code is much more attractive and readable than the equivalent code using the *Set* and *Get* methods.

Public properties are often associated with private fields, although they don't have to be. Properties are sometimes called "smart" fields because they can add a little code (such as consistency and validity checks) to getting and setting fields.

Properties are not actually part of the Common Language Specification (CLS), nor are they implemented in intermediate language. When you declare a property named *Year*, for example, the C# compiler fabricates methods named *set_Year* and *get_Year* that contain the property code. If you use a language that doesn't support properties (such as C++), you'll have to refer to properties using these method names. You can't have method names in your C# class that duplicate the names that the compiler uses with the property. (See the *C# Language Specification*, §10.2.7.1.) For example, if you declare a *Year* property, you can't also declare a method named *get_Year*.

Here's a declaration of a *Year* property that is functionally equivalent to the *SetYear* and *GetYear* methods I showed earlier:

```
public int Year
{
    set
    {
        if (value < 1)
            throw new ArgumentOutOfRangeException("Year");

        iYear = value;
    }
    get
    {
        return iYear;
    }
}
```

The property declaration begins with an optional access modifier and then the type of the property, which here is *int*. That's the type of the argument to the *SetYear* method, and the return type of the *GetYear* method. That symmetry is how both methods can be combined into a single property.

The name of the property is *Year*. A left curly bracket follows the name. That's how the compiler knows it's not a method or a field. If *Year* were a method, the name would be followed by a left parenthesis. If *Year* were a field, it wouldn't be followed by a left curly bracket. Properties can also include the *static* modifier or any other modifier used with methods.

Within the outer set of curly brackets are one or two sections (called *accessors*) that begin with the word *get* and *set*. Often both sections are present. If only a *get* accessor is present (which is common as well), the property is read-only. If there's only a *set* accessor (which is very rare), the property is write-only. The words *set* and *get* are not considered C# keywords because you can use the words as variable names. They have a special meaning only in this particular place in the property declaration.

Within the body of the property declaration, *set* and *get* are both followed by another set of curly brackets. In the *set* accessor, the word *value* refers to the value being set to the property; the *get* accessor must have a *return* statement to return a value.

I haven't shown code yet for the *Month* and *Day* properties, but I mentioned earlier that there was a subtle problem in the *SetYear* code, which I reused for the *set* accessor for *Year*. Suppose you create a *Date* object like so:

```
Date dt = new Date(2004, 2, 29);
```

That's OK. Because 2004 is a leap year, the date of February 29 is fine. But look what happens when the program then sets the *Year* property to something else:

```
date.Year = 2005;
```

As written, the *Year* property allows this year to be set, but the date is now invalid. You'd need to rewrite the *Year* property to check that the new year is consistent with the month and day:

```
if (value < 1 || (!IsLeapYear(value) && iMonth == 2 && iDay == 29))
    throw new ArgumentOutOfRangeException("Year");
```

That's not the only problem with consistency checking. Suppose a program using the *Date* class first creates a valid date:

```
Date dt = new Date(2004, 2, 29);
```

And then the program sets the three properties to something else:

```
date.Year = 2005;
date.Month = 3;
date.Day = 12;
```

Well, the program doesn't get quite that far because the revised *Year* property is diligent in rejecting the year 2005 even though it's obvious to us that eventually the new date will be just fine. Rearrange the statements and nobody objects:

```
date.Month = 3;
date.Year = 2005;
date.Day = 12;
```

In this case, surviving the validity checks requires that the *Date* fields be changed in a specific order.

This problem isn't really solvable. If you want to provide properties that allow a program to set the fields of the *Date* structure, and you want to prevent invalid dates, some sequences of code will work overall but won't work in the order that they're written. But the worst that can be said is that the code is overprotective.

Let's proceed to incorporate properties into the *Date* class. In general, I like structuring my classes like this: All instance fields go at the top, and they're usually private. Next, public properties provide access to the private fields. If possible, all the rest of the code in the class makes use of the properties rather than the fields. The constructors come next, followed by the methods.

Here's the new *Date* class that implements properties. Because this is the last version of *Date* I'll be showing you, I've isolated the class in its own file for possible use by other programs. I've added a static method named *IsConsistent* that's called by the *set* accessors of all three properties. Each *set* accessor calls *IsConsistent* using *value* (which is the value that the property is being set to) and the other two properties. At no time does this *Date* class allow an invalid date.

Date.cs

```
// -------------------------------------------------
// Date.cs from "Programming in the Key of C#"
// -------------------------------------------------
using System;

class Date
{
    // Private fields

    int iYear = 1;
    int iMonth = 1;
    int iDay = 1;

    // Public properties

    public int Year
    {
        set
        {
            if (!IsConsistent(value, Month, Day))
                throw new ArgumentOutOfRangeException("Year");

            iYear = value;
        }
        get
        {
            return iYear;
        }
    }

    public int Month
    {
        set
        {
            if (!IsConsistent(Year, value, Day))
                throw new ArgumentOutOfRangeException("Month");
```

```
                iMonth = value;
        }
        get
        {
            return iMonth;
        }
    }

    public int Day
    {
        set
        {
            if (!IsConsistent(Year, Month, value))
                throw new ArgumentOutOfRangeException("Day");

            iDay = value;
        }
        get
        {
            return iDay;
        }
    }

    // Private method used by the properties

    static bool IsConsistent(int iYear, int iMonth, int iDay)
    {
        if (iYear < 1)
            return false;

        if (iMonth < 1 || iMonth > 12)
            return false;

        if (iDay < 1 || iDay > 31)
            return false;

        if (iDay == 31 && (iMonth == 4 || iMonth == 6 ||
                           iMonth == 9 || iMonth == 11))
            return false;

        if (iMonth == 2 && iDay > 29)
            return false;

        if (iMonth == 2 && iDay == 29 && !IsLeapYear(iYear))
            return false;

        return true;
    }
```

```
// Parameterless constructor

public Date()
{
}

// Parametered constructor

public Date(int iYear, int iMonth, int iDay)
{
    Year = iYear;
    Month = iMonth;
    Day = iDay;
}

public static bool IsLeapYear(int iYear)
{
    return iYear % 4 == 0 && (iYear % 100 != 0 || iYear % 400 == 0);
}

static int[] aiCumulativeDays = { 0, 31, 59, 90, 120, 151,
                                  181, 212, 243, 273, 304, 334 };

public int DayOfYear()
{
    return aiCumulativeDays[Month - 1] + Day +
        (Month > 2 && IsLeapYear(Year) ? 1 : 0);
}

static string[] astrMonths = { "Jan", "Feb", "Mar", "Apr", "May", "Jun",
                               "Jul", "Aug", "Sep", "Oct", "Nov", "Dec"};

public override string ToString()
{
    return String.Format("{0} {1} {2}", Day,
        astrMonths[Month - 1], Year);
}
}
```

The constructors and all the instance methods use the properties rather than the fields. Even the property *set* accessors use the other properties when calling *IsConsistent*. This is not a requirement. Methods in a class can use either the class properties or the fields. But you'll see shortly why I like to structure my classes so that field accesses are kept to a minimum.

Here's a simple program that makes use of the *Date* class.

PropertyTest.cs
```
// ---------------------------------------------------
// PropertyTest.cs from "Programming in the Key of C#"
// ---------------------------------------------------
using System;

class PropertyTest
{
    static void Main()
    {
        Date dateMoonWalk = new Date();

        dateMoonWalk.Year = 1969;
        dateMoonWalk.Month = 7;
        dateMoonWalk.Day = 20;

        Console.WriteLine("Moon walk: {0}, Day of Year: {1}",
            dateMoonWalk, dateMoonWalk.DayOfYear());
    }
}
```

You can try setting the properties to invalid dates to see whether the consistency checking works.

Sometimes it's not clear whether a particular chunk of code should be a method or a property. Properties are often considered to be *characteristics* of the object, whereas methods often perform *actions*. A property is a noun; a method is a verb. If you can associate the words *get* and *set* with a method, you may want to make it a property. I'd be inclined to make *DayOfYear* a read-only property, for example. The only real rule is this: If it needs a parameter to get the value or an extra parameter to set the value, it's got to be method.

When we embarked on this project to encapsulate the date several chapters ago, we experimented with making *Date* either a class or a structure. But it soon became evident that doing it as a structure had some distinct problems. When an object is created from a *Date* structure using a parameterless constructor, there is no way to initialize the three fields to 1. Fields in a structure are always initialized to 0 or *null*.

Let's ask ourselves the question again: How can we implement *Date* as a structure and prevent an invalid date when the parameterless constructor is used to create the object?

Big hint: The *get* accessor of a property doesn't have to return simply the value of a field.

In fact, a *get* accessor can return the value of a field *plus one*. In other words, the private *iYear*, *iMonth*, and *iDay* fields can be zero-based, but the *Year*, *Month*, and *Day* properties can be one-based. Here's a revised *Year* property that uses this technique:

```
public int Year
{
    set
    {
        if (!IsConsistent(value - 1, Month, Day))
            throw new ArgumentOutOfRangeException("Year");

        iYear = value - 1;
    }
    get
    {
        return iYear + 1;
    }
}
```

The only difference is that the *set* accessor refers to *value* minus 1 rather than *value*, and the *get* accessor returns the field plus 1. The default *iYear* field is 0, but the *Year* property returns 1. Properties provide a type of buffer around fields that you can use to make the internals of a class or structure different than how it looks from outside.

A few other changes are required to convert *Date* from a class to a structure: First, most obviously, you'll change the *class* keyword to *struct*. The initialization of the three fields must be removed. Fields can't be initialized in a structure. The parameterless constructor would have to be removed because explicit parameterless constructors aren't allowed in a structure. You'll also need to add the following three lines to the beginning of the parametered constructor:

```
this.iYear = 0;
this.iMonth = 0;
this.iDay = 0;
```

Otherwise, there's a problem. When the constructor begins execution, the three fields are unassigned. The C# compiler won't let the constructor (or other code) use a property until values are assigned to all three fields. (The PropertyTestWithStructure project included with the Companion Content has the complete code of the *Date* structure.)

Before moving on from the subject of properties, I'd like to mention one other type of member. Although not appropriate for the *Date* class, C# supports a special member called the *indexer* that is declared somewhat like a property. An indexer is intended for classes or structures that store collections of items.

Programs using such a class can index an object of that class using square brackets as if the object were an array. The declaration of an indexer uses the keyword *this* followed by square brackets containing a parameter list:

```
public string this[int i]
{
    get
    {
        … // Return string value based on index i.
    }
    set
    {
        … // Save string value based on index i.
    }
}
```

The parameter list in the square brackets must have at least one item. These parameters need not be integers. I'll have an example of an indexer in the *NoteStreamArrayList* class in Chapter 41.

In the documentation of classes and structures in the .NET Framework, indexers are listed among the properties with the name *Item*. In your C# programs, you never use that word to refer to indexers. As with properties, C# fabricates indexers by creating methods named *get_Item* and *set_Item*. You must use these names when referring to indexers when programming in a language that doesn't support indexers, such as C++.

36

Inheritance

No class is an island. All classes are related to each other in some way. All classes, for example, automatically have methods named *ToString* and *Equals*. These two methods are declared in a very special class named *System.Object*— a class that's also known by the C# keyword *object*. All other classes also contain these two methods because all other classes ultimately *derive* (or *inherit*) from *System.Object*.

Inheritance is one of the primary features of object-oriented programming. When a new class derives from an existing class (or *subclasses* an existing class), it inherits all the nonprivate methods, properties, and fields declared in the existing class. The new class can then extend the existing class by adding to or replacing these methods, properties, and fields. The process is cumulative. A class contains all the nonprivate methods, properties, and fields declared in itself and all its ancestor classes going back to *System.Object*.

It's all about reusing code. Inheritance provides a structured way to reuse code that's already been written, but inheritance also provides a way to alter or enhance the code in ways that make it more useful or convenient.

The ability to inherit is one of the differences between classes and structures. Structures do not allow inheritance. All structures implicitly derive from *System.ValueType*, which derives from *System.Object*. But you can't declare a class that inherits from a structure, or declare a structure that inherits from another structure. Once you declare a structure, that's the end of the line.

There are many reasons why you'd want to use inheritance. For example, suppose you have a class that's fine for most of your requirements, but it needs just a few little changes. Even if you have access to the source code, you might not want to change the original class. Maybe the class is working well in some other application, and you'd just prefer not to mess around with it. Or perhaps you don't have access to the code. Maybe the class is available only in compiled form in a dynamic link library (DLL).

As another example of why you might want to use inheritance, suppose you're writing a book about object-oriented programming, and the class you've been using to demonstrate the various features of object-oriented programming has gotten a bit too long to show comfortably in the pages of the book. It makes sense to show future additions in a new class that derives from the original class.

Mostly, however, inheritance is used as an architectural mechanism that allows programmers to avoid duplicating code. Often a programmer will see that a particular job requires (for example) several classes. With further work and design, it appears that two of these classes would share about 75 percent of their code. It makes sense for one of these classes to inherit from the other, perhaps replacing a method or two, perhaps adding a method or two, whatever's required. Object-oriented design is an art (and a science) in itself, and this book will only scratch the surface.

With any luck, programmers who have come before you have used their skills to create object-oriented libraries that exhibit an intelligent structure of inheritance. If you'll eventually be writing Windows applications using the Windows Forms library (defined largely in the *System.Windows.Forms* namespace of the .NET Framework), you'll be working a lot with *controls*, which are visual user interface objects such as buttons, scroll bars, and so forth. These controls are declared in a vast hierarchy of inheritance, just a little bit of which is shown here:

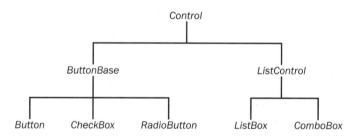

Typically, as classes inherit from other classes, they get less generalized and more specific. Windows Forms programs that you write can subclass from the predefined classes and make these controls even more specific—for example, a button that always has red italic text.

Let's begin our exploration of inheritance by examining how to declare a class that subclasses another class. In this chapter, I'll be creating a class named *ExtDate* (extended date) that inherits from the final *Date* class shown at the end of Chapter 35.

The simplest subclassing syntax is

```
class ExtDate: Date
{
}
```

The name of the *ExtDate* class is followed by a colon and then the name of the class that it's subclassing, in this case *Date*. *Date* is known as the *base* class to *ExtDate*. Many programmers put a space before the colon, but it's not necessary. If you don't indicate a base class when you're declaring a class, then the class is assumed to derive from *object*. A class can inherit from only one other class. Multiple inheritance—a feature of some object-oriented languages in which a class can inherit from multiple classes—is not supported by C#.

With this simple declaration of *ExtDate*, we have declared a new class that contains all the nonprivate methods, properties, and fields that are declared in *Date*.

What *ExtDate* does *not* inherit from *Date*, however, are the constructors. Highlight this sentence: Constructors are not inherited.

Because *ExtDate* does not declare any constructors (not yet, anyway), C# provides a parameterless constructor. You can create an *ExtDate* object like so:

```
ExtDate exdt = new ExtDate();
```

And you can then set the *Year*, *Month*, and *Day* properties that *ExtDate* inherits from *Date*. But you cannot use the three-parameter constructor declared in *Date* to create an *ExtDate* object.

If you'd like to provide a similar constructor in *ExtDate*, you must explicitly declare it. And if you do declare a three-parameter constructor in *ExtDate*, then *ExtDate* will no longer have an automatic parameterless constructor, so you must provide that one as well. Here's one approach that's identical to the constructor code in *Date*:

```
class ExtDate: Date
{
    public ExtDate()
    {
    }
    public ExtDate(int iYear, int iMonth, int iDay)
    {
        Year = iYear;
        Month = iMonth;
        Day = iDay;
    }
}
```

Notice that the three-parameter constructor uses the properties declared in *Date*. That's fine because *ExtDate* has inherited those properties. But a better way to declare the three-parameter constructor is to call the constructor in the base class, which involves a special syntax:

```
class ExtDate: Date
{
    public ExtDate()
    {
    }
    public ExtDate(int iYear, int iMonth, int iDay): base(iYear, iMonth, iDay)
    {
    }
}
```

Notice the colon following the parameter list. The colon is followed by the keyword *base*. The base class of *ExtDate* is *Date*. More specifically, in this context, the keyword *base* refers to a constructor in the base class. The keyword *base* is followed by three arguments in parentheses, so it refers to the three-parameter constructor in *Date*. When the *ExtDate* constructor executes, the three-parameter constructor in *Date* is called first, and then execution continues with the code in the body of the *ExtDate* constructor (if any).

I showed you a feature similar to this at the end of Chapter 33, but using the keyword *this* rather than *base*. Collectively the constructor calls are termed *constructor initializers*. A constructor initializer causes another constructor in the same class or the base class to be executed before the code in the body of a constructor.

Only one constructor initializer is allowed per constructor. If you don't include one, then one is implicitly provided for you that calls the parameterless constructor in the base class. In other words, you'll never need to provide a constructor initializer of *base()*. That initializer is provided automatically if you don't provide an alternative.

Imagine a series of classes. Class *Instrument* derives from *object*, and class *Woodwind* derives from *Instrument*, and class *Oboe* derives from *Woodwind*. All of these classes have parameterless constructors with no explicit constructor initializers. When you create an object of type *Oboe*, the constructor in *Oboe* first executes the parameterless constructor in *Woodwind*, which first executes the parameterless constructor in *Instrument*, which first executes the parameterless constructor in *object*. The final result in this chain of nested constructor calls is that the constructors are executed beginning with *object*, then *Instrument*, then *Woodwind*, and finally *Oboe*. This happens even if you're using a constructor in *Oboe* that has parameters. Just as long as that constructor has no explicit constructor initializers, the parameterless constructors in *object*, *Instrument*, and *Woodwind* are executed before the constructor code in *Oboe*.

In summary, if a constructor has no explicit constructor initializer, then the parameterless constructor in the base class is executed before the code in the body of the constructor. If the constructor includes a constructor initalizer (either *base* or *this*), then the code in that constructor is executed first. Nothing else happens automatically. In particular, a constructor with parameters does *not* automatically execute the parameterless constructor in the same class unless you specifically tell it to with a constructor initializer of *this()*.

Here's another way to think of it: whenever your program creates an object, the parameterless constructor in *System.Object* is called first, followed by constructors in the descendents of *object* leading up to the constructor in the class that you're using to create the object.

What's interesting is that you can never *prevent* execution of some constructor in the base class. Think about it. If you want to prevent a constructor from calling the parameterless constructor in the base class, you must provide a constructor initializer. If you don't want *any* constructor in the base class to execute, you must specify a constructor initializer that uses *this* rather than *base*. But you can't do that for every constructor in your class. You'll end up with a circular chain of constructor calls, which by common sense (and the *C# Language Specification*, §10.10.1) is prohibited.

It's important for *some* constructor in the base class to always be executed because that's how fields are initialized. Every constructor actually begins *first* by setting the values of initialized fields in that class and then by executing another constructor, either explicitly (with a constructor initializer) or implicitly by calling the parameterless constructor in the base class. If a constructor in the base class were never called, then the fields in the base class wouldn't be initialized, and that could cause problems.

Here's a program that contains a simple declaration of *ExtDate* that declares two constructors that call the corresponding constructors in the base class:

Inheritance.cs

```
// ---------------------------------------------------
// Inheritance.cs from "Programming in the Key of C#"
// ---------------------------------------------------
using System;

class Inheritance
{
    static void Main()
    {
        ExtDate dateMoonWalk = new ExtDate(1969, 7, 20);
```

```
            Console.WriteLine("Moon walk: {0}, Day of Year: {1}",
                dateMoonWalk, dateMoonWalk.DayOfYear());
        }
    }

class ExtDate: Date
{
    public ExtDate()
    {
    }
    public ExtDate(int iYear, int iMon, int iDay): base(iYear, iMon, iDay)
    {
    }
}
```

Because *ExtDate* inherits from *Date*, the Inheritance project must include the Date.cs file containing the *Date* class. The Inheritance.cs and Date.cs files must be compiled together, but you probably don't want to create a copy of Date.cs for this project. To include the original Date.cs file in the new project, you use a technique similar to that described in Chapter 17 for the AnotherProgram project. In Visual C# .NET, select Add Existing Item from the Project menu. Navigate to the Chap35\PropertyTest project (which is where the Date.cs file is). Click the down arrow on the Open button and select the Link File option. In Key of C#, select Link To Existing Source Code File from the Project menu, navigate to the Chap35\PropertyTest project, and select Date.cs.

The *Date* class contains constructors, methods, and properties with access modifiers of *public*, and also one method (*IsConsistent*) and several fields with no access modifiers, which is the same as having an access modifier of *private*. The *public* access modifier allows members of a class to be accessed from other classes. The *private* modifier prohibits the members from being accessed from other classes.

The *public* and *private* access modifiers apply to derived classes as well! The *ExtDate* class *cannot* call the *IsConsistent* method and cannot directly access any of the fields in *Date*.

Between these two extremes is the access modifier *protected*. A method, property, or field declared as *protected* is accessible in the class in which it's declared, and also in any classes that derive from that class. For example, if *Date* had a method declared as *protected*, then *Date* could use that method (of course) and *ExtDate* could use that method, and any other class derived from *Date* could use that method, but a class that is not derived from *Date* would have no access to that method.

Using *public*, *private*, and *protected* in an intelligent manner takes some thought and practice. Sometimes beginning programmers want to declare everything as *public* so that every class can access anything in any other class. (Microsoft Visual Basic actually fosters this attitude because class members are public by default.) But generally a class should have a bare minimum of public members. It's much easier to debug a class if other classes can affect it or access it in a very limited number of ways. When you're debugging, you're sometimes like a detective solving a crime and it's helpful to say: "The perpetrator could only have entered through this door or that window." Too many public members violates the concepts of hiding data and prevents the class from being a black box of code.

To declare something in a class as *protected* implies that you're giving some thought to what may be useful to classes that derive from the class. If you're declaring a bunch of related classes yourself, sometimes it will be obvious that certain methods or properties are useful to derived classes but not to other classes.

The next version of *ExtDate* I'm going to show you includes a new property named *CommonEraDay*. This property returns the number of days since the beginning of the common era. The date 1/1/1 has a *CommonEraDay* property of 1. The property will also let you set a date using the *set* accessor of *CommonEraDay*.

ExtDate.cs

```
// -------------------------------------------------
// ExtDate.cs from "Programming in the Key of C#"
// -------------------------------------------------
using System;

class ExtDate: Date
{
    // Constructors just execute constructors in base class.

    public ExtDate()
    {
    }
    public ExtDate(int iYear, int iMon, int iDay): base(iYear, iMon, iDay)
    {
    }

    // Private method for use by CommonEraDay property.
```

```
int DaysBeforeYear()
{
    int iYear = Year - 1;

    return (int) (365.25m * iYear) - iYear / 100 + iYear / 400;
}


// CommonEraDay sets/gets number of days since beginning of common era.

public int CommonEraDay
{
    get
    {
        return DaysBeforeYear() + DayOfYear();
    }
    set
    {
        Day = 1;      // Prevent inconsistencies during the calculation.

        // Year calculation if leap years were every four years.

        Year = (int) ((value - .125m) / 365.25m) + 1;
        int iDayOfYear = value - DaysBeforeYear();

        // Adjust for leap year anomalies every hundred years.

        if (iDayOfYear > (IsLeapYear(Year) ? 366 : 365))
        {
            iDayOfYear -= IsLeapYear(Year) ? 366 : 365;
            Year++;
        }

        // Find the Month and Day

        for (Month = 12; Month > 0; Month--)
        {
            if (iDayOfYear >= DayOfYear())
            {
                Day = iDayOfYear - DayOfYear() + 1;
                break;
            }
        }
    }
}
```

The code in the *CommonEraDay* property assumes that the leap year rules we currently observe were in effect from the beginning of the common era. In reality, much of the Western world celebrated leap years every four years without exception until the introduction of the Gregorian calendar in 1582. To reorient the calendar to compensate for the damage caused by the Julian calendar, 10 days were skipped. The date October 4, 1582 was followed by October 15, 1582. Algorithms that account for the switch from the Julian calendar to the Gregorian calendar are truly messy.[*] My approach isn't quite as bad, and doesn't conk out until the year 48,702. Don't worry if you don't quite get it. The nitty-gritties of the calculation aren't really the point of this exercise.

Here's a program that tests the *ExtDate* class. The CommonEraDayTest project contains this code, the ExtDate.cs file, and a link to Date.cs.

CommonEraDayTest.cs

```
// ----------------------------------------------------------
// CommonEraDayTest.cs from "Programming in the Key of C#"
// ----------------------------------------------------------
using System;

class CommonEraDayTest
{
    static void Main()
    {
        Console.Write("Enter the year of your birth: ");
        int iYear = Int32.Parse(Console.ReadLine());

        Console.Write("And the month: ");
        int iMonth = Int32.Parse(Console.ReadLine());

        Console.Write("And the day: ");
        int iDay = Int32.Parse(Console.ReadLine());

        ExtDate exdtBirthday = new ExtDate(iYear, iMonth, iDay);
        ExtDate exdtMoonWalk = new ExtDate(1969, 7, 20);

        int iElapsed = exdtMoonWalk.CommonEraDay - exdtBirthday.CommonEraDay;

        if (iElapsed > 0)
            Console.WriteLine("You were born {0} days before the moon walk.",
                              iElapsed);
        else if (iElapsed == 0)
            Console.WriteLine("You were born on the day of the moon walk.");
```

---

[*] For a taste of what's involved, see Chapter 5 of Meeus, Jean, *Astronomical Algorithms* (Willmann-Bell, 1991).

```
        else
            Console.WriteLine("You were born {0} days after the moon walk.",
                    -iElapsed);
    }
}
```

This program calculates a difference between two dates by subtracting one *CommonEraDay* property from another. We're actually coming very close to performing arithmetic on objects. In Chapter 38, you'll witness the final step.

37

Virtuality

As you saw in Chapter 34, concepts of equality that were intuitively clear earlier in this book have become somewhat muddied. Inheritance raises its own issues regarding equality and assignment. To what extent are classes that are related by inheritance equivalent to each other?

It turns out that object-oriented languages like C# provide some interesting features related to inheritance that culminate in the magic of virtual methods.

The most basic of these features involve conversion. In particular, C# provides implicit conversions from any object to any ancestral type. To explore these conversions, let's use the *ExtDate* class shown in Chapter 36, which derives from the *Date* class finalized in Chapter 35. The *Date* class implicitly derives from the *System.Object* class, also known by the C# keyword *object*. Both *object* and *Date* are ancestral types to *ExtDate*.

Let's begin by creating an *ExtDate* object:

```
ExtDate exdt = new ExtDate();
```

Because C# provides an implicit conversion from *exdt* to an object of any ancestral type, you can assign *exdt* to an object declared to be of type *Date*:

```
Date dt = exdt;
```

No new object is created by this statement. The only object we're dealing with here was created by the *new* expression in the preceding statement. That expression created an object of type *ExtDate* in the heap and returned a reference to it. Now the *dt* variable refers to that same object. In fact, the expression

```
exdt == dt
```

will return *true*.

C# allows a conversion from *ExtDate* to *Date* for two reasons: First, all references are the same size. The compiler has reserved space on the stack for both *exdt* and *dt* sufficient to store a reference, and there's no practical problem in copying this reference from one slot on the stack to another. Second, in this particular case, C# allows the conversion because *ExtDate* derives from *Date*. In a very real sense, an *ExtDate* object also qualifies as a *Date* object, and that's because an *ExtDate* object can do anything that's requested of a *Date* object. For example, the expression

```
dt.DayOfYear()
```

is no problem for an *ExtDate* object because *ExtDate* inherits the *DayOfYear* method from *Date*.

But this expression *is* a problem:

```
dt.CommonEraDay
```

Even though the *dt* variable is really referring to an instance of *ExtDate*, and *ExtDate* supports the *CommonEraDay* property, the C# compiler won't let this expression pass. The compiler knows that *dt* was declared to be an object of type *Date* and that *CommonEraDay* is not a property of *Date*. Hence, the expression is invalid.

Assigning an object to a variable of an ancestral type is sometimes known as *upcasting*, even though you don't need an explicit cast. The conversion is implicit, and it's always allowed.

Just as you can assign an *ExtDate* object to a *Date* variable, you can declare a variable of type *object* and assign an *ExtDate* object to it:

```
object obj = exdt;
```

You can assign any object to this *obj* variable because every object is created from a class or structure that derives from *object*. Every object is an *object*.

The *obj* variable to which we've assigned an instance of *ExtDate* still "knows" in some way that it's actually an *ExtDate* object. That information is part of what's stored in the heap along with the instance fields of the object itself. For example, if you pass *obj* to *Console.WriteLine*, as

```
Console.WriteLine(obj);
```

you'll see the date displayed. What's actually being called in this case is the *ToString* method. The compiler allows the *ToString* method to be called for *obj* because the *System.Object* class contains a *ToString* method. As you recall, *Date* overrode the *ToString* method, and that version was inherited by *ExtDate*. That the correct *ToString* method gets called is part of the magic associated with declaring and overriding virtual methods. That's what this chapter is about.

It will be convenient to refer to a particular variable by its *declared* type and its *actual* type. For example, consider the *obj* variable declared earlier. Its declared type is *object*. But because it was assigned an object of type *ExtDate*, its actual type is *ExtDate*. A variable's declared type never changes. In these examples, you'll always know a variable's declared type because the Hungarian Notation prefix will indicate that type. A variable's actual type, however, can change as the variable is assigned different objects. A variable's actual type is always its declared type or a descendent of its declared type.

Although C# provides an implicit conversion from any object to any ancestral type, going the other way (*downcasting*, it's sometimes called) requires an explicit cast:

```
ExtDate exdt2 = (ExtDate) obj;
```

Even if *obj* were never assigned an object of type *ExtDate* in the program, the C# compiler would still allow this cast based entirely on the declared types of *exdt2* and *obj*. Because *ExtDate* is derived from *object*, *obj* could conceivably be storing an object of type *ExtDate*, so the C# compiler awards that cast and assignment statement its good programming seal of approval.

However, there's still run time to consider. If at run-time *obj* is not actually an *ExtDate* object (or an instance of a class derived from *ExtDate,* if such a class existed), then the assignment statement throws an *InvalidCastException*.

If the actual type of *obj* is *ExtDate*, you can even cast it and access a property of *ExtDate* in the same expression:

```
((ExtDate) obj).CommonEraDay
```

The double parentheses are needed because casting is a unary operation and the period is a primary operation that has higher precedence than the unary operation. You can also cast *obj* to a *Date* object to access a property or call a method declared in *Date*:

```
((Date) obj).DayOfYear()
```

But you wouldn't be able to cast *obj* to a class that derives from *ExtDate*, if such a class existed. That cast would fail at run time, and it makes sense that it should, because a class that derives from *ExtDate* can do more than *ExtDate* can, and the actual type of *obj* is just *ExtDate*.

If *obj* isn't actually an *ExtDate* object (or a class that derives from *ExtDate*), and you try to cast it to an *ExtDate* object, you'll raise an exception. To avoid raising an exception, you can use the *as* operator instead:

```
ExtDate exdt2 = obj as ExtDate;
```

The *as* operator is similar to casting except that it doesn't raise an exception. If *obj* isn't really an *ExtDate* object (or a class that derives from *ExtDate*), then the *as* operator returns *null*. Programs that use the *as* operator should be prepared for a *null* result and check for it in code:

```
if (exdt2 != null)
```

Is it possible for a program to determine the actual type of *obj* before the program tries to cast or use the *as* operator? Yes, it is. The *System.Object* class implements a method named *GetType* that is inherited by all classes and structures. *GetType* returns an object of type *Type*. I know that sounds funny, but the *System* namespace includes a class named *Type*, and that's what *GetType* returns:

```
Type typeObj = obj.GetType();
```

The *Type* class has numerous properties and methods that a program can use to obtain information about the class of which *obj* is an instance, including all its fields, properties, methods, and so forth. *GetType* will raise a *NullReferenceException* if it's applied to a *null* object.

C# supports an operator named *typeof* that you can apply to classes, structures, enumerations, and so forth. You do *not* use *typeof* with objects. Like *GetType*, the *typeof* operator returns an object of type *Type*:

```
Type typeExtDate = typeof(ExtDate);
```

The documentation of the *Type* class in the .NET Framework says, "A *Type* object that represents a type is unique; that is, two *Type* object references refer to the same object if and only if they represent the same type. This allows … for comparison of *Type* objects using reference equality." This means that you can use the equality operators with *Type* objects. The expression

```
obj.GetType() == typeof(ExtDate).
```

is *true* if the actual type of *obj* is *ExtDate* (as it is in this example). But if the actual type of *obj* is *ExtDate*, the expression

```
obj.GetType() == typeof(Date)
```

returns *false*, despite the fact that *ExtDate* derives from *Date* and you can cast *obj* to a *Date* object.

Take a moment to grasp the difference between *GetType* and *typeof*. Both return objects of type *Type*. But *GetType* is an instance method that you call for a particular object whereas *typeof* is a C# operator that applies to a structure or class.

You can also determine whether an object is a particular type using the *is* operator. The expression

```
obj is ExtDate
```

return *true* if *obj* is an instance of *ExtDate*. One advantage of *is* over *GetType* is that it won't raise an exception if *obj* is *null*. It will simply return *false*. Another advantage is that it will return *true* for any class that *ExtDate* derives from. This expression is also *true*:

```
obj is Date
```

That's because *obj* can be cast to a *Date* object. You can also use *is* to determine whether the actual type of an object implements a particular interface. I mentioned interfaces in Chapter 26 in connection with the *foreach* statement. Although you'll use the *foreach* statement mostly with arrays and strings, *foreach* also works with any class that implements the *IEnumerable* interface. To implement an interface means to include several methods that the interface declares. (I'll discuss interfaces more in the next chapter.) If you want to determine if a particular object is an instance of a class that implements the *IEnumerable* interface, you can use the following expression:

```
obj is IEnumerable
```

There are some methods that are found in every class and structure in the .NET Framework and in every class and structure that you declare yourself. In Chapter 32, you saw how a class can include a *ToString* method to provide a text representation of the object. The *ToString* method is originally declared as a virtual method in *System.Object*:

```
public virtual string ToString()
```

To provide a *ToString* method in any class or structure, you use the *override* keyword:

```
public override string ToString()
```

Only methods and properties can be declared as *virtual*. Fields cannot. Any derived class can override a virtual method or property.

The *virtual* keyword is often used for methods and properties that are *intended* to be overridden. (Besides *ToString*, you'll see in the next chapter how a class can override the virtual *Equals* and *GetHashCode* methods also declared in *System.Object*.) You can't change a method's accessibility (that is, change the method from public to private) or return type when you override a virtual method. Any virtual method overridden with *override* remains a virtual method for further descendent classes.

There will be times when you'll derive a class from an existing class and you'll want to provide a new version of a method that is *not* declared as virtual in the base class. Or maybe you'll want to change a method's declared access, from private to public or the other way around. Or perhaps you need to change the return type of a method or property. Any member in a base class—and that includes fields as well as methods and properties—can be redefined in a derived class using the keyword *new*. This is sometimes known as *hiding* the base member.

Interestingly enough, the *new* keyword is not strictly required, but the compiler will warn you about its omission. The warning is helpful: The compiler tries to prevent you from hiding a member of the base class inadvertently.

If necessary, methods or properties can make calls to overridden members in the base class by prefacing the method or property name with the keyword *base*. (See the *SoundEngineer* class later in this chapter for an example.) Of course, a class can reference methods in its base class that it inherits but does not override simply with the method name.

The *override* and *new* keywords have significantly different effects, as this short program demonstrates.

InheritedMethods.cs

```
// -----------------------------------------------------------
// InheritedMethods.cs from "Programming in the Key of C#"
// -----------------------------------------------------------
using System;

class InheritedMethods
{
    static void Main()
    {
        DerivedClass dc = new DerivedClass();
        BaseClass bc = dc;

        bc.VirtualMethod();
        bc.NonVirtualMethod();
    }
}
class BaseClass
{
    public virtual void VirtualMethod()
    {
        Console.WriteLine("VirtualMethod in BaseClass");
    }
    public void NonVirtualMethod()
    {
        Console.WriteLine("NonVirtualMethod in BaseClass");
    }
}
```

```
class DerivedClass: BaseClass
{
    public override void VirtualMethod()
    {
        Console.WriteLine("VirtualMethod in DerivedClass");
    }
    public new void NonVirtualMethod()
    {
        Console.WriteLine("NonVirtualMethod in DerivedClass");
    }
}
```

The class *DerivedClass* derives from *BaseClass* and inherits two methods: *VirtualMethod* (which of course is declared as *virtual*) and *NonVirtualMethod*. *DerivedClass* also declares these same two methods, using *override* with *VirtualMethod* and *new* with *NonVirtualMethod*. Both methods simply display some text identifying what and where they are. The *Main* method creates an instance of *DerivedClass* and then assigns it to an object of type *BaseClass*:

```
DerivedClass dc = new DerivedClass();
BaseClass bc = dc;
```

The declared type of *bc* is *BaseClass*, but the actual type is *DerivedClass*. Next, *Main* calls the two methods using *bc*:

```
bc.VirtualMethod();
bc.NonVirtualMethod();
```

The results are interesting:

```
VirtualMethod in DerivedClass
NonVirtualMethod in BaseClass
```

Despite the fact that you're referring to the *DerivedClass* object with a *BaseClass* variable, the actual type of the object is *DerivedClass*. Any virtual methods you call will be those in *DerivedClass*, which is the actual type. The nonvirtual method is different. The method that's called is based on the declared type, not the actual type.

This characteristic of virtual methods is sometimes called *polymorphism*, a word derived from the Greek for "many forms." Virtual methods take on many forms as they are overridden in descendent classes.

Suppose *dt* is an instance of the *Date* class. Consider the following method call:

```
Console.WriteLine(dt);
```

If you look in the .NET Framework documentation of the *Console* class and scan through all the overloads of *WriteLine*, you won't find one that takes a *Date* argument. How could it? The *Date* class wasn't invented before Chapter 31 of this book. It didn't exist back when the .NET Framework was put together. But the *Console* class does have a *WriteLine* method that takes an *object* argument, and that's the one that gets called when you pass the *Date* object to *WriteLine*. The *Date* object is upcast to an *object* for purposes of the *WriteLine* call. Somewhere in the body of *WriteLine*, the *ToString* method of this *object* parameter is called:

```
public static void WriteLine(object obj)
{
    …
    … obj.ToString() …
    …
}
```

Because the actual type of *obj* is *Date*, and because *ToString* is a virtual method, the version of *ToString* that gets executed is the one that's in the *Date* class.

The difference between virtual and nonvirtual methods may become clearer when you consider the role of the compiler. Suppose your program contains a declaration of an object:

```
SomeClass someobject;
```

Or perhaps *someobject* appears in a parameter list to a method. Later on, your code contains the following method call:

```
someobject.SomeMethod();
```

But there's a little problem here. The *someobject* variable could be an instance of *SomeClass* like it's declared, or it could be an instance of a class that derives from *SomeClass*.

What's the compiler to do when it attempts to compile your C# code? The first thing it does is examine the declaration of *SomeMethod* in *SomeClass*. If *SomeMethod* is not part of *SomeClass*, the compiler examines the class that *SomeClass* inherits from, and so forth, until it finds *SomeMethod*. (If the compiler never finds *SomeMethod*, then that's a compile error.) Once the compiler finds *SomeMethod*, it checks whether the method is virtual; that is, does it have a *virtual* modifier or does it have an *override* modifier to override a virtual method in an ancestral class? If the method is not virtual, the compiler has it easy. The compiler knows *exactly* which method should be invoked when *SomeMethod* is called for the *someobject*. It's the one that's declared in *Some-Class* or that *SomeClass* inherits. The compiler can match up the code with the method call.

If *SomeMethod* is a virtual method, however, the compiler has a problem. The compiler doesn't have enough information to figure out which version of *SomeMethod* should be invoked. It depends on the actual type of *someobject*, and, in general, that's not known at compile time. The actual type of *someobject* is known only when the program is run. Only at run time can the correct version of *SomeMethod* be invoked. Only at run time can that call to *ToString* in *Console.WriteLine* be hooked up to the appropriate *ToString* method. This process of hooking up a method call with a virtual method is known as *late binding* because it takes place while the program is running.

Virtual methods are an essential part of object-oriented programming. Without virtual methods, an expression such as

```
obj.ToString()
```

would be worthless. But because virtual methods require some additional overhead when a program runs, they shouldn't be used indiscriminately.

You'll probably want to use virtual methods in situations where you have a general case, and then variations of that general case, and you want to use the same property or method names with these variations, but you want the implementations to be different.

For example, here's a general case that contains a virtual method:

```
class BaseClass
{
    ...
    public virtual int DoSomething()
    {
        ...
    }
}
```

The first variation derives from *BaseClass* and overrides the virtual method:

```
class FirstVariation: BaseClass
{
    ...
    public override int DoSomething()
    {
        ...
    }
}
```

The second variation does likewise:

```
class SecondVariation: BaseClass
{
    ...
```

```
public override int DoSomething()
{
    …
}
}
```

You can make as many of these descendent classes as you need.

Because *FirstVariation* and *SecondVariation* derive from *BaseClass*, objects of those types can be converted to objects of type *BaseClass*. These conversions to *BaseClass* have astonishing implications. For example, you can store objects of type *FirstVariation* and *SecondVariation* in an array of type *Base-Class*. Or you can pass these objects to a method that has a *BaseClass* parameter. Even though you're treating these objects as if they were *BaseClass* objects, whenever you call *DoSomething*, the version of *DoSomething* in *FirstVariation* or *SecondVariation* will execute. You can always determine what the actual type of the object is by using the *GetType* method or the *is* keyword, but you may just find it convenient to treat these objects uniformly without worrying about the actual type.

Most importantly, you can later declare additional descendents of *Base-Class* with minimal impact to the rest of your code.

For a more concrete example, let's look at an orchestra that pays its musicians a flat $100 per performance (public funding of the arts being what it is). Here's a simple class containing a constructor to store the musician's name and a *CalculatePay* method that returns the decimal value 100.

Musician.cs

```
// --------------------------------------------------
// Musician.cs from "Programming in the Key of C#"
// --------------------------------------------------
class Musician
{
    public string strName;

    public Musician(string strName)
    {
        this.strName = strName;
    }
    public virtual decimal CalculatePay()
    {
        return 100;
    }
}
```

Notice that *CalculatePay* is a virtual method. It's virtual because not every musician is paid $100. The harp players, for example, are paid based on the weight of their harps.

Harp.cs

```
// ------------------------------------------------
// Harp.cs from "Programming in the Key of C#"
// ------------------------------------------------
class Harp: Musician
{
    int iWeight;

    public Harp(string strName, int iWeight): base(strName)
    {
        this.iWeight = iWeight;
    }
    public override decimal CalculatePay()
    {
        return 1.5m * iWeight;
    }
}
```

The *Harp* class subclasses the *Musician* class. It declares its own constructor for both a name and a weight and then uses a constructor initializer to execute the constructor in *Musician* to store the harpist's name. The *Harp* class itself stores the weight of the harp. The new *CalculatePay* method has an *override* modifier and implements its own pay formula.

Violinists are paid a little more than the other musicians, but they're also penalized if they break a string during performance.

Violin.cs

```
// ------------------------------------------------
// Violin.cs from "Programming in the Key of C#"
// ------------------------------------------------
class Violin: Musician
{
    int iBrokenStrings;

    public Violin(string strName, int iBrokenStrings): base(strName)
    {
        this.iBrokenStrings = iBrokenStrings;
    }
    public override decimal CalculatePay()
    {
        return 125 - 50 * iBrokenStrings;
    }
}
```

The French horn is a notoriously difficult instrument, and the players are paid based on the number of correct notes and flubbed notes.

FrenchHorn.cs

```
// ------------------------------------------------------
// FrenchHorn.cs from "Programming in the Key of C#"
// ------------------------------------------------------
class FrenchHorn: Musician
{
    int iGoodNotes, iFlubbedNotes;

    public FrenchHorn(string strName, int iGoodNotes, int iFlubbedNotes):
        base(strName)
    {
        this.iGoodNotes = iGoodNotes;
        this.iFlubbedNotes = iFlubbedNotes;
    }
    public override decimal CalculatePay()
    {
        return 1.5m * iGoodNotes + 0.75m * iFlubbedNotes;
    }
}
```

Somehow the sound engineer has managed to get paid 125 percent of whatever the generic musician is paid.

SoundEngineer.cs

```
// -------------------------------------------------------
// SoundEngineer.cs from "Programming in the Key of C#"
// -------------------------------------------------------
class SoundEngineer: Musician
{
    public SoundEngineer(string strName): base(strName)
    {
    }
    public override decimal CalculatePay()
    {
        return 1.25m * base.CalculatePay();
    }
}
```

Notice the use of the *base* keyword to reference the *CalculatePay* method in the *Musician* class.

All these classes are part of the PayTheMusicians project, which also contains the following class with the *Main* method.

PayTheMusicians.cs

```
// -------------------------------------------------------
// PayTheMusicians.cs from "Programming in the Key of C#"
// -------------------------------------------------------
using System;

class PayTheMusicians
{
    static void Main()
    {
        Musician[] amus =
            {
                new Musician("Leonard"),
                new Harp("Sam", 62),
                new Violin("Sydney", 0),
                new FrenchHorn("Janet", 46, 23),
                new Musician("Chuck"),
                new Harp("Arien", 78),
                new Violin("Jason", 2),
                new FrenchHorn("Deirdre", 52, 25),
                new SoundEngineer("Fitz")
            };

        foreach (Musician mus in amus)
            Console.WriteLine("Pay {0} the amount of {1:C}",
                mus.strName, mus.CalculatePay());
    }
}
```

The program creates nine objects based on *Musician* and its descendents, and stores all these objects in an array of type *Musician*. Despite the fact that five different classes are involved here, a single array stores them all. The *foreach* statement then loops through the array, displaying the musician's name and calling the *CalculatePay* method. The results reveal that each musician gets paid a correct (if not quite appropriate) amount:

```
Pay Leonard the amount of $100.00
Pay Sam the amount of $93.00
Pay Sydney the amount of $125.00
Pay Janet the amount of $86.25
Pay Chuck the amount of $100.00
Pay Arien the amount of $117.00
Pay Jason the amount of $25.00
Pay Deirdre the amount of $96.75
Pay Fitz the amount of $125.00
```

What's interesting about virtual methods is that there's obviously a lot going on behind the scenes. Without virtual methods, tailoring calculations like this would probably require a bunch of *if* statements or a *switch*. With virtual methods, we get the same effect in a much cleaner way. You can easily add alternate pay scales by declaring new classes that derive from *Musician*. You don't have to touch the *foreach* loop or any other code that uses objects of type *Musician*.

Eventually, *all* the musicians may have special pay scales, and then you really won't be creating objects of type *Musician*. In that case, you can use the *abstract* modifier for the *Musician* class:

```
abstract class Musician
{
    ...
}
```

An abstract class can't be instantiated. The C# compiler won't allow a *new* expression involving an abstract class. However, you can still declare a variable of type *Musician*, and you can still have an array of type *Musician*. Everything else about the program would remain the same.

If a descendent of *Musician* doesn't override the *CalculatePay* method, the descendent ends up with the version of *CalculatePay* declared in *Musician*. It could be that you want to declare *Musician* as an abstract class and also force every descendent of *Musician* to implement its own *CalculatePay* method. In that case, you can also use the *abstract* keyword for the *CalculatePay* method in *Musician*:

```
public abstract decimal CalculatePay()
{
}
```

An abstract method (or property) is implicitly virtual. Because this method is never called, it must have an empty body. In such a situation, a call from the *CalculatePay* method in a derived class to the base class method (such as in *SoundEngineer* class) would not be allowed.

You can see a real-life example of an abstract class and abstract methods in the *Calendar* class used in conjunction with the *DateTime* structure. I discuss this class a bit in Chapter 40.

The opposite of an *abstract* class is a *sealed* class. An abstract class *must* be subclassed to have any value to a program; a sealed class *cannot* be subclassed. Classes that contain only static fields, properties, and methods (such as *Console*, *Convert*, and *Math*) are often sealed. There's no real advantage to inheriting from these classes. Structures are implicitly sealed because structures can't be subclassed.

I began this chapter by noting that C# allows implicit conversions of objects to any ancestral type. Because every object ultimately derives from *object*, a variable declared as type *object* can be assigned any object. An array of type *object* can store any object. A method with an *object* parameter (like *WriteLine*) can be passed any object.

Any object. Even value types such as *int*, *decimal*, *bool*, and whatever structures you declare. For example,

```
decimal mPi = 3.14159m;
object obj = mPi;
```

Is this right? The more you study those two simple (and completely legal) statements, the stranger they may seem. To store *mPi*, the C# compiler allocates 16 bytes on the stack. For *obj*, the C# compiler allocates enough space on the stack to store a reference. On today's machines, that's probably 4 bytes. Normally, *obj* would be a reference to memory allocated from the heap, but the absence of a *new* expression here seems to indicate that no heap memory has been allocated.

So how on earth can a 4-byte *obj* store a 16-byte *decimal?*

The answer is a technique known as *boxing*. Whenever a value type is assigned to a variable of type *object* (and that's the only reference type a value type can be assigned to), memory is allocated from the heap sufficient to store the value type. In this example, that's 16 bytes for the *decimal* value plus whatever is needed to store information about the object's type. The *decimal* value is then copied from the stack into the heap. That's how the *obj* variable can refer to the *decimal*. When the reverse operation takes place, as in

```
mPi = (decimal) obj;
```

then the value type is *unboxed*. The value is extracted from the heap and copied back to the stack.

Boxing and unboxing take some time and could affect the performance of your programs. For that reason, you should be wary of any code in which you are converting many value types to *object*. For example, if you have a method that has an *object* parameter and you're passing many value types to that method, consider writing overloads specifically for those value types. Take a look at *WriteLine*. *WriteLine* has overloads for all the C# simple types besides the version with an *object* parameter. *WriteLine* tries to avoid boxing, and you should as well.

38

Operator Overloading

You got your first taste of operator overloading in the AddingTextStrings program in Chapter 9. That program used the plus operator—customarily associated only with numbers—to concatenate two strings. In C#, operator overloading is generalized. Any class or structure you write can specify how the C# operators are supposed to work on objects of that type.

Although operator overloading is a very powerful feature, it's easily abused. It doesn't make much sense to multiply two *Font* objects, for example, so you shouldn't even be tempted to implement a multiplication operator in a *Font* class.

An object representing a date, however, is a different story. Although I'm not sure what it would mean to multiply two dates, the CommonEraDayTest program at the end of Chapter 36 showed how useful it is to subtract one date from another to find the number of days between the two dates. The Common-EraDayTest program used the *CommonEraDay* property of the *ExtDate* class to perform this calculation, but it would certainly be more convenient to perform the operation on the objects directly.

The CommonEraDayTest program also showed how useful it is to perform equality and relational operations on dates. Yet, Chapter 34 demonstrated that even the simple equality operator doesn't work for objects created from structures and only compares references for objects created from classes. If you want these operators to work differently, you'll have to define them to do what you want.

The operators that a class or structure can overload are listed in the *C# Language Specification*, §7.2.2 and §10.9. The overloadable unary operators are +, -, !, ~, ++, --, *true*, and *false*. The overloadable binary operators are the arithmetic operators (+, -, *, /, and %), the logical and bitwise operators (&, |, and ^), the equality operators (== and !=), the relational operators (<, <=, >, and >=), and the shift operators (<< and >>). Because the compound assignment operators (such as +=) are defined in terms of the corresponding binary operators, you get those for free. You can't overload the conditional operators && and ||, but they will be applicable for your class if you define & and | as well as *true* and *false*. See the *C# Language Specification*, §7.11.2, for details.

Let's look at some examples. At the end of this chapter, I'll show you a complete class that includes all the operator declarations I'll be discussing. This class will inherit from *ExtDate* and be called *SuperDate*, so the examples in this chapter will refer to *SuperDate* objects.

Operator declarations always include the modifiers *public* and *static* and the keyword *operator* followed by the operator itself. Here's a possible declaration of the equality operator:

```
public static bool operator == (SuperDate sdLeft, SuperDate sdRight)
{
    return sdLeft.Year == sdRight.Year && sdLeft.Month == sdRight.Month &&
            sdLeft.Day == sdRight.Day;
}
```

Notice that the return type is *bool*. I often forget to include the return type when declaring operators; I suppose it's because I figure the return type is implied by the operator itself, but that's not the case. The return type is always required. The two operands that are placed to the left and right of the operation appear as parameters. At least one operand must be the same type as the class in which the operator is declared. For that reason, you never need a *new* modifier to declare an operator already declared in an ancestral class. The operands in the two declarations can never be the same, so they constitute distinct methods. Operators are never declared as virtual; C# prohibits it.

The above declaration of the equals operator uses the *Year*, *Month*, and *Day* properties to determine the return value. Because *SuperDate* inherits the *CommonEraDay* property from *ExtDate*, it's easier to use that property when defining the equality operator:

```
public static bool operator == (SuperDate sdLeft, SuperDate sdRight)
{
    return sdLeft.CommonEraDay == sdRight.CommonEraDay;
}
```

If a *SuperDate* class includes such a declaration, a program can compare two *SuperDate* objects directly:

```
if (sdBirthday == sdMoonWalk)
```

A class that includes a declaration of the equality operator must also include the inequality operator, which you can define in terms of equality:

```
public static bool operator != (SuperDate sdLeft, SuperDate sdRight)
{
    return !(sdLeft == sdRight);
}
```

Similarly to the way you declared the equality operators, you can declare a relational operator:

```
public static bool operator < (SuperDate sdLeft, SuperDate sdRight)
{
    return sdLeft.CommonEraDay < sdRight.CommonEraDay;
}
```

You can then declare the opposite relational operator using logical negation:

```
public static bool operator >= (SuperDate sdLeft, SuperDate sdRight)
{
    return !(sdLeft < sdRight);
}
```

You'll want to declare the greater than operator and the less than or equal to operator similarly.

Here's a subtraction example. Notice that the subtraction operation occurs between two objects of type *SuperDate* but returns an *int*:

```
public static int operator - (SuperDate sdLeft, SuperDate sdRight)
{
    return sdLeft.CommonEraDay - sdRight.CommonEraDay;
}
```

What about addition? Does it make sense to add two dates? Well, not really. But it makes a whole lot of sense to add a date and an *integer*. That calculation would tell you what date was a certain number of days after a particular date. The return value is another *SuperDate* object. Here's how the declaration would begin:

```
public static SuperDate operator + (SuperDate sdLeft, int iRight)
```

At least one of the parameters in a binary operator declaration must be the same type as the class, but the other parameter can be anything. You can even write multiple addition overloads for addition of various types.

This addition method needs to return an object of the type *SuperDate*, so it must create an object of that type. It sounds a bit odd for a class to create an object of the class type, but there's no problem doing it. Here's a possible implementation of the addition operator:

```
public static SuperDate operator + (SuperDate sdLeft, int iRight)
{
    SuperDate sdReturn = new SuperDate();
```

```
    sdReturn.CommonEraDay = sdLeft.CommonEraDay + iRight;
    return sdReturn;
}
```

The method begins by creating an object of type *SuperDate* and then sets the object's *CommonEraDay* property to the calculated value of the addition. The method then returns that object.

The addition operator would be even easier if *SuperDate* had an additional constructor—one that creates a *SuperDate* object based on an argument indicating the common era day:

```
public SuperDate(int iCommonEraDay)
{
    CommonEraDay = iCommonEraDay;
}
```

Now the body of the addition operator can be written in one line:

```
public static SuperDate operator + (SuperDate sdLeft, int iRight)
{
    return new SuperDate(sdLeft.CommonEraDay + iRight);
}
```

Addition between a date and an integer is commutative, of course, but the C# compiler doesn't know that. When you want to define a commutative operation between two different types, you need two declarations of the operator to account for commutativity. Here's the second addition operator that exploits commutativity by being written in terms of the first version:

```
public static SuperDate operator + (int iLeft, SuperDate sdRight)
{
    return sdRight + iLeft;
}
```

Now that you've implemented addition, you might want to reconsider subtraction. We've already declared a subtraction operator between two *Super-Date* objects. It also makes sense to subtract an integer from a date:

```
public static SuperDate operator - (SuperDate sdLeft, int iRight)
{
    return new SuperDate(sdLeft.CommonEraDay - iRight);
}
```

But it doesn't make sense to subtract a date from an integer.

You can also declare the two unary increment and decrement operators for *SuperDate*. Here's the increment operator:

```
public static SuperDate operator ++ (SuperDate sd)
{
    return new SuperDate(sd.CommonEraDay + 1);
}
```

The decrement is similar. I arrived at these versions of the increment operator only after some experimentation. At first, I wasn't quite sure if the increment and decrement operator needed to create a new object. My first version of the increment operator looked like this:

```
public static SuperDate operator ++ (SuperDate sd)     // No good!
{
    ++sd.CommonEraDay;
    return sd;
}
```

This version alters the *CommonEraDay* property of the parameter and then returns the parameter. However, the postfix version of the increment operator didn't work right when I tested the operator using code like this:

```
SuperDate sdMoonWalk = new SuperDate(1969, 7, 20);
Console.WriteLine(sdMoonWalk);
Console.WriteLine(sdMoonWalk++);
Console.WriteLine(sdMoonWalk);
Console.WriteLine(++sdMoonWalk);
Console.WriteLine(sdMoonWalk);
```

I tried several variations, but came to the conclusion that creating a new *Super-Date* object was necessary in the increment operator. Also, make sure you don't alter the parameter. Don't define your increment operator like this:

```
public static SuperDate operator ++ (SuperDate sd)     // No good!
{
    return new SuperDate(++sd.CommonEraDay);
}
```

I think that's about as far as we can go with unary and binary operators that make sense for dates. But we're not quite finished with *SuperDate*. The inclusion of the *CommonEraDay* property—that is, making a date equivalent to an integer—raises a question: Do you want an implicit or explicit conversion between *SuperDate* objects and integers? I'd shy away from implicit conversion, where you could convert between *SuperDate* objects and integers directly:

```
int i = sdMoonWalk;
```

It would be too easy to introduce bugs in your programs. But explicit conversion using casting seems reasonable to me.

The syntax for declaring explicit conversions involves the *explicit* keyword and looks like this:

```
public static explicit operator int (SuperDate sd)
{
    return sd.CommonEraDay;
}
```

This declaration allows an explicit conversion from a *SuperDate* to an *int*. If *sd* is a *SuperDate* object in your program, you can have the statement:

```
int i = (int) sd;
```

Similarly, this declaration allows explicit conversions from integers to *Super-Date* objects:

```
public static explicit operator SuperDate (int iCommonEraDay)
{
    return new SuperDate(iCommonEraDay);
}
```

You'd use the keyword *implicit* to declare implicit conversions.

If you declare equality or inequality operators, you'll get a warning message from the compiler about your failure to also declare overrides for the virtual *Equals* and *GetHashCode* methods declared in *System.Object*. As we discovered in Chapter 34, the *Equals* method in *System.Object* implements reference equality; the *Equals* method in *System.ValueType* (from which all structures derive) implements bitwise equality, also known as value equality.

The *Equals* method is declared in the *System.Object* class like this:

```
public virtual bool Equals(object obj)
```

This is an instance method. The body of the method must compare the current instance with the parameter. If we were writing a brand new *Equals* method for *SuperDate*, the parameter would obviously be a *SuperDate* object. Some classes (like *String*) do precisely that: the *String* class includes a new *Equals* method that has a *String* parameter. But the *Equals* method that is to be overridden has a parameter that is of type *object*. No problem. As we discovered in the preceding chapter, if necessary, C# implicitly converts any object to *object*.

The documentation of the *Equals* method in the *System.Object* class indicates that the method must not raise an exception. In particular, if the argument to *Equals* is *null* or not of the correct type, *Equals* should simply return *false*. Here's a rather lengthy *Equals* method for *SuperDate*:

```
public override bool Equals(object obj)
{
    if (obj == null || GetType() != obj.GetType())
        return false;
    SuperDate sd = (SuperDate) obj;
    return CommonEraDay == sd.CommonEraDay;
}
```

If *obj* is *null*, then the method returns *false*. If *obj* is non-*null*, then the rest of the *if* statement compares the type of the instance with the type of the parameter. It could alternatively have compared the type of the parameter with *typeof(SuperDate)*. If the parameter passes this test, it's cast to an object of type *SuperDate*. Finally, the method returns *true* if the *CommonEraDay* properties of the instance and the argument are the same.

Here's a simpler implementation that makes use of the equality operator already declared in *SuperDate*:

```
public override bool Equals(object obj)
{
    return obj is SuperDate && this == (SuperDate) obj;
}
```

If *obj* is *null* or not an object of type *SuperDate*, the *return* statement returns *false*. Otherwise, the method returns a comparison of the current instance (indicated by the keyword *this*) to the method parameter cast to a *SuperDate* object.

The other virtual method in *System.Object* that the C# compiler wants you to override is *GetHashCode*, which returns a 32-bit integer. A hash code is a number that programs can use to assist in storing and retrieving objects. Two objects that are equal according to the *Equals* method must return the same integer from *GetHashCode*. However, unequal objects need not return unique hash codes. (It's certainly *preferable*, but it's not required.) And if you think about it, it's simply not possible for most classes and structures to return unique hash codes for unique objects. If the class or structure is capable of more than 2^{32} unique objects (which is the case for *long*, *double*, and *decimal*), then there are more unique objects than possible return values of *GetHashCode*.

In such cases, *GetHashCode* usually performs some kind of operation on the fields of the class or structure. For example, suppose you declared a *Point* class or structure that had two *int* fields named x and y. Here's how *GetHash-Code* might be implemented for such a class:

```
public override int GetHashCode()
{
    return x ^ y;
}
```

Two *Point* objects that are equal obviously have the same hash codes. But it's possible for the same hash code to be associated with unequal objects.

With the *SuperDate* class, we've lucked out. A *SuperDate* object can be represented by a unique integer, which is the *CommonEraDay* property. *Get-HashCode* can be implemented as simply as:

```
public override int GetHashCode()
{
    return CommonEraDay;
}
```

While we're on a roll here, let's add yet another method that might prove useful somewhere down the road. Suppose you have an array of *SuperDate* objects, and you want to sort them. You could write a sorting algorithm yourself (which would certainly be a good exercise) or you can use one of the static *Sort* methods of the *Array* class. But to use *Sort*, the elements of the array must implement the *IComparable* interface.

What does it mean to "implement the *IComparable* interface"? *IComparable* is declared in the *System* namespace, probably as simply as this:

```
public interface IComparable
{
    int CompareTo(object obj);
}
```

Interfaces are entirely overhead! The interface declaration looks something like a class or a structure, except for the *interface* keyword. All interfaces defined in the .NET Framework begin with a capital *I*, but that's just a convention. You can name your own interfaces anything you like.

An interface is generally a collection of methods without bodies. An interface can also contain other types of members, such as properties. The *IComparable* interface has a single method named *CompareTo* that returns an *int*. The documentation of *CompareTo* also comes with rules:

- If the instance is less than the parameter, *CompareTo* returns a negative number.

- If the instance is equal to the parameter, *CompareTo* returns 0.

- If the instance is greater than the parameter, *CompareTo* returns a positive number.

- If the parameter is *null*, *CompareTo* returns a positive number.

- If the parameter is the wrong type, *CompareTo* throws an *ArgumentException*.

If the first three rules look familiar, it's because the *String* class implements the *IComparable* interface, and I discussed the *CompareTo* method at the end of Chapter 20.

To make *SuperDate* implement the *IComparable* interface, you start at the very top of the *SuperDate* class declaration and list *IComparable* along with *ExtDate*, which is the class that *SuperDate* inherits from:

```
class SuperDate: ExtDate, IComparable
```

A class can inherit from only one other class, but it can implement multiple interfaces, which must be separated with commas.

A class that implements an interface must include all the methods in that interface. To implement the *IComparable* interface, *SuperDate* must declare a *CompareTo* method in accordance with the rules listed earlier. Here's the *CompareTo* method:

```
public int CompareTo(object obj)
{
    if (obj == null)
        return 1;

    if (!(obj is SuperDate))
        throw new ArgumentException();

    return this - (SuperDate) obj;
}
```

CompareTo actually returns the difference between the instance and the parameter by taking advantage of the definition of the subtraction operator. The keyword *this* refers to the current instance.

And here we have it—the complete *SuperDate* class. All this code should now look familiar:

SuperDate.cs

```
// -----------------------------------------------
// SuperDate.cs from "Programming in the Key of C#"
// -----------------------------------------------
using System;

class SuperDate: ExtDate, IComparable
{
    // Constructors

    public SuperDate()
    {
    }
    public SuperDate(int iYear, int iMon, int iDay): base(iYear, iMon, iDay)
    {
    }
    public SuperDate(int iCommonEraDay)
    {
        CommonEraDay = iCommonEraDay;
    }

    // Equality operators
```

```csharp
public static bool operator == (SuperDate sdLeft, SuperDate sdRight)
{
    return sdLeft.CommonEraDay == sdRight.CommonEraDay;
}
public static bool operator != (SuperDate sdLeft, SuperDate sdRight)
{
    return !(sdLeft == sdRight);
}

// Relational operators

public static bool operator < (SuperDate sdLeft, SuperDate sdRight)
{
    return sdLeft.CommonEraDay < sdRight.CommonEraDay;
}
public static bool operator > (SuperDate sdLeft, SuperDate sdRight)
{
    return sdLeft.CommonEraDay > sdRight.CommonEraDay;
}
public static bool operator <= (SuperDate sdLeft, SuperDate sdRight)
{
    return !(sdLeft > sdRight);
}
public static bool operator >= (SuperDate sdLeft, SuperDate sdRight)
{
    return !(sdLeft < sdRight);
}

// Arithmetic operators

public static SuperDate operator + (SuperDate sdLeft, int iRight)
{
    return new SuperDate(sdLeft.CommonEraDay + iRight);
}
public static SuperDate operator + (int iLeft, SuperDate sdRight)
{
    return sdRight + iLeft;
}
public static int operator - (SuperDate sdLeft, SuperDate sdRight)
{
    return sdLeft.CommonEraDay - sdRight.CommonEraDay;
}
public static SuperDate operator - (SuperDate sdLeft, int iRight)
{
    return new SuperDate(sdLeft.CommonEraDay - iRight);
}
```

```
// Unary operators

public static SuperDate operator ++ (SuperDate sd)
{
    return new SuperDate(sd.CommonEraDay + 1);
}
public static SuperDate operator -- (SuperDate sd)
{
    return new SuperDate(sd.CommonEraDay - 1);
}


// Explicit casts

public static explicit operator int (SuperDate sd)
{
    return sd.CommonEraDay;
}
public static explicit operator SuperDate (int iCommonEraDay)
{
    return new SuperDate(iCommonEraDay);
}


// Overrides of methods in System.Object

public override bool Equals(object obj)
{
    return obj is SuperDate && this == (SuperDate) obj;
}
public override int GetHashCode()
{
    return CommonEraDay;
}


// Implementation of IComparable interface

public int CompareTo(object obj)
{
    if (obj == null)
        return 1;

    if (!(obj is SuperDate))
        throw new ArgumentException();

    return this - (SuperDate) obj;
}
}
```

The following OperatorTest program is similar to the CommonEraTest program in the last chapter, but it uses a few of the operators declared in *Super-Date*. OperatorTest compares and subtracts the objects directly.

OperatorTest.cs

```
// ---------------------------------------------------
// OperatorTest.cs from "Programming in the Key of C#"
// ---------------------------------------------------
using System;

class OperatorTest
{
    static void Main()
    {
        Console.Write("Enter the year of your birth: ");
        int iYear = Int32.Parse(Console.ReadLine());

        Console.Write("And the month: ");
        int iMonth = Int32.Parse(Console.ReadLine());

        Console.Write("And the day: ");
        int iDay = Int32.Parse(Console.ReadLine());

        SuperDate sdBirthday = new SuperDate(iYear, iMonth, iDay);
        SuperDate sdMoonWalk = new SuperDate(1969, 7, 20);

        if (sdBirthday > sdMoonWalk)
            Console.WriteLine("You were born {0} days before the moon walk.",
                            sdBirthday - sdMoonWalk);

        else if (sdBirthday == sdMoonWalk)
            Console.WriteLine("You were born on the day of the moon walk.");

        else
            Console.WriteLine("You were born {0} days after the moon walk.",
                            sdMoonWalk - sdBirthday);
    }
}
```

The OperatorTest project must contain SuperDate.cs as well as links to Date.cs and ExtDate.cs. Obviously this program doesn't perform an exhaustive test of all the operators in the *SuperDate* class, but it's a start.

Now let's test the *IComparable* interface. I mentioned that one reason to implement *IComparable* was to easily sort arrays. The static *Array.Sort* method sorts arrays. Because arrays can contain any type of object, *Sort* needs some way to determine if one element of the array is less than, equal to, or greater than another element. *Sort* can't figure that out on its own. For this reason, *Sort* requires that the argument to *Sort* be an array whose elements implement the *IComparable* interface. What the *Sort* method *really* wants is to call *CompareTo* on the elements of the array. That's the only way *Sort* knows how to sort an array of objects it's not familiar with.

Let's try this out. The following program contains an array of famous composers alphabetized by last name. A corresponding array of *SuperDate* objects contains the birth dates of these composers. The program sorts the arrays by birth date and displays the results. The DateSorting project must have links to Date.cs, ExtDate.cs, and SuperDate.cs:

DateSorting.cs

```
// ------------------------------------------------------
// DateSorting.cs from "Programming in the Key of C#"
// ------------------------------------------------------
using System;

class DateSorting
{
    static void Main()
    {
        string[] astrComposers =
            {
                "John Adams",           "Johann Sebastian Bach",
                "Bela Bartok",          "Ludwig van Beethoven",
                "Hector Berlioz",       "Pierre Boulez",
                "Johannes Brahms",      "Benjamin Britten",
                "Aaron Copland",        "Claude Debussy",
                "Philip Glass",         "George Frideric Handel",
                "Franz Joseph Haydn",   "Gustav Mahler",
                "Claudio Monteverdi",   "Wolfgang Amadeus Mozart",
                "Sergei Prokofiev",     "Steve Reich",
                "Franz Schubert",       "Igor Stravinsky",
                "Richard Wagner",       "Anton Webern"
            };
        SuperDate[] asdBirthDates =
            {
                new SuperDate(1947, 2, 15),  new SuperDate(1685, 3, 21),
                new SuperDate(1881, 3, 25),  new SuperDate(1770, 12, 17),
                new SuperDate(1803, 12, 11), new SuperDate(1925, 3, 26),
                new SuperDate(1833, 5, 7),   new SuperDate(1913, 11, 22),
                new SuperDate(1900, 11, 14), new SuperDate(1862, 8, 22),
                new SuperDate(1937, 1, 31),  new SuperDate(1685, 2, 23),
                new SuperDate(1732, 3, 31),  new SuperDate(1860, 7, 7),
```

```
                new SuperDate(1567, 5, 15),   new SuperDate(1756, 1, 27),
                new SuperDate(1891, 4, 23),   new SuperDate(1936, 10, 3),
                new SuperDate(1797, 1, 31),   new SuperDate(1882, 6, 17),
                new SuperDate(1813, 5, 22),   new SuperDate(1883, 12, 3)
            };

        Array.Sort(asdBirthDates, astrComposers);

        for (int i = 0; i < astrComposers.Length; i++)
            Console.WriteLine("{0} was born on {1}.",
                astrComposers[i], asdBirthDates[i]);
    }
}
```

The *Array* class contains eight overloads of the static *Sort* method. The simplest version simply sorts a single array, which is not quite enough for this program. We need the second simplest version, which has *two* array arguments. The arrays are assumed to be of equal size. The *Sort* method sorts both arrays the same way based on the elements of the first array. When two arrays are used in such a way, the elements of the first array are referred to as the *keys*. Here's the result:

```
Claudio Monteverdi was born on 15 May 1567.
George Frideric Handel was born on 23 Feb 1685.
Johann Sebastian Bach was born on 21 Mar 1685.
Franz Joseph Haydn was born on 31 Mar 1732.
Wolfgang Amadeus Mozart was born on 27 Jan 1756.
Ludwig van Beethoven was born on 17 Dec 1770.
Franz Schubert was born on 31 Jan 1797.
Hector Berlioz was born on 11 Dec 1803.
Richard Wagner was born on 22 May 1813.
Johannes Brahms was born on 7 May 1833.
Gustav Mahler was born on 7 Jul 1860.
Claude Debussy was born on 22 Aug 1862.
Bela Bartok was born on 25 Mar 1881.
Igor Stravinsky was born on 17 Jun 1882.
Anton Webern was born on 3 Dec 1883.
Sergei Prokofiev was born on 23 Apr 1891.
Aaron Copland was born on 14 Nov 1900.
Benjamin Britten was born on 22 Nov 1913.
Pierre Boulez was born on 26 Mar 1925.
Steve Reich was born on 3 Oct 1936.
Philip Glass was born on 31 Jan 1937.
John Adams was born on 15 Feb 1947.
```

In the past several chapters, I've been using the *Date*, *ExtDate*, and *Super-Date* classes to demonstrate object-oriented programming. Over the course of these chapters, I progressively added methods, constructors, properties, and operators to these classes. It was very convenient to use inheritance to break up this material into separate chapters. Without inheritance, the size and contents of the overall class would have been too much to tackle in one big chapter.

In the real world, inheritance is not often used to restrict the size of a class to something short enough to be discussed in the chapter of a book. In fact, you'd probably use a structure rather than a class to represent a date. Structures are more closely associated with objects that have particular numeric values; therefore, operator overloading is much more common in structures than in classes.

Structures cannot be inherited, and that's actually an advantage when the structure contains operator declarations. Operators in classes can be problematic when the class is inherited.

For example, suppose you declared another class named *HyperDate* that inherits from *SuperDate*. In a program, you declare a *HyperDate* object:

```
HyperDate hdSputnik = new HyperDate(1957, 10, 4);
```

HyperDate inherits all the methods and operations declared in *SuperDate*, but some of them are no longer quite as easy to use. Try this:

```
hdSputnik = hdSputnik + 7;
```

This statement makes use of the addition operator declared in *SuperDate*. The appropriate overload has two parameters, a *SuperDate* object and an integer. Passing a *HyperDate* object to the addition operator in *SuperDate* is no problem, because a *HyperDate* can be implicitly converted to a *SuperDate*. The problem is the return value, which is assigned to the *HyperDate* object. The return value of the addition operator is a *SuperDate*, and there is no implicit or explicit conversion from a *SuperDate* object to a *HyperDate*. To make such a statement work, *HyperDate* would have to declare its own addition operator.

39

Classes and Libraries

Inheritance can sometimes be tricky. For example, consider a program in which you need both two-dimensional and three-dimensional coordinate points. This sounds like an ideal application of inheritance, and it is.

At first, it seems reasonable that the three-dimensional point class should inherit from the two-dimensional point class. After all, 3-D points have everything 2-D points have, plus more (a whole other dimension). Here's some code illustrating this hierarchy.

PointsDemo.cs

```
// -------------------------------------------------
// PointsDemo.cs from "Programming in the Key of C#"
// -------------------------------------------------
using System;

class PointsDemo
{
    static void Main()
    {
        Point2D ptA = new Point2D(10, 20);
        Point2D ptB = new Point2D(20, 30);

        Console.WriteLine(ptA - ptB);

        Point3D ptC = new Point3D(10, 20, 10);
        Point3D ptD = new Point3D(20, 30, 10);

        Console.WriteLine(ptC - ptD);
    }
}
```

```
class Point2D
{
    public double x, y;

    public Point2D()
    {
        x = y = 0;
    }
    public Point2D(double x, double y)
    {
        this.x = x;
        this.y = y;
    }
    public static double operator - (Point2D ptL, Point2D ptR)
    {
        return Math.Sqrt(Math.Pow(ptL.x - ptR.x, 2) +
                         Math.Pow(ptL.y - ptR.y, 2));
    }
}
class Point3D: Point2D
{
    public double z;

    public Point3D()
    {
        z = 0;
    }
    public Point3D(double x, double y, double z): base(x, y)
    {
        this.z = z;
    }
    public static double operator - (Point3D ptL, Point3D ptR)
    {
        return Math.Sqrt(Math.Pow(ptL.x - ptR.x, 2) +
                         Math.Pow(ptL.y - ptR.y, 2) +
                         Math.Pow(ptL.z - ptR.z, 2));
    }
}
```

Obviously there are other members you might want to add to the *Point2D* and
Point3D classes, but the minus operator (which calculates the distance between
two points) is enough to demonstrate the problem: The *Point3D* class can't use
the minus operator in the *Point2D* class because it only involves two dimensions. The *Point3D* class needs its own minus operator.

A better approach is for *Point2D* to inherit from *Point3D*. Remember: class
hierarchies generally precede from the *general* to the *specific*. A 3-D point is

more general that a 2-D point. Two-dimensional points are specific types of 3-D points, where the z-coordinate equals 0.

Here's an example of a better hierarchy:

BetterPoints.cs

```
// ----------------------------------------------------
// BetterPoints.cs from "Programming in the Key of C#"
// ----------------------------------------------------
using System;

class BetterPoints
{
    static void Main()
    {
        Point2D ptA = new Point2D(10, 20);
        Point2D ptB = new Point2D(20, 30);

        Console.WriteLine(ptA - ptB);

        Point3D ptC = new Point3D(10, 20, 10);
        Point3D ptD = new Point3D(20, 30, 10);

        Console.WriteLine(ptC - ptD);
    }
}
class Point3D
{
    public double x, y, z;

    public Point3D()
    {
        x = y = z = 0;
    }
    public Point3D(double x, double y, double z)
    {
        this.x = x;
        this.y = y;
        this.z = z;
    }
    public static double operator - (Point3D pt1, Point3D pt2)
    {
        return Math.Sqrt(Math.Pow(pt1.x - pt2.x, 2) +
                Math.Pow(pt1.y - pt2.y, 2) +
                Math.Pow(pt1.z - pt2.z, 2));
    }
}
```

```
class Point2D: Point3D
{
    private new double z = 0;

    public Point2D()
    {
        z = z;      // Prevents a warning message
    }
    public Point2D(double x, double y): base(x, y, 0)
    {
    }
}
```

Now the *Point2D* class is quite simple. The *Point2D* class redeclares the *z* field using the *new* keyword:

```
private new double z = 0;
```

Even without the *private* access modifier, the field would still be implicitly private. The *new* modifier essentially allows a class to hide the inherited member and provide a new declaration.

The parameterless constructor contains a do-nothing statement that sets *z* to *z*; but without it, the compiler gives a warning message about the *z* field never being used. The two-parameter constructor simply uses a constructor initializer to invoke the three-parameter constructor in the base class with the third parameter set to 0. Best of all, the *Point2D* class doesn't require a declaration of the subtraction operator. The version in *Point3D* is generalized enough to work just fine.

One application of object-oriented programming that might not be immediately obvious is to give a more prominent identity to measurements that would otherwise be treated as mere numbers. You may recall the incident in September 1999, when a Mars orbiter was lost due to confusion between metric and English units. It's easy to say that errors such as this would be eliminated if everybody would just switch to one set of units or another, but until that time comes, a few simple classes or structures might help.

For example, you might need to work with temperatures in one of your programs. Should you use the Fahrenheit, Celsius, or Kelvin scale? It really depends on the context. If you were eventually displaying the temperatures for American users to read, you'd probably want to convert to Fahrenheit at least. But it's important to realize that Fahrenheit, Celsius, and Kelvin are not three different things. They're all just one thing—the temperature. If you created objects of type *Temperature*, you might avoid dealing with the particular temperature scale until you needed to.

Let's make a structure of type *Temperature*. I'm choosing a structure rather than a class because the temperature is very much like a simple value, and I don't anticipate any inheritance to be required. A user of this structure will be able to create an object of type *Temperature* like this:

```
Temperature temp = new Temperature();
```

A structure declaration can't include an explicit parameterless constructor or explicitly initialized fields. When a program creates an object based on a structure, all fields are initialized to zero or *null*. It makes sense for a default *Temperature* object to represent absolute zero—zero degrees Kelvin, the lowest temperature possible. So, the single field in the *Temperature* structure (which I've made private) stores a temperature in the Kelvin scale:

```
struct Temperature
{
    double dKelvin;
    ...
}
```

The field is private. The *Temperature* structure will also require some properties to get access to this field. The *Kelvin* property could simply access the field with no conversion:

```
public double Kelvin
{
    set { dKelvin = value; }
    get { return dKelvin; }
}
```

For simple properties, I sometimes like to consolidate the curly brackets and accessor bodies on a single line. It saves a lot of space, but it's still quite readable.

But wait. If zero degrees Kelvin is the lowest possible temperature, why are negative values allowed? You might want to prevent negative degrees Kelvin by throwing an exception:

```
public double Kelvin
{
    set
    {
        if (value < 0)
            throw new ArgumentOutOfRangeException();

        dKelvin = value;
    }
    get { return dKelvin; }
}
```

The *Celsius* and *Fahrenheit* properties are fairly straightforward. The *Celsius* property makes use of the *Kelvin* property:

```
public double Celsius
{
    set { Kelvin = value + 273.15; }
    get { return Kelvin - 273.15; }
}
```

And the *Fahrenheit* property makes use of the *Celsius* property:

```
public double Fahrenheit
{
    set { Celsius = 5 * (value - 32) / 9; }
    get { return 9 * Celsius / 5 + 32; }
}
```

One of the crucial parts of the *Temperature* structure is the declaration of *ToString*. This method must provide a readable rendition of the temperature. You can declare a new version of *ToString* that has a parameter that indicates if the temperature should be displayed in Fahrenheit, Celsius, or Kelvin. It's convenient to first declare an enumeration:

```
enum TemperatureUnits
{
    Kelvin,
    Celsius,
    Centigrade = Celsius,
    Fahrenheit
}
```

Just to make it interesting, I decided to add another member to this enumeration, *Centigrade*, which is the old term for Celsius. The two members have the same numeric value.

And here's *ToString* consisting largely of a *switch* statement:

```
public string ToString(TemperatureUnits tu)
{
    switch (tu)
    {
    case TemperatureUnits.Kelvin:
        return String.Format("{0}\u00B0 K", Kelvin);

    case TemperatureUnits.Celsius:
        return String.Format("{0}\u00B0 C", Celsius);

    case TemperatureUnits.Fahrenheit:
        return String.Format("{0}\u00B0 F", Fahrenheit);
    }
    return "";
}
```

Because of the parameter, this is a new *ToString*—not an override of the parameterless *ToString* declared in *System.Object*. The Unicode character '\u00B0' is the degree sign. Because the *Centigrade* member of the enumeration is the same numeric value as *Celsius*, it's not required in the *switch* statement and is actually prohibited. The final *return* statement is required or the compiler will complain that not all code paths return a value. (A *default* case for the *switch* statement would also avoid that problem.)

The standard parameterless *ToString* for *Temperature* simply displays the Celsius temperature:

```
public override string ToString()
{
    return ToString(TemperatureUnits.Celsius);
}
```

The *Temperature* structure can also contain another constructor that requires a temperature value and the *TemperatureUnits* enumeration. That constructor and the rest of *Temperature* are shown here:

Temperature.cs
```
// ------------------------------------------------------
// Temperature.cs from "Programming in the Key of C#"
// ------------------------------------------------------
using System;

namespace Petzold.KeyOfCSharp
{
    public struct Temperature
    {
        double dKelvin;

        public double Kelvin
        {
            set
            {
                if (value < 0)
                    throw new ArgumentOutOfRangeException();

                dKelvin = value;
            }
            get { return dKelvin; }
        }
        public double Celsius
        {
            set { Kelvin = value + 273.15; }
            get { return Kelvin - 273.15; }
        }
```

```
public double Fahrenheit
{
    set { Celsius = 5 * (value - 32) / 9; }
    get { return 9 * Celsius / 5 + 32; }
}
public Temperature(double dTemp, TemperatureUnits tu)
{
    dKelvin = 0;      // Avoid compiler message.

    switch (tu)
    {
    case TemperatureUnits.Kelvin:
        Kelvin = dTemp;
        break;

    case TemperatureUnits.Celsius:
        Celsius = dTemp;
        break;

    case TemperatureUnits.Fahrenheit:
        Fahrenheit = dTemp;
        break;
    }
}
public override string ToString()
{
    return ToString(TemperatureUnits.Celsius);
}
public string ToString(TemperatureUnits tu)
{
    switch (tu)
    {
    case TemperatureUnits.Kelvin:
        return String.Format("{0}\u00B0 K", Kelvin);

    case TemperatureUnits.Celsius:
        return String.Format("{0}\u00B0 C", Celsius);

    case TemperatureUnits.Fahrenheit:
        return String.Format("{0}\u00B0 F", Fahrenheit);
    }
    return "";
}
    }
}
```

You might want to add some operators to this structure if you need them. Most of the structure should look familiar or reasonable, but I've also thrown in a couple new features because I'm going to put this class in a dynamic link library (DLL).

First, I've enclosed the entire structure in a pair of curly brackets preceded by the *namespace* keyword and a namespace name of *Petzold.KeyOfCSharp*. This namespace name is in accordance with the recommended practice: Company name first (the closest equivalent is my last name) followed by a period and product name (in this case, an abbreviation of this book's title). A namespace declaration isn't required when you put classes and structures into DLLs, but it's a good idea so that the class and structure names don't clash with other DLLs.

Secondly, I've given the structure itself an access modifier of *public*. Any class or structure in a DLL that is to be accessed from outside the DLL (as this one will be) needs to be public.

For classes and structures in a DLL, you can also use the access modifiers *internal* and *protected internal* for properties, methods, and fields, as well as classes and structures themselves. These two access modifiers are similar to *public* and *protected* respectively except that they apply only to other classes and structures in the same DLL. From outside the DLL, they are equivalent to *private*.

The Temperature project also includes the enumeration declared with the same namespace and an access modifier of *public*:

TemperatureUnits.cs
```
// -------------------------------------------------------
// TemperatureUnits.cs from "Programming in the Key of C#"
// -------------------------------------------------------
namespace Petzold.KeyOfCSharp
{
    public enum TemperatureUnits
    {
        Kelvin,
        Celsius,
        Centigrade = Celsius,
        Fahrenheit
    }
}
```

Temperature.cs and TemperatureUnits.cs are the only two files in the Temperature project. There's no *Main* method because this isn't going to be a program. It's going to be a dynamic link library that other programs can use, which you'll need to specify before you compile the Temperature project.

If you're running Key of C#, choose Compiler Options from the Project menu. Change the Output Type to Dynamic Link Library.

If you're running Visual Studio .NET (as opposed to Visual C# .NET), invoke the Project Properties dialog box by right-clicking the project name in the Solution Explorer and choosing properties from the context menu, or selecting Properties from the Project menu. On the left, select General. On the right, change Output Type to Class Library.

If you're running Visual C# .NET, the Project Properties dialog box does not allow you to change the output type. (That's one of the things you sacrifice by not paying the big bucks for Visual Studio .NET.) But it's easy to get around this little restriction and persuade Visual C# .NET to create the DLL. Anytime after you create the Temperature project, close the solution. Then, using Notepad, find the Temperature.csproj ("C Sharp Project") file and load it in. Change the line reading

```
OutputType = "Exe"
```

to

```
OutputType = "Library"
```

Save the Temperature.csproj file from Notepad and then reload the Temperature solution in Visual C# .NET.

Now you can compile. Rather than a file named Temperature.exe, you'll get a file named Temperature.dll.

Now let's make use of that DLL. A project named TemperatureDemo contains only this file:

TemperatureDemo.cs

```
// ----------------------------------------------------------
// TemperatureDemo.cs from "Programming in the Key of C#"
// ----------------------------------------------------------
using System;
using Petzold.KeyOfCSharp;

class TemperatureDemo
{
    static void Main()
    {
        Temperature temp = new Temperature();
        Console.WriteLine(temp);

        temp = new Temperature(100, TemperatureUnits.Centigrade);
        Console.WriteLine(temp.ToString(TemperatureUnits.Fahrenheit));
    }
}
```

Notice the new *using* directive. (Without it you'd need to preface every mention of *Temperature* and *TemperatureUnits* with the namespace name.) Before compiling this program, you'll also need to specify that the program requires Temperature.dll.

If you're running Key of C#, select the Add Reference item from the Project menu. Click Browse and navigate to the Temperature.dll file, which will be in the Temperature directory.

If you're running Visual C# .NET, choose Add Reference from the Project menu. Select the Projects tab. Click the Browse button and navigate to the Temperature.dll file. (It will be in the Temperature\bin\Debug or Temperature\bin\Release directory.) Select that file.

When a program like TemperatureDemo makes use of classes and structures in a particular DLL, the DLL comes into play twice. As you can see, the compiler itself needs access to the DLL. The compiler automatically accesses mscorlib.dll, but if the program needs any other DLLs, you must explicitly indicate them to the compiler. The compiler accesses the DLLs to obtain *metadata*, which is information about the contents of the DLL. Accessing Temperature.dll is the only way for the compiler to determine if the DLL really contains a *Temperature* class and a *TemperatureUnits* enumeration, and what members are available. The compiler also embeds information in TemperatureDemo.exe indicating that the program needs access to Termperature.dll when it runs. When you run TemperatureDemo, the DLL comes into play a second time. The Common Language Runtime (CLR) links up the program with the DLL so the program can use the *Temperature* class.

If you have a project that requires you to use DLLs from other companies, you might someday encounter a problem in which two DLLs have used the same name for two different classes, both of which are useful to your program. Fortunately, these two companies will have used two different namespace names for these classes, and you can use the namespace to fully qualify the class name. You can shorten your typing with a variation of the *using* directive that lets you specify an alias for the namespace:

```
using pw = Proseware.ProsewareLibrary;
```

Now you can preface the class name with *pw* rather than the long namespace name.

Now that you've seen how namespaces are declared, you can get a better feel for the overall structure of declarations you can make in C#. Within a namespace declaration, you can declare five types of items. You can also declare these five items if you don't use a namespace declaration:

■   The *class* is the basic organizational element of code and data.

■   The *struct* is similar to the class but is a value type.

- An *interface* is similar to a class but consists only of declarations without implementations.

- A *delegate* declares a signature for a method used as an event handler. I'll discuss event handlers in the next chapter.

- An *enum* is an enumeration of related words with constant numeric values.

Declared within a class or a structure are members:

- Constructors are executed when an object is created.

- Destructors are executed when an object is freed from the heap. I'll discuss destructors in the last chapter.

- Methods are collections of code with optional parameters and return values.

- Fields are variables accessible to all methods.

- Constants are similar to fields but have the same value for the duration of the object.

- Properties are accessible like fields but contain code like methods.

- Indexers are properties that allow an object to be indexed like an array.

- Operators allow the class to overload arithmetic and logical operations.

- Events allow a class to call event handlers in other classes. I'll talk about events in the next chapter.

In addition, although it's not common, a class or structure can contain declarations of other classes, structures, interfaces, delegates, or enumerations.

40

Framework Essentials

The .NET Framework contains numerous classes and structures, many of which you'll probably never have occasion to use, but some of which find their way into many programs. In this chapter, I'd like to briefly explore some of these common classes and structures. You should explore them more fully on your own, not only because you'll have occasion to use them, but because they may give you ideas about how to structure your own classes.

The *DateTime* structure declared in the *System* namespace is used throughout the .NET Framework. As its name suggests, an instance of *DateTime* represents not only a date, but also a particular point in time.

As you explore *DateTime*, you might be interested to see how the structure handles validity checking, which is something that we struggled with when creating our own *Date* classes. You create a *DateTime* object using one of the numerous *DateTime* constructors. However, all the *DateTime* properties (such as *Year*, *Month*, *Day*, *Hour*, *Minute*, and *Second*) are read-only. Once you create a date, it's immutable and cannot be changed. All validity checking occurs in the constructors.

Some of the constructors of *DateTime* let you create dates using other calendars, such as Hebrew or Hijri, which is another term for the Islamic calendar. You do this by passing an instance of a *Calendar* object to the *DateTime* constructor. But *Calendar* (declared in the *System.Globalization* namespace) is an abstract class. You actually need to instantiate one of the classes that derive from *Calendar*, such as *HebrewCalendar* or *HijriCalendar*. These classes convert dates in these calendars to dates in the Gregorian calendar (which is what the *DateTime* structure stores). You can also use these classes to convert Gregorian dates to dates in other calendars. *Calendar* is an excellent application of an abstract class.

Where *DateTime* really puts *SuperDate* to shame is in displaying the date and time in various formats. Even the standard *ToString* method uses preferences the user has specified in the Regional Options dialog box in the Control Panel. The *ToShortDateString*, *ToLongDateString*, *ToShortTimeString*, and *ToLongTimeString* methods display the date and time in isolation in both short and long versions.

DateTime also has a *ToString* method with a single argument, which is a short text string that lets you get much more specific about formatting the date and time. (You can also use these short text strings in the formatting string of *String.Format* or *Console.WriteLine* calls.) An optional second argument to *ToString* can be either *CultureInfo.CurrentCulture* to display something appropriate for the user's language and display conventions, or *CultureInfo.InvariantCulture* for a format that's independent of the user's locale. See the *DateTimeFormatInfo* class in the .NET documentation for details.

The *DateTime* structure also allows you to obtain the current date and time. (*DateTime* obviously accesses the Windows operating system to obtain this information.)

The static *DateTime.Now* property returns the local date and time at the moment the property is called. If you want to write a clock program—which is much less common in console environments than in graphical user interfaces such as Windows—you'll need to call *DateTime.Now* multiple times and display the result.

It might first occur to you to put the call in an infinite loop:

```
while (true)
    Console.WriteLine(DateTime.Now);
```

This code displays line after line of date and time text. You can terminate the program by clicking the close box in the console window or by typing Ctrl-C.

You might want to keep the display tidier by restraining the display to just a single line:

```
while (true)
    Console.Write("\r{0}     " + DateTime.Now);
```

Notice the change from *WriteLine* to *Write*. The *Write* method doesn't skip to the next line. Instead, the string argument begins with an explicit carriage return character to move to the left margin. Each display writes over the previous display. The formatting string has a few extra blanks so that the previous text is fully erased when the length of the date and time text becomes shorter (for example, when the time switches from two-digit hours to one-digit hours).

One problem is that an infinite loop updates the display continuously, but the displayed time probably changes only every second. The program is doing much more work than it needs to and might even hamper the performance of other applications. It also has an annoying flicker.

You probably want to call *DateTime.Now* and *Console.Write* only once per second, in effect, slowing the program down. One approach to slowing the program down is to make a call to the static *Sleep* method of the *Thread* class:

```
while (true)
{
    Console.Write("\r{0}    ", DateTime.Now);
    Thread.Sleep(1000);
}
```

You'll also need a *using* directive for the *System.Threading* namespace. The argument to *Sleep* is a time in milliseconds (thousandths of seconds). The *Sleep* method doesn't return until the specified period of time has elapsed. During the time the program is asleep, it's not doing any work and other programs get a chance to run.

Another approach is to install a timer. A timer has the capability of calling a method in your program at regular intervals.

Using the *Timer* class is different from anything you've seen before in this book. You've seen lots of examples of your programs calling methods in the .NET Framework, starting in Chapter 5 with *Console.WriteLine*. Starting in Chapter 17, you've also declared your own methods and written code to call those methods. You've also seen how you can declare certain methods in your classes, like *ToString*, that are called by other methods such as *String.Format* or *Console.WriteLine*.

The *Timer* class calls methods in your program, but it's different because you need to tell the *Timer* class exactly what method in your program you want the class to call. This method can have any name, but it must have a specific return type and parameter list. Traditionally, such a method has been termed a *callback*, but in C# a better term is an *event handler*. An event handler is a generalized mechanism for one class to request that a certain method in that class be called from another class. Classes in the Windows Forms library use events and event handlers extensively to inform programs when users click buttons, select menu items, scroll scollbars, and perform numerous other user input actions.

There are actually three classes named *Timer* in the .NET Framework. The *Timer* class in the *System.Windows.Forms* namespace is an interface to the standard Windows timer for use by Windows Forms applications. Non-Windows applications can use the *Timer* class in the *System.Threading* namespace or the *System.Timers* namespace. I'm going to demonstrate how to use the one in *System.Timers*, but only because it's structured more in accordance with other classes in the .NET Framework and with the Windows Forms timer.

The *System.Timers* namespace consists of three classes and one *delegate*. A delegate looks very much like a method with no body. The *Elapsed-EventHandler* delegate declared in the *System.Timers* namespace looks like this:

```
public delegate void ElapsedEventHandler(object objSender,
                                ElapsedEventArgs eea);
```

Notice the keyword *delegate*. The second parameter is an object of type *ElapsedEventArgs*, a class that is also declared in *System.Timers* and consists of a single property named *SignalTime* that is of type *DateTime*.

To use the *Timers* class, you must declare a method in your program that has the same return type and parameter list as *ElapsedEventHandler*. You can name it whatever you want:

```
void TimerHandler(object obj, ElapsedEventArgs eea)
{
    ...
}
```

This is the method in your program that the timer will call at periodic intervals. If you're creating the timer object in a static method, then *TimerHandler* must also be static.

To use the timer, you first create an object of type *Timer*:

```
System.Timers.Timer tmr = new System.Timers.Timer();
```

or, if you've wisely put a *using* directive for the *System.Timers* namespace at the top of your program:

```
Timer tmr = new Timer();
```

Now you specify the callback method. The syntax of this statement is unique to event handlers:

```
tmr.Elapsed += new ElapsedEventHandler(TimerHandler);
```

Elapsed is a member of the *Timer* class, but it's not a field and it's not a property (although it may look like one). *Elapsed* is an *event*. The use of the compound assignment statement is a special syntax for use with events, and the process is referred to as *attaching* the handler to the event. On the right is the name of the event handler in your program (*TimerHandler* in this example) seemingly passed as an argument to what looks like a constructor but which involves the delegate name (*ElapsedEventHandler*). The compiler complains if the signature of your event handler doesn't match the signature of the delegate. You can also detach a handler from the event using similar syntax:

```
tmr.Elapsed -= new ElapsedEventHandler(TimerHandler);
```

You can attach multiple handlers to the same event.

The *Timer* class also has a property named *Interval* that you use to specify the timer interval. Set the Boolean property *Enabled* to *true* to start the timer. At that time, the *Timer* class will begin making periodic calls to the event handler in your program. Alternatively, you can call the *Start* method to start the timer and the *Stop* method to stop it.

Here's a complete clock program using the timer:

Clock.cs

```
// ------------------------------------------------
// Clock.cs from "Programming in the Key of C#"
// ------------------------------------------------
using System;
using System.Timers;    // Requires System.dll

class Clock
{
    static int iStringLength;

    static void Main()
    {
        Console.WriteLine("Press Enter to end program");
        Console.WriteLine();

        Timer tmr = new Timer();
        tmr.Elapsed += new ElapsedEventHandler(TimerHandler);
        tmr.Interval = 1000;
        tmr.Start();

        Console.ReadLine();
        tmr.Stop();
    }
    static void TimerHandler(object obj, ElapsedEventArgs eea)
    {
        Console.Write(new String('\b', iStringLength));

        string str = String.Format("{0} {1} ",
                            eea.SignalTime.ToLongDateString(),
                            eea.SignalTime.ToLongTimeString());
        iStringLength = str.Length;

        Console.Write(str);
    }
}
```

All previous programs in this book have used classes and structures in the .NET Framework that have resided in mscorlib.dll (Multi-language Standard Common Object Runtime Library). Everything in the *System.Timers* namespace is instead in System.dll. (You can determine where a particular class or structure resides by checking the Assembly line of the first page of the documentation of the class or structure.) You need to specify this DLL when compiling the program.

If you're running Visual C# .NET, choose Add Reference from the Project menu, or right-click the References line under the project name in the Solution

Explorer pane at the right side of the screen and choose Add Reference. Find System.dll in the list and click the Select button. Then click OK.

If you're running Key of C#, choose Add Reference from the Project menu and click System.dll.

In the Clock program, *TimerHandler* uses the *SignalTime* property of the *ElapsedEventArgs* object passed to the handler. This property is the time that the *Timer* class called the *TimerHandler* method. I used that property rather than *DateTime.Now* just to demonstrate how event handlers can use their parameters. The event handler parameters often include useful information. The first parameter to *TimerHandler* is the *Timer* object created in *Main*, and which is responsible for calling the event handler.

TimerHandler uses the *ToLongDateString* and *ToLongTimeString* to display the date and time. Because the string lengths are so variable (for example, in the transition from February to March), I decided to erase the previous display by backspacing. The first *Console.Write* displays a number of backspaces equal to the length of the previously displayed string.

Take a look at *Main*. What's important to realize here is that the call to the *Start* method of the *Timer* class returns immediately. If that *Start* call were the last statement of *Main*, the program would then terminate! It's necessary for *Main* to avoid ending so that the *Timer* class gets a chance to call the *Timer-Handler* method. *Main* delays termination by calling *Console.ReadLine*, which will only return when the user presses the Enter key. (The program begins by telling the user that this is how the program is to be ended.) When the user presses Enter, the program stops the timer and exits.

By creating a *Timer*, the Clock program has implicitly created a second *thread of execution*. Windows is a multitasking operating system, which means that Windows switches among different programs very quickly, giving the illusion that the programs are running simultaneously. In addition, programs can split themselves into multiple threads of execution that also seem to run simultaneously. The *System.Threading* namespace has a bunch of classes for creating multiple threads of execution and synchronizing among them.

The event handler in the Clock program is a second thread of execution. The thread seems to run simultaneously with the code in *Main*, which spends most of its time deep within the *Console.ReadLine* call. If you need to control the interaction between more active threads, you can make use of the *lock* statement in C#, or more sophisticated semaphores in *System.Threading*. I'll show you some examples in the last chapter.

Another important .NET Framework namespace is *System.ID*. If a C# program needs a lot of memory, it can generally obtain that memory just by creating a large array. Arrays that are several million bytes in size are no problem on today's multi-megabyte machines. But once the program ends, all the information stored in that array is lost as the memory is freed for use by other applications.

If a program wishes to store information that persists beyond the termination of the program, it must use *files*.

A file is a collection of data stored on a disk (or some other medium, such as flash memory, that mimics a disk) and identified by a filename. Disks are organized into a hierarchical system of directories. A *fully-qualified filename* includes the disk drive and the complete directory path of the file along with its name, such as c:\Documents and Settings\Username\My Documents\Key of C#\TemperatureDemo\TemperatureDemo.cs. Files can also be stored on a network or the Internet, with fully-qualified names such as *http://www.charles petzold.com/key/index.html*.

The .NET Framework makes a distinction between a file and a *stream*. A file is a collection of data stored on disk. A stream is a series of bytes that a program reads or writes. A stream is the mechanism a program uses to read from or write to a file. A stream generally refers to an *open* file—a file that a program is currently accessing.

The world of files is divided into two main groups: binary files and text files. A simple way to determine if a file is binary or text is to load the file into Windows Notepad. If you see text, it's a text file. If you see "junk," it's a binary file.

Binary files include executable (EXE) files, image files (such as JPEG and GIF), and many proprietary data formats (such as Microsoft Word's DOC format). Plain vanilla text files created in Notepad often have the extension TXT, but text files don't have to consist solely of common written languages. C# source code files (CS) are also text files. Several types of text files allow the representation of formatted text. These include the Hypertext Markup Language (HTML) and the Rich Text Format (RTF). Extensible Markup Language (XML) is a generalized text format becoming popular for the storage of many different kinds of information. The Temperature.csproj file in the previous chapter is an XML file.

In preparation for writing to (or reading from) a file, a program *opens* a file. This process makes the file available to the program. After the program is finished using the file, it *closes* the file. Thus, writing data to a file generally involves three steps:

1. The program opens an existing file or creates a new file. In doing so, it obtains a stream.

2. The program uses the stream to write data to the file.

3. The program closes the file.

While a file is open and being written to, it's in a rather precarious state; if the electricity fails, the file could be left in an unusable condition. For this reason, programs try to open and close files as quickly as possible or to use procedures that protect against lost data. Reading from a file is similar to writing but is considerably less dangerous because the file doesn't have to be altered.

Often programs must modify existing files. Adding data to the end of a file is fairly easy; more problematic is inserting stuff into the middle of a file. Generally, this job requires the file to be entirely rewritten to the disk. If the file is small enough, the program can read the entire file into memory, perhaps into an array, make the necessary changes, and then write it back out. For longer files that may not fit in available memory, you'll want to open the existing file and create a new file. Then you gradually read the existing file in pieces, make changes, and write out the changed data to the new file. You finish up by deleting the first file and renaming the second file to the original name.

A C# program that works with files uses classes declared in the *System.IO* ("input/output") namespace. (Programs dealing with XML can make use of the *System.Xml* namespace; programs using sophisticated databases will probably spend time with the *System.Data* namespaces.)

Text files are often convenient for storing simple data, and are very similar to using console I/O. A program can create a text file by creating an object of type *StreamWriter* and specifying the filename:

```
StreamWriter sw = new StreamWriter(strFilename);
```

If a file exists of that name, it will be deleted; an optional Boolean argument allows you to open an existing file for appending to the end of the file.

To write to the text file, you generally use methods named *Write* and *WriteLine* that are declared in the *TextWriter* class and inherited by *StreamWriter*. These methods are the same as the *Write* and *WriteLine* methods in the *Console* class.

When you're finished writing to the file, you call the *Close* method:

```
sw.Close();
```

This call indicates that the program is finished using the file and directs the operating system to update directory listings and other tables on the disk drive. Following the *Close* call, you can no longer write to the file using this *StreamWriter* object. You would have to reopen the file to make any changes.

Opening a file for reading requires creating an object of type *StreamReader*:

```
StreamReader sr = new StreamReader(strFilename);
```

If the file does not exist, an exception is thrown. After the file is open, you read from it using *Read* (to read individual characters), *ReadLine* (to read sequential lines), or *ReadToEnd* (to read to the end of the file). Here's *ReadLine*:

```
strLine = sr.ReadLine();
```

If *ReadLine* returns *null*, the program is attempting to read past the end of the file. Very often in reading files, you'll want to use a *while* loop that looks something like this:

```
while ((strLine = sr.ReadLine()) != null)
{
    // Process each line of the file.
}
```

The code in parentheses following the *while* keyword reads another line from the file using *ReadLine*, stores it in *strLine*, and checks if *strLine* is not equal to *null*. The parentheses around the assignment statement are required because the inequality operand has a higher precedence than the assignment operator.

Although you're not modifying the file by reading from it, you should close the file when you're finished:

```
sr.Close();
```

Often a program must read lines from a text file and store them in an array. Yet, the program doesn't know how large this array should be until the file is entirely read. The program might also be adding to this array as the user works with the file. In such a case, if you need an array whose size varies as your program is running, you should consider the *ArrayList* class in the *System.Collections* namespace. *ArrayList* stores elements like an array, but it can dynamically change its size as needed.

You can explore *ArrayList* more fully on your own. In the next chapter, I'll show a program that uses just a couple of methods and properties of *ArrayList*. You add elements to an *ArrayList* object using the *Add* method. These elements can be of any type. The elements are converted to *object* for storage. You can use *Remove* to remove a particular element or *RemoveAt* to remove an element based on its index in the *ArrayList*. The *Count* property indicates the number of elements currently stored. *ArrayList* also has an indexer that you can use to *get* and *set* elements, but the index can't be greater than *Count* minus one. In other words, you can only use the *get* indexer to replace elements. If you need to add new elements without replacing existing elements, use *Add*.

The next program is a C# implementation of a program I first saw in a BASIC version over 20 years ago. The program begins with the following statement:

```
Think of an animal and press Enter.
```

After you press Enter, the program asks:

```
Is it a cat (Yes/No)?
```

If that's not right, you type No (or just N) and press Enter. The program then asks:

```
What animal were you thinking of?
```

You type in (for example)

```
Dog
```

and press Enter. The program asks:

```
And what yes/no question might distinguish a dog from a cat?
```

There are many possibilities for such a question, but you type:

```
Does it meow?
```

The program then asks:

```
And what's the answer for a dog (Yes/No)?
```

You type N and press Enter. The program asks:

```
Would you like to play again?
```

You decide you want to. The program displays the initial prompt again:

```
Think of an animal and press Enter.
```

Now the program begins by asking:

```
Does it meow?
```

You get the idea. The more you play, the more the program "learns."

This program cries out for a data structure known as a *linked list*. Each question that the program is capable of asking is known as a *node*. The user can answer Yes or No to this question. Each node is potentially linked to two other nodes, one for Yes and the other for No. That node contains the next question. Here's a diagram showing five nodes:

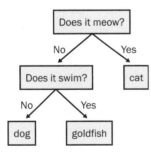

And here's a simple implementation of a node class for this program:

```
class AnimalNode
{
    public string strQuestion;
    public AnimalNode anYes;
    public AnimalNode anNo;
}
```

Notice that this class contains two fields that are instances of the same class. Each instance of the *AnimalNode* class potentially has references to two other instances. These links allow a program to leap from one question to another. It looks like the links could go on forever, but they really can't. At the beginning, there is always a *root* node. That's the first question the program asks. At the end of each path through the links is an *AnimalNode* object where *strQuestion* is actually an answer—the string "cat" or "dog" or "goldfish" or whatever—and *anYes* and *anNo* are *null*. That's the end of that list of links. There can never be a node where *anYes* is *null* but *anNo* is not, or *anNo* is *null* but *anYes* is not.

Here's a more extensive implementation of *AnimalNode*:

AnimalNode.cs

```
// ------------------------------------------------------
// AnimalNode.cs from "Programming in the Key of C#"
// ------------------------------------------------------
using System;
using System.IO;
using System.Text;

class AnimalNode
{
    private string strQuestion;
    public AnimalNode anYes;
    public AnimalNode anNo;

    public string Question
    {
        set
        {
            StringBuilder sb = new StringBuilder(value);
            sb.Replace(',', ' ');
            sb.Replace('(', ' ');
            sb.Replace(')', ' ');
            strQuestion = sb.ToString();
        }
        get { return strQuestion; }
    }
    public void WriteNode(StreamWriter sw, int iLevel)
    {
        sw.Write("{0}({1},", new string(' ', iLevel * 4), Question);

        if (anYes != null)
        {
            sw.WriteLine();
            anYes.WriteNode(sw, iLevel + 1);
        }
```

```
            sw.Write(",");

            if (anNo != null)
            {
                sw.WriteLine();
                anNo.WriteNode(sw, iLevel + 1);
            }
            sw.Write(")");
        }
        public static AnimalNode ReadNode(StreamReader sr)
        {
            char ch;

            do
                ch = (char) sr.Read();
            while (Char.IsWhiteSpace(ch));

            AnimalNode an = new AnimalNode();

            while ((ch = (char) sr.Read()) != ',')
                an.Question += ch;

            if ((char) sr.Peek() != ',')
                an.anYes = ReadNode(sr);

            ch = (char) sr.Read();

            if ((char) sr.Peek() != ')')
                an.anNo = ReadNode(sr);

            ch = (char) sr.Read();    // This is the closing parenthesis.

            return an;
        }
    }
}
```

In this version, *strQuestion* is private; the *Question* property strips all commas and parentheses from any text the user may type in. (You'll see the reason for this shortly.) The *StringBuilder* class helps out here because it has a *Replace* method that replaces all occurrences of a character or string with another character or string.

The *AnimalNode* class has *WriteNode* and *ReadNode* methods that store the information in a file and later retrieve it. In the file, each saved node is enclosed in parentheses; the three components of the node are separated by commas. (If the question the user types in has commas and parentheses itself, that would confuse the program. That's why they're stripped from the question text.) Each of these methods is recursive. If the argument to *WriteNode* is the root node, then the method ends up writing the whole file. Similarly, if *Read-Node* begins at the beginning of the file, it reads the whole file and returns the root node. After you play with the program awhile, you'll want to take a look at the data file. Each node is displayed on a new line with indentation for your convenience in examining the file.

Here's the program:

GuessTheAnimal.cs

```
// --------------------------------------------------------
// GuessTheAnimal.cs from "Programming in the Key of C#"
// --------------------------------------------------------
using System;
using System.IO;

class GuessTheAnimal
{
    static void Main()
    {
        string strFilename = "GuessTheAnimal.txt";
        AnimalNode anRoot;

        try
        {
            StreamReader sr = new StreamReader(strFilename);
            anRoot = AnimalNode.ReadNode(sr);
            sr.Close();
        }
        catch
        {
            anRoot = new AnimalNode();
            anRoot.Question = "cat";
        }

        do
        {
            // Start playing.

            Console.Write("Think of an animal and press Enter.");
            Console.ReadLine();
            AskQuestion(ref anRoot);

            // Save the file.

            StreamWriter sw = new StreamWriter(strFilename);
            anRoot.WriteNode(sw, 0);
            sw.Close();
```

```
            // Possibly play again.

            Console.Write("Would you like to play again? ");
        }
    while (GetYesNo());
}
static void AskQuestion(ref AnimalNode an)
{
    if (an.anYes != null)     // Ask a question; get an answer.
    {
        Console.Write(an.Question + " ");

        if (GetYesNo())
            AskQuestion(ref an.anYes);
        else
            AskQuestion(ref an.anNo);
    }
    else     // End of the line; time to wrap up this game.
    {
        Console.Write("Is it a " + an.Question + " (Yes/No)? ");

        if (GetYesNo())
        {
            Console.WriteLine("I guessed it!");
        }
        else
        {
            Console.Write("What animal were you thinking of? ");
            string strAnimal = Console.ReadLine();

            Console.WriteLine("And what yes/no question might " +
                            "distinguish a " + strAnimal +
                            " from a " + an.Question + "? ");
            string strQuestion = Console.ReadLine();

            Console.Write("And what's the answer for a " +
                        strAnimal + " (Yes/No)? ");
            bool bAnswer = GetYesNo();

            AnimalNode anNewAnimal = new AnimalNode();
            anNewAnimal.Question = strAnimal;

            AnimalNode anNewQuestion = new AnimalNode();
            anNewQuestion.Question = strQuestion;

            if (bAnswer)
            {
                anNewQuestion.anYes = anNewAnimal;
                anNewQuestion.anNo = an;
```

```
                }
                else
                {
                    anNewQuestion.anYes = an;
                    anNewQuestion.anNo = anNewAnimal;
                }
                an = anNewQuestion;
            }
        }
    }
    static bool GetYesNo()
    {
        while (true)
        {
            string strAnswer = Console.ReadLine().Trim().ToUpper();

            if (strAnswer.Length > 0 && strAnswer[0] == 'Y')
                return true;

            else if (strAnswer.Length > 0 && strAnswer[0] == 'N')
                return false;

            Console.Write(" Try again: ");
        }
    }
}
```

The *Main* method begins by attempting to read the file. If the file doesn't exist, it simply creates a root node consisting of the *Question* property set to "cat." The recursive *AskQuestion* method does much of the work in this program. If it doesn't guess the animal, it must construct a new node and insert it into the linked list. The *GetYesNo* method simply gets a response from the user and returns *true* if Yes was typed and *false* if No was typed.

The final program in this book deals with yet two more text files, but these files store not linked lists, but musical compositions in the key of C#.

41

Coda

C# may be a fine language for programmers, but the key of C# is not so hospitable for musicians. While the do-ri-me C major scale consists of just the white keys of the piano (C, D, E, F, G, A, B, C), the C# major scale is half a step higher: C#, D#, E#, F#, G#, A#, B#, C#. The key is confusing because on many modern instruments, E# is the same as F and B# is the same as C. Almost nobody writes music in C# major, and if they do, they use the equivalent (and somewhat easier) key of D-flat major. (The C# minor scale, which is C#, D#, E, F#, G#, A, B, C#, is much more common than C# major. Beethoven's 14th piano sonata, nicknamed the Moonlight Sonata, is in the key of C# minor.)

One composer who took up the C# challenge in an aesthetically triumphant manner was Johann Sebastian Bach (1685–1750), whose 1722 work *Das Wohltemperirte Clavier* (*Well-Tempered Keyboard*) consists of 24 preludes and fugues in all 12 major and minor keys. In this work, Bach had no hesitation writing music for treacherous keys such as C#, and he repeated the feat by writing a second set of 24 preludes and fugues about 20 years later. The *Well-Tempered Keyboard* is generally played today on a harpsichord or piano, but almost any keyboard instrument will do.

Interestingly enough, it's not clear what Bach was trying to prove with this work. Some believe that he was demonstrating the advantage of *equal temperament*, a tuning in which all the notes of the instrument are equally spaced by a factor of the 12th root of 2. Others believe that Bach was advocating a *well-tempered* tuning, which uses non-uniform intervals between each note. Well-tempered tunings can accommodate all 24 keys, but the different keys have somewhat distinctive sounds. All existing recordings of the work are performed on equally tempered pianos, harpsichords, or clavichords.

In this chapter, I'm going to show you a program named CSharpBach that plays the Prelude and Fugue in C# Major from the first book of the *Well-Tempered Keyboard*. Because this is a computer program playing the music rather than a human being, it sounds a bit mechanical, but Bach seems to survive this rude treatment better than most composers.

The program makes use of Window's support of the Musical Instrument Digital Interface (MIDI). The MIDI standard was developed by a consortium of manufacturers of electronic music synthesizers in the early 1980s as a protocol for connecting electronic music instruments among themselves and with computers. The standard is maintained by the MIDI Manufacturers Association (MMA), which has a Web site at *www.midi.org*.

MIDI has been supported by Windows since Windows 3.1. Most sound boards on today's computers contain MIDI synthesizers, and recent versions of Windows can even simulate a MIDI synthesizer in software.

MIDI devices communicate among themselves using short *messages*, which are simply numeric codes. Each message is generally one, two, or three bytes in length. Often a MIDI controller (such as a keyboard) sends messages to a MIDI synthesizer to play notes on the synthesizer. When a MIDI synthesizer is attached to a computer, a program can send messages to the synthesizer. The most important of these messages are Note On, which begins playing a particular note at a specified volume, and Note Off, which stops playing that note. Another important message is called Program Change, and is used to specify the instrument sound for a series of notes. The code to specify the instrument can range from 0 to 127; the instrument sound associated with each code is defined by the General MIDI standard. See *www.midi.org/about-midi/gm/gm1sound.shtml* for the complete list. The codes in this list begin at one. The program in this chapter uses zero-based instrument codes.

All three types of messages I've described (Note On, Note Off, and Program Change) include a code to indicate one of 16 MIDI *channels*. Because each channel can be assigned a different instrument sound, in effect MIDI allows 16 different instrument sounds at any time.

The MIDI Manufacturers Association also defines a MIDI file format. MIDI files generally have an extension of MID or MIDI and store entire musical compositions. The Windows Media Player can play MIDI files; using Media Player (or another program) to play MIDI files is the customary way that people play MIDI music on their computer. To make this project more interesting, I've decided to ignore the standard MIDI file format and make up my own (much simpler) format.

For using MIDI without using MIDI files, the Windows application programming interface (API) includes a set of *low-level* MIDI functions that allow a program to send individual MIDI messages to the computer's synthesizer. These functions begin with the prefix *midiOut* and are located in the WINMM.DLL dynamic link library. A Windows program calls *midiOutOpen* to gain exclusive access to a MIDI device, *midiOutShortMsg* to send it messages, and *midiOut-Close* to close the device and make it available to other applications. My book *Programming Windows, Fifth Edition* (Microsoft Press, 1999) has a more extensive discussion of the Windows API support of MIDI.

Unfortunately, the .NET Framework itself has no MIDI or other multimedia support. A C# programmer wishing to use multimedia can either take advantage of the managed code version of DirectX 9.0 or call the Windows API functions directly.

The program I'll show you in this chapter takes the latter approach, if only to demonstrate how you can use your C# programs to call arbitrary functions in Windows DLLs that are not part of the .NET Framework.

The MIDI synthesizer is a shared resource among all programs running under Windows. A program that gets exclusive access to a MIDI device must properly relinquish that access when it's finished so that other applications can use the device. Handling this process correctly in your C# programs requires learning a little bit more about automatic memory management and garbage collection.

A C# program implicitly allocates memory from the managed heap whenever it creates an array or any object based on a class. This memory could be just a few bytes or, for large arrays, it could be several megabytes in size. Generally, a C# program doesn't have to worry about freeing this memory when the object is no longer needed by the program. If memory becomes scarce, the common language runtime (CLR) performs garbage collection on the program's managed heap. All objects stored in the heap that are no longer referenced by the program are eligible to have their memory reclaimed. This memory is thus made available for future objects.

What does it mean for an object to no longer be referenced by a program? Here's a simple example:

```
MyClass mc = new MyClass();
mc = null;
```

At the completion of the first statement, memory has been allocated from the heap and *mc* refers to that memory. The second statement that sets *mc* to *null* removes all references to that memory block. The memory is eligible for garbage collection.

Objects that are local to a method are generally eligible for garbage collection when the method completes. However, if the method stores the local object somewhere else—a field perhaps—then even when the method finishes, there's still a reference to the object by the field. The object is not eligible for garbage collection. Sometimes eligibility for garbage collection is somewhat subtle. For example, if a program installs an event handler for a particular object (perhaps a *Timer* object), then the *Timer* object is still in use even if the object itself goes out of scope. It is the responsibility of the CLR and the garbage collector to determine when an object is no longer referenced.

Let me emphasize that an object's memory is not immediately reclaimed by the garbage collector at the moment the object becomes unreferenced by the program. The object only becomes *eligible* for garbage collection. Garbage collection might not occur at all while the program is running. As the program terminates, all memory from the program's heap is freed for use by other programs.

A program cannot directly free an object's memory from the heap. However, there's a class named *GC* ("garbage collection") in the *System* namespace that provides several static methods that a program can use to run the garbage collector on demand. That process results in the freeing of memory used by unreferenced objects.

A class knows when an object of that class is being created because one of the class's constructors is called during object creation. But nothing I've discussed so far indicates how a class can know when the memory that an object occupies is being freed from the heap. That we have come so far in this book without worrying about the freeing of heap memory indicates just how convenient it is to have a garbage collector that works behind the scenes.

However, there are times when a C# program must deal with an *unmanaged* resource. An unmanaged resource is something outside the control of the CLR. An unmanaged resource might access hardware or it might use memory that's not part of the managed heap. Or perhaps a program uses a DLL that was created before the .NET era. Whenever your program needs access to unmanaged resources, it must get involved with cleaning up those resources when they are no longer needed by the program. In part, this requires that the class know when an object is being freed from the heap.

A class can be informed when an object is freed from the heap by implementing the opposite of a constructor, which is called a *destructor*. In the .NET documentation, you'll often see destructors referred to as *Finalize* methods, which is the name the C# compiler uses to represent a destructor when creating intermediate language.

In your classes or structures, you declare a destructor using the name of the class preceded by the tilde character, a character normally used in C# as the bitwise complement operator. The syntax of the destructor comes from C++. The destructor has no access modifier, no return type, and no parameters:

```
class MyClass
{
```

```
    ...
    ~MyClass()
    {
        ...
    }
    ...
}
```

The destructor is called only when an object is being freed from the managed heap, either as a result of garbage collection while the program is running or as the program is terminated. You can't call the destructor directly. If the class with the destructor derives from other classes that have destructors, the destructors in the ancestral classes are also called in order, ending with the destructor in *object*. That sequence is the opposite order as constructors.

Classes that provide access to files have destructors; so do classes in the Windows Forms library that encapsulate Windows objects such as windows, buttons, and fonts. These are all classes that deal with unmanaged resources.

Don't use destructors indiscriminately. Destructors require some overhead on the part of the CLR. The CLR must keep special track of objects with destructors, and then call those destructors during garbage collection. Fortunately, it's possible for a class to avoid this overhead by preventing a destructor from executing if the resource has already been cleaned up.

Although not strictly required, it's recommended that classes that implement destructors also include methods that a program can call directly to clean up unmanaged resources. These methods are generally named *Dispose* or *Close*. We've already encountered a *Close* method in the *StreamWriter* and *StreamReader* classes. In fact, you should probably think of the destructor mostly as a safeguard in case the *Dispose* or *Close* methods never get called by the program.

A parameterless *Dispose* method is the sole method of the *IDisposable* interface. It's helpful for a class that includes a destructor to implement the *IDisposable* interface so that other classes can use the *is* operator to easily determine if the class has a *Dispose* method.

A *Dispose* method has a *void* return value and no parameters:

```
public void Dispose()
{
    ... // Clean up unmanaged resources.
}
```

You can simply call *Dispose* from the destructor so that the two methods perform the same job:

```
~MyClass()
{
    Dispose();
}
```

A *Dispose* method should be written so that it can be called multiple times without a problem. You might want to have a field named *bDisposed* initialized to *false* that you use to make sure that code in the *Dispose* method is executed only once:

```
public void Dispose()
{
    if (!bDisposed)
    {
        … // Clean up unmanaged resources.
        bDisposed = true;
    }
}
```

I mentioned that destructors add some overhead to the work the CLR must do in keeping track of objects. There's a special static method in the *GC* class that *Dispose* can call to prevent the destructor from executing if *Dispose* has already cleaned up the unmanaged resources:

```
public void Dispose()
{
    if (!bDisposed)
    {
        … // Clean up unmanaged resources.
        GC.SuppressFinalize(this);
        bDisposed = true;
    }
}
```

Suppose you're writing a class that encapsulates an unmanaged resource, and which also has a field (such as a *StreamWriter* object) that itself encapsulates an unmanaged resource. The unmanaged resource that the *StreamWriter* class encapsulates is a disk file. The *StreamWriter* class has a destructor (indicated in the .NET documentation as a *Finalize* method) and both *Dispose* and *Close* methods.

From the perspective of your class, the *StreamWriter* object is a managed resource because it is part of the .NET Framework. Whenever you use a *StreamWriter* object (or any other file I/O object) in any of your programs, you should call the object's *Dispose* or *Close* method when you're finished with the file. If your class also encapsulates an unmanaged resource, your class's *Dispose* method should call the *Dispose* or *Close* method of this *StreamWriter* object if the file is still open at that time. But you shouldn't call the *Dispose* or *Close* method of the *StreamWriter* object during the destructor. By then it's too late and the destructor in *StreamWriter* has to deal with closing the file.

The recommended approach in dealing with such a situation involves declaring a second *Dispose* method with a single *Boolean* parameter like so:

```
protected void Dispose(bool bDisposing)
{
    ...
}
```

Both the destructor and the parameterless *Dispose* methods of your class call this version of *Dispose*. The argument is *false* when called from the destructor and *true* when called from *Dispose*. Here's a complete scheme of a destructor and *Dispose* methods:

```
~MyClass()
{
    Dispose(false);
}
public void Dispose()
{
    Dispose(true);
    GD.SuppressFinalize(this);
}
public void Dispose(bool bDisposing)
{
    if (bDisposing)
    {
        ... // Call Dispose on managed objects stored as fields.
    }
    ... // Clean up unmanaged resources.
}
```

The second *Dispose* method could also have logic shown earlier using the *bDisposed* field. If you also desire a *Close* method, it can simply call the parameterless *Dispose* method:

```
public void Close()
{
    Dispose();
}
```

In a program that uses this class, calling the *Dispose* method is similar to calling the *Close* method of the *StreamReader* or *StreamWriter* classes:

```
MyClass mc = new MyClass();
// Use the object.
mc.Dispose();
```

Generally, an object is not very useful after you've called its *Close* or *Dispose* method.

C# provides an alternative approach to explicitly calling *Dispose* that you can use with objects that implement the *IDisposable* interface. The *using* statement (not to be confused with the *using* directive that appears at the top of your source code files) calls the *Dispose* method implicitly at the end of the block:

```
using (MyClass mc = new MyClass())
{
    … // Use the object.
}
```

The *using* statement provides a couple of advantages over the earlier approach. First, the object is not visible outside the block. You can't accidently use an object that's been disposed of in this manner. Secondly, if an exception is raised by any statement within the block, the *Dispose* method of *mc* will be called even if the program terminates as a result of the exception. It's as if the *Dispose* call were in a *finally* block.

Now that we know how to properly clean up unmanaged resources, let's examine how a C# program can get ahold of one.

You saw with the *Temperature* class in Chapter 39 the ease with which a class can be made part of a DLL, and how easy it is to specify that a program makes use of that DLL. It wasn't always this easy. If you want to access unmanaged DLLs (the ones that make up much of Windows, for example), you'll need to use some special code.

The class I'll show you shortly gets access to three Windows API functions that are part of the WINMM (Windows multimedia) DLL. One of these functions is *midiOutShortMsg*. If you look at the documentation of this function, you'll encounter several obscure uppercase identifiers. The function has two parameters that are defined in the API documenation as an *HMIDIOUT* and a *DWORD*, and the function returns a variable of type *MMRESULT*. If you further explore how these types are defined in the API, you'll find that they are all 32-bit values. They are actually *unsigned* 32-bit values, but in a C# program you can refer to them all using the C# *int* type.

In a C# program, you should be able to call *midiOutShortMsg* as if it were a method declared like so:

```
public static int midiOutShortMsg(int hMidiOut, int iMessage)
```

The first argument to *midiOutShortMsg* is a *handle* (hence, the 'h' prefix). A handle is simply a number that (in this case) is used within Windows to refer to a MIDI output device. A program obtains this handle from an API function named *midiOutOpen* and uses it in the other *midiOut* functions. Handles are unnecessary in object-oriented languages because objects serve the same purpose in a more-generalized manner.

Normally the C# compiler gets information about the classes and methods implemented in a DLL from the DLL metadata. But regular Windows DLLs don't have metadata. You need to insert code in your program that informs the compiler of the function's parameters and return types. You also need to indicate the DLL in which the function is located. This latter requirement involves the use of an *attribute*, which is information enclosed in square brackets preceding a declaration. Attributes are a general-purpose mechanism to provide more information about a method declaration beyond its parameters and return type. The particular attribute you use is *DllImport*, which is supported by the *DllImportAttribute* class in the *System.Runtime.InteropServices* namespace, a namespace that contains other classes related to *interoperability*. Interoperability refers to the general ability of C# programs to work with dynamic link libraries that are not part of the .NET Framework. You'll need a *using* directive for the *System.Runtime.InteropServices* namespace and a declaration of each API function you want to use. The declaration uses the *extern* keyword to indicate that the function is external to the class. The declaration has no body:

```
[DllImport("winmm.dll")]
static extern int midiOutShortMsg(int hMidiOut, int iMsg);
```

Put these two lines in a class and you'll be able to call *midiOutShortMsg* from that class.

Here's my complete *Midi* class that provides declarations of the API functions *midiOutOpen*, *midiOutClose*, and *midiOutShortMsg*, and includes some C# methods that put a friendlier face on these functions. Such a class is sometimes called a *wrapper* because it encapsulates or wraps an alternative interface around an existing interface:

Midi.cs

```
// -------------------------------------------------
// Midi.cs from "Programming in the Key of C#"
// -------------------------------------------------
using System;
using System.Runtime.InteropServices;

class Midi: IDisposable
{
    [DllImport("winmm.dll")]
    static extern int midiOutOpen(out int hMidiOut, int iDevice,
                        int uiCallback, int uiInstance, int uiFlags);

    [DllImport("winmm.dll")]
    static extern int midiOutClose(int hMidiOut);

    [DllImport("winmm.dll")]
    static extern int midiOutShortMsg(int hMidiOut, int iMsg);
```

```
int hMidiOut;

public Midi()
{
    // Most midiOutOpen arguments are not used here.
    int iResult = midiOutOpen(out hMidiOut, -1, 0, 0, 0);

    if (iResult != 0)
        throw new Exception("midiOutOpen error number " + iResult);
}
~Midi()
{
    Dispose(false);
}
public void Dispose()
{
    Dispose(true);
    GC.SuppressFinalize(this);
}
protected void Dispose(bool bDisposing)
{
    if (hMidiOut != 0)
    {
        midiOutClose(hMidiOut);
        hMidiOut = 0;
    }
}
void Close()
{
    Dispose();
}
public void Message(int iStatus, int iData1, int iData2)
{
    // Combine parameters into a single message.
    int iMsg = iStatus | iData1 << 8 | iData2 << 16;
    int uiResult = midiOutShortMsg(hMidiOut, iMsg);
}
public void Instrument(int iChannel, int iInstrument)
{
    Message(0xC0 | iChannel, iInstrument, 0);
}
public void NoteOn(int iChannel, int iNote, int iVelocity)
{
    Message(0x90 | iChannel, iNote, iVelocity);
}
public void NoteOff(int iChannel, int iNote)
{
    NoteOn(iChannel, iNote, 0);
}
```

```
public void NoteOn(int iChannel, string strNote, int iVelocity)
{
    if (strNote.ToUpper()[0] == 'R')     // Rest
        return;

    int iNote = " C D EF G A B".IndexOf(strNote.ToUpper()[0]);
    int i = 2;        // assumed index of octave number in string

    if (strNote[1] == '#')
        iNote++;

    else if (strNote[1] == 'b')
        iNote--;

    else
        i = 1;      // index of octave number in string

    iNote += 12 * Int32.Parse(strNote.Substring(i));
    NoteOn(iChannel, iNote, iVelocity);
}
public void NoteOff(int iChannel, string strNote)
{
    NoteOn(iChannel, strNote, 0);
}
}
```

The constructor is responsible for opening the MIDI output device by calling *midiOutOpen*. The second argument of –1 indicates a MIDI device known as MIDI_MAPPER, which is the default MIDI output device for the system. If *midiOutOpen* encounters a problem, it returns a non-zero value, and the constructor raises an exception.

The *Dispose* method with a parameter is responsible for closing the MIDI output device. It calls *midiOutClose* only if *hMidiOut* is not equal to 0, and then sets *hMidiOut* to 0, which indicates that the device is closed. Both the destructor and the parameterless *Dispose* call this method.

The *Message* method in this *Midi* class is a generalized method for sending messages to the MIDI output device. Each MIDI message is constructed of one to three bytes. I've also written higher-level *Instrument*, *NoteOn*, and *NoteOff* methods that simply call *Message*. The final two overloads of *NoteOn* and *NoteOff* work on an even higher level. The argument is a short text string such as "C#5" to indicate a note and an octave. The string "C#5" is the C# above middle C. The method converts these strings to a MIDI note code that ranges from 0 through 127.

The *Midi* class is capable of playing individual notes. A later class, called *MidiPlayer*, is capable of playing a series of notes based on a simple text file format that I devised for storing music compositions.

These music files store notes in the same text format that's valid for the *NoteOn* overload in the *Midi* class. Each note is followed by a duration in terms of *ticks*. A quarter note is 16 ticks, an eighth note is 8 ticks, and a sixteenth note is 4 ticks. Durations can be omitted from the file if they're the same as the previous duration. Here's a simple string that plays a sequence of four quarter notes that comprise a C# major chord:

```
C#5 16 E#5 G#5 C#6
```

There's a considerable amount of simplification in storing notes like this. Each note is assumed to end when the next note begins. There's no way to indicate any degree of staccato or legato in the file, and no accommodation for any changes in volume.

This format is restricted to playing only one note at a time. Notes do not overlap. With very few exceptions, Bach compositions are polyphonic with two or more parts that play simultaneously. The file format must accommodate these multiple parts. I decided to store multiple parts in the file by terminating each part by a vertical bar character. A program can extract each part by just searching for that character. The parts must then be played simultaneously.

The two files containing Bach's Prelude and Fugue in C# are named BachCSharpPrelude.txt and BachCSharpFugue.txt. They won't be reproduced here, but they are stored in the CSharpBach project along with the program files, and you can look at them with Notepad. In these two files, each text line of notes and durations is one measure of music.

The next class I'm going to show you is called *NoteStream*. A *NoteStream* object primarily stores a field named *strNotes* that contains the whole sequence of notes and durations for a single part of the composition. As the composition plays, the *iIndex* field points to the current position in the file. The two methods *GetNextNote* and *GetNextDuration* are responsible for parsing the *strNotes* string and returning the next note and next duration in the sequence, adjusting *iIndex* in the process.

NoteStream.cs

```
// ---------------------------------------------------
// NoteStream.cs from "Programming in the Key of C#"
// ---------------------------------------------------
using System;

class NoteStream
{
    // Public fields
```

```
public int iChannel;
public int iInstrument;
public int iVolume;
public bool bMute;
public int iCountdown;
public string strNotePlaying;
public bool bStopped;

// Private fields

string strNotes;
int iIndex;
int iLastDuration;

// Constructor

public NoteStream(int iChannel, string strNotes, int iInstrument,
                  int iVolume, bool bMute)
{
    this.iChannel = iChannel;
    this.strNotes = strNotes;
    this.iInstrument = iInstrument;
    this.iVolume = iVolume;
    this.bMute = bMute;

    Reset();
}

// Methods

public void Reset()
{
    iIndex = 0;
    bStopped = false;
    strNotePlaying = null;
}
public string GetNextNote()
{
    int iNoteIndex = SkipWhiteSpace(strNotes, iIndex);

    if (strNotes[iNoteIndex] == '|')
        return null;

    iIndex = SkipNonWhiteSpace(strNotes, iNoteIndex);

    return strNotes.Substring(iNoteIndex, iIndex - iNoteIndex);
}
```

```
    public int GetNextDuration()
    {
        int iDurationIndex = SkipWhiteSpace(strNotes, iIndex);

        if (!Char.IsDigit(strNotes, iDurationIndex))
            return iLastDuration;

        iIndex = SkipNonWhiteSpace(strNotes, iDurationIndex);

        int iDuration = Int32.Parse(
            strNotes.Substring(iDurationIndex, iIndex - iDurationIndex));

        iLastDuration = iDuration;
        return iDuration;
    }
    static int SkipWhiteSpace(string str, int i)
    {
        while (i < str.Length && Char.IsWhiteSpace(str, i))
            i++;

        return i;
    }
    static int SkipNonWhiteSpace(string str, int i)
    {
        while (i < str.Length && !Char.IsWhiteSpace(str, i))
            i++;

        return i;
    }
}
```

You'll notice that *NoteStream* contains a number of other fields as well as *strNotes* and *iIndex*. The *iChannel, iInstrument, iVolume,* and *bMute* fields are all set by the *NoteStream* constructor and represent other information associated with this particular sequence of notes. (I used the *bMute* field when testing the program and left it in just in case I ever needed it again.) The *iCountdown, strNotePlaying,* and *bStopped* fields will be used by the *MidiPlayer* class coming up shortly.

Because each *NoteStream* object represents a single sequence of non-overlapping notes, a polyphonic composition is generally a collection of *NoteStream* objects. To accommodate multiple *NoteStream* objects, the *NoteStreamArrayList* class derives from the *ArrayList* class:

NoteStreamArrayList.cs

```
// -----------------------------------------------------------
// NoteStreamArrayList.cs from "Programming in the Key of C#"
// -----------------------------------------------------------
using System.Collections;
```

```
class NoteStreamArrayList: ArrayList
{
    public void Add(int iChannel, string strNotes, int iInstrument,
                    int iVolume, bool bMute)
    {
        Add(new NoteStream(iChannel, strNotes, iInstrument, iVolume, bMute));
    }
    public new NoteStream this[int i]
    {
        get
        {
            return (NoteStream) base[i];
        }
    }
}
```

I described *ArrayList* in the last chapter. *NoteStreamArrayList* provides a new *Add* method that simply creates a new *NoteStream* object and adds it to the collection. *NoteStreamArrayList* also provides a new indexer that casts the object to a *NoteStream*.

A *NoteStreamArrayList* basically encapsulates an entire composition with multiple parts. The major job that remains is to play this composition, and that's the job of the *MidiPlayer* class. As you might guess, a timer is involved. I decided to use the same *Timer* class in the *System.Timers* namespace that I demonstrated in the *Clock* program in Chapter 40.

The *MidiPlayer* class has two constructors. The first has just one parameter, which is a *Midi* object. The second constructor also includes a filename of a composition file (in the format I described earlier): a code ranging from 0 to 127 to indicate the instrument to be used for the composition, and a volume, which can range from 1 to 127. This second constructor is responsible for opening the file, breaking it down into parts, and then calling the *Add* method for each part. Alternatively, a program could call the first constructor of *MidiPlayer* and then call *Add* for each part. This second approach (which my sample program doesn't use) allows each part to have a different instrument and volume. The *Add* method simply calls the *Add* method in *NoteStreamArrayList*.

MidiPlayer.cs

```
// ----------------------------------------------------
// MidiPlayer.cs from "Programming in the Key of C#"
// ----------------------------------------------------
using System;
using System.IO;
using System.Threading;
using System.Timers;      // Requires System.dll
```

```
class MidiPlayer
{
    Midi midi;
    NoteStreamArrayList nsal = new NoteStreamArrayList();
    System.Timers.Timer tmr = new System.Timers.Timer();
    ManualResetEvent[] amre;

    // Constructors

    public MidiPlayer(Midi midi)
    {
        this.midi = midi;
    }
    public MidiPlayer(Midi midi, string strFileName, int iInstrument,
                      int iVolume): this(midi)
    {
        StreamReader sr = new StreamReader(strFileName);
        string strLine, str = "";

        while (null != (strLine = sr.ReadLine()))
        {
            if (strLine.Length == 0 || strLine[0] == '/')
                continue;

            str += strLine + " ";
        }
        sr.Close();

        int iStart = 0;
        int iEnd = str.IndexOf('|', iStart);

        for (int i = 0; iEnd != -1; i++)
        {
            Add(i, str.Substring(iStart, iEnd - iStart + 1), iInstrument,
                               iVolume, false);
            iStart = iEnd + 1;
            iEnd = str.IndexOf('|', iStart);
        }
    }

    // Add method adds NoteStream objects to the composition.

    public void Add(int iChannel, string strNoteStream, int iInstrument,
                    int iVolume, bool bMute)
    {
        if (!tmr.Enabled)
            nsal.Add(iChannel, strNoteStream, iInstrument, iVolume, bMute);
    }
```

```csharp
// Play method starts the composition playing.

public ManualResetEvent[] Play(int iTempo)
{
    // Initialize semaphores.
    amre = new ManualResetEvent[nsal.Count];

    for (int i = 0; i < amre.Length; i++)
        amre[i] = new ManualResetEvent(false);

    // Set instrument for each channel.
    foreach(NoteStream ns in nsal)
        midi.Instrument(ns.iChannel, ns.iInstrument);

    // Convert tempo to milliseconds per tick.
    tmr.Interval = 60000 / (16 * iTempo);
    tmr.Elapsed += new ElapsedEventHandler(TimerCallback);
    tmr.Start();

    return amre;
}


// Stop method stops the timer.

public void Stop()
{
    tmr.Stop();
    tmr.Close();
}


// TimerCallback plays the next notes if they're ready to be played.

void TimerCallback(object obj, ElapsedEventArgs eea)
{
    lock(this)
    {
        for (int i = 0; i < nsal.Count; i++)
        {
            if (nsal[i].bStopped)
                continue;

            if (nsal[i].iCountdown == 0)
            {
                if (nsal[i].strNotePlaying != null)
                    if (!nsal[i].bMute)
                        midi.NoteOff(nsal[i].iChannel,
                            nsal[i].strNotePlaying);
```

```
            string strNote = nsal[i].GetNextNote();

            if (strNote == null)
            {
                nsal[i].bStopped = true;
                amre[i].Set();    // Signal the semaphore.
                continue;
            }

            if (!nsal[i].bMute)
                midi.NoteOn(nsal[i].iChannel, strNote,
                            nsal[i].iVolume);

            nsal[i].strNotePlaying = strNote;
            nsal[i].iCountdown = nsal[i].GetNextDuration();
        }
        nsal[i].iCountdown--;
    }
   }
  }
 }
```

Once a program has initialized *MidiPlayer* with the composition, it calls *Play* with a tempo value that indicates the number of quarter notes per minute. The *Play* method starts a *Timer* going based on that tempo. The *TimerCallback* method obtains the notes to play from each *NoteStream* object and passes those notes to methods in the *Midi* class. *TimerCallback* uses the durations from the *NoteStream* objects to initialize the *iCountdown* values, which are decremented on each call to *TimerCallback*. When *iCountdown* is 0 for a *NoteStream*, it's time to stop the previous note and play the next note.

When the *GetNextNote* method in *NoteStream* returns *null*, the end of the sequence of notes has been reached. The *TimerCallback* method sets the *bStopped* field in the *NoteStream* object to *true* and thereafter skips the rest of the method for that part.

One problem is that *MidiPlayer* is playing an entire composition of multiple parts, and these parts may end at different times. A listener can usually tell when a composition has completed, but how does the program know? It could periodically check all the *bStopped* fields of all the *NoteStream* objects. If they're all *true*, then the composition has completed. But this approach would be awkward.

A better approach is to use *semaphores*. Semaphores are a signaling mechanism that threads can use to communicate with each other. The use of semaphores in this application makes sense because the *Timer* callback method runs in its own thread of execution.

The semaphore class I've chosen for this job has a name of *Manual-ResetEvent* and is declared in the *System.Threading* namespace. The *ManualResetEvent* class derives from *WaitHandle* and additionally declares two methods named *Set* and *Reset*. Conceptually, a *ManualResetEvent* object has two states, which are called *signaled* and *nonsignaled*. The *Set* method sets the state to signaled and the *Reset* method sets it to nonsignaled. The *ManualResetEvent* constructor requires a Boolean argument to indicate the initial state, *true* for signaled and *false* for nonsignaled:

```
ManualResetEvent mre = new ManualResetEvent(false);
```

Generally, one thread controls whether the *ManualResetEvent* is signaled or not. Another thread might then call the *WaitForOne* method that *ManualResetEvent* inherits from *WaitHandle*:

```
mre.WaitForOne();
```

If *mre* is signaled, then *WaitForOne* returns immediately. If *mre* is not signaled, then *WaitForOne* doesn't return until the object is signaled.

What's most useful for our purposes is the static *WaitAll* method that *ManualResetEvent* inherits from *WaitHandle*. The argument is an array of *ManualResetEvent* objects:

```
ManualResetEvent.WaitAll(amre);
```

The *WaitAll* method doesn't return until all the *ManualResetEvent* objects in the array are signaled. This is an ideal way for the *MidiPlayer* class to indicate that it has finished playing a composition.

To indicate when a composition has ended, the *Play* method in *Midi-Player* creates an array of *ManualResetEvent* objects, one for each track. Each *ManualResetEvent* is initialized to an unsignaled state. *Play* then returns this array to whatever code may need to use it. Whenever a track finishes, the *TimerCallback* method sets the corresponding *ManualResetEvent* object to its signaled state.

I also discovered a need in *TimerCallback* for another type of signaling mechanism, but this one was simple enough to let me use the C# *lock* statement. When using the final program, I discovered that the timer implemented in the *System.Timers.Timer* class could be slowed down if there were other activity going on in Windows. (That still happens in the final program.) Sometimes, however, *TimerCallback* would itself be interrupted and begin execution at the top again. This would sometimes cause the different parts to fall out of sync. That I could not tolerate.

The C# *lock* keyword allows a program to have exclusive access to a block of code. The argument to *lock* can be any reference type; for instance methods in classes, it's convenient to use *this* (which refers to the current object).

Finally, we need a program to put these four classes to work. Here's the CSharpBach.cs file. The CSharpBach project also includes the four previous files.

CSharpBach.cs

```
// -------------------------------------------------
// CSharpBach.cs from "Programming in the Key of C#"
// -------------------------------------------------
using System;
using System.IO;     // For File.Exists method
using System.Threading;

class CSharpBach
{
    static void Main()
    {
        string strPrelude = CheckIfFileExists("BachCSharpPrelude.txt");
        string strFugue = CheckIfFileExists("BachCSharpFugue.txt");

        if (strPrelude == null || strFugue == null)
        {
            Console.WriteLine("Cannot find music files.");
            return;
        }

        int iInstrument = GetInteger("Enter instrument 0 through 127\r\n" +
            "\t(0 = Grand Piano, 6 = Harpsichord, 20 = Reed Organ)\r\n" +
            "\t\tor press Enter for piano: ", 0, 127, 0);

        int iVolume = GetInteger("Enter volume 1 through 127" +
            " or press Enter for default of 127: ", 1, 127, 127);

        int iPreludeTempo = GetInteger("Enter tempo for prelude" +
            " (70 through 280 quarter notes per minute)\r\n" +
            "\tor press Enter for default of 140: ", 70, 280, 140);

        int iFugueTempo = GetInteger("Enter tempo for fugue" +
            " (55 through 220 quarter notes per minute)\r\n" +
            "\tor press Enter for default of 110: ", 55, 220, 110);

        using (Midi midi = new Midi())
        {
            MidiPlayer mp = new MidiPlayer(midi, strPrelude,
                                            iInstrument, iVolume);

            ManualResetEvent[] amre = mp.Play(iPreludeTempo);
            Console.Write("Playing the Prelude... ");
            ManualResetEvent.WaitAll(amre);
```

```
            mp.Stop();
            Console.WriteLine("");
            foreach (ManualResetEvent mre in amre)
                mre.Close();

            mp = new MidiPlayer(midi, strFugue, iInstrument, iVolume);

            amre = mp.Play(iFugueTempo);
            Console.Write("Playing the Fugue... ");
            ManualResetEvent.WaitAll(amre);
            mp.Stop();
            Console.WriteLine("");
            foreach (ManualResetEvent mre in amre)
                mre.Close();
        }
    }
    static string CheckIfFileExists(string strFilename)
    {
        if (File.Exists(strFilename))
            return strFilename;

        strFilename = "..\\..\\" + strFilename;

        if (File.Exists(strFilename))
            return strFilename;

        return null;
    }
    static int GetInteger(string strPrompt, int iMin, int iMax, int iDef)
    {
        Console.Write(strPrompt);
        int iReturn;

        try
        {
            iReturn = Int32.Parse(Console.ReadLine());

            if (iReturn < iMin || iReturn > iMax)
                iReturn = iDef;
        }
        catch
        {
            iReturn = iDef;
        }
        return iReturn;
    }
}
```

The *Main* method begins by looking for the two composition files. If you compiled the program using Key of C#, the CSharpBach.exe file will be in the same directory as the other project files. But if you've compiled the program with Visual C# .NET, the EXE file will be two nested subdirectories away from the other project files, so the program needs to look two directories up the hierarchy. *Main* continues by getting information from the user regarding the desired instrument, volume, and tempo. If you just press Enter, the program will use its defaults.

Main next has a *using* statement for the *Midi* object. That statement ensures that the *Dispose* method in *Midi* gets called so the class can call the *midiOutClose* API function.

Within the *using* block the program creates a *MidiPlayer* object, calls *Play*, and then uses the *ManualResetEvent* array returned from *Play* in a call to *ManualResetEvent.WaitAll*. Without this call (or some other way for this thread to stop executing for awhile), the program would quickly exit the *Main* method and the program would terminate before the first note of music would be played.

When *WaitAll* returns, *Main* stops the timer (which is not doing much at this point) by calling the *Stop* method of *MidiPlayer*. *Main* then calls *Close* for all the *ManualWaitEvent* objects in the array returned by *Play*. The *WaitHandle* class that *ManualWaitEvent* derives from encapsulates unmanaged Windows resources, so it's a good idea to call *Close* on these objects when you're finished using them.

This is not an easy program. There's a lot going on and much interaction between the various classes and the multiple threads of execution that make the program difficult to understand. This program took longer to work out than any other program in this book. I rearranged the classes several times before I was moderately satisfied, and I'm still not entirely convinced that I got it right.

But I think the results are worth the effort. Because between the flash of initial inspiration and the sweat of execution, between the joy of coding and the grind of debugging, between the periods of complete mystification and the moments of triumph, it's always nice to listen to a little music.

Index

Get a **Free**
e-mail newsletter, updates,
special offers, links to related books,
and more when you

register online!

Register your Microsoft Press® title on our Web site and you'll get a FREE subscription to our e-mail newsletter, *Microsoft Press Book Connections.* You'll find out about newly released and upcoming books and learning tools, online events, software downloads, special offers and coupons for Microsoft Press customers, and information about major Microsoft® product releases. You can also read useful additional information about all the titles we publish, such as detailed book descriptions, tables of contents and indexes, sample chapters, links to related books and book series, author biographies, and reviews by other customers.

Registration is easy. Just visit this Web page and fill in your information:

http://www.microsoft.com/mspress/register

Microsoft®

Proof of Purchase

Use this page as proof of purchase if participating in a promotion or rebate offer on this title. Proof of purchase must be used in conjunction with other proof(s) of payment such as your dated sales receipt—see offer details.

Programming in the Key of C#:
A Primer for Aspiring Programmers
0-7356-1800-3

CUSTOMER NAME

Microsoft Press, PO Box 97017, Redmond, WA 98073-9830

Charles Petzold

Charles Petzold (*www.charlespetzold.com*) is a full-time freelance writer who has been programming for Microsoft Windows since 1985 and writing about Windows programming for nearly as long. He wrote the very first magazine article about Windows programming for the December 1986 issue of *Microsoft Systems Journal* (now *MSDN Magazine*). His book *Programming Windows* (first published by Microsoft Press in 1988 and currently in its fifth edition) taught a generation of programmers how to write applications for Windows. More recently, his books *Programming Microsoft Windows with C#* and *Programming Microsoft Windows with Microsoft Visual Basic .NET* show programmers  how to use the Microsoft .NET Windows Forms library to write Windows programs. He is also the author of a unique introduction to the inner workings of computers entitled *Code: The Hidden Language of Computer Hardware and Software*. Petzold is currently researching a book on the pre-twentieth-century origins of computer hardware and software.

C# Keywords			
Types	**Statements**	**Modifiers**	**Other**
bool	break	abstract	as
byte	case	const	base
char	catch	event	explicit
class	checked	extern	false
decimal	continue	internal	implicit
delegate	default	override	is
double	do	private	namespace
enum	else	protected	new
float	finally	public	null
int	fixed	readonly	operator
interface	for	sealed	out
long	foreach	static	params
object	goto	unsafe	ref
sbyte	if	virtual	sizeof
short	in	volatile	stackalloc
string	lock		this
struct	return		true
uint	switch		typeof
ulong	throw		using
ushort	try		
void	unchecked		
	while		

Susie Martinez is a professional counselor with a private counseling practice in Lakewood, Colorado. She has been married to her husband, Joe, for twenty-two years and has two teenage children. Susie adores her family, her Kitchen Aid mixer, and her purple PT Cruiser. In her free time, she enjoys shopping with her daughter, taking long walks, and home decorating. Susie also struggles with a particular weakness for palm trees and white sandy beaches.

Bonnie Garcia is a busy mother of three sons. She works as a part-time pediatric nurse, where she enjoys working with newborns and their parents. In her free time, she enjoys downhill skiing and reading. An Iowa native, Bonnie has been married to her husband, Steve, for twenty-six years. She is active in her local church, where her husband is the senior pastor. After recent trips to Greece and Israel, Bonnie has discovered that she is hooked on international travel.

Vanda Howell is a busy mom who works part-time as a kitchen design consultant. Vanda is a Denver native and has been married to her husband, Mike, for twenty-seven years. She is absolutely in love with (a.k.a. addicted to) dark chocolate, espresso lattés, and going to movies. In her free time, she enjoys gourmet cooking, gardening, and wakeboarding with her husband and teenage son.

More Tasty, Make-Ahead and Easy-to-Prepare Recipes

Three experienced cooks share simple and economical alternatives to take-out and prepackaged foods. You will love these quick and healthful home-tested recipes.

 Revell

a division of Baker Publishing Group
www.RevellBooks.com

Available Wherever Books Are Sold
Also Available in Ebook Format